HEIDEGGER
AND NAZISM

HEIDEGGER AND NAZISM

VICTOR FARÍAS

Edited, with a Foreword, by
Joseph Margolis and Tom Rockmore

French materials translated by Paul Burrell,
with the advice of Dominic Di Bernardi

German materials translated by Gabriel R. Ricci

TEMPLE UNIVERSITY PRESS

PHILADELPHIA

Temple University Press, Philadelphia 19122
Published in French by Éditions Verdier under the title
Heidegger et le nazisme; copyright © 1987
English translation copyright © 1989 by Temple University
All rights reserved
Published 1989
Printed in the United States of America

The paper used in this publication meets the minimum requirements of American
National Standard for Information Sciences—Permanence of Paper for printed
Library materials, ANSI Z39.48-1984

Library of Congress Cataloging-in-Publication Data
Farías, Victor, 1940–
[Heidegger et le nazisme. English]
Heidegger and nazism / Victor Farías; edited, with a foreword, by
Joseph Margolis and Tom Rockmore; French materials translated by Paul Burrell,
with the advice of Dominic Di Bernardi; German materials translated by Gabriel
R. Ricci.
      p.   cm.
Translation of: Heidegger et le nazisme.
Bibliography: p.
Includes index.
ISBN 0-87722-640-7
1. Heidegger, Martin, 1889–1976—Views on national socialism.
2. National socialism.   I. Margolis, Joseph, 1924–   .
II. Rockmore, Tom, 1942–   .   III. Title.
B3279.N49F3413   1989
193—dc20   89-32963
                                                                        CIP

Contents

Foreword

by Tom Rockmore and Joseph Margolis

The dual purpose of this foreword is to describe briefly the importance of Victor Farías' work, *Heidegger and Nazism*, which we here present in English translation, and to indicate the nature of this particular version of the text. In part, the importance of the book depends on the importance attributed to Heidegger, who, as this century draws to a close, looms ever larger as one of the principal philosophers of our age—perhaps, as some argue, the author of the most important philosophical work since Hegel's *Phenomenology*. There is no question that Heidegger is a most significant thinker, although the nature of his contribution has been called into serious question since the end of World War II because of his link to Nazism. Heidegger stands before us as a singular case, philosophically *sui generis,* the source of one of the most influential currents of philosophical thought in our century, the only major thinker to opt for Nazism, the main example of absolute evil in our time—possibly of any time. The combination is without any known historical precedent.

The link between Heidegger and Nazism has been known in part for many years. In France, where Heidegger's thought has been in steady ascendance since the "Letter on Humanism" addressed to Jean Beaufret some four decades ago, it is a matter of record that the Nazi connection has been discussed on two separate earlier occasions: in 1946–1948, in a swift-moving controversy in the pages of *Les Temps Modernes,* and again, in the mid-1960s, in a debate ending with the emergence of François Fédier as a self-anointed defender of the official faith. The early French discussion is instructive, since it adumbrates four main strategies of the developing debate: the necessitarian thesis, originally advanced by Karl Löwith, which argues for an intrinsic link between Heidegger's thought and Nazism; the contingency thesis, originally advanced by Alphonse de Waelhens and still maintained in its pristine form by Fédier, according to which the relation between Heidegger and Nazism is merely and entirely transitory; third, the learned form of the contingentist defense, also originated by Waelhens, which holds that Heidegger's detractors are insufficiently aware of the entire body of his thought to criticize it. More recently, in the wake of Farías' book, a fourth line of thought has emerged, combining features of the three preceding approaches. The new strategy, illustrated by the writings of Jacques Derrida and Philippe Lacoue-Labarthe, simply concedes the essential connection between Heidegger's thought and Nazism, but maintains that the uninitiated, those whose philosophical being is not bound up with Heidegger in an essential way, cannot really measure the importance or full significance of Heidegger's work.

Farías' book is important because, arguably, for the first time, it renders an arcane discussion accessible to any thoughtful reader and, in doing that, calls into immediate question the received or official version of Heidegger's link to Nazism. What we may call the official view includes at least the following claims: the link between Heidegger and National Socialism was never a principled adherence but at best a necessary compromise; the main reason for the assumption of the rectorate was to defend the German university; Heidegger severed his links to the movement when he realized its true nature and criticized it in his later writings; he was never a racist and went out of his way to defend various Jews, including Husserl; he never abandoned the discipline of serious philosophical inquiry for any more immediate political goal.

This version of events is obviously flattering to Heidegger, who then appears at worst naive—a worthy successor of Thales perhaps, the legendary founder of philosophy who, in a much-publicized incident, fell into a well while looking at the stars. On the analogy, Heidegger, in a moment of political inattention but with the kindness of heart of a devoted scholar, acceded to the importuning of his colleagues and acted to defend the university against an evil of as yet unknown proportions. This version, which has for years been disseminated by Heideggerians, is largely due to Heidegger himself. Although during his lifetime he never publicly took a stand either on the holocaust or on his own role as rector of the University of Freiburg in 1933/34, he did on two occasions provide materials (published only after his death) that were definitely intended to shape public opinion on the political import of his life. In an article written at the end of the war, which appeared only in 1983, on the fiftieth anniversary of Hitler's rise to power (possibly timed to coincide with that event), Heidegger suggested that his asssumption of the rectorate was intended to seize the occasion for the sake of the destiny of the German people, by accepting personal responsibility for directing the university to this grave task, but that his relation to Nazism in all of that was at best distant. In the better-known *Spiegel* interview, published some ten years after the event, on the occasion of his death, Heidegger strengthened his self-defense by insisting that his main motive had been to defend the very institution of the German university.

To be sure, this view has always had its detractors. Heidegger may himself have unwittingly contributed to a deconstruction of his own defense, for instance through the republication, in 1953, of *An Introduction to Metaphysics*, written in 1935—where one cannot fail to notice the incriminating insistence, after so many years, on the intrinsic essence and greatness of National Socialism. This strange statement, however, which appears so flatly to contradict a break with Nazism in any but the most narrow sense, could perhaps, if suitably isolated, be explained or explained away by Heidegger's supporters and, if necessary, by reference to the words of the master himself. But other equally troubling materials had to be regularly passed over in silence to make the case stick—such as the unfortunate statement in an obscure unpublished lecture on technology in which Heidegger compares the extermination technology of the concentration camps to various forms of agricultural technology. Still other materials were actually suppressed through the simple but effective process of restricting, or even refusing, access to archives known to contain relevant documents.

For the most part, prior to Farías' book, Heidegger's deeds and misdeeds were largely insulated from general scrutiny. Meanwhile, to be sure, isolated scholars continued to chip away at the official view. Guido Schneeberger, for instance, assembled a collection of Heideggeriana relevant to the problem, which appeared in 1962. But Schneeberger was impeded from publishing his work except by his own private means. So he was effectively prevented from giving his work the wide circulation it deserved. He also could not get permission to use certain important materials. Bernd Martin, Rainer Marten, and Hugo Ott pursued additional research, but their work has received almost no attention outside certain extremely specialized circles. Although some scholars knew that there was a problem to be faced, most were not really aware of its depth and profound significance. Indeed, we are hardly aware or fully aware even now of the entire matter; and "damage control," if that is the correct term, has been effectively functioning for a long time in concealing from us the very nature and complexity of the problem.

Farías' book has changed all that. It has done so in a way that makes it unlikely—arguably, impossible—ever again to confine the discussion of the theme of Heidegger and Nazism to the pale pages of scholarly debate. The fact is that Farías' book has evoked an unprecedented reaction in the public media of many countries. In Europe especially, the book received a noisy, even tumultuous, reception in the daily newspapers, the magazines, interviews, televised debates, collections of papers that do not mention it but would never have existed but for its appearance. It is difficult to measure the extent of the discussion that has resulted from its publication without a simple enumeration of the places in which that has occurred and the many forms that it has taken. Discussion still continues, of course, and with an intensity usually reserved for matters of considerably less scholarly concern. We may mention one example among many: the bitter exchange, in Italy, between Gianni Vattimo, a well-known specialist on Heidegger's later thought, and Roberto Maggiori. In a review of Farías' book, Maggiori pointed out that Farías' argument directly contradicted Vattimo's claim that there was no intrinsic connection between Heidegger and Nazism. Vattimo responded that Heidegger's thought was stronger than that of its detractors and that nothing, absolutely nothing, had yet been established of a fundamentally detrimental nature. Nevertheless, that Vattimo was able to reaffirm the familiar claim of innocence in the face of Farías' unprecedented documentation—for instance, that, during the war, Heidegger had denounced several colleagues as Jews, including at least one who was not Jewish—manifests a degree of faith, an identification with a form of thought, that no counterevidence could be expected to shake.

We should perhaps point out the asymmetrical character of the discussion evoked by Farías' book in West Germany and France: in West Germany, hardly any philosopher wishes to comment on the Heidegger problem; in France, hardly any can actually avoid making a comment.

At least four reasons may be advanced to explain the intensity of the immediate reaction to the Farías book—what the French, by a sort of conceptual analogy, refer to as *réaction à chaud*. To begin with, there is the obvious failure of every effort at academic damage control—visible more recently in the Paul de Man case—which led to cries of outrage and frustration among scholars concerned to preserve reputations seemingly safely in place, also among scholars concerned to justify the nature and usefulness of their own scholarly pursuits. The fury of the lover scorned has not infrequently been matched here by the emotion of scholars who have invested their entire lives in the pursuit of a certain failed conception of the scholarly task.

Second, there are the questions about the full meaning of Heidegger's thought that arose almost instantly in the conceptual space produced by puncturing the official myth. These concern a whole variety of themes, including: Heidegger's turn to Nazism; the turn away from Nazism; the relation of Nazism to the turning in his thought in general; his later attachment to a personal, supposedly authentic alternative form of National Socialism; his view of anti-semitism and racism in general; the precise relation between his philosophical thought and National Socialist ideology.

A third reason, identified by Christian Jambet in his introduction to the original French edition of Farías' book, concerns the presumed link, which philosophers have always maintained, between philosophy and virtue. Almost as old as philosophy's concern with reason is its persistent but less frequently voiced concern with the social relevance of reason. For several millennia since Socrates claimed that the unexamined life is not worth living, philosophers have offered rather different views of the utility of their own pursuit. It is true that very few among us have actually stepped forward to defend truth when called upon; and only a few have dared to break a lance for freedom. For every Socrates who died for the truth there have always been others, like the master of Königsberg (Immanuel Kant), who have regularly affirmed that philosophical discretion was preferable in troubled times. In Europe, where philosophy is apparently still held in high esteem, the case of Heidegger seemed to point (if any case could ever be said to do so) to the finding that philosophy has little or no relevance. After all, philosophy seems to have no reliable resource for escaping ideological entanglements.

A final reason, specific to the French intellectual scene, explains in part the unusual intensity of the immediate French response. There is a distinct tendency in France to pursue serious and systematic thought in the shadow of a single position, in the shadow of a master thinker who dominates all thought by providing the conceptual horizon within which various positions, modes, and counter-modes acquire a distinctly dialectical shape. It has been shown in some detail that, in France, since the late 1930s until the end of the 1960s, which saw the emergence of structuralism, poststructuralism, modernism, and so on, philosophy may be construed as a series of reactions to Hegel. It is not sufficiently well understood that, roughly since the publication of Jean-Paul Sartre's *Being and Nothingness* during the war, momentum for a general reaction against the French form of left-wing Hegelianism has been building in favor of

Heideggerianism, itself regarded as an expression or a program of anti-humanism. It would be fair to say that, during the last twenty years, Heidegger's influence has increased to the point where it now justifies his famous claim that when the French begin to philosophize they think in German: Heidegger's thought now dominates French philosophy to an extent unsurpassed, in fact unequaled, by its influence in any other country. A further reason, then, why the reaction to Farías' book was so violent and swift in France lies in the fact that it was seen as a direct menace to the Heideggerianism everywhere current in contemporary French philosophy, whether in the study of Aristotle or Descartes or Hegel. For, in attacking Heidegger, given the extent to which French philosophy tends to identify with Heidegger's position, Farías was perceived to have launched an assault on French philosophy in general.

These remarks on the reaction to Farías' study do not, however, tell us much about the nature of the book itself—its intent and its importance. The book, which is the result of more than a decade of solitary study in a variety of archives, pursued very much against the fashions of the day, concerns five principal biographical themes: Heidegger's background prior to his initial teaching post; the link with Ernst Krieck that was intended to establish a new university organization by bringing in candidates approved by Alfred Rosenberg; Heidegger's own explanation of why he was elected rector of the University of Freiburg; his relations with students and student organizations; the story of how Heidegger applied for various chairs at Berlin and Munich. Each of these issues isolates an important facet of the larger theme of Heidegger's relation to Nazism. Each deserves the most careful scrutiny.

According to Farías, Heidegger's joining the Nazi Party was not the result of opportunism, since he had already manifested Nazi sympathies well before he became rector. Farías effectively combats those who argue that the link to Nazism was merely contingent; the latter argue even against Heidegger, who always acknowledged that his turn to Nazism was rooted in his own deeply felt position. Like the Freiburg historian Hugo Ott, Farías shows in great detail that the connection to Nazism is also rooted in Heidegger's social and cultural background and in the themes of *Being and Time*. Farías' discussion of Krieck confirms that Heidegger's interest in the National Socialist effort to reform the university clearly preceded and continued after the period of the rectorship. Heidegger's relation to students and student groups clarifies just how he attempted to use students—much as Marx had suggested the proletariat could be set in motion by philosophy—to fulfil the Nazi program. Finally, Farías' account of the busy maneuvering undertaken within the German academic community helps us understand Heidegger the man, the man in his own world.

Our summary hardly conveys the spirit and tone of the work. It is also too quick for any serious impression of its importance. In our view, the book is decisive for at least two reasons. First, against the prevailing temper of nearly half a century of discussion, Farías utterly deflates the myth of Heidegger the good samaritan, Heidegger the conceptual resistance fighter against Nazism, Heidegger the kindly scholar, by showing that, in the final analysis, this brilliant philosopher was and must be seen to be what he always was: a convinced Nazi, a philosopher whose genuine interest in Nazism *survived* his apparent disillusionment with Hitler's particular form of National Socialism. In this respect, Farías has introduced a permanent caesura, a rupture in the discussion, an unbridgeable gap between earlier and later efforts to come to grips with the connection between Heidegger's thought and his times. Before Farías, it was arguably still possible, however difficult, to claim that the link between Heidegger and Nazism was tangential at best. After Farías, that is no longer possible—except under the condition of bad faith, under the condition of denying what one simply knows to be true. There will, of course, still be honest disputes about the nature of Heidegger's relation to National Socialism and the force of particular interpretations. But if ever a scholarly dispute of this complexity could be settled, Farías has now closed the door on reasonable doubts about all forms of the contingentist reading of Heidegger's relation to the Nazi movement.

Obviously, the assertion that Farías has produced a basic divide in Heidegger studies risks casting him in a rather exclusive company. In this century, for instance, there is no more than a very small number of writers who could be mentioned whose contribution to the interpretation of an even smaller number of genuinely great thinkers could be said to have changed the direction of subsequent studies. Examples that come to mind include Werner Jaeger's account of Aristotle, which has influenced most if not all later studies of the Stagyrite in this century; or Alexandre Kojève's book on Hegel, which raised Kojève to prominence in France and still represents, together with Georg Lukács' book, the most exciting left-wing approach to Hegel scholarship. Now Farías, to be sure, functions on a lesser plane. He is neither as scholarly as Jaeger nor as penetrating a commentator as Kojève. His book is controversial and was admittedly marred, at least in its original version, by a variety of factual, possibly even interpretive, errors. But to concede that much is not to abandon our large claim for Farías' book, which, even with its weaknesses (now very largely overcome), transforms the discussion of Heidegger—thought by many to be the pre-eminent philosopher of our century—in a way that can never be undone. No doubt, the discussion of Heidegger and Nazism will attract progressively less and less attention. Scholars will turn to other pursuits. New affairs will flare up in the academic world. Still, we insist: although the steady proclamation of Heidegger's innocence by the faithful could always be heard in the past above the scholarly din, that is no longer possible. The strong case Farías has assembled now quite properly affects the reading of Heidegger's *philosophy*.

Farías' book is a specimen of that rare sort of scholarly text that points beyond itself to a naggingly real problem in the social world. Its ramifications are serious ones. As concerns Heidegger in a narrow way, it is now relatively easy to pick out important questions that demand closer analysis. One such question centers on the "official" view of Heidegger's relation to Nazism. As already noted, the "official" view is mainly due to Heidegger himself. It was formulated in two places: in the posthumously published article on the rectoral period, and in the posthumously published magazine interview. But Heidegger, who is of course the author of his own view, cannot be said to have any privileged standing as the authorized interpreter of that view. It is certainly arguable that Heidegger's two accounts are not consistent with one another; also, that they are inconsistent as well with the famous rectoral address. Accordingly, Farías' work suggests the need for a closer look and, if necessary, a "deconstruction" (in Heidegger's language, an *Abbau*) of Heidegger's own version of his link to Nazism.

There are other questions that Farías raises that invite further research (beyond Farías' own work). A second question concerns the precise link between Heidegger and National Socialism. Heidegger indicates that the link involves no more than an insignificant episode. The point is favored by a number of his supporters. But the interpretation is threatened on various grounds. For one thing, Heidegger always insisted on an essential and intrinsic link between his thought and the activity of the rectoral period, since he claimed to have been led to the rectorship itself as a seamless extension of his view of science and engaged thought. For another, Farías has usefully shown Heidegger's continued cooperation with Krieck, even after he resigned as rector, in the union of German academics concerned with recasting the entire university system. The suggestion is clear that there must have been a more durable, longer-lasting link than Heidegger cared to acknowledge.

What *is* the link? Arguably, the famous turning *(Kehre)* in Heidegger's thought was invoked in the "Letter on Humanism" and, even earlier and at much greater length, in the recently published *Beiträge zur Philosophie,* for at least two reasons: to convey the impression that his thought had changed in a fundamental way—presumably by the turn away from an approach to Being *(Sein)* through Dasein to an approach to Being as essentially not mediated by Dasein; and to indicate that whatever it was that led him to Nazism had been eliminated from his mature position.

As a first pass at an analysis of the nature of the true link to Nazism, we endorse the mention of the concept of the turning. But we do so in order to sort out a triple turning in Heidegger's evolving thought: a turning toward National Socialism on the basis of his early thought; a turning away as he became disillusioned; and a turning toward another non-standard "utopian" version of Nazism that he envisaged and supported as viable even after he turned away from the actual forms Nazism took.

Another complicated question concerns the evolution of Heidegger's thought after he gave up the rectorship. If the link between his thought and the project of the rectorship was merely transitory and contingent, as Heideggerians so often argue, then there is probably no real connection that could be plausibly made out between the two; but there must be an intrinsic connection if Farías and other recent critics are right. The recent appearance of the famous but so far nearly inaccessible *Beiträge zur Philosophie* should help determine the nature and extent of the continuity between the various phases of Heidegger's thought, before, during, and after the rectoral period. This is obviously a complex matter. Heidegger's philosophy clearly contains any number of ideas that weave in and out throughout its entire career and that also change over time. One relevant strand, for instance, is the traditional philosophical concern with the social utility of philosophy. Heidegger changed his view on this theme in a dramatic way. Leading up to and including his commitment during the rectorate, he seems to have stressed very vigorously the decisiveness of the role of philosophy in commitment and engaged action. Later, he seems to have favored the inutility of philosophy (or of thought that surpasses philosophy) with regard to action other than thought itself (thought as a form of serious reception)—in short, a change from *Entschlossenheit* to *Gelassenheit*. Although the issue cannot be decided here, one may well wonder whether the turn from activity to passivity, which Heidegger attributes to his discovery of the role of technology, is not also a piece of strategy intended to explain the failure of the effort to seize control of the German future in Germany's turn to Nazism.

Returning to our original tally, we may claim that Farías' book is important in a second respect: in picking out another kind of issue, the general issue of the political responsibility of intellectuals. We may begin to review the matter by turning to the French discussion. Now, the French discussion is a special but most instructive affair. One must recall the Gaullist view that sought to secure the direction of the political present by turning to a glorious past; one must recall the painful problems of collaborationism, the nature of the resistance movement, the precise role of the Vichy government, the extent of French complicity in the deportation of French Jews, and so on. These factors all prove pertinent in the context of the French discussion. In examining the import of the link between Heidegger and Nazism, French thinkers are themselves placed in question. If we acknowledge Heidegger's importance in the formation of the horizon of relatively recent French philosophy, we cannot fail to understand the unusual—indeed, extraordinary—attention Farías' book has provoked since its publication. No fewer than six books on the topic have appeared in France, from the first October in which Farías' work appeared to the following May.

The question that is raised, possibly most acutely in the French intellectual world, but surely not an exclusively French question, concerns what we have rather blandly called the responsibility of intellectuals. The difficult discussion of the matter in France shows that there must be a deeper question raised by the theme of Heidegger's relation to Nazism than the one centered in recent French self-examination. Beyond the interpretation of Heidegger's own thought, we must discern the elusive but persistent second-order question of *how* philosophers and others *can* think through and rationally resolve the matter of their responsibility as intellectuals, how they can (and must) come to grips (as the de Man case reminds us) with discerning and naming evil and acting conformably with that understanding.

In this regard, the link between Heidegger and Nazism is indeed transparent: Nazism is universally recognized to be the very embodiment of evil that it was. How is it, then, that, at this late hour, there are those who still cannot grasp the implication of Heidegger's professional life? In that sense, we ourselves, reading and applying Heidegger as we seem bound to do, are also placed in mortal question.

Farías' book is unusual not merely for its effect, for its *succès de scandale,* but because of the very nature of the text. Most translations begin with a fixed text that does not change in the course of the process. In Farías' case, it has been necessary to translate "a moving object." The first French edition was quarried from a mass of Spanish manuscripts. In that sense, this book literally came into existence *in* translation, since the original materials have so far not been published; they may never appear in their original form. The present translation is based, as are those in Italian, Portuguese, and Dutch, which appeared in the interim, on the French version. When the first draft of the translation into English was nearly finished, Farías was kind enough to send us the proofs of the German edition—in effect, the second edition—in which he had rewritten a number of important passages and added much new material. We saw at once that, in order to offer the best possible version of the work, we could not go forward without incorporating the improvements. Accordingly, our final edition has combined large parts of the original French text, which preserve the historical importance of the original publication, and the key new and improved materials from the German, which implicitly respond to the best of the intervening critical discussion of the entire issue. Every effort has been made to correct this new English-language edition, based on a careful study of the original Spanish manuscript, the French book that that eventually became, together with appropriate use of improved translations from other languages. As concerns the French version, which is now widely known but in part superseded, there are two main differences in the text we now offer. First, the endnotes, which Farías was unable to verify in the original edition, since he did not see the proofs, have been painstakingly corrected to the best of our ability. Second, we have replaced old materials altogether with Farías' newly rewritten passages or we have simply inserted additional new material from the German edition wherever we thought the text would be improved. But we have not deleted or abandoned any part of Farías' original argument, including the much-criticized materials on Abraham a Sancta Clara (which we were urged to excise).

We are pleased to acknowledge the help and encouragement of a large number of colleagues and friends. We received splendid cooperation and encouragement from Jane Cullen, Philosophy Acquisitions Editor, and David Bartlett, Director, Temple University Press. Without them we could not have begun this incredible adventure or completed it on time. Their quick grasp of the historic importance of the project enabled us to acquire the English-language translation rights from Éditions Verdier, for which other presses, some with stronger financial resources, were earnestly competing. In addition, we were greatly aided by Mme. Colette Olive, Éditions Verdier, who has consistently helped us dissolve any number of problems as they arose. A colleague, who wishes to remain anonymous, carefully compared the Spanish manuscript and the French edition and offered a great number of useful suggestions and corrections. Herr Günther Busch, the director of S. Fischer Verlag, publishers of the German translation, graciously granted us permission to make use of materials that have appeared only in the Fischer edition. The translation from the French was prepared at record speed by Paul Burrell, Professor of French Language and Literature at the University of Cincinnati. His translation was reviewed by Dr. Dominic Di Bernardi, Associate Editor of *The Review of Contemporary Fiction*. The additional German texts were rendered into English by Dr. Gabriel R. Ricci. Professor Theodore Kisiel, Philosophy, Northern Illinois University, reviewed the German materials and advised us on questions of factual accuracy in an extremely generous way. All the texts and notes were finally compared, corrected, and edited by Joseph Margolis and Tom Rockmore. We have also benefited from the remarkable editorial resourcefulness and skill of Doris Braendel, the Press's in-house editor, and several of her staff, including Richard Gilbertie and Kim Rakosky. The final editing was, to say the least, a unique accomplishment; and the text as it now stands is a unique selection of Farías' materials.

Farías himself was very nearly unknown until the book's appearance. He is obviously not the most expert chronicler. One wonders how he came to write the book. As an outsider, something of a marginal figure, he was not really susceptible to the usual professional prudence or "correction." What sets him apart from the better archivists—and there are a good many—are the immense candor and courage and compelling unity of his perception of Heidegger. We may guess that Farías was, and is, a somewhat alienated observer, a Chilean Jew stranded in a post-war Germany that cannot yet confront its own history with an equal directness. Farías himself is a man who (perhaps) could come to terms with the irony of his own isolation only by putting in order and sharing his unique penetration of Heidegger's spirit, the perception of a young philosopher in whose work Heidegger had apparently taken an affectionate interest, forced by the seeming incoherence of his encounter with Heidegger to find its essential nerve and to breach once and for all the spell of the world's half-silence. He sustains an unblinking steadiness that the reviewers have not been particularly happy to discover.

It is also usual, of course, to say that responsibility for inaccuracies must be assumed by the editors alone, although we are bound to add, with no intention of excusing ourselves, that we have made every effort, under often difficult circumstances, to produce the most satisfactory text of what we very strongly believe to be a historic, most significant work.[1]

1. The materials that, with permission from the publishers, we have included from Victor Farías, *Heidegger und der Nationalsozialismus* (Frankfurt am Main: S. Fischer Verlag, 1989), either by addition to or replacement of the French materials, are the following: Chapters 1 and 3, Part I; Chapter 1, Part II (the section on Albert Leo Schlageter); Chapter 2, Part II; Chapter 4, Part II (the section on

Heidegger and the Association of German Universities); Chapter 2, Part III (the section on "The Introduction to Metaphysics" and the lectures on Nietzsche's philosophy); Chapter 3, Part III (the sections on Hölderlin and on Parmenides and Heraclitus and the section titled "Echoes"). The French version appeared as: Victor Farias, *Heidegger et le nazisme* (Lagrasse: Éditions Verdier, 1987). The Notes have been adjusted accordingly.

HEIDEGGER
AND NAZISM

Introduction

When we study the relationship between a philosopher and a political system, we are led to go beyond the borders of a pure analysis of ideas and abstract meanings. In fact, philosophical and political ideas in themselves bring us back not only to the world in which they exist but also to the practical objectives of the person defending them. For these reasons, a work of interpretation necessarily requires three levels of analysis. First there is the objective historical context, next the concrete practice of the philosopher who had made one or another political decision, and finally the systematic significance of the ideas he or she formulated. This significance is certainly not to be deduced from a given objective context, since that context itself cannot be completely understood without taking into account the context in which the ideas grew and the direction of their application.

In 1962, Guido Schneeberger published some texts, until then unknown, that gave evidence of the full and total adherence of Martin Heidegger to National Socialism during the years 1933–1934.[1] It was this publication that moved me to begin to think about my subject. The documents urgently demanded to be placed in their historical context as well as in the context of Heidegger's political practice. But the studies that followed Schneeberger's were exclusively concerned with treating the question on a purely abstract level. Although the documents furnished by Schneeberger were published years after the works by Karl Löwith and Georg Lukács,[2] all the studies that came out afterwards, whether meant to stress Heidegger's links to National Socialism[3] or to deny them,[4] failed to examine the available documents concerning the affair.

After several years of systematic research, I offer these first results.

What I have done will in part need to be completed later, for some important sources are still closed.[5] From my first reflections on Schneeberger's documents, I knew that it was impossible to achieve any really solid results without taking into account historical events that determined Heidegger's adherence to National Socialism or analyzing his political engagement in the light of his later political and philosophical evolution.

My central thesis is the following: When Heidegger decided to join the National Socialist Party, he was following an already-prepared path whose beginnings we will find in the Austrian movement of Christian Socialism, with its conservatism and anti-semitism, and in the attitudes he had found in his native region (Messkirch and Konstanz), where he had begun his studies. By considering the historical context and the texts he wrote in his youth (especially his first writing concerning the Augustinian preacher Abraham a Sancta Clara, dating from 1910), we can see the progressive connections in a thought process nourished in traditions of authoritarianism, anti-semitism, and ultranationalism that sanctified the homeland in its most local sense. This sacralizing tendency was closely tied to a radical populism and carried strong religious connotations. From the systematic point of view, this development is linked to Heidegger's reflections in *Being and Time* (*Sein und Zeit,* 1927)—on historicity, "authentic" being-in-community, and his own links with the people, the hero, and the struggle (§74)—and his rejection of democratic forms of social life, a rejection inspired by the ideas of Paul Yorck von Wartenburg and Wilhelm Dilthey (§77).

Heidegger's decision to join the NSDAP was in no way the result of unexpected opportunism or tactical considerations. The decision was clearly linked with his having already acted in a way consonant with National Socialism prior to becoming rector of the University of Freiburg and with his actual political practices as rector and member of the party.

His actions in favor of a National Socialist reform of the universities and his writings at the time make it clear that Heidegger was politically active within a faction of the party that during the years 1933–1934 was trying to take power and lead the movement. In these years, when the general political line of Nazism was still in flux and violent struggles were taking place between factions, Heidegger chose the faction headed by Ernst Röhm and his Storm Troops (*Sturmabteilung,* or SA) and tried to base this variant of National Socialism on his own philosophy, openly in opposition to the racist and biological line of Alfred Rosenberg and Ernst Krieck. At the level of persons, this opposition became a bitter struggle for the ideological leadership of the Nazi movement.

In June 1934, Hitler and the rightist faction eliminated Röhm, thus getting rid of a project whose radical requirements had almost triggered a military intervention funded by big industrial and financial capital. One consequence of this purification was the collapse of the intellectual and political apparatus that until then had supported Heidegger's political actions (especially his attempts to direct the Nazi student movement), and another was to isolate this movement, which from then on had no voice in official party politics.

From this situation was born the philosopher's conviction that, beginning in June 1934, the Nazis had become traitors to the truth that was at the root of their movement. In Heidegger's eyes it was not the movement but the National Socialist leaders who had taken positions of authority who had abandoned the truly Nazi ideas. On its side, the regime continued to watch him, even to fight against him, but simply as a factional element, not as an unyielding opponent.

Martin Heidegger never broke the organic links tying him to the National Socialist Party. Documents kept in the NSDAP archives[6] show, among other things, that he remained an active member until the end of the war, continuing to pay his dues, and that he was never subject to discipline nor internal political trials within the party.

It is only by examining Heidegger's political practice that we can accurately reconstruct what links tied him to National Socialism and what convictions drew him to it. I have studied several thematic lines that I judge to be crucial.

The first of these are Heidegger's activities within the movement whose goal was to destroy the Association of German Universities and replace it with one of a totally militant bent. It was in concert with the most radical sectors of the National Socialists that Heidegger sent a telegram to Hitler calling for a complete neutralization of German universities, which according to Heidegger were insufficiently "revolutionary."

The second theme is his efforts to establish a new university organization, which was to be held in reserve until it could replace the Association, which Heidegger judged inadequate to assume the responsibilities needed for the new era. Here, Heidegger collaborated with Ernst Krieck long before he became rector, and he did his best to join forces with this parallel association until certain crucial moves were made by the office Alfred Rosenberg directed.

A third broad theme is Heidegger's election to the rectorship at the University of Freiburg, as well as some episodes that clarify how he exercised his functions as rector.

We shall then analyze Heidegger's relationship to the National Socialist student movement, which was directed by the Röhm faction and represented a totally radical, avant-garde Nazism. Then we shall examine Heidegger's political activities, which, in general, were closely and essentially linked to the intrigues of the student base. A sort of special political pact united the spiritual Führer and this "popular" base, whose growth was meant to transform the "ankylosed" structures of the traditional German university.

The fifth group of questions, particularly critical, is linked to Heidegger's nomination to two important universities of the Reich, Berlin and Munich. It is true that Heidegger refused both chairs, yet an examination of the process of the nominations clarifies Heidegger's relationship to the regime during 1933–1934 and later. For this reason, it seems important to compare these nominations with the nomination process in place prior to National Socialism. Under the Weimar Republic, Heidegger had been nominated to teach at Marburg, Freiburg, Göttingen, and Berlin. My research confirms that, despite differences, in its official dealings the Nazi regime never thought of Heidegger as an unyielding opponent, and that he himself did not act like one.

That the harmonious relationship between Heidegger and the regime was never broken is demonstrated by various of his activities after his resignation from the rectorship. His declaration at the time of Hindenburg's death in favor of Hitler's accession to the chancellorship and to the position of chief of state naturally comes to mind. There is also the affair of the Academy of Professors of the Reich: Not only did the Ministry of Education beg Heidegger to formulate a detailed plan for the Academy, but the documents I examined show that the Ministry considered naming Heidegger president of the Academy, whose function was to select, according to political criteria, the new generation of university professors.

It is also significant that, along with Rosenberg and other high officials, Heidegger was asked by Hans Frank, Reichsjustizkommissar, to become a member of the Commission for the Philosophy of Law, an important decision-making body of the Academy for German Law, which was formed and directed by Frank himself and which had been established to replace Roman law by the new, "German" law. At the same time, Heidegger was giving speeches at the highest political school of the regime—the Advanced School for German Politics, at Berlin—with Rudolf Hess, Joseph Goebbels, Herman Göring, and Alfred Rosenberg. Heidegger continued his speeches at least into 1935.

Another theme concerns Heidegger's literary activities during the Nazi period and how his writings were received by the general public and particularly by the regime. This analysis illuminates not only the chronology of his editions but also the political context of his publications. For example, I have been able to affirm not only that the Rector's Address of 1933 was reedited in 1937, but that the text, "Hölderlin and the Essence of Poetry," published in the review *Das innere Reich*, was the text of a speech delivered in Rome in 1936, as part of the collaboration between the German and Italian governments at the German Institute in Rome. Also, the publication of "Remembrance of the Poet" in 1943, on the occasion of celebrating the centenary of Hölderlin's death, was made possible thanks to official support, which not only arranged to publish the volume containing Heidegger's article but to coopt the Hölderlin Society as well. We also need to keep in mind how the text "Plato's Doctrine of Truth" came to be published in a regular annual collection edited by Ernesto Grassi. In spite of an official veto by Rosenberg, Heidegger's article was published through Mussolini's direct intervention with Goebbels in 1943. This indicates not only the political friends Heidegger had and the influence he exercised at that time, but also the contradictions tied to the permanent struggle for power in the movement that never ceased to be part of official actions.

These lines of inquiry present Heidegger's political and philosophical activities in a different light and enable us to consider their systematic implications in a new way. It would all be insufficient, however, if we did not take into account Heidegger's subsequent philosophical and political evolution. My own research has led me to the conclusion that, even had Heidegger seen things differently after his "break" with the genuine National Socialist movement, we ourselves could not really understand his later development without taking account of his evident loyalty to a certain principle that rightly belongs to National Socialism and is conveyed in a manner and style that also belong to it. I offer as testimony of this not only the fact that in 1953 Heidegger was careful not to deny his opinion of "the grandeur and internal truth" of the Nazi movement but even more the facts about his clear and repeated refusal to make amends, given the monstrous crimes perpetrated during the Hitler regime, which by that time were widely acknowledged. If we review the whole interval beginning with the courses on Nietzsche's philosophy right up to the posthumously published interview with the weekly *Der Spiegel* (in which, for example, he claims that, when the French begin to think, they find they must speak German), it is clear that Heidegger always remained faithful to a whole spate of doctrines characteristic of National Socialism.

A genuine understanding of Heidegger's thought is impossible if one ignores this fidelity: as in his radically discriminatory attitude regarding the intellectual superiority of the Germans, rooted in their language and their destiny; in his belief in the primacy of his own thought, much like Hölderlin's, taken as a paradigm and guide for the spiritual development of humanity itself; in his radical opposition to any form of democracy. In opposition to frequent attempts to minimize the importance of Heidegger's connections to National Socialism, my own research has led me to conclude that, through this link, Heidegger found a way to connect himself and his past to the past of an entire epoch, and that, through that link as well, one could trace the subsequent evolution of Heidegger's thought in an essential way.[7]

I

From youth to the
rectorship (1889–1933)

1 Messkirch, origins, and the religious problem

In studying the genesis of any philosopher's thought, we can hardly doubt that the setting of his birth and early life will provide an important element. This principle is especially important in the case of Martin Heidegger. The connection with his place of origin, with the fatherland *(Heimat)*, is, in fact, a central theme of his reflections, a distinct determinant in all his philosophical work. Given the object of this study, it takes on greater importance. In effect, Heidegger's relationship with National Socialism was so closely tied to the question of *Heimat* that, in his eyes, its meaning could be explained only in terms of the notion of the German nation and one's place of origin.

Heidegger's hometown, Messkirch, has not been the object of any serious historical research. Other than the work by G. Tümbült[1] and the *Zimmerische Chronik*,[2] the only study worth mentioning is by Paul Motz,[3] who has done several studies on this part of southern Germany. His account of Messkirch, although brief, has a special interest for us because he was a fellow student of Heidegger's at the Konstanz *lycée* between 1903 and 1906 and stayed in close contact with Heidegger his whole life. He succeeded in periodically bringing together his old comrades, including Heidegger.

Motz's work indicates that the origins of Messkirch are very old. The region was already inhabited in the Bronze Age, and the oldest chroniclers emphatically report again and again the remains of Roman bridges and walls. From about the year 260, the Alemanni conquered territories north of Konstanz and the Rhine, peopled the area, and gave it different place names. The first reference to Messkirch does not appear, however, until 1080, in the chronicle of the life of Saint Hemereid, written by the monk Ekkebert, who was affiliated with the monastery at Hersfield, but was also a native of Messkirch. The place name "Messkirch" refers to a certain Masso, who founded a church there, no doubt in the seventh century, a time when Christianity was expanding to the east. It developed into an important town when it became the parish for a number of neighboring settlements. From the beginning of the thirteenth century, it held the rank of *forum,* and chronicles in 1261 call it *civitas* and *oppidum.* The first lords of Messkirch were the Counts of Rohrdorf, whose residence in the eleventh century was north of the town. They extended their holdings in the thirteenth century to Lake Konstanz, occupying Konstanz and an establishment on the Rhine. After the disappearance of this family line, Messkirch passed into the hands of the Walburgs (until 1300), to the Zimmern (fourteenth century), to the Helfensteins (until 1627), to the Fürstenbergs, until 1806, when it finally became part of the county of Baden.

Like all the territories between Lake Konstanz and the Danube, Messkirch saw the movement of a number of active armies and suffered the harsh consequences. In 1634, the town was invaded by the Swedish general Horn fighting against Swabian troops. Toward 1800, French and Austrian troops held the town in turn. In addition to the lord's chateau and administrative buildings, in 1814 the town could count 200 houses for 1,176 inhabitants and, in 1843, 309 houses for 1,696 inhabitants. Subsequent development of the town was due to the construction in 1870 of a rail line linking Radolfzell and Sigmaringen.

It was here that Martin Heidegger was born in 1889. During his earliest childhood, he was surrounded by the violent struggles then taking place between Catholics and Old Catholics *(Altkatholiken).* The dogma of papal infallibility, decided by the Council of 1870, had raised a serious controversy at the heart of German Catholicism. The majority of the bishops as well as the Catholic Centrist Party *(Zentrum)* in the Congress *(Reichstag)* finally accepted the dogma. But a dissident minority, which met in Munich to found Old Catholicism in 1871, did, in their first congress, denounce the new dogma as an ultramontane conspiracy fomented by the Jesuits. This opened the door to schism. Old Catholics were enthusiastically supported by "enlightened" and anti-Catholic members of the central government seeking German unity under the ecclesiastical hierarchy of Prussia. In 1872, they held a second congress, after which they requested the Prussian government to make them the sole official representatives of the Catholic Church and to allow them to proceed with a reform of the religious service and ecclesiastical administration. In 1873, Old Catholicism set up its own hierarchy, using the power of the bishops elected by a constituent assembly. The principal bishop named by this assembly was the theologian Josef H. Reikins, who was confirmed that same year by the movement's ministry. In 1873, at Konstanz, the third congress also created a communitarian synodal order. Among other things, the Synod of 1878 accepted the abolition of obligatory celibacy for churchmen. In 1901, the state recognized sixteen Old Catholic parish priests in Prussia, twenty-one in Baden, four in Bavaria, and two in Hesse. At that date Old Catholicism may have counted some 50,000 faithful. The Messkirch church was administratively attached to Konstanz, where Wessenberg had been able to assemble around himself a number of Old Catholic believers.[4]

Conrad Gröber has done the only study of the struggles between Old Catholics and Catholics at Messkirch.[5] Like Motz's article, it has some documentary value apart from its useful information because the author was intimately associated with Heidegger. Gröber, later archbishop of Freiburg, had been director of religious teaching at the *lycée* at Konstanz and had also directed the Saint Conrad residence where Heidegger lived during his Konstanz years. Consequently, Gröber's interpretation of this religious conflict and its effects at Messkirch (independent of its objective interest) allows us to see how the young Heidegger may have perceived them. First, Gröber understood Old Catholicism as a southern German would—as an attempt to destroy regional traditions that had profound ties to Catholicism. Thus, he denounced Old Catholicism as a movement radically opposed to the Roman Church and its hierarchy, but favorable to liberalism and the Enlightenment, close to freemasonry, and sufficiently distant from any popular base that it was becoming elitist and closer to the aristocracy than to the people. Only the privileged would find it acceptable—the privileged, who, he said, are naturally unbelievers.[6] With the support of Prussia and Bismarck, Old Catholicism could become a political force directed against the province and the local fatherland and especially against the hierarchical power of the Roman Catholic Church.[7] Gröber went so far as to call it violent and aggressive, emphasizing the group's tendency to violate law and custom. He gave several causes for the growth of this schism, the principal one being the failure of Catholics to take their faith seriously—that is, their lack of militant piety, their inability to confront the enemy with a strong political sense stiffened by an authentic, living faith.[8] Gröber turned their own accusations against the Prussian government—namely, that Catholics had been the "internal enemy," fighting national unity and freedom of conscience and seeking only the dissolution and fall of the Reich. It was, on the contrary, the destruction of Catholicism that seemed to Gröber to be the real threat to national unity. Gröber found clear proof of the fundamentally evil nature of Old Catholicism in its opportunism, which drew it into an alliance of doubtful quality with the "true internal enemy" of the Reich, Social Democracy.[9]

We see here the development of an ideology that combines the primacy of the local fatherland, opposition to rationalism and liberalism, a basic populism that considers Social Democracy the ultimate "internal enemy," and, finally, an unconditional adherence to the Roman Catholic Church and its hierarchy. This was the spiritual and political atmosphere that saturated Heidegger's childhood. Certainly by the 1890s, Old Catholicism in Messkirch was in retreat as a result of a strong Catholic counteroffensive. Still, anti-Catholic persecution continued to produce effects: "We know from bitter experience the pain children had to endure at this time. Catholic kids, for the most part the poor ones, were hit, mocked, and excluded by the richer kids, the privileged Old Catholics."[10]

Martin Heidegger could not avoid this struggle. His family was Catholic, his father a sacristan. At Messkirch, the sacristans were extremely active in the fight. Hunted by the police,[11] they often had to leave their parish dwellings. Only after a long period of such strife were they able again to lead stable, normal lives. One anecdote shows just how difficult those struggles must have been for the very young boy, for they threatened the very ground of his material and spiritual existence. At a particularly tense time, a certain sacristan, who was obliged to flee, entrusted the keys to the parish house to the five-year-old Heidegger, asking him to pass them on to his father.

Martin Heidegger was born into a poor family; his father worked as an artisan to earn the family's living, and his mother was the daughter of farmers in the area. Heidegger was able to study at Konstanz only through a stipend granted by the lords of Fürstenberg. His move from the Messkirch school to the *lycée* at Konstanz was due chiefly to the Catholic pastor, Camille Brandhuber,[12] who was also an important political figure. Brandhuber was active in the Catholic Centrist Party. He was a persuasive preacher and a member of the Prussian Parliament from Hohenzollern from 1908 until 1918, when he became president of the local Hohenzollern Parliament, a position he held until 1922.[13] The records of the Parliament show Pastor Brandhuber's populist connections.[14] The scholarship granted the young Heidegger came from the Weiss Foundation, created by someone with connections to the Catholic integrist movement, whose ostensible leader was Richard von Kralik.

From documents located in the archives of the *lycée* at Konstanz, we learn that the majority of Heidegger's fellow students were the sons of doctors, professors, wealthy farmers, civil servants, and evangelical ministers. Children of artisans or modest peasants were in the minority. During his years at Konstanz (1903–1906), Heidegger lived at Saint Conrad, a student residence founded in 1864 by the archbishop of Freiburg to give religious training to students who were to take orders in the Roman Church. These students received the rest of their education at the preparatory school at Konstanz.[15] This residence had also suffered from religious clashes. It was closed in 1874, and not reopened until 1888.[16] The Catholic hierarchy had considered it an important bastion ever since the *Kulturkampf* struggles, and during the years Heidegger spent there, the place was also seen as an asset in the fight against the growing influence of Protestantism and the liberalism of the area. Nor was the preparatory school at Konstanz spared. From its foundation in 1604 by the Jesuits, it had had to fight against lively resistance from the civil servants of the town.[17] In about 1880, there was a move to suppress religious schools in the provinces of Baden, Hesse, and Nassau, placing direction of the *lycées* in the hands of the state. Thus, it is probable that, with the school's change in ideology, the Church would try even harder to develop a militant Catholic consciousness in the boarders at Saint Conrad, where the young Heidegger was staying. In an ambience clearly pervaded by humanist notions, Heidegger belonged to a Catholic community that was fighting to maintain and enlarge its position.

Günther Dehn,[18] who was a pupil at the Konstanz *lycée* at nearly the same time as Heidegger, has left us enlightening memoirs of this interval. Among the professors held in most esteem by the majority of the students, Dehn names Pacius (modern languages), a democrat and a freethinker and pacifist, as well as Wilhelm Martens (history) and Otto Kimming (Greek, Latin, and German). The last two were Protestants, but not assigned to pastoral work, and the same was true for the two directors, Böckel and Mathy. Martens, whose books were used in the history classes at Konstanz, was an admirer of Lessing and did his best to communicate his enthusiasm to his students. Kimming was a humanist and idealist and preached the virtues of freedom of thought. Dehn describes in the following way how these two professors influenced him: "Only much later did I understand how much they unintentionally contributed to pulling me out of the ideal world of Christianity, which scarcely existed in their eyes."[19] Listen to his description of Saint Conrad and how the future seminarians were seen by their fellow students at the school:

We always looked down on them. They were badly dressed and, I must say, unwashed. Though we knew we were their superiors, we didn't fail to exploit them. At their residence they were forced to do their school work with the greatest care, and therefore we pushed them to do translations for us, and at recreation we copied their language and math homework. . . . These young kids lived completely isolated from the rest of the world. They were subjected to a harsh discipline that scarcely left them a single free hour in the day. After so many years, I now reproach myself for not having shown more fellowship with them. . . . Without knowing where the expression came from, we used to call them "Capuchins."[20]

Dehn's words are important for a number of reasons. By depicting the attitudes of his fellow students toward the group that included Heidegger, he helps us form an idea of what that group's reactions must have been. He also evokes the populist theme of Heidegger's later attraction to National Socialism. Heidegger's admiration for Abraham a Sancta Clara (the "Capuchin preacher" in Schiller's *Wallenstein*), the "son of the people" who captivated the imperial court at Vienna, may well be linked to the antagonistic social situation he knew at Konstanz. His identification with Abraham a Sancta Clara could only be reinforced by the fact that the monk was from the same region and had been a student at the same Latin school at Messkirch where Heidegger would much later begin his own studies.

Another characteristic of life at Saint Conrad was that conservative and "patriotic" pedagogic principles were combined with progressive and forward-looking elements. A chronicle of activities at the residence kept by the students themselves remains in the archives. The students could elect a kind of parliament of their own that had been empowered to voice suggestions to the religious and administrative authorities. We find in the chronicle the following lines written at the time Heidegger was living there: "It was an especially pleasant fact that this year our group will have six graduates. Even more important, five of them opted for the 'black'— I don't mean that in the political sense. But that they must become 'blacks' in the political sense as well could hardly be doubted by this chronicler." In other words, the five graduates who chose to become priests (black-robes) could not do otherwise than become members of the Centrist Party, the "blacks," as they were called. This was the political option governing education at Saint Conrad, a rather important matter for the writer of the chronicles.

I must also describe the lectures organized by the oldest students for their fellows. The chronicle of these years contains a list of them, and though it seems that Heidegger did not speak, they give us a good idea of the educational atmosphere in the residence. Certain titles suggest in fact that these talks were aimed at strengthening the Catholic consciousness of the students, helping them to stand up against the lay notion of the world that was common at the school. We note one talk on the "Salpeterer," a youth movement with ideas of a libertarian and radically democratic nature that spoke highly of mountain climbing and had links with a group called "Jacobins of Southern Germany."[21] Another such talk was "Is Goethe's *Iphigenia* a pagan-Christian figure or a Christian-German one?" One student, Max Josef Metzger, spoke on "History of the Monastery of Reichenau," another on "Scenes of Hegau" (at the time of Napoleon's campaigns), and another on "History of Lake Konstanz from the End of the Xth Century to the End of the Thirty Years' War." Shortly after, Metzger did an exposé on "Humanism." Another group of talks deserves attention because of titles that must have sparked the interest of the young Heidegger: a talk on "Views of a Landscape in Different Eras" or one by a student named Rombach on "Etymology in General and Particularly in the German Language." During Heidegger's stay at Saint Conrad, study trips were organized along the Rhine, through Mannheim and Cologne, and another in the valley of the Danube.

With all this in mind, we can at least claim that Heidegger found himself directly faced, during these important formative years, with the alternative, Religion versus Humanism, and obviously found no univocal resolution to the question. We know for certain that he was to choose at first the path to the Catholic priesthood, with all that that decision meant at that time, ideologically. But it is no less certain that some crisis then brought him to leave the seminary and abandon militant Catholicism, revealing a serious doubt not resolved until then.

This polarity does not necessarily convey some unconditional message. We would need to examine closely, for instance, the extent to which the liberal humanism of Heidegger's professors, and in general at the school in Konstanz, indicated true humanist convictions. Indeed, at this time, in southern Germany, just as in Austria, an anti-clericalism was growing that would later have direct links to fascism. A similar line of research could be profitably pursued regarding the reigning conservatism at Saint Conrad, because out of it would also be born political positions radically opposed to National Socialism. One example features Heidegger's fellow student Max Josef Metzger, mentioned above, who became a chaplain during the First World War, and was shot by a firing squad during the

Second, in 1944, for involvement in plots against Hitler. On the other hand, another of his fellow students, Albert Leo Schlageter, became a Nazi hero when France was invaded. Schlageter was a boarding student at Saint Conrad and was in the school at Konstanz, as well as at the Berthold Gymnasium at Freiburg, where Heidegger continued his secondary studies, beginning in 1906. It was Schlageter to whom Heidegger dedicated one of his most significant speeches in 1933.

Heidegger's move to Freiburg seems to have taken place at the time of a crisis at Saint Conrad, a crisis ending with the removal of the principal, Conrad Gröber, who was relegated to a parish in the region. This institutional crisis must have been matched, at the same time, by a personal crisis on Heidegger's part, and possibly also a sense of the difficulty of continuing this sort of life. The move meant additional expense for Heidegger's father, who, as we have seen, was a man of modest means. Conrad Gröber later became archbishop of Freiburg and for a time was one of the most enthusiastic supporters of Hitler's regime, one of those who crafted the Concordat between the Vatican and Germany.[22] It was he who gave Heidegger in 1907 the book by Franz Brentano, *The Manifold Meaning of Being,* a book Heidegger claimed played an important role in his philosophical evolution.[23] It was also at Konstanz that Heidegger had his first contact with philosophy through a manual used by the school, *Grundzüge der philosophischen Propädeutik* by Professor Richard Jonas, published in Berlin in 1891. This work is a very succinct introduction to logic and psychology, permeated by Kantianism. Although it defends Christian positions on the whole, it is far from approaching philosophy as would a text destined for future seminarians.[24]

Heidegger's moves to secondary school and to the seminary at Freiburg were made possible by a scholarship from the foundation in Messkirch established in the will of the theologian Christoph Eliner, who had been professor of theology and rector at the University of Freiburg in the sixteenth century (1567). At his death he had left his fortune to be used for scholarships for two students from Messkirch to study theology at Freiburg. Heidegger held this honor until 1911.[25] Heidegger entered the Berthold Gymnasium in 1906 and remained there until 1909. I have been unable to learn the circumstances of this period of his life because, according to the present administration, the archives were destroyed during World War II. But the young Heidegger's decision, in 1909, to enter the seminary leads me to suppose that during these three years the motivation that led him to live at Saint Conrad had not changed.

2   The Jesuit novitiate and the seminary at Freiburg

Heidegger decided, in 1909, to enter the Jesuit novitiate of Tisis at Feldkirch. The records of the school indicate that he spent only a very brief time there as a novice, from September 30 to October 13, without taking minor orders. This fact, however, does not mean at all that he had rejected plans to become a priest. In fact, he immediately became an intern *(Konvikt)* in theology at the archbishopric of Freiburg, where he studied until 1911.[1] The available documents appear to show that Heidegger decided to drop his studies at Freiburg for the same reasons that brought him to quit the Jesuit novitiate: heart problems of psychosomatic origin. Although he had followed a special treatment and had been exempt from all hard work, Heidegger had had to interrupt his studies about mid-February 1911 and go home to Messkirch to rest until his condition improved. But on his return to Freiburg the pains returned, obliging him to give up the internship once and for all.

The clinical reports of these troubles become enlightening when tallied with the conflictual situation he had known since beginning his studies at Konstanz. Such cardiac ailments with no physiological cause often appear in people who suffer from a dilemma they are unable to solve at the conscious level. When these patients make a decision that they neither really want nor are able to carry out, their ambivalence takes a somatic character. The cardiac muscle threatens to cease beating, thereby revealing the unconscious rejection of the decision and the desire to reverse it.

The symptom is often linked to more or less serious problems between fathers and sons. We may conjecture that the young Heidegger's religious vocation, although it was viewed as quite natural by his family, especially by his father, had rather too quickly caused an internal conflict reinforced somewhat by external influences rather distant from priestly ideals. It is possible that some of the devastating experiences he endured during his studies at Konstanz may have contributed to his conflict. In any case, his choice of the priesthood, perhaps compensatory in some way, proved essentially unstable. It is worth trying to reconstruct the bases of Heidegger's decision to enter the novitiate and then to become a Konvikt at Freiburg. We can get a better idea of how the Jesuits with whom Heidegger was in contact would think by consulting one of their most representative reviews published at Freiburg by Herder—the *Stimmen aus Maria Laach: Katholische Blätter*. Issue number 16, for 1909, for example, carried a series of articles whose ideological slant is clear. One of these, by Father H. Koch, SJ, concerns the principles that Koch says should guide the administration of the Reich in its colonial policies.[2] Koch accepts economic considerations as legitimate factors in transforming Germany into a colonial power, though only, he adds, if the government guarantees to spread the faith as part of political domination. Colonization must be at the same time a missionary undertaking. Koch regards German culture as a gift to "inferior" peoples, and he treats the gift of faith as the living element of that culture: "Under the protection of the flag of the fatherland, our mission can function successfully in ethical and religious activity as well as in the social and economic work created by colonizing."[3] The state must above all be vigilant in protecting missionary faith from the hostile intrusions of colonial administrators. The authorities must especially bear in mind "that Islam, dominant in East Africa, in Togo and the Cameroons, is an inimical cultural power to be fought by every means possible."[4] Koch adds: "It would be a grave error to think that Islam is a cultural stage that allows the natives to escape from paganism and an absence of culture to European civilization."[5] For him, Islam is a rigid form of life reduced to purely formal practices that cannot curb the lower passions. Polygamy and prostitution will quite naturally proceed from the base nature of this religion.[6] "Muslims are not able to discover for themselves superior forms of economic activity. Enemies of farm work and all serious labor in general, they demonstrate their ability and cunning only in that sort of commerce that often degenerates into mere exploitation and theft. In political matters, Arabs can never be trusted. Believing that Allah will make them masters of the world, they are never willing to be the loyal subjects of a European power."[7] To misconstrue these facts is proof not only of a misplaced romanticism but also of a false tolerance with respect to primitive peoples. Father Koch concludes that all colonization straying from these rules of conduct will wind up by confusing everything and amounting to nothing but pure economic exploitation.[8]

Two other articles, both by Father V. Cathrein, SJ—"Materialismus und Sozialdemokratie" and "Die sozialdemokratische Moral"—strongly criticize the political program of revisionist Marxists, especially Kautsky and Bernstein, for their theoretical inconsistencies as well as for their aggressive attitudes toward the Church and its rights. Cathrein hotly contests the concept of history cast in class terms, which, he says, leads to the destruction of the most fundamental social institutions: family, private property, and legitimate hierarchical order.[9] Social Democratic leaders seek to establish a "revolutionary party," which, since it lacks morality, must necessarily become a perverse and demoniacal agent.[10]

It is clear that the young Heidegger, entering the Society of Jesus as a novice, could not be antagonistic to the political and philosophical ideas favored by this review. We must not lose sight of the fact that Heidegger's decision to join the Jesuits was in part at least dictated by his desire to become part of a cultural and social world he would have had the utmost difficulty approaching in any other way. It is significant that in these two attempts to undertake a religious career, Heidegger turned first to the Jesuits, primarily a teaching order, and then to a diocesan seminary. Evidently, he was more attracted to the active than to the monastic and purely contemplative life that he would have found, for instance, at the Benedictine monastery at Beuron.

Heidegger's studies in theology at Freiburg have been examined in a short essay by B. Casper.[11] Casper notes that the young student had a profound interest in questions of exegesis, an interest shown by his choice of courses, and also that Heidegger probably got his taste for hermeneutics from Gottfried Hoberg. From Heidegger himself,[12] we learn that it was Carl Braig's teaching, especially in dogmatics, that stimulated him to reflect on the relationship between being and language. That much is clear. But the documents discovered by Casper also reveal Heidegger's explicit interest in strictly historical questions and his orientation toward professors who defended well-defined political positions. Casper's findings allow us to define important influences in Heidegger's ideological education at this time.

Casper reports that Heidegger not only chose to take Julius Mayer's courses on the Catholic notion of property but took courses as well from the historians Heinrich Finke ("The Age of the Renaissance") and Georg von Below ("The Constitutional History of Germany from the Sixteenth Century to Our Time"). Later I will examine the consequences of Hei-

degger's and Finke's relationship, especially with regard to the time Heidegger first tried to be nominated for the chair of philosophy in the
theology faculty. At this point, I will only describe roughly the ideological
situation around 1910.

Heinrich Finke occupied the chair of history at Freiburg at the end of
the last century.[13] His findings, supported by voluminous archival work
on the history of the Christian church during the Middle Ages, indicate
his total commitment to the national state: Bismarck's founding of the
Reich in 1870–1871 was for Finke an event of colossal significance. Finke
viewed the modern state as the inheritor of the medieval *imperium* and
consequently extolled "world imperialism" as the greatest work of the
"Germanic peoples," who, by integrating the national principle with universal history, would bring to a successful conclusion a mission of incomparable importance.[14] Finke was a distinguished member of the Catholic
Centrist Party.

Von Below, a native of East Prussia who had come to Freiburg in
1905, was to the right of Finke. Well known for having brought economic
history into the realm of the historical disciplines,[15] von Below held that
acknowledging the state in the form of a national state was the true foundation of history as a science. The state appeared to him as the most
important link between peoples, the essential organization of each people, and the source of all culture. Basing his ideas on such philosophies
as Wilhelm Dilthey's and Heinrich Rickert's, von Below also insisted on
the central role of particular individuals in history, rejecting the idea that
the science of history can abstract any laws of history without first considering the exemplary actions of certain figures.

Even before the advent of the Weimar Republic, von Below was famous for his extreme views. He considered democracy the worst danger
for Germany and its people. He had always been in favor of the most
aggressive expansionism, and he extolled a society divided into orders.
Moreover, he fed virulent anti-semitism by holding Jews responsible for
spreading anti-national, liberal, and democratic ideas.[16] He went so far as
to assert that, among educated Christians of German origin, only those
with clear deficiencies could have Marxist leanings, while among Jews this
tendency was the rule.[17]

Toward the end of World War I, von Below was one of the principal
leaders of the Deutsche Vaterlandspartei, an extremist group that advocated continuing the war to its ultimate end. In the town and at the University of Freiburg, he was naturally an important figure. Later he co-
published the review *Deutschlands Erneuerung* with the ideological racist
H. Stuart Chamberlain, who as early as the 1920s had spoken in favor of

the incipient National Socialist Party.[18] Earlier von Below had given free rein to his militant anti-semitism in another review, the *Konservative Mon- atsschrift*.[19] From this information, it appears evident that the young stu- dent Heidegger got his first scientific political education from professors holding positions that would become, in different ways, factors in the fascist takeover of power.

3 Abraham a Sancta Clara and Martin Heidegger's first written work

The context we have outlined in the preceding chapter will help us understand and interpret Heidegger's first writing and see how it is linked to his early spirituality and ideological evolution. The piece "On the Occasion of the Inauguration of a Monument to Abraham a Sancta Clara at Kreenheinstetten, August 15, 1910" was published in the review *Allgemeine Rundschau*.[1] Because the text brings together all the determining elements of Heidegger's ideological evolution and also contains certain motifs that proved critical in the future, we need to linger over their significance.

The Augustinian monk Abraham a Sancta Clara was a famous writer and the most important Catholic preacher in Germany during the Baroque era. An extraordinary satirist and a biting critic of contemporary morality, he became the official preacher of imperial Austria, wielding considerable influence over the political and religious life of the time, especially in Vienna. His fame lives even in our time, mostly in southern Germany. He was born in 1644 in the Swabian village of Kreenheinstetten, not far from Messkirch. His given name was Johann Ulrich Megerle. His first education was at the Latin school in Messkirch, Heidegger's home town. He continued his studies at the Jesuit house at Ingolstadt, then with the Benedictines at the Salzburg Gymnasium,[2] where he received the best intellectual education a young Catholic could expect at that time.

Megerle came from a modest family, of neither a peasant nor a poor artisan background. His father kept a tavern. Earlier, an ancestor, Abraham von Megerle, had been raised to the nobility by Frederick III and had served as a notary and church canon at Altötting.[3] In 1662, Ulrich Megerle joined the discalced monks at Taxa in Bavaria, received orders in 1666, and became a pastor at Taxa. When he returned to the monastery in 1668, he began his career as preacher. His talent quickly earned him the admiration of Leopold I, who named him court preacher. This was an extremely important post, the highest in fact that anyone could receive without being a member of the nobility.[4]

An outbreak of the plague in 1679 and then the seige of Vienna by the Turks in 1683 were decisive for Abraham a Sancta Clara's life and success. His *Merck's Wien (Beware Vienna!)* was the first chronicle of the plague, and his war pamphlet *Auf, auf Ihr Christen (Rise, You Christians!)* was written during the period of the resistance against the Turkish invasion.

A prolific writer, with some twenty volumes attributed to him, he had great vitality and energy and bordered on fanaticism both in speech and writing. His influence was a determining factor in the manner of preaching in Austria and southern Germany. In 1680, he became the superior of his monastery, and he was made provincial of the order in 1690. He died in 1709 at the height of his fame and creative powers. All his books, epistles, and sermons consisted of forthright criticism of behavior in Vienna and the court, and even society at large. His rhetorical style came from his Jesuit training, which focused his diatribes on religious questions.[5] Friedrich Schiller was so taken by his strong personality that he used him for the character of the "Capuchin preacher" in his play *Wallenstein* (1799).

The image of Abraham a Sancta Clara as "court plebian" was a later creation, hardly a historical reality, but it does show with some faithfulness his own political machinations. His political concerns focused exclusively on two themes: Turks and Jews. For him, both were archetypes of the Evil threatening Viennese Christianity. In the guise of pursuing religious matters he preached an extreme xenophobia: "What is a Turk? A true Antichrist, a famished tiger, a consummate Satan, a damned aggressor of everything that he is not, a monster of sinister cruelty, an insatiable and vindictive beast, a poison from the East, a raging dog, a tyrant, the opposite of a man. The Turk is the flail of God."[6] And Abraham praised those "warriors who steep their daggers in the barbarian blood of the enemy."[7]

Anti-semitism had already had a long history, and now again it reached a peak with Abraham's labors. Cruelly persecuted and then finally expelled from Vienna in 1491, Viennese Jews had returned to live in relative calm, but were again expelled in 1669. Exploited, pursued, and oppressed, at times even sent to the stake (Salzburg), Jews were held responsible for economic troubles in a system where they had no power, and were even blamed for natural catastrophes.

Abraham a Sancta Clara was preaching after their second exile, which made his violent anti-semitism somewhat peculiar. No doubt its purpose was to justify Leopold after the fact, and also to keep alive a keen hatred of Jews. "The Jew is an atheist without honor, conscience, virtue, faith, and even reason, and is incurably so." The Jew is the mortal enemy of all that is Christian, and "his blackguard behavior would fill books and books." In his chronicle of the plague, Abraham accused witches and Jews of being the willing and direct causes of this frightful tragedy: "It is clear that our pestilential scourge is the work of perverted enemies, Jews, gravediggers, and witches."[8] From the pulpit, he proclaimed the truth of those medieval legends according to which Jews would spit on consecrated hosts and sacrifice baptized children for their devil worship: "This damned diseased crew ought to be chased wherever they go. . . . And because of what they did to Jesus, every Holy Thursday the nostrils of their male children fill up with worms, they are born with pigs' teeth, and the sons of those Jews who flogged the Christ are born with the right arm shorter than the left one."[9] And more: "Other than Satan, the worst enemy of mankind are the Jews. . . . Their beliefs are such that they all ought to be hanged, even burnt."[10] Anti-semitic literature was rich at the time, but Abraham's was particularly notable, according to O. Frankl[11] and others who have expressed an opinion about how Abraham was regarded during the time when Heidegger published his article.

Abraham's anti-semitism and xenophobia came at a time when nationalism was undergoing a bitter struggle. Since Austria was part of the German world for him, the preacher explained his criticism of behavior by offering as a criterion of moral judgment "the purity of the Swabian peasant" and all that was *Teutsch* (Teuton, German), as opposed to the infiltrating alien practices of peoples like the French, the Italians, and the Spanish. In *Centifolium Stultorum*, Abraham warned against the dangers of using foreign languages: learning a language other than German meant adopting other habits, and it was not rare to find that those who set aside their mother tongue ended by becoming traitors to the fatherland. In *Lauberhütt II*, he claimed that young Germans who traveled to other countries "to study and become refined" most often returned with nothing more than "a disease or a dagger in their bodies, or with the low wiles of the Italians or the effrontery of the French." Adults who traveled returned having lost "valor, wealth, life, and soul. Believers who go to France return atheists; they replace their character and good habits with doubts and idle ideas."[12] In *Reimb dich,* he wrote that "Germans are the most peaceful and upright of humans. Yet many nations who live in fear of the light like bats are jealous of us and treat us like dogs. Perhaps that is because we've so often nipped at their heels."[13] Germans were not only the best thinkers and inventors but also the best painters known to mankind.[14] Naturally, Abraham put the fatherland in God's hands: "God has never forsaken a German [a Teuton]."[15]

Historians have generally acknowledged that anti-semitic currents in Austria and southern Germany hark back to Abraham a Sancta Clara.[16] His greatest influence may be found in Catholic areas, where anti-semitism is rife mostly among the middle classes and intellectuals of a nationalist bent. Catholic anti-semitism has its medieval roots and sees Abraham as one of its chief ideologues.[17] Radical anti-semitism and xenophobia deriving from Abraham found new life in the writings of the founders of Austrian Christian Socialism, the priests Josef Scheicher and Sebastian Brunner. The latter was influenced from childhood by Abraham and cited him in his public pronouncements as the perfect authority.[18] It is thanks to Brunner that, even during an era of liberalism there was a very considerable recovery of all the anti-semitic prejudices and superstitions of earlier times—of the Baroque age, of the period called the period of "the Court Jew" (1673–1782), and of the time of Josephism.[19]

The Christian Socialist movement came from Catholic romantic sources and, like romanticism, viewed the Enlightenment as its chief enemy. The spiritual father of the movement was the Redemptorist priest Clemens Maria Hofbauer (1751–1820), who was quickly canonized. His disciples resurrected the Movement of Catholic Restoration in 1848, which Sebastian Brunner joined.[20] The movement quickly found a leader in Karl Lueger, who was born in Vienna. Lueger's father was of lower Austrian peasant stock; his mother came from a family of artisans. His political followers had similar backgrounds. Lueger received a doctorate in law and began a political career as the major defender and flag-carrier for the "little people," who formed the majority in the Viennese suburbs. In 1887, with the priests A. Latschka and L. Psenner, he founded the anti-semitic sheet *Österreichischer Volksfreund.* He began his public career with a speech that broke all prevailing constraints on anti-semitism.[21]

Backed by the majority of young Viennese priests, who smarted under the conservative monarchic hierarchy, and helped by the Jesuits, Lueger and his Christian Socialism got almost as many votes as the liberals in the local elections of 1901. Lueger became the chief of the anti-semites in the local Parliament,[22] where one of the members, Ernst Schneider, moved an addendum to a bill granting a bounty to those who would kill birds, stipulating that there would be an additional bounty for those who killed a Jew.[23]

At this time, Parliament did not play a large role in the country. On the other hand, the mayoralty of Vienna was a powerful post, and the Christian Socialists fought to win it. Filled with trite expressions, Viennese dialect, and attacks against the liberals, their oratory resonated among the populist masses. Their promise to eliminate "the Jewish private interests theatening to strangle the economy and the population" was received with enthusiasm by the civil servants of the city and, even more significantly, among many of the inhabitants of the suburbs. These people were all the more susceptible to such propaganda because they were suffering from the oppressive growth of population in Vienna, which posed terrible problems of lodging, health, and sanitation. In fact, Austria's capital city came to house the highest proportion of tuberculosis cases in all Europe.

As the unchallenged leader of anti-semites and anti-liberals, Lueger fought the alliance formed by the Catholic hierarchy, the aristocracy, and the liberals, taking the populist side in a sort of "class struggle" within the Church and within Viennese society. Several times he won the election for mayor of Vienna. Frightened by what he thought Lueger could do as mayor, however, the Emperor refused to confirm his election until it became evident that the real menace was the growth of Social Democracy, not only because of its call for violent revolution but also because of claims that it had been infiltrated by Jews, whom Lueger and his friends denounced. This is how Karl Lueger finally became mayor of Vienna in 1897 and could finally begin to establish populist reforms. With the fiscal purse now at his disposal, Lueger bought from England a city-wide sewer system, had a gas distribution system installed, brought trams to Vienna, extended city water distribution, had hospitals and schools built, and even had a public slaughterhouse erected, which brought into play some elementary norms of sanitation.[24]

Lueger was close to the international anti-semitic movement and received from Leon Daudet on his sixtieth birthday the following wishes: "I am happy to shout: Down with Jews!" When Lueger died in 1910, crowds of Viennese, as well as German admirers and many from other countries, came to offer their last homage. Emotion was especially strong in south Germany—for example, at Konstanz (*Konstanzer Nachrichten,* March 12), at Sigmaringen (*Hohenzollerische Volkszeitung,* also March 12), and at Messkirch (*Heuberger Blatt,* again March 12). Among the spectators at the burial was the young Adolf Hitler, who later wrote his youthful memories and the first stammerings about National Socialism in *Mein Kampf:*

When the imposing funeral procession of the Burgomaster set out from City Hall toward the Ringstrasse, I found myself among the hundreds of thousands of people attending this ceremony. Along with my inner emotions there was the mixed feeling that all the work of this man had been in vain because fortune was leading this State inexorably toward its death. If Doctor Lueger had lived in Germany, he would have had a first place among our notables. It is too bad for him and for his work that he had to live in this impossible State.[25]

What did Hitler consider inadequate in Lueger's political work? Certainly Lueger knew how to promote and direct a true mass movement, which Georg Ritter von Schönerer, the chief anti-semite at that time, did not. But Hitler criticized Lueger for not having achieved an ideology comparable to the one Schönerer had and for his failure to develop the theory needed for the movement.[26]

Martin Heidegger's first writing described the inauguration of the monument dedicated to Abraham a Sancta Clara and analyzed its significance. The circumstances surrounding the erection of the monument have made this long introduction necessary. For instance, the population of Kreenheinstetten had not been able to collect the necessary funds, and essential financial contribution had come from the central administration of Vienna, where Lueger reigned. After considering the request from Kreenheinstetten, the Viennese Council decided in its favor on July 12, 1901. The two hundredth anniversary of the Augustinian preacher "who had such close ties with the Viennese community" would be funded with one thousand crowns.[27] Shortly after, the same group agreed to underwrite the cost of publishing the works of Abraham a Sancta Clara.[28] After numerous discussions and other steps that cost some years of effort by the ad hoc committee at Kreenheinstetten, the monument was finally ready for its official inauguration on August 15, 1910.[29]

The festival for the occasion produced considerable repercussions throughout the region. All the newspapers carried articles about it: the *Hohenzollerische Zeitung* (August 16) and the *Neue Konstanzer* and the *Konstanzer Nachrichten* (August 13, 16, 17), as well as the Vienna *Reichspost* (August 20). The two dailies at Messkirch, the *Oberbadische Grenzbote* and the *Heuberger Volksblatt* (August 16), emphasized the solemn spirit and the immense popular support it generated. It was an event without precedent in the region, the fatherland of Abraham a Sancta Clara. For this magnificent day—"it was as if the skies were aware of the meaning of this celebration"—all the houses of the village were decorated with flowers

and banners with quotations from Father Abraham. Flags were everywhere.

The day began with high mass for the region's faithful. The city of
Vienna sent as representatives the deputy Dr. Tomola and Professor
Zimmermann. The festivities were also attended by a delegation of monks
from the monastery at Beuron, by Karl Bertsche (the best-known specialist on Abraham a Sancta Clara), and by young Catholics from Messkirch dressed in their traditional colors:

> The crowd began marching behind a herald and four horsemen,
> all wearing multicolored costumes from the time of Father
> Abraham, as well as breastplates. School children carried different
> flags and flowers. The military club and a group of bicyclists with
> banners brought up the rear. At the foot of the monument, the
> groups were received by the writer Marquart, who spoke in the
> name of the city, and by Pastor Gessler of Engelswies, who
> officially unveiled the statue and made the gift to the town. Dr.
> Tomola from Vienna spoke of the "aid given by Vienna as a
> natural mark of thanks and a response to the generosity of
> Kreenheinstetten, which had sent them such an extraordinary
> person to fight the Turks and the French. We are proud that
> Father Abraham came from the same popular groups as all those
> present, for we know that the great men of a people do not
> come from palaces, but are born in the humble dwellings of
> peasants and city folk." Dr. Tomola also said that he did not want
> to recall only the connections between Father Abraham and Karl
> Lueger (whose mother was also Swabian) but also "the blood
> uniting Kreenheinstetten and Vienna, who stand today hand in
> hand to salute the work accomplished by Abraham for the
> German spirit." The ceremony ended with students reading
> poems from the *Blütenlese* by Karl Bertsche.

The Catholics from Kreenheinstetten, and even Beuron, belonged to
a fringe of German Catholicism that held the same political and religious
positions as the Christian Socialists around Karl Lueger. The traditional
group, unswervingly faithful to the conservative hierarchy, held other
political views. We find this difference in several articles printed at the
time of Lueger's death in the *Historisch-politische Blätter*, a review belonging to the Görres family.[30] The article "To the memory of Doctor Lueger," for example, acknowledges the successes of Christian Socialism, but

criticizes Lueger's anti-semitism, warning against any general identification of Catholicism with this movement.

The piece by Martin Heidegger, "Abraham a Sancta Clara," has two
principal parts. In the first part, Heidegger discusses the speeches already presented and describes the atmosphere of the ceremony. In the
second, he expresses his own views about the meaning attached to Abraham a Sancta Clara and the inauguration. Unlike the journalists covering
the event, he begins by emphasizing the simplicity of the small town and
the surrounding territory, and also of the ceremony itself: "What gives
this ceremony its particular character is the natural, healthy, and fresh,
even unpolished accent. . . . This country of unmarked frontiers, dark
forests with pines in the fog, bright sun in spots, and rocky outcrops,
makes for an odd atmosphere. . . . The inauguration ceremony is like
the place: simple, clear, and true."[31]

Heidegger next speaks about the addresses, using the words of the
pastor from Engelswies, who had expressed his thanks to the city of Vienna for having done so much "to save the honor of her preacher." Heidegger also speaks of the Viennese orator, who had said that Abraham a
Sancta Clara had been sent by Providence, as had "Clemens Maria Hofbauer and the unforgettable Lueger": "The care with which the Austrian
chose his words, his clear convictions, his love of the people worked like
a spell."

Commenting on the words of the principal speaker, Pastor Mart from
Eigeltingen ("also a son of the craggy mountain of Heuberg"), Heidegger
emphasizes "that through him are expressed the strength, the unshakable
faith, the love of God held by those born Catholic." And he adds, "We
must know the area of Kreenheinstetten, penetrate its depths so as to
think and live with the people of Heuberg to understand the singular
attraction emanating from Father Abraham."

Heidegger then describes the statue, expressing his own impression of
it and Abraham himself through it:

> The head of genius (so similar as to be mistaken for the old
> Goethe) helps us imagine the profound and inexhaustible spirit of
> untamed energy behind that broad and expressive forehead able
> to engage every tempest with an insatiable thirst for fruitful
> action. The health of the people, in soul and body, that's what this
> genuinely apostolic preacher longed for.

So Abraham a Sancta Clara becomes an exemplary figure of the en-
ergetic guide, working for the health of the people in body and soul.
"Literary and cultural history has revised its judgment of the man once

called the 'farceur.' His humor marked by malice, his shining barbs of
wit, his often biting irony, expressed briefly and concisely in supple language, cannot be understood but as oratorical genius." According to Heidegger, this genius who knows how to forge his own law ought to become
a model for opposing today's culture:

> If only our totally superficial culture of today, which loves rapid
> change, could visualize the future by turning to look more closely
> at the past! This rage for innovation that collapses foundations,
> this foolish negligence of the deep spiritual content in life and art,
> this modern concept of life as a rapid sequence of instant
> pleasures, . . . so many signs of decadence, a sad denial of health
> and of the transcendent character of life.

It is quite clear that the criticism of culture extolled here by Heidegger
goes well beyond a conservative traditionalism. By inscribing the problem
in a frame that opposes health to sickness (authentic values of the past to
present secularized and liberal values), he invites a "spiritual" counteroffensive having, at the very least, aggressive possibilities. Even more so
when he uses Abraham as the very model of action and reaction: "Great
people like Abraham a Sancta Clara ought to remain alive in us, working
silently in the soul of the people. Would to God that his writings were
found more often among us, that his spirit . . . could become a powerful
ferment to conserve—and, even more urgently, to restore—the health of
our people."

The original text indicates that Heidegger's first talks on the preacher
were drawn from the *Blütenlese* by Karl Bertsche, published in 1910. This
book may be considered a sourcebook, therefore, especially because of
the interpretation given by Bertsche in the introduction. It is in conformity with Christian Socialism and served as a model for Heidegger. Bertsche
takes the quote from Abraham's *Judas*—"He who is born in a thatch hut
does not have just thatch in his head"[32]—and applies it to Abraham himself, saying that "truth finds the fatherland the surest among its compan-
ions, as also in small towns not yet contaminated by the hypocrisy that
destroys palaces." Bertsche also cites passages that express the bitter
struggles of nationalism.[33] He uses euphemisms when speaking of Abraham's anti-semitism: In the arguments against those "of another faith,"
Abraham was "a son of another time," speaking "in ways that seem harsh
and gross to refined twentieth-century ears."[34] Bertsche arranges the text
by themes: "City Life,"[35] "Vanity of Life Here,"[36] "Rich and Poor,"[37]
"Death,"[38] "Conscience."[39] Unfortunately the importance of this text in
Heidegger's philosophical and political formation is not clear to the reader

who proceeds in quite good faith to read the text in the *Collected Works*,[40] because, without our being given any reason, the text that is provided there omits the quotes Heidegger included in the original text of 1910 from Bertsche's *Blütenlese*.

This is an important matter because in 1943 Bertsche published in Vienna the posthumous writings of Abraham at Vienna with the support of Baldur von Schirach, Hitler's Reichsstatthalter in occupied Austria. We will return to this when we analyze Heidegger's second text on Abraham in 1964.

We must also consider the review that published this first writing, the *Allgemeine Rundschau*. Founded in 1904 by Dr. Armin Kausen and loyal to the Catholic Centrist Party, it accentuated the clearly anti-semitic and Christian Socialist programs. In the twelfth issue, some months after the one that included Heidegger's article, is an obituary for Lueger: "When Lueger was elected to the local Parliament, he could immediately see the corruption and its source. To free the fatherland, he knew he had first to crush liberalism dominated by Jews, and then to found a new party, one that would later bring him to the mayoralty. . . . From 1875 to 1896 the grand struggle continued against Jewish liberalism, an excrescence of Viennese life for generations. . . . First he thought he could succeed in the democratic party, but his disgust with the Jews already effectively installed made him leave"—that is, to found the Christian Socialist movement. Beginning in 1913, the *Allgemeine Rundschau* became even more radical in its anti-semitism and attacks on Social Democracy. Here are some titles: "The Jewish Press and Social Democracy," "German Nationalism and Social Christianity," "Richard Wagner," "Radicalism in Baden."[41] Later, however, the paper would refuse to support the growing National Socialist movement, and in 1932 it wrote against legalizing the NSDAP.[42]

Now we must return to Heidegger's connections with the cult of Father Abraham as it existed in his region. In spite of his youth, Heidegger was already known in Baden, hence his participation in the celebration for the Augustinian monk. Messkirch's Catholic daily, *Heuberger Volksblatt*, mentions, on July 21, 1909, that "young Martin Heidegger, bright and talented son of Friedrich Heidegger, sacristan, obtained his baccaulaureat at Freiburg, with honors, and plans to devote himself to theological studies."

On September 20, 1909, the same paper notes that "enthusiasm for Abraham a Sancta Clara has found good harvest among students, who have planned a celebration in his honor." This took place September 6 at nearby Hausen im Tal and attracted a number of people. We find in the same paper on September 10 that many were students:

All came with the same intention, to honor our compatriot, Abraham a Sancta Clara, to remember his work and to draw a great enthusiasm from it, to find a new ideal for professional life. . . . From the beginning we were conscious of the difficulties to be overcome if this celebration was to take place. First we needed time to raise enthusiasm and to quicken everyone's energy, which actually took only a little time. Next we needed speakers as well as helpers to be responsible for arrangements. The earlier ceremony proved a happy decision. . . . The presidency was exercised with a good deal of skill and judgment by the theology student Martin Heidegger from Messkirch. He began the festivities with words bordering on poetry, and in his short talk recalled the ideas that brought people here to render homage to Abraham a Sancta Clara, writer and preacher.

Then the reporter described high points of the day and finally said about Heidegger's speech:

After hymns were sung, President Heidegger spoke in a proper classical style about recent literary polemics in German Catholicism. He explained clearly the disputes between the reviews *Hochland* and *Gral*, showing how *Hochland* was going too deeply into the waters of modernism and by its exaggerated criticisms of Catholic writers was ruining the plans of its own founder, Karl Muth. We hope that this very objective speech that illuminates the positive and negative aspects of both camps will be known widely. At the end, Heidegger forcefully encouraged his listeners, particularly the students, to subscribe to *Gral* and to join the organization publishing the review. His remarks evoked thunderous applause.

The *Heuberger Volksblatt*, the organ of the Catholic Centrist Party, next reported the reading of passages from Abraham's *Judas the Scum* by the philosophy student Neusch. "After Heidegger had thanked all who had helped with the celebration, it ended with another song." There was a second celebration by the students at the Realschule of Messkirch in December 1909.[43]

The polemic that was central to Heidegger's speech was the *Literaturstreit*, a deep wound for German Catholics at the time because it placed in opposition ultraconservatives and the Catholic integrists, led by the Viennese ideologue Richard von Kralik and the modernists, led by Carl Muth. Their respective reviews, *Der Gral* and *Hochland*, supported explicitly opposing views about how German Catholics ought to react to mod-

ern culture and the problems modern culture posed for the Church and
its dogmas. According to von Kralik, Catholic culture had to return to its
source and give birth to a specifically Catholic science and literature, always in absolute conformity with Rome.[44] Von Kralik's review denounced
the views of Muth and his *Hochland*, which was advising integration with
non-Catholic society. Von Kralik called this position a betrayal of Catholic
ideas, which by nature are true and superior.[45] Pope Pius X entered the
quarrel directly and wrote a supporting letter to von Kralik.[46] Von Kralik
was at that time the leading figure of the Catholic integrist movement,
which was powerful in southern Germany but counted Vienna as its ideological bastion.

Von Kralik's supporters set up a militant organization, the Gralbund,
which the young Heidegger joined. He seems to have had an important
part to play in it. The group's name clearly refers to the somewhat parallel bundist movement, which was linked to the youth group (*Jugend
bewegung*), later to be the Völkisch, an immediate predecessor of National
Socialism. In Austria, the Bund movement (*bündisch*) first appeared
among the middle class, somewhat like the support groups of German-
speaking Austrians fighting for a "Germanic" national identity in the midst
of the mixed peoples who made up Austria.[47] The Bund gathered its
young members into a "community" that opposed civilization and technology by leading a "simple life" and by trying to realize a unique mission
based on the lived experience (*Erlebnis*) of that community and run by
charismatic guides (*Führer*). The point was to link themselves with the
real people (*Volkstum*) and their traditions.[48] Von Kralik's Catholicism appeared as flaming Germanism:

> As we read in the Book of Daniel, each nation has it own angelic
> principle, its guardian angel, its genius as guide. But just as
> each member of our organic body (even though not all with the
> same dignity) has a different function, so Divine Providence
> has charged different people and different states with different
> missions. The psychology of peoples shows that there are
> active and passive people. . . . Tacitus . . . placed the Germans
> of his time above all others because he admired the German *spirit*.
> This fact establishes, as Jacob Grimm saw it, an honor for
> Germans of all times.[49]

All this was tied to the ideal of a new Germanic Roman Empire directed by Catholic Austria. Of the two possible Germanic spiritual centers, Gothic Aryan Protestantism or Franconian (*fränkisch*) Catholicism,
von Kralik saw historic vitality only in the latter. Opposed to Prussian

Protestantism, von Kralik claimed that the Carolingian kings, especially Charlemagne, had created German grandeur by close collaboration with Rome and the papacy. The Greater German ideology (*grossdeutsch*) was in essence Catholic. That nationalism was not a move to isolate Germany, but, on the contrary, to reunite it with German Danes, the Slavs of Bohemia, and the Hungarians, who had early accepted Germanic principles:

> The German people does not die, its substance is healthy, is growing and developing, and is adapted for life. It constitutes one people more effectively *[völkischer]* than the French and other rivals. . . . It is not by chance that "deutsch" means the same as "völkisch," because since the *Germania* of Tacitus the German people is the only one worthy of that name in the entire post-classical world. Everything that has value in a people *[völkisch]*, all political and cultural value since antiquity, whether in Italy, Spain, Gaul, Britain, Russia, or elsewhere, derives from Germanic influence. Since the time of Christ, the world progress is becoming German and Christian. . . . The concept of the Great Germanic Empire is indestructible.[50]

In this way, von Kralik's "revolutionary" ideas (also conservative) were explicitly added to principles proposed by Richard Wagner, whom von Kralik considered his ancestor,[51] and by Austrian neo-romanticism, whose precursors were the Redemptorist Clemens Maria Hofbauer and Friedrich von Schlegel.[52] "The idea of the Reich is inextricably tied to German romanticism, which ought rightly to be called Germanism. The ideal took form with Wagner in 1871 in opposition to Bismarkism. Bayreuth, the *Nibelungen, Parsifal* form the ground on which should be grafted the new poetry, the new art, the new Catholic science."[53] "It is from Austria, land of the song of the Nibelungs, of Walther von der Vogelweide, of Grillparzer and Raimund, as well as from Germany, land of the Weimar classics, that the German spirit will take life, so as to create the true *grossdeutsch* form, or, better, to recreate it."[54] "This ought not be understood as imperialism because the German peoples are the only peoples having a genuinely universal dimension. The English and the Americans are just German rejects who know only what they have learned from Germans. Their mother was always Germany." Von Kralik ends by saying: "German literature is the only universal literature in that it alone is able to take over the literatures of all other peoples by means of that incomparable instrument, the German language. It is the most perfect language of all. . . . It is only when humanity will listen to the guides of Germany and Austria that they will know what politics is, for until now they have no idea of it at all."[55]

In this sense, it pays to recall the function von Kralik assigned Abraham a Sancta Clara,[56] as well as his anti-semitism, which, even if only implied, serves as the basis of his social and religious opinions. Von Kralik did not hide his total agreement with Lueger and his anti-semitic Christian Socialism.[57] In the archives in Vienna are many of von Kralik's unedited papers. In some of them are references to the Gralbund, to his program, his organization, and his political preferences. In *Der Wiener Gralbund* (February 1920), von Kralik says that the work and spirit that propelled the Gralbund is "the same spiritual current that won the Christian Socialist victory of Mayor Lueger" and that one of the first promoters of the Gralbund was the poet Franz Eichert, "the author of several fighting songs of the movement."

We find in von Kralik the notion of the determining role of language and literature in history.[58] This notion implies a criticism of modern art and culture, a criticism the young Heidegger would absorb almost literally in his own 1910 article, for he uses the same terminology. In addition, the concepts of "soul of the people" and "tradition," which Heidegger employs in the article, are analogous in form and context with those found in von Kralik's writings.[59]

Von Kralik's group included J. Weiss (1820–1899), a Catholic historian and theologian who gave his name to the foundation that granted Heidegger the scholarship to finance a part of his studies. Weiss was the author of a monumental historical work in twenty-two volumes,[60] which after his death was completed by Kralik. Other important figures include Karl Bertsche, who wrote on Abraham a Sancta Clara in the *Gral*,[61] and Josef Nadler, also a writer for the *Gral* and an associate of von Kralik's.[62] Von Kralik's correspondence with Nadler, located in the Viennese archives, reveals how the integrist "patriarchs" influenced the youth of the time. We find evidence that the "youth movement" obeyed certain ideological directives originating outside the movement that were linked to certain conservative social and political forces.

4   Heidegger's contribution to the *Akademiker*

The clarification of Heidegger's ideological development between 1910 and 1913, the year of his promotion, reveals some unknown
works of importance, which Hugo Ott has pointed out, that Heidegger
published in the periodical *Der Akademiker*. At issue are eight texts: three
collective reviews and five short individual reviews. The collective reviews
carry the titles: "Per Mortem ad Vitam (Reflections on Jörgensen's *Lebenslüge und Lebenswahrheit*),"[1] "Toward a Philosophical Orientation for Academics,"[2] and "Religious Psychology and the Unconscious."[3] The individual reviews deal with F. W. Foerster's *Authority and Freedom: Thoughts
on the Problem of Culture in the Church*,[4] and A. J. Cüpper's *Sealed Lips: An
Account of the Life of the Irish People in the Nineteenth Century*,[5] J. Jörgensen's
Travelbook: Light and Dark Nature and Spirit,[6] J. Gredt's *Elementa Philosophiae Aristotelico-Tomisticae*, vol. 1,[7] and Hellinghaus' *Library of Worthwhile
Novels and Tales*.[8]

The periodical *Der Akademiker: Monatsschrift des Katholischen Akademiker-
Verbandes* was a private publication of the Catholic Academic Association
in Munich from 1908 until 1917, when publication ceased. It was Dr.
Arnim Kausen, who directed the *Allgemeine Rundschau*, in which Heidegger published his essay on Abraham a Sancta Clara, who characterized
the *Akademiker* as a "general organ for Catholic academics and different
corporate groups" open to "all areas of student life, pure scholarly interests in religion and social concerns, artistic questions in literature and
fiction, [and] its own standing interests."[9]

The journal unequivocally provided Catholics with insight into their role in academia. Vis-à-vis modernism the journal championed official Church policy[10] and supported ultramontane Catholic interests in the battle with the Old Catholics.[11] The controversy between Catholics and Old Catholics provided a forum for von Kralik's integrists and Muth's followers to explain their views.[12] The journal declared war on Marxism and further applied itself to popularizing the Church's social teaching.[13] It did not concentrate on presenting theoretical questions, but energetically encouraged Catholic students and academics to take part in meetings and to join Catholic organizations.[14] Since the young Heidegger was in Freiburg at this time, it is important to note that the student groups there played a leading role in those activities.[15] There was talk of forming an alliance with workers and apprentices that would be modeled after the cooperation between the Catholic students and the Christian Socialist Party in Austria. Thus guided, the students promoted in various issues of the journal the Catholic conception of mission involving German colonial policy. The journal also invited students to take part in this work.[16]

World War I spurred the journal on. The *Akademiker* even established a permanent column titled "War Literature" in which reviews on war literature appeared. In 1915 an article titled "The Prophecies of the World War, 1914/15" appeared in which the "Zionist" poet Robert Hamerling was assailed.[17] Also included in the issue was a tribute to H. Stuart Chamberlain[18] and a commentary on "Heinrich Mohr's Field Letters" by Engelbert Krebs, Heidegger's advisor.[19]

The anti-semitism that was imprinted on the Church and public life in the last phases of the Kaiser's rule[20] found its way onto the pages of the *Akademiker*. Not only did it manifest itself in literary and historical analysis; it was politically applied. The journal called attention to the significance of Karl Lueger's death for the student population and also drew the connection between his work and the romantic tradition and Richard Wagner.[21] Lueger's life proved to be a special source of inner strength for the people.

> Just as Schiller, the idealist par excellence, might have declared in words suggested by Karl Moor: A curse on the pen-pushing Saeculum, a curse on the limp castrated century, a curse on the unjustified and the sinners—the same sentiment vibrated in the soul of the young Lueger. Such was the vengeance he brooded over. The reform he wanted was the banishment of all sickness and frivolity from his homeland.

The author of these words, Joseph Eberle, was the publisher of the Catholic periodical *Schönere Zukunft* and was one of the best-known publishers between the wars and on into the Nazi era.[22] His book *Grossmacht Presse* is a "classic work" of anti-semitism.[23] For Eberle the question concerning the Jews was the "question of all questions." He saw the solution to this issue in the "restriction of Jews from all branches of culture and the economy with corresponding population quotas." In the journal *Das Neue Reich,* which appealed to Catholic academics, Eberle began to shape a vendetta against the Jewish people. Richard von Kralik also published a text in the journal in which he proposed a hymn to be disseminated among the people: "God conserve, God protect our land from the Jews! Power through the pillars of belief, Christians take your stand. Let our rightful Father shield us from our worst enemies. Let not our people come to ruin, let them remain unified in their Faith!"[24] After Kristallnacht, Eberle wrote, "It is frequently the children who first pay for the sins of the fathers."[25]

Other authors in the *Akademiker* did not keep their anti-semitism a secret. M. G. Lap, in a review "Neuere Klassikerausgaben, "praised the distinction of Lenaus . . . , whose romantic discontent was a tool for greatness in opposition to the Jewish poet Heine's."[26] The young Heidegger sharply attacked Heine, a move that matched the journal's political posture,[27] which after all had turned to the spiritual and pedagogical significance of Abraham a Sancta Clara.[28]

The *Akademiker* filled an important function for the organization of young Catholic graduates. Complete editions of the periodical would be devoted to promoting a greater Catholic unity, and contributors would comment on each other's efforts. This was especially the case for the Akademische Piusvereine.[29] The Piusvereine were founded in March 1848;[30] in 1907, the year the *Akademiker* was founded, the Jesuit Father Viktor Kolb, on the occasion of the Austrian Katholikentages, called a Piusverein into existence "as a war union . . . to repel the world-encompassing alliance of Israel,"[31] which had taken control of the press in Austria, as well as in other parts of Europe, in order to carry out a "world-plan,"—namely, "the destruction of the religious, moral, and material foundation of Christianity and on the very ruins of the Christian people to build a new Zion."[32] Kolb succeeded in bringing 75,000 members into his organization.[33]

The *Akademiker* published a message from Pius X in 1909 to the Akademische Piusvereine Deutschlands.[34] Besides this the journal propagated the goals of other significant Catholic associations like the Sankt-Klemens-Maria-Hofbauer-Verein,[35] the Verein Südmark,[36] the Katholische Akademiker-Ausschuss,[37] the Gral,[38] the Sozial-caritativen Vereinigungen katholischer Studenten Deutschlands, and the Vinzenzverein.[39]

Heidegger's contributions to the *Akademiker* are marked by their unconditional support of the reactionary positions of Catholic integralism, an aggressive critique of modernism, and a defense of the *Akademiker*'s theological and philosophical offspring as well as of Christian social values in general. Indeed, by 1912 Heidegger had already touched on such newer goals, which grew out of his interpretation of Thomistic philosophy. However, in his interpretation of history and society he remained true to the more conservative principles he had taken from the Church. This is displayed in his essay on Jörgensen, in which he is occupied with the author's conversion to Catholicism. In his description of this process ideological elements appear that had already been manifest in Heidegger's treatment of Abraham a Sancta Clara. The young Heidegger had presented Abraham as a commanding personality, a leader *(Führer)* of people, though certainly not in the ordinary sense of the word. For he had sharply criticized the cult of personality that prevailed at the time:

In our day one speaks a great deal of "personality." And philosophers always find new value concepts. Besides critical, moral, and aesthetic value we now deal with the "value of personality," especially in literature. The artistic personality is coming into prominence. So now we hear of such interesting men: Oscar Wilde, the dandy, [Paul] Verlaine, the "genial drunk," [Maxim] Gorky, the great vagabond, the Nietzschean superman. And if, when one of them were, in a moment of Christian grace, to become conscious of the Big Lie of his rootless life, the altars of the false gods would be shattered, they would then call it insipid and disgusting.[40]

The conditions for developing a "personality" lie, Heidegger continues, neither within the terms of one's own ability nor of one's own freedom. Individual freedom and personal power are gained to the fullest extent only if one turns to tradition and the authority of an unquestionably higher superpersonal power, which Heidegger finds embodied in the doctrines and institutions of the Church. In this regard he writes: "At the age of eighteen Jörgensen was an atheist. Soon he found himself swimming in a free-thinking movement in which (even in his seventies Georg Brandes, the Danish Heine, was also caught up: for free inquiry and free thought had become the battle cry of modern Danish literature." Heidegger viewed the enlightenment and liberalizing tendencies, as represented by Heine and Brandes, as the most disastrous temptations of the spirit. This outlook parallels the opinion of others in the *Akademiker:* for instance, M. G. Lap, who denied "the Jew Heine's" greatness, and A. von Roth, who with extreme chauvinism attacked the aesthetic position of von Kralik, saying, "The expression 'I am a German poet' sounds a bit strange for a man who received a pension from the French government for his sympathetic stories. He was not ashamed of this. In his description of the war of liberation as a kick ventured by Prussian asses against dangerous lions, dirty Teutonic boots could once again profane the holy ground of the Parisian boulevard."[41]

Heidegger took Brandes to be an agent of liberalism and thought he enabled the "spirit of Nietzsche and Zola," transported to Denmark, to be "all powerful." "Consider Denmark's greatest atheist, J. P. Jacobsen. He was too weak to live and not sick enough to die. He dragged himself through life. There's the model of decadence facing Jörgensen while he was in school."[42] The critique of the foundations of aesthetics that Heidegger was schooled in faithfully followed von Kralik's integrist principles:

> In beauty the artist finds his heart and his art. But what is it that we find beautiful that a mere rule or an intention might acquaint us with? The unfortunate author of "Niels Lyhne" gives the answer: "I find the wilderness beautiful, the untamed and the untameable Nature, the hot, never-satisfied passion of the Renaissance men." The purest Cesar-Borgia-like enthusiasm of a Nietzsche! Sin and the false idols of abomination overwhelm us with flattery. The golden calf, fame, and the Babylonian Venus stand before the altars. And what should your poetry be? The pleasures the people fawn over. . . . That was what "Supernaturalism" tossed over its shoulder. The enemy of obscurantism, the great "personalities," that had brought the Ego to complete development. Life was an ecstasy. And on and on one drifts downwards, until one is drawn to death and despair and "calls for holy corruption."

Pain and decay follow conversion: What a wonder! "Every morning God's help is needed. A strong hand stirs him. He sees. The Darwinist bustles about. With iron discipline he steps forward and up." Thus does Heidegger diagnose Jacobsen's inadequacies with utter contempt. His every spiritual resource is assessed. Natural power and divine grace apparently concur—a veritable spiritual and supernatural Darwinism:

Luck is only possible through life's lies. Was Ibsen correct in
maintaining this proposition? No; he was repeating a biological
law. The truth must naturalize into luck; lies, into destruction.
That is the productive premise. Here we are led to the truth that
you will be punished for your transgressions. Now, however,
who have more energetically pursued the truth, who have thrown
all their prejudices overboard, broken all their chains, who have
not established their convictions with the "spiritual and ethical
sovereignty of the Ego"? Have the great "personalities" found luck?
No, despair and death look upon this line of witnesses; having
gone astray, they find a revolver pointed at their heads. So none
of them have the truth; their individualism is a false norm for life.
Then ban the flesh's inclinations, worldly doctrines, the pagan
world.

For "the higher forms of life are conditioned by the destruction of the
lower forms. The plants use inorganic material for growth. Animals live
only on the death of plants and so the line continues. And do you want
a spiritual life? Do you want to gain your happiness? Then die, kill the
base things in you, work with supernatural grace and you will be resurrected." In Jörgensen's conversion Heidegger not only sees the power of
Catholicism at work but also love of homeland. In his commentary on
Jörgensen's *Travelbook* he connects Jörgensen's turning to God with his
reconciliation with homeland: "He saw in the old German cities the shaded
bay window, the familiar images of the Madonna mounted on houses.
He heard the murmuring of sleepy springs and eavesdropped on mel-
ancholy folk songs. The German June evening, in which one might be
lost in dreamy silence, hovers over his beloved books. The convert's God-
filled and fulfilling longings for home might well constitute the most
powerful impetus for his art."[43]

The review of F. W. Foerster's book is significant in a number of respects for Heidegger's development. The importance the *Akademiker* gave
Foerster makes it worth our while to scrutinize the journal's editorial policies rather closely,[44] not just on this account but because Foerster played
a substantial role in the pacifist movement before, during, and after World
War I.[45] For this reason not only would he be beset in Prussia but even
after the war he would be quite a key figure in the debate over war rep-
arations.[46] Since we cannot establish Heidegger's positions up to World
War I and since the majority of German intellectuals supported the war,
it should be clarified whether Heidegger (under the influence of Foerster)
maintained a certain distance from the war. The matter has some ur-

gency, since Heidegger would later advocate (in his speech on Schlageter) the aggressive politics of the Nazis. In his review, at least, Heidegger does not go into this central aspect of Foerster's work; rather, he concentrates on features of Foerster's publications that reveal his beliefs as a reactionary ideologue. He emphasizes every circumstance that he had raised in his observations on Jörgensen's conversion and had radicalized in a most extreme way:

> The glaring conflicts of our time—here the reality-passion *[Wirlichkeitsfanatismus]* for the naturalistic, socialistic order of life; there, a new world of ideas and notions of life-values formed in accord with an immanence philosophy—are the final results of an unbridled autonomy. Foerster raised the question of competence when he asked if modern individualism was legitimate and capable of solving the deepest problems of religious and ethical life as he saw them. In an inductive manner, he came to a decisive No.[47]

His first reason, which is explicitly anti-democratic, is mentioned by Heidegger: "It is already an almost crushing fact that most people turn out to be for themselves and not interested in discovering the truth or attaining it; they would rather be nailed to the cross and removes every justification for an individualistic ethic." The similarity between this argument and the anti-democratic posture Heidegger later formulated in *Being and Time* (1927), under the influence of Paul Yorck von Wartenburg, is obvious. The second reason that Heidegger proposes was already contained in his opinion of Jörgensen:

> Furthermore the fundamental truths of life cannot be construed a priori in a scientific manner. Rather a rich and deep life experience, the very source of freedom, is needed in order to oppose the world of instinct. Only then can the famous cult of personality prosper at all, by remaining in close contact with the richest and deepest source of religious and ethical authority. In the nature of things this can hardly happen without a suitable embodiment. And the Church, true to its eternal truth, will with justice oppose the correcting influence of modernism, which is quite unaware of the deep conflict between its world view and the ancient wisdom of the Christian tradition.

The praise that Heidegger bestows on Foerster's book highlights every ideology that he himself fought at every opportunity:

Those who never place a foot on the path of error, never allow themselves to be dazzled by the misleading appearance of the modern spirit, those, however, who venture through life in a truer, deeper well-grounded *Entselbstung* in the brightness of truth, will herald this book as a great joy. It will make surprisingly clear the great good luck of possessing the truth. One keeps in mind while enjoying reading this book the words of the great Görres: "Dig deeper and you will strike Catholic ground." Foerster was bold enough not to shrink from any consequences in order to dig deeper.

In his paper "Toward a Philosophical Orientation for Academics" Heidegger pits two philosophical concepts against one another:

Philosophy, in truth a mirror of eternity, today only reflects subjective opinions, personal views and wishes. Anti-intellectualism allows philosophy to become no more than "inner experience"; one has turned it into impressionism, tied it to the "value of the moment," linked it with dark impulses as a sort of "Eclecticism," the most inconsistent sort of thought for a world view. The system is finished. There must be a system in it, since it "produces world views" today. A strong, ice-cold logic opposes the delicate modern soul. "Thought" can no longer be allowed to force into the unchanging, eternal bounds of logical principles. But, of course, we already have them. To this strong logical thought, closed to any real influence from the hermetic mind, to every *genuine* presuppositionless scientific work, belongs a certain depth of ethical power, the power of self-control and self-renunciation.[48]

This radical contradiction, Heidegger contends, reverses conceptual inclinations: "Today, world views are cut out of life, rather than the other way around. Because of this wavering, because of the encroachment of a certain excessive refinement in handling philosophical questions, despite so much conviction and smugness, there erupts an unperceived craving for complete and final answers to the questions of Being. It sometimes flashes so abruptly that some days there is left only a weight of lead lying on the tortured, rudderless soul." The young Heidegger thus emphasizes his intention; that is, young academics ought to be strengthened in their Catholic beliefs. He recommends taking an active religious course organized by the Catholic student unions, which was regularly alluded to in the *Akademiker:*

There can be no doubt about the urgency of a thorough
grounding in Christian apologetics. A timely thought like that
could be translated into action through a scheme of religious-scientific
lectures; the eternal greatness of the fundamental truths of
Christianity would be expounded in a fine manner; we would
kindle enthusiasm in the soul of the Catholic student, to remind
him of "what we have," and to prepare him more keenly to
consider his own individual potential.

All the same, this purely theoretical objective is not quite enough. Heidegger turns to his fellow students with great vigor in order to stir in
them a sympathy for the search for truth:

Actual self-possession of this wealth of truth, however, implies an
undaunted, indefatigible self-motivation that can never be
replaced by listening to lectures. The young spirit, propelled by an
inner magical urgency toward the truth, seeks to secure the
necessary experience by assimilating the requisite principle for
himself. He is then confronted by the critical problem of working
out and grasping a genuine world view for himself, for that is
the only true means in which the goodness of truth is gained.

Heidegger's review of the book *Sealed Lips* by A. J. Cüpper shows its
author to have been completely taken with Richard von Kralik's integrist
aesthetic, which affirmed Catholicism to be the principal guide for in-
structing its people:

The author does not permit himself to be swept up in mere
literary trends. Uninfluenced, he travels the tranquil path of his
wholesome, popularly edifying art. One is constantly tempted by
the story alone to attribute to Cüpper a dramatic capability.
The nobility of the deep trust in God demonstrated by the priest
in this book is all the more uplifting when we contrast it to the
distortions and tendentious designs we come across in our
own literature that are invested in no more than the sensational
and the titillating.[49]

Heidegger's articles in the *Akademiker* are also proof of his early efforts
to distance himself from scholastic philosophy, especially in his commentary on J. Gredt's textbook *Elementa Philosophiae Aristotelico-Tomisticae*, about
which Heidegger expresses many reservations: "The definition of philos-

ophy (p. 1) is much too cheap. The scholastic logic ought to be gradually extricated from its rigidity and apparent isolation."[50] This ought to happen, Heidegger says, because "philosophy is not a mere sum of settled teachings that one could confidently carry home in his memory or in black and white." Heidegger is steadfast in holding to the goals of Aristotelian logic and opposes Gredt's attempt to cast it as the "science of all sciences." Heidegger's own philosophy, starting with the study of Edmund Husserl's *Logical Investigations* and its handling of the problem of psychologism, hardly led him to revise his basic assumptions about the nature of history and society that he had adopted in his own Catholic integrist phase. On the contrary, his later secularization of these themes conferred on his initial ideology its distinctively sharp contours.

5   From Freiburg to Marburg

Studies at the University of Freiburg

Heidegger's connections with the *Allgemeine Rundschau*—that is, with the radical fringes of the Catholic Centrist Party—had probably been encouraged by the historian Heinrich Finke, an eminent member of the organization. The article by B. Casper discussed in Chapter 2 implies that Heidegger and Finke must have been close when Heidegger was a student of theology at Freiburg and took classes from Finke. Casper notes that, after leaving the Catholic seminary at Freiburg, Heidegger, in spite of his interest in history, registered at the recently opened school of mathematics and natural sciences,[1] studies that he dropped in the summer of 1913.[2] He remained in close contact with Finke at this time. Casper cites from biographical notes written by a common friend, Professor Engelbert Krebs, the following pertinent paragraph dated November 14, 1913: "This afternoon [Martin Heidegger] came to see me and said that Finke had stopped him on the street to urge him to choose a historical-philosophical thesis. Finke implied that, since the chair of that department was at present empty, he ought to hurry to prepare himself to take advantage of the opportunity."[3] Engelbert Krebs, professor of dogmatics in the theology faculty, was also close to Heidegger, probably because of Heidegger's strong Catholicism. Krebs was one of the spiritual directors of the seminarians while Heidegger was studying philosophy at Freiburg. It was Krebs, around 1913, who tried harder than anyone else to bring Heidegger into the professorial body of the university by offering him the chair in Catholic philosophy.

Heidegger's doctoral thesis in philosophy ("The Doctrine of Judgment in Psychologism," Freiburg, 1914), which he defended in 1913, was directed by a young Catholic professor, Arthur Schneider. This fact reveals how close Heidegger was to both faculty and Church. He chose not to work with Heinrich Rickert, the most prestigious professor of philosophy, but with a relatively unknown teacher whose single book was *The Psychology of Albert the Great*.[4] Heidegger received the diploma *(venia legendi)* on July 31, 1915, which made him a Privatdozent at the university. The essay he wrote for the habilitation was "The Doctrine of Categories and Meaning in Duns Scotus," directed by Rickert, if we can trust a report Heidegger sent to Georg Misch concerning appointments at the University of Göttingen, a subject we shall discuss later.

In his dissertation on judgment in psychologism, Heidegger directs his criticism at the claim that there is an intentional consistency in the laws of logic, a claim that derived from Edmund Husserl's understanding of psychic phenomena. Heidegger must have read Husserl's *Logical Investigations* during his seminary studies,[5] but Heinrich Rickert's influence is surely also a factor. Casper tells us that Heidegger was in Rickert's course "Introduction to Logic and Metaphysics" during the summer of 1913 and also attended his seminar on "Exercises on a Theory of Knowledge, Concerning the Doctrine of Judgment."[6]

World War I

During World War I, Heidegger's philosophical, political, and religious development went through several important stages. According to data he himself sent to the *Führer-Lexikon* (1933–1934), Heidegger enlisted in August 1914 and was released in October of the same year. From 1915 to 1917, he was part of the postal service in Freiburg and, in 1918, was in combat training and at the front as a rifleman in a quartermaster batallion of the 11th infantry regiment. At the end of the war, according to this source, he was in the weather service with the troops at Verdun.

Documents I have consulted in the Krankenbuchlager at Berlin differ somewhat from Heidegger's report in the National Socialist *Lexikon*. I can find, in fact, only his entry as rifleman on September 18, 1915, stationed at Mullheim, and his dismissal as not fit for combat on October 16, 1915. I have not found evidence of any earlier military service. Knowing his later work, I find it difficult to believe that his war efforts were limited to what I have managed to verify. The sources also offer nothing about what he might have published about the war. His later general reflections on war, especially concerning his former friend Albert Leo Schlageter, lead me to believe that Heidegger must have made reference to the war in public pronouncements or in correspondence. This is most likely because all the German university personnel who were of the same ideological bent as Heidegger, and even the moderates, were outspoken in their support of the aggressive politics of the Reich, even before the beginning of hostilities.[7]

This was especially true for those close to Heidegger. Karl Bertsche published a selection of texts from Abraham a Sancta Clara—*War, Nourishment of the Soul* (Freiburg, 1917)—as a religious weapon for soldiers at the front. In the introduction, Bertsche writes:

> Like its sisters, death, malady, and poverty, war has the high mission of testing the pilgrims of life, of making a selection among them . . . , because in peacetime men become slothful, but war brings out an inner strength that permits them to do the impossible. . . . It is said that Abraham was a "moral swordsman." How true this is. He spoke as a soldier, as a warrior. His very nature was warlike through and through, filled with personal courage, never knowing fear, inspired by the spirit of sacrifice for the fatherland. This is how Abraham is a good friend of the soldiers, an active chaplain.

The text is a pastiche of Abraham's sermons and writings on the Turks and Jews, which Bertsche "modernizes": "Let the enemy with its black, white, and even yellow savages strike! With its half and quarter savages! We have no fear of them because God is on our side! . . . Rise, German Christians! Avenge the blood of your fellow Christians devoured by the savage beast, by the Russian beast thirsting for blood."[8]

Similarly, Heinrich Finke actively participated in organizing Catholics in the universities to answer attacks from French bishops and their French faithful, who accused German Catholics of "Germanic arrogance and contempt of Latin peoples."[9] Finke organized a permanent committee for the defense of German and Catholic interests in World War I that circulated documents in an attempt to counter the enemy's positions. The member of the committee responsible for the *Monatshefte* was precisely Professor Engelbert Krebs, who also wrote often on the war—notably, *The Secret of Our Strength: Reflections on the Great War,* in which he made religion an element of war.[10] He also wrote, in French, *How War Prisoners Live in Germany.*[11] At the same time, Georg von Below was playing a large part in the Deutsche Vaterlandspartei, the most violent group of the period, which condemned other rightest German groups for refusing to use violence.

Against the prevailing anti-war feeling in Germany, the Deutsche Vaterlandspartei opposed to the bitter end every move favoring a "shameful peace" and called for a superhuman effort to gain a cease fire that would guarantee Germany the positions she had held at the beginning of the war.[12] Since we are interested in Rickert's influence on Heidegger, we must consider his views on the war: We see them clearly in his correspondence with his student and Heidegger's friend, Emil Lask, who was at the front. Rickert wrote to Lask on May 28, 1915:

I do not share the sense of great disappointment that Italy's move has brought to many, even wounding them profoundly. Italy is a proud country, yet Italians I have known seem nasty and offensive. I believe that the Italian government has acted just like Florentine coachmen do: if we give one of them exactly what the fares require, he puts on a mask of "moral indignation," considers it a threat to his "most sacred patrimony," and then calls to his defense an unsavory mob. We are then obliged to accede to his demands to escape a nasty scene. As to what Italy's actions mean for the outcome of the war, I can't say. But I try to think as little as possible about the Triple Alliance, null from now on. It makes no sense to look back.[13]

Finally, we should consider the position of Lask, to whom Heidegger later dedicated his habilitation work, in memory of Lask in his distant soldier's tomb. The young soldier wrote to his mother in November 1914: "Finally it's time to leave. I've been terribly impatient with everything in jeopardy, feeling that I was being inactive instead of using absolutely all my available strength when *everything* is at stake. It's unbearable not to be able to contribute, not even in the smallest way."[14]

Martin Heidegger, teacher of Catholic philosophy: the crisis of modernism and the break with the Church

No doubt it was Engelbert Krebs's high regard for Heidegger that brought the theology faculty to hire Heidegger to teach philosophy classes. In the winter semester of 1915–1916, he chose to do a history of

ancient philosophy. During the summer semester of 1916, he directed
(with Krebs) a seminar on some texts of Aristotle. In the winter of 1916–
1917, the Baden Ministry of Culture asked him to offer instruction on
"Catholic philosophy," which issued a course on "Fundamental Questions
of Logic."[15] The friendship between Krebs and Heidegger went well beyond that of the academy. Krebs blessed the union of Martin Heidegger
and Elfride Petri in the cathedral of Freiburg in 1917. Elfride Petri was
the daughter of an Army officer; she was Protestant by birth and remained so.

Everything indicated that Heidegger would begin his university career
on the theology faculty of the University of Freiburg. It was not to go
this way, however, and Joseph Geyser was appointed to the chair by the
faculty and the Archbishop's Office in the summer semester of 1917.[16]
This was a great disappointment for Heidegger, perhaps responsible for
his first move away from the Church. There were, however, also doctrinal reasons. While Heidegger was teaching at Freiburg, violent quarrels were taking place at the heart of Catholicism, notably on the question
of modernism, which from about 1900 had a strong influence on the
philosophy and social doctrines of the Church. Beginning with analyses
of the philosophy of religion, the history of dogma, apologetics, and exegesis of scriptures, the modernists came out in favor of the possibility of
a natural experience of divinity, quietly putting aside the supernatural
character of both dogma and Church. One reason for this stand was to
allow for the rational examination of religious experience. Consequently,
church and state seemed to become two spheres without any necessary
connection.

Pope Pius X condemned modernism in 1907 in the encyclical *Pacendi
dominici gregis* and decreed in 1910 that all clergy, including all those who
taught Catholic philosophy and theology, were to take an "anti-modernist
vow" if they were to be allowed to do the work of the Church.[17] This
touched off violent arguments in the German universities. The Organization of University Professors, meeting at Dresden in 1911, decided that
colleagues who took this vow would be excluded from the universities. In
the region of Baden, where the move seems to have started, several professors went so far as to exclude from the universities those who submit-
ted to the decision of the Pope. At first the government acceded to the
request of the body of professors, but under pressure from Prussia quickly
reversed itself. We can guess that the faculty of theology at Freiburg was
at this time in a rather isolated position. Yet it is true that, according to
what Georg Misch reported about Heidegger (apparently from information Heidegger had given him), Heidegger must already have left the

theology faculty and even the Church because of his disgust at Rome's decision. The situation is, however, far from clear, for we may note in Misch's report that in distancing himself from the Church Heidegger may have strengthened his chances with the philosophy faculty at Göttingen.

Karl Braig, like Krebs, had been a spiritual counselor to the seminarians of Freiburg at the time Heidegger was studying there, and was the most vocal defender of the papal decree. In his work *Modernism and the Freedom of Science*,[18] Braig denies that the modernists were authentically interested in freedom of thought and true rational research. Other writings of Braig's warn Catholic intellectuals against the dangers hidden in this modernist apostasy.[19]

Finally, all these factors succeeded in distancing Heidegger from the faculty of theology as well as from the Church. Writing to Krebs on January 19, 1919, Heidegger gave his reasons for deciding from now on to work only in philosophy. Epistemological notions, he says, relating to the theory of historical knowledge, have made the *system* of Catholicism problematic and unacceptable in his eyes, but not Christianity or metaphysics (this last item now certainly taken in a new sense). Heidegger claims to have grasped the values held by medieval Catholicism "better perhaps than its official interpreters" and gives assurance that his forthcoming researches on phenomenology of religion will bear witness to his high regard for the Catholic world. After reaffirming his friendship, Heidegger takes his leave of Krebs, telling him that he believes in his own philosophical vocation and that he is convinced that, thanks to this vocation, he will be able "to justify his existence and his work before God."[20]

Before receiving the offer from the University of Marburg (which he would take), Heidegger gave three courses on subjects closely allied to theology: in the winter semester, 1919–1920, "Philosophical Bases of Medieval Mysticism"; during the winter of 1920–1921, "Introduction to the Phenomenology of Religion"; during the summer of 1921, "Saint Augustine and Neoplatonism."[21] Thus, although Heidegger's break with Catholicism took place about 1919, he maintained an ambivalent connection with the Church. Surprisingly, despite the virulent anti-clericalism he would express during the crisis with the student association Ripuaria, he clearly declared himself a Catholic on questionnaires from the Ministry of Education.[22]

Here we must add another factor that perhaps contributed to Heidegger's break with the Catholic Church. The German defeat and the establishment of the Weimar Republic brought changes in German society in the 1920s and had immediate effects on university politics. Since professors were ultimately named by the Ministry of Education, a center of republican power, the Church no longer had any voice in these decisions. We can guess that most scholars starting their careers adapted to the new situation, taking positions outside their beliefs, at least in dealings with the Ministry.

Heidegger's ambivalence toward the Church can perhaps (with some caution) be summed up best by a quotation from the diary of Engelbert Krebs, professor of theology and spiritual director at the seminary, a diary held in the Krebs collection of the faculty of theology. In the diary Krebs mentions Heidegger's move to Marburg. On Saturday, June 23, 1923, Krebs wrote, "Heidegger has been named *ordinarius* in philosophy at Marburg. This will influence his notion of the world." Then, on September 1, 1923, Krebs remarked, "After dinner this evening, we saw our colleague Heidegger. . . . I asked him if he had not yet come back to the Catholic faith and dogmas, and he answered, 'Absolutely not at this time.' But he does work a great deal on Augustine and Thomas, and Aristotle. I had the impression during our talk that I was hearing my friend of the past, and was sitting across from the truly Catholic sage. I believe that this evening has joined us forever."

Husserl at Freiburg

When Edmund Husserl arrived at Freiburg in 1916 to replace Rickert, who had left for Heidelberg to replace Windelband, this meant a new period in the life of Heidegger. Not only did Husserl personally direct the research and teaching of a generation of young thinkers, but Heidegger's own work and interests were close to Husserl's thought and would grow in precision and coherence as a result. The meeting of the two thinkers has already been widely discussed. What has not really been studied, however, is the philosophical and political milieu in which this meeting took place. This is understandable, at least in the case of Heidegger, because the work of the two philosophers moved to a level that seemed to leave no place for historical reflection or for reflection of a specifically philosophico-political sort. In fact, this phase of phenomenology inspired no work favoring such considerations. It remains nonetheless true that the political options to which the most eminent academics adhered clearly reflected the ideological orientation of the majority of German university professors at the time. Even if later events (including those of National Socialism) led along paths quite different for the "phenomenologists" at Freiburg, we are forced to the conclusion that, at the time of World War I, they were all unconditionally in favor of the

Reich's positions, with all that implies about their notions of the state, the German nation, and society. In 1915, for instance, Max Scheler, a recent convert to Catholicism, published a work on *The Genius of War and of the German War*,[23] where he attributes to war the value of a "metaphysical awakening" in that it permits the birth of a true spirit of sacrifice, devotion, and love, thus leading to God. Scheler posits a substantial relationship between "political emotions" and "religious and spiritual contents."[24]

Positions like Scheler's often were formulated in an immediate and empiric context, but they faithfully reflect the philosophico-political milieu within which Heidegger began his research and teaching in the entourage of Husserl and his colleagues. When we realize this, we must realize the inaccuracy of the view according to which Heidegger's thought evolved in a politically aseptic milieu, concerned with only abstract questions.

6 Marburg, *Being and Time,* and the various appointments

For our purposes it is of the utmost importance to review the events of Heidegger's appointments. For not only did academic appointments play a considerable role in the university life of Germany, which was distinctly dependent on government influence; in Heidegger's case the appointments cast some further light on his own political activities.

In his post as an Extraordinariat (associate professor) at Marburg, Heidegger prospered in evangelical Prussia as he had not as a member of the Catholic theology faculty at Freiburg. The call to Marburg came after the University of Göttingen, likewise a traditional Prussian university, had placed Heidegger second on a list to succeed Hermann Nohl, who had been promoted to the position of professor of education. The appointments committee, headed by Georg Misch, named Moritz Geiger as the first candidate on November 2, 1922. But being named as the second candidate at Göttingen opened the door to being considered for further appointments. As the documents in the Göttingen archives show, Heidegger's candidacy was supported by Husserl, whose support carried great weight, since Husserl had been a professor at Göttingen until 1916.

The commission's report presenting the candidates' qualifications for the philosophy post, which appears in the same archive, was written by Georg Misch.[1] In retrospect its report is particularly instructive, for it indicates the beginning of Heidegger's relationship with the most important proponents of Lebensphilosophie. (Misch was not only the son-in-law of Wilhelm Dilthey but also Dilthey's most important student.) Misch emphatically supported the candidacy of Heidegger, whom he describes

in the report as an "unusually strong personality." He also refers expressly to the reasons that Heidegger had given for distancing himself
from Catholicism and the church, apparently using biographical information provided by Heidegger as the basis of his own report. Doubtless
he did this in order to increase Heidegger's chances with the faculty, who
were not unwilling to take a stand against religious and Church interests.
From this we can gather what sort of role a candidate's religious affiliation played in his evaluation as a scholar and especially as a philosopher.
Misch wrote on Heidegger: "Heidegger has freed himself from that strict
doctrinal affiliation in which scientific interests were bound, and, when
the modernist oath was required, he decided to leave the seminary and
his theological studies behind." In his report Misch emphasizes that Heidegger's lectures and seminars at Freiburg have, "in spite of heavy intellectual demands," made Heidegger a philosophical star and a distinct attraction for students. An indication of Heidegger's stand at that time with
regard to phenomenology and Lebensphilosophie can be seen from Misch's
report:

> One gets an impression of his lecture plan from his writings: he
> links history and systematic philosophy, and he favors the present
> form of "Lebensphilosophie" in which Husserl's logical, extremely
> carefully formed hermeneutic system and Dilthey's philosophical
> use of cultural history meet and complement each other. He
> brings to all of this an absolute originality that stems from his own
> development and his consciousness of the historicity of human
> life.

Heidegger was also mentioned for the post of associate professor in
philosophy at Marburg in 1920. The appointment, however, went to Nicolai
Hartmann, and Heidegger was placed third on another list to succeed M.
Wundt. In the committee's deliberations for the earlier appointments Paul
Natorp voted to award Heidegger a post, while Jaensch opposed him.
Both judgments are worth mentioning, since they bear in an important
way on the reconstruction of Heidegger's later academic-political career.
With Natorp, Heidegger developed a limited relationship in which he
was undoubtedly impressed with Natorp's political outlook. Jaensch's view
is relevant because after 1933 he became one of Heidegger's most vocal
opponents in the factional struggles within the NSDAP. As we have seen,
Edmund Husserl had also wholeheartedly supported Heidegger in his
first bid for an appointment at Marburg. The concluding report of the
appointment commission indicates that Husserl had mentioned in a letter

that Heidegger was his most valuable assistant.[2] Furthermore, the report to the Ministry emphasized Heidegger's interest in medieval philosophy and noted that he could not be reproached for religious prejudice, although one could not also say as yet whether beyond the study of the Middle Ages he had a perceptive grasp of cultural problems.[3]

Two years later the same Marburg faculty together with the Prussian Ministry for Science, Art, and Popular Education placed Heidegger at the head of the list, rating Heinz Heimsoeth and Richard Kroner second and third. In their report the professors and others refer to Heidegger's originality among phenomenologists and especially praise his work on Aristotle. They describe Heidegger as a phenomenologist who made the phenomenological method productive for historical research. The fact that Heidegger had only a few publications to show was effectively offset by his intense activities as a teacher. The commission had before it only a part of Heidegger's investigation of Aristotle, but for them it established the quality of his work. It surpassed similar works of the nineteenth century, for Heidegger managed to confirm the relevance of Aristotle for modern philosophy.[4] The Ministry granted its approval on August 1, 1923, and summoned Heidegger to become director of the Philosophy Seminar. On August 17 Heidegger accepted the call.

During his five years of teaching at Marburg, until his appointment to Freiburg in 1928, Heidegger did not limit himself to philosophy. At this time his interest grew in the university as a distinct type of scientific study and historical documentation, particularly the history of his specialty. This interest produced his essay "Zur Geschichte des philosophischen Lehrstuhls seit 1866."[5] At this time as well he reestablished his connection with the student body, which bears upon his later involvement with National Socialism. Even Jaensch, in a document that will be discussed later, underscores the excellent relations Heidegger maintained with his students outside the classroom. In the setting of the interfactional battles being waged within the NSDAP just when Jaensch was writing, Jaensch's report is unquestionably meant as a denunciation of Heidegger and must therefore be regarded with caution, yet even that report notes that Heidegger always made himself available to students for intellectual and spiritual guidance. The intensity and the touching quality of his teaching at Marburg is recounted from memory by Hans-Georg Gadamer:

> One cannot adequately present the dramatic appearance of
> Heidegger at Marburg. Nothing he did was intended to cause a
> sensation. In his appearance at lectures he had an air of
> unconscious security, but the force of his person and teaching

rested in the fact that he would throw himself fully into his work and he transmitted this energy. There was always something totally new in his lectures; they were no longer the typical "lessons" of a professor whose real efforts were invested in mere research and publication.[6]

During his Marburg years Heidegger appears to have had a close connection with a student group that called itself Akademischer Vereinigung. Its members wholeheartedly recommended attendance at Heidegger's lectures. According to documents in the archives of Hesse, the Akademischer Vereinigung described itself in its statutes as an independent religious and political corporation without political or ideological preferences. The group was to serve one purpose, to give its members access to Kultur. In spite of its alleged ideological independence, however, the union observed the letter of certain "National Socialist anti-Jewish legislation" *(Arier-paragraph)* that most German student associations, and most Austrian ones, took to heart, requiring their groups to restrict membership solely to students "belonging to German states and having German origin" and to exclude Jews and blacks. The rapport between Heidegger and the student population was a symbol of the new life of the youth movement in the Weimar Republic and in its range of influence, especially through its reactionary wing. Once again Heidegger had hit upon ideological tendencies that were imprinted upon him in his youth. His later development also accords with the general purpose of another part of the youth movement, which sought to compensate for a political vacuum that World War I created—namely, to reconstitute a fresh relationship with Nature as well as human society.

Being and Time

Being and Time was published during Heidegger's tenure at Marburg. In order to arrive at a systematic view of his major work we must treat it in the light of the circumstances surrounding its publication, for there is every indication in it of his later turn to National Socialism. In 1923 Heidegger was named associate professor. In 1926 he could have risen in the university hierarchy by succeeding Nicolai Hartmann. In a proposal from the faculty dated August 5, 1925, Heidegger was placed first on the list, the others named being Heinz Heimsoeth and Alexander Pfänder. The faculty had based its decision, above all, on Heidegger's teaching performance since taking his post in 1923: "When we placed

him two years ago in first place for the associate professorship, our judgment was supported by the mediation of Husserl and the chapters of the
work on Aristotle." In the meantime, they noted, this judgment has been
bolstered; a new manuscript "titled *Being and Time* has been placed before
us . . . that shows Heidegger from another side as an original and con-
structive thinker. This work is nothing less than a new unraveling of the
latest and deepest ontological questions presented in the form of a phenomenological synthesis detached for the first time from every mere subjectivism, but an analysis that makes use of the best of ancient, medieval,
and modern metaphysics."[7] The report placed Heidegger at the top of
the list of philosophers of his generation and ascribed to him a role rather
similar to Paul Natorp's, because of his achievement of a groundbreaking
synthesis of historical and systematic elements in his philosophy (*Wissenschaft*).

Nonetheless, the Ministry's reaction was mostly negative. The minister,
Carl Becker, answered on February 7, 1925, that "in spite of Professor
Heidegger's obvious teaching success" he can hardly gain such an important chair until his publications can attract some special recognition from
his colleagues. Becker demanded a revised list. Only after the publication
of *Being and Time* in Husserl's *Jahrbuch* in 1927 did the Ministry agree to
Heidegger's appointment.[8] As Heidegger later wrote, the faculty put his
name forward as the only candidate, which shows that they were prepared to support him in spite of the Ministry's opposition.

The usefulness of *Being and Time* for the theme of the present work
lies in its treatment of the concept of *Existenz*. On this notion depends
everything else regarding Heidegger's intervening philosophical and political discoveries. In no sense can we read National Socialism into *Being
and Time,* but we can identify philosophical beliefs that foreshadow Heidegger's later convictions.

The characteristic concept of existence in *Being and Time*—overcoming
the dichotomies of substance among the Scholastics on the one hand and
the transcendental subjectivism of Husserlian phenomenology on the
other—affords an original perspective on the nature of cognition. On the
one hand, as "Dasein" functions, existence becomes that horizonal site
from which Heidegger means to understand "Being" *(Sein)*, that "tran-
scendence" that is implicated in every judgment of reality. On the other
hand, existence refers to the horizon of understanding Being through a
reflexive analysis that yields a "categorial" system (of existentialia) through
which existence comes to understand its own being. Existence cannot be
reduced here either to thinking or to empirical practice. The question of
the basic activity through which existence is constituted as the site for an

implicit understanding of Being is at the same time an essentially "ontic" act that is indispensable in trying to grasp the Being of human beings. Human Being is expressly defined as an ontic being essentially concerned with the question of Being. Dasein is not a being like other beings or a being simply included among others. Dasein's condition is precisely that it defines itself and decides upon a task of its own making, by which it grounds its own being. When Dasein inquires about "Being," it inquires about itself.[9]

This original relationship that Heidegger establishes between empirical and transcendental referents allows him to identify another kind of reality that is neither subjective nor empirical but rather cast in terms of an affirmative and effective practice that embraces all occasions of transcendentality without sacrificing any important elements of genuine action. This central definition is decisive for understanding Heidegger's further intellectual development, for otherwise one is tempted to confront his terribly convenient and rash theses with the mention of a more familiar "Reality." By the same token, one should not give in to the temptation to exonerate Heidegger's philosophy from mere political noise *(Grundgeräuschen)*. The radical transcendentalizing that Heidegger assumes from the beginning of *Being and Time* allows him to pursue two essential strategies in regard to our present theme. First, he manages to detach his reflections from historical empiricism; second, he manages to treat particular sets of historical events as unique, paradigmatic, and transcendental-historical moments. In short, Heidegger means to give history an ontological basis. He sets in motion the ontologizing of historical phenomena beyond the point of Dilthey's and Rickert's theories. Since *Being and Time* provides a distinction between a philosophical interpretation of history (proceeding from the historicity of Dasein itself) and a simple identification of facts (paragraphs 72 and 73), there is really no strict difference between history and philosophy. Also, Heidegger had tried earlier to link up ontology and facticity. He proceeds further, producing a synthesis of philosophy and "life" at a new level of transcendental practice in which the "meaning" of history is conceived anew. This way the act of philosophizing and the person of the philosopher acquire a privileged status with respect to the Being *(Sein)* of human existence. Heidegger transforms history, not by offering a variety of philosophies (a history of philosophy), but by construing philosophy (as a distinct way of understanding being) as the most meaningful articulation of the "openness to Being" that he identifies as "Dasein." He must seek out the roots of his political commitments, not in the usual external motives, but deep within the consistent radicalization of his thinking.

Karl Löwith[10] and Ernst Tugendhat[11] have correctly remarked that Heidegger's relationship to National Socialism is grounded in an interpretation of truth as formulated in *Being and Time*. Heidegger's decision to enter into the question of Being in a pre-predicative context in which the "showing-in-itself" *(Sich-an-ihm-selbst-zeigende)*, the "opening" *(Erschlossenheit)* (paragraphs 7 and 44), is supposed to allow thought the opportunity to discover verifiable or falsifiable criteria of judgment within some form of consensual objective and effective rationality. This justifies a transcendental facticity in which there is only the possibility of seeing or not seeing what is "indicated" *(zeigt)* without being able to examine or sort out the greatness or the misery of actual particular historical occurrences. This critique agrees with the assessments of Theodor Adorno and Jürgen Habermas.[12]

Hans Ebeling insists we can conclude that the concept of freedom in *Being and Time* has an affinity to that in National Socialism, for this concept of freedom sanctions the "turn to the dominance of caprice" *(Hinwendung zur Herrschaft der Willkür)* and leads to a radical denial of equality of peoples:

> The egocentric solipsism that recognizes only the *in*equality of
> peoples, not their equality, was entrenched in 1927 in as total a
> way as it was in 1933. There is in *Being and Time* a kinship
> with ruthless anarchy just as there is in Heidegger's Rector's
> Address a kinship with the totalitarian state. In both cases the
> power of acknowledging the other as the other, as essentially
> equal, is missing, and for that reason it only remains to oppress
> the other without any leniency.[13]

This critique requires some expansion. It brings to bear, of course, the *positive* factor of Heidegger's position from 1933 on, but it hardly does so in an adequate way. It claims only that there is a *possibility* that Heidegger adopted National Socialist ideas without giving the reasons for making such a claim. To complete this critique methodically we need to see that relevant positive elements in *Being and Time* form a pattern that will help us understand Heidegger's later development. In other words: we must ascertain the inner continuity of Heidegger's thinking between 1927 and 1933 beginning with whatever elements of his philosophy then or later are pertinently valid and for which he provides an "objective" justification within his own system. This requires first of all that we dismiss the more or less widespread conviction that Heidegger's deliberations in *Being and Time* are devoted solely to the matter of his individual, isolated, and forlorn personal existence together with its *Angst*. The year

1927 was essential for Heidegger's distinction between "eigentlich" (authentic) and "uneigentlich" (inauthentic) existence. It is worth mentioning that Heidegger draws the distinction of inauthentic *(uneigentlich)* life entirely from his analysis of the nature of individual existence, which yields no other approach to social life than by way of addressing the phenomenon of "loss of personal identity" *(Vermassung)*. Still, on the other hand, the possibility of authentic existence becomes secure within the context of a communal life, from which the loss of personal identity is entirely excluded. Heidegger matter-of-factly finds an historical-ontological connection between individual and collective existence in something he calls "tradition" in which authentic *(eigentlich)* existence finds a home and which it takes over as its rightful "heir."

It is not necessary that in resoluteness one should *explicitly* know the origin of the possibilities upon which that resoluteness projects itself. It is rather in Dasein's temporality, and there only, that there lies any possibility that the existential potentiality-for-Being upon which it projects itself can be gleaned *explicitly* from the way in which Dasein has been traditionally understood. The resoluteness that comes back to itself and hands itself down then becomes the *repetition* of a possibility of existence that has come down to us. *Repeating is handing down explicitly*—that is to say, going back into the possibilities of the Dasein that has-been-there.[14]

Practical directions cannot impart the call to conscience, "because it calls Dasein to existence in its own potentiality-for-being-its-self."[15] The tradition has something to offer, however, because it is connected with *heritage.* "The resoluteness in which Dasein comes back to itself discloses current factical possibilities of authentic existing and discloses them *in terms of the heritage* which that resoluteness, as thrown, *takes over.* In one's coming back resolutely to one's thrownness, there is hidden a *handing down* to oneself of the possibilities that have come down to one, but not necessarily as having thus come down."[16] Collective existence, understood as actual community, can and should regulate its own ongoing activity, for tradition always incorporates it and its heritage extends it. For Heidegger, its historical deeds are neither "happenings" in some irrational, merely occurrent sense or in the sense of anarchic outbreaks, but qualitative, unexpected, encompassing resolutions occurring in some "objective" but undetermined direction. Tradition and heritage are certainly two forms of reality; they appear to Heidegger as forms of the people *(Volk),* and hence also of the community *(Gemeinschaft).* The *destiny (Ges-*

chick) of existence, which in the case of individualized existence seems quite independent—just what a blind and anonymous majority of people is accustomed to think—nevertheless, when greater events suddenly befall, does become legitimate, actual, and true.

> If Dasein, by anticipation, lets death become powerful in itself, then, as free of death, Dasein understands itself in its own superior power, the power of its finite freedom, so that in this freedom, which "is" only in its having chosen to make such a choice, it can take over the *powerlessness* of abandonment to its having done so, and can thus come to have a clear vision of the accidents of the situation that has been disclosed. But if fateful Dasein, as Being-in-the-world, exists essentially in Being-with-Others, its historicizing is a co-historicizing and is determinative for it as *destiny [Geschick]*. This is how we designate the historicizing of the community, of a people. Destiny is not something that puts itself together out of individual fates, any more than Being-with-one-another can be conceived as the occurring together of several Subjects.[17]

Here Löwith's and Tugendhat's criticism of Heidegger's irrationality reveals its comprehensive structure (of the people), which is said to possess a completely "objective" regulation (its own exclusive tradition) and which for that reason is supposed to be able to ensure its own authentic deeds (its historical heritage). With the introduction of a (so-called) community of people, with its own tradition and heritage, Heidegger comes close to the interpretations that circulated widely under National Socialism (albeit, there, in a specifically racial way). Heidegger himself marked the similarity after 1933 as a symbol of his own ultranationalism.

However, the similarity between Heidegger's ideas in *Being and Time* and those of National Socialism is not yet exhausted. In order to become aware of their special possibilities, so the argument goes, a people must break through to an exceptional commitment that is neither an acceptance of traditional values from the past nor the bare continuation of orderly institutions and customs. For *Being and Time* the activity in which "authentic being-with" *(eigenliche Mitsein)* is constituted and pale individuality overcome is called the "struggle" *(Kampf)*. Within this struggle "decision" *(Entscheidung)* turns into act, instantiating thereby the ontological category of "resoluteness" *(Entschlossenheit): "*In affirmation and struggle does the power of fate first become free."[18]

The double structure of authentic community and a people's struggle in the face of the most extreme likelihood of death (the immanence of death) completes, even in a terminological sense, the philosophical and political project that already in 1927 anticipates Heidegger's later positions. To be sure, in *Being and Time* the tradition, heritage, and struggle are not taken to be embodied in any particular people. Still, the model for the community's quest for self-identity is designated by Heidegger as the *hero (Helden)*. The "having-been" *(gewesene)* of existence that Dasein should select as a model is said to be the heroic: "The authentic repetition of a possibility of existence that has been—the possibility that Dasein may choose its hero—is grounded existentially in anticipatory resoluteness; for it is from resoluteness that one first chooses the choice which makes one free for the struggle of loyally following in the footsteps of that which can be repeated."[19]

In any case the issue is not one of a traditionalist returning to the past or of a reactionary re-living of something expired; rather, for Heidegger, it is an inventive correspondence with the active possibilities still living in the former manifestations *(Gewesene)* of a people (in its tradition) and, by that token, still effective in the present. Yet, precisely because a community is in itself a possibility and because its potentialities are continually being inscribed in the future, the validity of its tradition does not arise from the past but actually comes to it as a task *(Aufgabe)* from the future. The people *(Volk)* should function in the future as their heroes had done within the tradition. The past (as *Gewesene)* becomes the paradigm and goal for a people's action. And because it is necessary to turn to "one's own" *(Eigenen)*, a people must refer to itself for its task and must preserve its exclusive "ownness" *(Eigenheit)*. What in the pejorative vision of anonymity (of the impersonal "they") implicates a critique of genuine culture *(Kultur)* is explained by Heidegger by means of an ideological schema for suppressing conservative traditionalism. The schema is "revolutionary" insofar as it does not involve the mere repetition of past values but rather the futural transformation of German society in the struggle "for ownness."

If we examine in detail the categories Heidegger used around 1927 for his analysis of inauthentic existence, we shall find that, at that moment, Heidegger's thinking overcame the disadvantages of an avowedly decadent individualism in favor of a distinct conservative-revolutionary solidarity. Hence, in the context of *Being and Time* and its ontological questions, pertinent political positions emerge with a clarity we can presume to read as an intended model for political society. Heidegger lends support to this thesis with quotations from the correspondence between Count Yorck von Wartenburg and Dilthey,[20] holding in effect that every

interpretation of historicity must be linked up with this sort of commitment, as it is in Dilthey's case (paragraphs 76 and 77). Yorck's views expressed in his letters to Dilthey had had an early influence on Heidegger's conception of history, society, and the state. This is apparent in
Heidegger's correspondence with Erich Rothacker (of Bonn), a philosopher who later belonged to "orthodox" National Socialism. Not only does
Heidegger talk about the impression that the reading of the correspondence between Yorck and Dilthey had made on him in a letter dating
from January 4, 1924; he also mentions in *Being and Time* (paragraph 77)
what Yorck's message for the future would be.[21] The text from Yorck
that Heidegger cites is:

> But you are acquainted with my liking for paradox, which I justify
> by saying that paradoxicality is a mark of truth, and that the
> *communis opinio* is nowhere in the truth, but is like an elemental
> precipitate of a halfway understanding that makes generalizations;
> in its relationship to truth it is like the sulphurous fumes that the
> lightning leaves behind. Truth is never an element. To dissolve
> elemental public opinion and, as far as possible, to make possible
> the molding of individuality in seeing and looking, would be a
> pedagogical task for the state. Then, instead of a so-called public
> conscience—instead of this radical externalization—individual
> consciences—that is to say, conscience—would again become
> powerful.[22]

The implications of this passage and Heidegger's agreement with it
are clear: the political intrusion of the state is postulated. Yorck and Heidegger not only distinguish between "the masses" and "the truth"; they
insist on the weakening of public opinion as an essential stage in the
development of society and the state. Accordingly, both emphasize that
there should be only the least public access (which "paradox" appreciates)
to the "truth," which the state and society alone should direct and control.

The concrete political implications of Yorck's theses, which Heidegger
adopts, were first revealed in Hitler's programmatic struggle against par-
liamentarianism and the "growing Jewish influence [*Verjudung*] in the
press." In *Mein Kampf* Hitler says:

> There is absolutely no principle, objectively considered, that is so
> wrong as that of the parliament. One can still completely
> disregard the manner in which the vote of a sovereign people's

representative is permitted, as it is primarily its new function and new source of dignity that matters. Only the smallest fraction of a population really negotiates over the fulfillment of a general need or wish. It's quite clear that the political understanding of the wider masses is hardly developed enough to form definite political views or to select future leaders.

In essence Hitler's critique agrees with Yorck's and Heidegger's position: "What we call 'public opinion' is based only to a small degree on self-acquired experience or even on the knowledge of any individual. It depends rather on an illusion that emerges from often endless insistent impressions and a kind of 'Enlightenment.' " It rests in its interpretation "not in the hands of the state but in the claws of those with the most inferior powers . . . the infamous Jewish race. . . . This rabble constitutes more than two-thirds of the so-called 'public opinion' from whose delusions the parliamentarian Aphrodite arises." The principle of personal responsibility, which Yorck appeals to, was accentuated by Hitler: "Whatever standard really towers over a large cross-section of the population must, more often than not, be declared in a personal voice to be effective in world history."[23]

From this point of view, it is not enough to describe the consequences of Heidegger's philosophy before 1933, as Georg Lukács does, solely as the disarming of the German intellectual vis-à-vis fascism. Beyond the conscious role Heidegger played in training a whole generation of young academics, his philosophy distinctly influenced the ideological continuity of later historical developments. Drawing from the texts we have looked at, we can enumerate various ways in which, around 1927, Heidegger brought to full expression certain themes that he was occupied with from the start: the distinction between authentic and inauthentic existence in the face of decisive alternatives (like struggle and death), the refusal to acknowledge public opinion, the notions of value that originated in the youth movement, as well as the now revolutionary conservative values of Catholic neo-romanticism (especially the Austrian variety). Heidegger secularizes this code of values and defines it more exactly. With Heidegger, "Being" ceases to be a mere object of speculation; it appears in the "horizon" of "Dasein," in which it is said to be actualized and realized without forfeiting its transcendent character. In *Being and Time*, Heidegger adopts the central romantic categories—categories like the We, struggle, destiny, the historical mandate of the people, community, and, above all, the exemplary leader, who in this situation is expected to point out the path that the people will follow.

7 The return to Freiburg and the Berlin temptation

On February 26, 1928, Heidegger informed the Ministry of Education at Berlin that the Ministry in Baden had offered him the chair at Freiburg just vacated by Husserl.[1] The faculty of philosophy at Marburg said they "found Heidegger to be the immediate successor and beneficiary in Marburg's great tradition of philosophy," and three days later wrote to beg the Ministry to "do everything necessary" to keep Heidegger at his present post. The administrator at the University of Marburg also wrote to the Ministry on March 2, 1928, to propose a large increase in salary for Heidegger in the hopes that he would refuse the Freiburg offer. In spite of these efforts, on March 21 Heidegger advised the faculty and the interested parties at the Ministry in Berlin that his decision to return to Freiburg was final. The principal argument he gave was that his master, Husserl, had requested his collaboration in pursuing research together.

I have been unable to reconstruct the precise circumstances of Heidegger's return to the faculty at Freiburg because the relevant papers are not accessible. But we can assume that Husserl strongly supported Heidegger's return. When we think about the later relationship between these two thinkers, we realize how interesting these inaccessible documents may be.

After a period of intense activity teaching at Freiburg, Heidegger received another offer, this time from Berlin, where Ernst Troeltsch's death had left the chair empty. After much negotiation, Heidegger finally turned the post down. Heidegger had already gained a reputation beyond the confines of the world of German philosophy, as we see in the *Frankfurter Zeitung* for January 25, 1929, where the journalist Krakauer wrote about Heidegger's speech "Philosophical Anthropology and the Metaphysics of Existence," given in Frankfurt before the Kant Society: "We end this report by saying that the personality of the speaker brought a great crowd of spectators, who were no doubt unversed in the problems of philosophy, but who put themselves at risk and entered the complex world of subtle definitions and distinctions."

Thus it is not surprising that Heidegger's return to Freiburg was an event for the small world of Baden. The possibility that this young but already famous philosopher might again abandon his "land" became almost a public affair in the region's cultural circles. The matter was fraught with real political implications. Heidegger's position already exhibited at that time radical traits that were known and manifest to the public at large. He had in effect helped to spread word about the well-known encounter at Davos where he had taken stock of Ernst Cassirer, where Cassirer's wife had made the blunt remark, "We were not unaware of Heidegger's anti-semitism."[2] It is fitting to report here an anecdote told to Guido Schneeberger by one of the participants at the encounter: "During the discussion, a man entered who suffered from serious and visible nervous problems resulting from service in World War I. This man claimed that the unique task of twentieth-century philosophy was to avoid another war, and Heidegger answered him with quiet disdain, saying that one could endure these times only with toughness. For his own case, combat would have been beneficial."[3] The significance of making such a declaration was considerable. To have done so in front of an audience including illustrious representatives of European intellectual life was to take a position identical to that of the anti-liberal and anti-republican rightist militarists who were currently intensifying their own efforts to destabilize the Weimar Republic utterly.

The circumstances surrounding Heidegger's refusal to go to Berlin can be clarified in part by the events of the celebration of the Day of the Baden Fatherland at Karlsruhe on July 11–14, 1930. Heidegger took part, like the other well-known personalities and representatives of the cultural and political world of Baden. He read his article "On the Essence of Truth." The writer Heinrich Berl, who gave the opening talk, made perfectly clear the political significance of the meeting, especially organized in the context of the "historic occasion for the liberation of occupied territories," that is, of those territories on the far bank of the Rhine that Germany had ceded to France after World War I.[4]

A local organization, Badische Heimat (Baden Fatherland), with headquarters in Freiburg, had organized the meeting. An analysis of its program, as well as of the previous political involvements of its most active participants, reveals the true meaning of the event. The honorary president of the committee was Eugen Fischer, founder and director (after 1927) of the Institute for Racial Purity in Berlin, whose sinister activities came to light later when the Institute became the scientific infrastructure for experiments done by the SS in the concentration camps. Perhaps this conference was the beginning of the friendship between Fischer and Heidegger, a friendship that lasted beyond the era of National Socialism up to Fischer's death. Both took part in the ceremony at Leipzig to offer support to Hitler, and Heidegger often visited Fischer, who was a fellow Freiburger. At Christmastime 1960, Heidegger sent Fischer a copy of his book *Hebel, der Hausfreund* (1958), with the dedication: "For Eugen Fischer with friendly greetings for Christmas and the New Year. Martin Heidegger." (I would like to thank Fischer's grandson, Eberhard Fischer of Zurich, for giving me a copy of this greeting.)

Many of the participants in the Karlsruhe ceremony had later connections to National Socialism. One speaker was the dramatist and professor Otto zur Nedden, who gave a talk on "Music at Konstanz around 1500." Zur Nedden, who probably joined the Nazi Party in 1931 at Pforzheim, was known for his violently anti-semitic play *The Jew of Malta*, which the official press seems to have praised after 1933 as the "best and the most representative anti-semitic dramatic work of world literature."[5] Following zur Nedden's speech was a concert directed by Franz Philipp, conductor and director of the Academy of Music at Karlsruhe. Philipp joined the NSDAP in 1933 and was the author of the "German Patriotic Hymn to the Glory of Work," sung at the first celebration of the National Socialist Day of Work, May 1, 1933, where Hitler also gave a famous speech. Also present was August Rumm, who contributed a portrait of Heidegger (signed by the philosopher) as the centerfold of the *Badische Presse*'s issue dedicated to the festival. Rumm joined the Nazi party in 1940.[6] His portrait of Heidegger was used along with a portrait of Ernst Krieck, also by Rumm, in a book with a preface by Heinrich Berl.[7]

The series of speeches began with "Baden Culture, Especially Within Germanic Cultural Space" by Josef Mussler, teacher at the Offenburg Preparatory School; Mussler joined the Association of National Socialist Professors (NSLB) on January 1, 1934.[8] Another, "The Soul of the Baden Peasant," was given by Anton Fendrich, a writer from Freiburg and member of the Social Democrats until 1932, who would soon see Hitler as "sent by Providence" and who became an unconditional partisan.[9] The traditional play for the conference was *Fatherland and the Foreigner*, staged by Hans Blum, who became a member of the SS in 1934.[10] Music was presented by two choirs from the Academy of Music of Karlsruhe, directed by Gustav Etzkorn, who joined the NSDAP in May 1933. The evangelical pastor from Baden-Baden, Dr. Karl Hesselbacher, gave a speech on "The Significance of Baden Poetry." He also joined the Nazis in May 1933. Leopold Ziegler, who delivered the important speech "The Myth of the Reich," was the author of the two-volume work *The Holy German Empire* (1925), in which he made the Reich a transcendental entity that "beyond any historical change will always remain the destiny and particular mission of Germans."[11]

In the same series of speeches that included Heidegger's were Friedrich Muckle's "Changes in World Culture and the Mission of the German Spirit" and Ernst Krieck's "The German Ideal in Education." Muckle taught at the University of Heidelberg and in 1923 had published an anti-semitic book, *The Spirit of Jewish Culture and the West*.[12] Krieck was the most assertive Nazi pedagogue and a National Socialist from the beginning. We will examine his political ideas more fully later on.

Another important speaker at the conference was the well-known writer Hermann Burte ("The Alemannic Dialect"). A contributor to the review *Deutschlands Erneuerung,* directed by Georg von Below and H. Stuart Chamberlain, Burte continued to proclaim his sympathies with Nazism well after World War II. At the festivities in 1954 honoring E. G. Kolbenheyer (an official Nazi poet), organized by the Kolbenheyer Society, the Sudetendeutsche Landsmannschaft, and the Deutsches Kulturwerk europäischen Geistes, Kolbenheyer himself greeted the audience with the Hitler salute, drawing applause that was then redoubled when Burte complimented him for "being a man who would not grovel."[13] Finally we might mention Jacob Bleyer from Budapest, whose talk was "German Culture Abroad, Notably in Hungary."[14] Bleyer was a university professor, a former Hungarian minister, and director of the Movement of Germans Abroad.[15]

This list includes more than 80 percent of the speakers and their speeches; it gives a pretty good idea of the conference's composition and political stripe.

Heidegger's speech was awaited eagerly because people expected to learn something about the offer to teach in Berlin. Heinrich Berl describes the situation and the general atmosphere in his 1946 book *Conversations with Famous Contemporaries.* "There was the Berlin offer. Everyone was asking, 'Would Heidegger take the offer of Troeltsch's chair?' For a time he remained quiet, but those who knew him knew that he'd do nothing: 'What would a buddy from the Black Forest do on the Berlin asphalt?' Then something nice happened: Heidegger accepted the invitation to come to the conference for the Baden region, where he gave his talk, 'The Essence of Truth.' Icy heights of abstraction, and then he came down to earth and dared to take the step: Truth and Reality become one on the soil of the Fatherland. This was his answer to the call from Berlin."[16]

"The Essence of Truth" was published for the first time at Frankfurt in 1943.[17] As Heidegger acknowledged, the original text was somewhat "touched up over time,"[18] and we do not have access to the original 1930 text. Berl's description of it, however, is clear and is corroborated by accounts in the dailies *Karlsruher Tageblatt* and *Karlsruher Zeitung* for July 16, 1930: "The final leap by which Heidegger indicates the foundation of truth is decisive: the connection with the land *(Bodenständigkeit)* is the foundation of all truth *(Wahrhaftigkeit)*. . . . This was not the first time that Heidegger would speak of the seriousness of our relationships with the fatherland."[19] It is almost certain that the speech that Heidegger delivered at Karlsruhe had some essential differences from the text given elsewhere. At Baden-Baden, he emphasized patriotism.

Heidegger delivered a speech with the same title at Bremen in October 1930. As reported by his disciple and friend H. W. Petzet in *Bremer Nachrichten* for October 11, 1930,[20] there is no allusion to the patriotic "finales" that those who heard the speech at Baden-Baden mention. However, Petzet attributes a political dimension to Heidegger.[21] Heidegger's philosophy goes beyond the nihilism that the "socialist" H. de Man attributes to the "classes [who are] devoted to decadence and who have a tendency to turn mysticism and the irrational into the divine." But the philosophy also goes beyond the answers given by Spengler, Klages, and Scheler. One proof of this is the vigorous student movement that grew up around Heidegger and the great influence he had on younger generations.[22]

Reconstituting the circumstances that brought the offer from the Ministry at Berlin is important for several reasons. First of all, this was the first time that Heidegger had found himself in competition with other reputable philosophers. In fact, even though he did receive the proposal from the Ministry, he lost this competition. In addition, the contest not only shows the public acclaim that Heidegger enjoyed but also clarifies certain aspects of German university politics during the Weimar Republic.

Of the twenty-three universities with a philosophy faculty, Berlin's was without question the most important, because of both its prestige and its size. Between 1928 and 1933, there were nasty struggles among the different factions, with the result that a coalition was formed of forces clearly favorable to the conservative nationalists *(deutschnationale)*. This kept the Ministries of Education from imposing their choice of professors.[23] The process for Heidegger's nomination began with Minister Becker's request, December 6, 1929, to the effect that he, Becker, be allowed to choose the successor to Troeltsch.[24] Becker did not hide the fact that Nicolai Hartmann was his choice. An ad hoc committee was established, consisting of Professors von Fischer (Dean), H. Maier, Max Dessoir, E. Schmidt, Eduard Spranger, Köhler, Max Planck, W. Sombart, Werner Jaeger, and Wechsler. At a meeting on February 12, 1930, they drew up a list of four candidates: Ernst Cassirer, Paul Tillich, Georg Misch, and Nicolai Hartmann. The committee allowed that Heidegger's name "could be considered," but pointedly did not place it on the list. Spranger, for example, wondered whether Heidegger's popularity might not come more from his personality than from his actual philosophy, since this philosophy was hardly one that could be taught or studied.

Although Max Planck and Werner Jaeger preferred to have the chair remain empty, the committee as a whole stated its preference for Cassirer: "Of all the professors on the list, only Ernst Cassirer should be considered."[25] The report explained that, after the death of Troeltsch, the faculty had initially thought of sending in Cassirer's name, but had hesitated in the hope of finding a replacement among the rising generation of young philosophers. When this had failed, they had decided to nominate Cassirer. Although Becker's choice, Hartmann, was on the list, the committee judged that his standing was in fact inferior to Cassirer's.

The report does also speak of Heidegger:

> For some time there has been much talk about Martin Heidegger at Freiburg. Although there are questions about his publications, it is clear that he has his own notions and especially that his personal attraction is powerful. Yet even his partisans recognize that hardly any of the students who flock to him can in fact understand him. This is a time of crisis for Heidegger; it would be best to wait for its outcome. To have him come now to Berlin would be wrong. What he needs is tranquillity, which he would never find in Berlin. Also, even the students who would be impressed by his teaching would not get a strong philosophical grounding.

There had still been no decision when Becker was replaced at the Ministry by Adolf Grimme, a former student of Husserl's at Göttingen who admired him and considered him a dear friend.[26] This changed the direction of events completely.

We can imagine that Grimme was swayed, if only indirectly, by the influence of his former teacher. At any rate, he went against the express will of the committee and the faculty by choosing Heidegger as Troeltsch's successor. Heidegger acknowledged the offer by letter (March 23, 1930), saying that he would come to Berlin to discuss the appointment.[27] On April 10, Heidegger signed a contract noting that he would take up his post October 1, 1930, and giving his salary as well as certain privileges. In a letter of April 14, Heidegger said he would return to Berlin and that his wife and friends were searching for suitable living quarters. In a note to the Minister of Finance, Grimme begged him to do what he could to give Heidegger special financial perquisites. He mentioned some of his reasons for appointing the philosopher from Freiburg, "even though this bothered the public more than such questions usually do."[28] Grimme said also that Heidegger would be reticent "because his close communion with nature forms the very foundation of his philosophical work"; Heidegger made as a condition of his employment that "he was to be allowed to live and work in peace, without the problems of urban life." This nomination, Grimme insisted, ought not be lost for reasons of financial economy.[29]

In spite of all Grimme's efforts, however, Heidegger eventually refused the offer. But if it is true that the relationship with his native land was of great importance for Heidegger, this was certainly not the reason for his refusal. The sources make it clear that, when faced with the overt antagonism of the most eminent faculty in Germany toward a minister who was forcing their hand, Heidegger's only option was to refuse the offer. We find no documents indicating that Husserl would have pressured Grimme; so it seems Grimme pressed Heidegger's nomination on his own. This may explain why after Heidegger's first refusal and the pressures from the faculty and public opinion, Grimme continued to press for quite a while for the appointment in hopes of getting the philosopher to change his mind. In his letter of refusal, Heidegger thanked Grimme for his confidence.

Grimme continued to insist and told Heidegger that his state secretary, Dr. Richter, would be in Freiburg May 14 to renew the discussion. He begged Heidegger not to make his refusal public until after this meeting.[30] On May 17, Heidegger answered that it would be impossible for him to take the chair, although he was pleased to know that in the highest administration, where German spiritual life was being developed, there was a will that understood that the German university could never renew itself without a certain inner strength that was needed for a true mutation. Only after unsuccessfully sending Richter to Freiburg to try to persuade Heidegger did Grimme finally send the offer to Nicolai Hartmann,

who accepted it.[31] Cassirer's nomination, the first choice of the committee, was never again mentioned. There is not a word about it in the documents. The anti-semitic forces in Berlin had been opposed from the
start to Cassirer.[32]

The unusual stir provoked by public opinion at Grimme's decision in
favor of Heidegger, which Grimme mentions in a letter to his colleagues
in the Finance Ministry, definitely originated with strong faculty resistance to a ministerial decision that went diametrically against them. We
find echoes of all this even in the press. A violent article in the review
Monistische Monatshefte[33] complained that "a socialist minister wanted to
bring to Berlin a cultural reactionary, a theologizing irrationalist, who is
unable to educate our students with the perfect objectivity of the scientific
mind." Not without irony, the author called attention to the satisfaction
in traditionalist circles with Grimme's decision and called on the faculty
to double its efforts to stop Heidegger's nomination. This allusion to traditionalist circles certainly referred to commentaries on the affair in the
Berliner Tageblatt, the *Berliner Börsen-Courier*, the *Frankfurter Zeitung*, and
the *Vossische Zeitung* that had appeared on March 28 and 29, 1930. In the
Frankfurter Zeitung, for example, Hermann Herrigel had greeted with ef-
fusion Heidegger's arrival in Berlin. In 1933, the same Herrigel found
the highest terms to applaud Heidegger's speech when he took the rectorship at Freiburg.[34]

The fact that the Berlin faculty had resisted Heidegger, no doubt
causing his eventual refusal, makes it clear how this whole affair must
have strengthened his determination that a radical reform of the universities was necessary, and must also have convinced him to keep his close
ties with the student world, who regarded him (in Hannah Arendt's words)
as "the uncrowned king of the empire of thought."[35] The context helps
us understand as well the encounter with Cassirer at Davos, because, at
least among the philosophy faculty, Cassirer had clearly been the winner
in the Berlin competition.

This judgment by Arendt, who had studied with Heidegger at Marburg, makes clear a fundamental aspect of Heidegger's personality
and his university and political position in the 1930s. It also helps us
understand the decisive importance of this stage for the positions he would
take in 1933. In fact, it is clear from his activities at Marburg and Georg
Misch's report for the Göttingen faculty, as well as the report of the Berlin faculty (not to mention the press reports), that Heidegger enjoyed an
enormous popularity and that his personality was extremely attractive to
students. This era was marked not only by a deep bitterness among the
extremely nationalistic young people over the defeat of World War I, but

also by their dissatisfaction with the "bottomless pit" of scholastic rationalism.[36] The appearance of a strong personality like Heidegger who would "guide" young minds to a radical questioning of the presuppositions of traditional thought could only be a powerful force. Although Heidegger had not yet articulated his notions in systematic form, and although his works were often handed around in the form of notes and papers from the seminars, his new attitudes, his freshness, his unpolished style, which provoked and demanded active participation from his students at every moment, all this appeared truly revolutionary during those years, which, except for Husserl's dense technical attempts, saw nothing new happening in the field of German philosophy.[37] Added to this style was a demand for discipline in the service of "things themselves," which made philosophical activity quite different from apprenticeship in a "trade."

We can imagine that this "uncrowned king of the empire of thought" would not fail to excite jealousy and uneasiness among his aging colleagues. But this phrasing, familiar in the academic setting, also says something about the way Heidegger must have seen himself.

His popularity among the students was certainly due to his youthfulness. He was only thirty-nine when he returned to Freiburg, and forty-four when he became rector.

II

The rectorate
(1933–1934)

II

8   Heidegger, rector at Freiburg (1933)

The German student movement and its avant-garde role

To understand Martin Heidegger's commitment to National Socialism and his activities during the Hitler regime, we first need to explore the student movement. This will help us understand the discussions about university reform and the problems they created. Faced with these problems, Heidegger decided to commit himself to the political combat.

We should recall, however, that Heidegger's sympathies for the rising National Socialist movement dated from before Hitler's taking power. According to Carl Friedrich von Weizsäcker, a student of Heidegger's during the 1930s, it was known "before 1933 that Heidegger had already grounded his hopes on National Socialism."[1] A colleague of Heidegger's in history at Freiburg, Gerhard Ritter, shared this opinion: "Heidegger was elected rector because people thought that his long-time sympathy with National Socialism made him the best candidate to watch over the interests of science during the Third Reich."[2]

The political orientation of the youth movement, especially the student movement, with its potential for growth, had been noticed by Hitler since 1930: "Nothing makes me more certain of the victory of our ideas than our success in the universities."[3] Hitler spoke of how his party had infiltrated the student organizations. The number of members was far above the number in other organized university groups, just as it was in non-student National Socialist organizations.[4] Professors of philosophy, history, and economics were for the most part convinced that the German people were "a metaphysical people who violently opposed the superficiality of Western democracy,"[5] but it was the students themselves who were the most committed and active. After the demise of the Weimar Republic, the growing numbers of National Socialist students often used terrorist tactics[6] as a way of taking advantage of the weaknesses of the Republic's tentative politics.

Before 1933, the National Socialists were a minority, but took strength from their connections with the SA, the storm troops.[7] Student organizations fell into the hands of the Nazis long before the government institutions did. The first federation to elect Nazi officers was organized at the University of Erlangen in 1929.[8] Some figures about their comparative strength in the different universities during the winter semester 1930/31 may help to make the situation clear: At the Technical University in Berlin, Nazis had five of ten votes; in the Graduate Veterinary School in Berlin, twenty of thirty; at Breslau University, twenty-two of thirty; at Erlangen, ten of twenty-five; at Giessen, fourteen of twenty-five; at Greifswald, nine of fifteen; at Jena, eight of twelve; at Leipzig, eight of fifteen; at Rostock, seven of eleven. The virus was also rife beyond the frontiers of the Reich: At the Graduate Veterinary School in Vienna, the Nazis had seven of twelve votes; at the Technical University of Brünn, eight of twenty.

At the Conference of German Students, the National Socialists gained an absolute majority, as well as the post of first president.[9] There had been a tradition of anti-semitism and militarism in the student organizations since 1919, when all the German student groups, Austrian and Sudeten-German as well, were brought into the same organization, an early sign of the supranational unity of the Reich, or Greater Germany, that Hitler was to impose by force.[10] In 1927, the student organizations were united as German-Austrian Aryan Societies to assure their anti-semitism and to exclude Jews from these groups. When Hitler took power, a limitation was added regarding the number of Jewish students permitted in the universities.[11]

Students had an extremely important role in National Socialism; "the living generation," they affirmed, not only ought to be "revolutionaries" in the universities but also ought to become models of how to transform German society through National Socialism.[12] Controlling student leaders was only the first step; the central idea was "to revolutionize" other students and the whole university world. The National Socialist students declared that in this way "the university front" would be "the sector with the greatest importance for the general offensive during the first years of National Socialism."[13] "The transformation of the liberal bourgeois university into a military-style National Socialist university could not be imposed from without; it would have to grow by drawing on the cultural reserves of the living generations."[14]

This task fell to the teaching corps. H. J. Düning made the accusation: "There was no National Socialist teaching corps until the coup. Attempts to establish such a group would probably have fallen apart, because of a lack of militant members."[15] He called for a precise plan: "The faculty could never for an instant be a force for change, for that would be contrary to its interests, even to its functions. Only the students could do that or, more precisely, only the National Socialist student groups could take that role. Young people must be trained before acting and working, for only in this way are they liberated."[16] "With only a few exceptions, the university revolution was achieved, not with the help of the teaching body, but often in spite of its pathetic opposition. The representatives of German science found their solidarity in scientific notions of absolute objectivity that derived from the antiquated specter of rationalism. . . . Thus representatives of classical liberalism were radically opposed, with an instinctive sense of having detected the enemy, to a movement whose program was the destruction of the self-governing university as well as the synthesis of politics and science. The collision between the new spirit and the old was inevitable."[17]

The success of one group of Nazi students in electing leaders encouraged a strong and violent "grass-roots" movement; student groups became an essential support for the government, which next abolished the autonomy of the universities and introduced the Führer principle to the administration of German universities. A result of the new legislation was the expulsion of about 7.5 percent of the university teachers, with Freiburg among the most gravely hit. At Berlin, Frankfurt am Main, Heidelberg, Breslau, Göttingen, Freiburg, Hamburg, and Cologne, the percentage was between 18 and 32.[18] Even before the reforms of 1934, avant-garde National Socialist students denounced and boycotted Jews in teaching positions and fought to have them replaced by "new forces."[19] At the same time, four thousand lawyers, three thousand physicians, two thousand civil workers, and two thousand actors also lost their jobs.[20] In the next section we will outline the particulars at Freiburg during this time.[21] Here we note the names of Ernst Krieck, Alfred Bäumler, and Heidegger. Each of these men had somewhat different convictions, and each had different ideas of how to bring the universities into the National Socialist movement. The struggle to transform the universities after the coup essentially lay in the balance as these three forces engaged in open conflict. The period was clearly anarchic; student radicalism and fights between opposing student camps precluded any stable consensus. Disorder subsided rather quickly once Ernst Röhm and his SA were purged—that is, after the most "revolutionary" and most radical in the student movement had been eliminated.

The seizure of power in the region of Baden:[22] Freiburg

The Nazi Party organized some extraordinary propaganda efforts in Baden, a promise of their later ability to reach a wide audience. This, however, does not mean that the NSDAP easily controlled the majority of the population from the beginning. Although it was the majority party in the region, the NSDAP did not get an absolute majority in the 1932 elections. The situation was treated as a challenge and inspired renewed efforts.[23] In March 1933, Baden's National Socialist newspaper, *Der Alemanne*, took up the current national denunciation of Communists and Social Democrats as those responsible for the fire at the Reichstag. Violent persecution of leftist groups throughout the Reich resulted in the prohibition of all their political activities, the closing of their presses, the destruction of their organizational structures, and the imprisonment or assassination of their leaders and most eminent members. The persecution was also felt in Baden. After the National Socialist Party's success in the election of March 5, a success that immediately eliminated the constitutional protections then in place, Minister of the Interior Wilhelm Frick named Robert Wagner, who was the Gauleiter of the regional NSDAP, as Reichskommissar of the region of Baden. Initially the appointment might have been considered a normal part of filling government slots, because, as late as March 7, the Nazis and the Centrist Party began talks about a possible coalition. When, however the police were put under the control of a Nazi Reichskommissar on May 9, and on May 11 a Nazi government was nominated, this broke the rules. To form a unified police system, Wagner recruited five hundred members of the SA, the SS, and the Stahlhelm, which increased the persecutions of all the opposition groups, including the Social Democrats.[24]

Added to these actions directed from above were attacks from the lower levels of National Socialism. Before finally being closed on March 9, 1933,[25] the coalition of workers' unions came under attack. On March 17, two policemen assassinated Nussbaum, a well-known Social Democrat and member of Parliament.[26] The NSDAP organized a rally in front of the cathedral in Freiburg, called Demonstration Against Marxism, announcing (in the words of Dr. Franz Kerber, mayor of Freiburg) that they "were going to destroy this evil at the root."[27] The police were given the power to act immediately against any "terrorist acts." All Social Democratic members of Parliament and local representatives were imprisoned, their presses closed, their organizations suppressed. All political and union groups in Freiburg were made to toe the line well before the rest of Germany.[28] The history professor G. Tellenbach makes clear in his memoirs that these were public acts: "We looked in consternation at the photos of the leading Social Democrats who were being taken to concentration camps. I recall a photo of Remmele, respected minister of the interior of Baden, now sitting in a truck surrounded by those brutes of the SA and the SS."[29]

During Heidegger's rectorship at Freiburg, there were already two concentration camps in the region of Baden, both at Heuberg, near Messkirch. When the second one was opened, the official National Socialist newspaper, *Völkischer Beobachter* (south German edition, June 1, 1933), gave the following information:

> After opening a camp at Heuberg some months ago for politically dangerous persons, we have now opened a second KZ, also at Heuberg, for prisoners still held in the prison at Karlsruhe. . . . These are all Communist agitators, Social Democrats, and pacifists, civil servants and members of Parliament—like all those who endanger public order and in whom one could not expect to see a change of heart even if they were to be freed. Civil servants and the police must keep under surveillance those who have been released until they can show that they are now ready to become what they ought to be—Germans.[30]

The concentration camps at Heuberg were torn down in 1935 and the prisoners sent to the death camp at Dachau.[31] The goods and properties of all the banned organizations were appropriated and distributed among the SA, the SS, and the Hitler Youth. The Central Union was reopened in May 1933 for the Celebration of Work organized by the Nazis. The "self-dissolution" of bourgeois political parties took place on June 23, 1933, and the prohibition of any party other than the NSDAP was made law on July 14, 1933.

The Jewish population in Freiburg was caught between institutionalized terror and the terrorism of loosely organized "grass-roots" groups.

On March 11, 1933, Mayor Kerber directed the SA of Freiburg to begin the boycott of Jewish businesses, and published lists of Jewish physicians and lawyers, also to be boycotted.[32] No official voice was heard in protest against this campaign.[33] On April 7, 1933, the law to "restructure the public sector" was promulgated, which required that Jews be expelled from public posts and the universities. In 1940, this "cleansing" was achieved when the last 5,617 Jews from the region of Baden were first sent to KZ Gurs in the French Pyrénées, then transferred to the death camps in the east.[34]

Heidegger as rector of the University of Freiburg

What was called "coordination of German society" was to involve the crucial step of taking over the universities and transforming them according to the vision of the NSDAP. When Heidegger was given the post of rector at Freiburg, the event had national and international import, as his prestige as a philosopher offered powerful support for the new regime. His election as rector and appointment as Führer of the university coincided with his publicly joining the Nazi Party.[35] His party membership card, located in the Berlin Document Center, notes that Heidegger became a member on May 1, 1933 (no. 3125894, Gau Baden), and that by paying his dues regularly he kept his membership until 1945.

The papers concerning his election to the rectorship have been carefully studied by the Freiburg historian Hugo Ott.[36] Unlike Heidelberg University, its sister in the Baden region, which kept its rector for a while (the historian Willy Andreas), Freiburg was in the avant-garde of the National Socialist training process. Professor Wilhelm von Möllendorf, a famous professor of medicine, was named rector before Heidegger, but he served only for a few days. His political fate was tied to that of the mayor, Dr. Hans Bender, a militant member of the Centrist Party,[37] who was violently attacked in *Der Alemanne* by Kerber, who was then the local Nazi chief.

Kerber demagogically accused Bender of being responsible for Nussbaum's assassination and announced that, precisely because of his association with Bender, Möllendorf was not competent to supervise the "cultural renewal of Germany," which demanded unquestioning commitment. The election of Möllendorf, claimed Kerber, meant an unwillingness to collaborate with the "national revolution," and certainly not a harmonious relationship with the students, since a majority were National Socialists.[38] At the same time, the students sent a letter supporting Kerber's accusations.[39] Concurrently, Reichskommissar Wagner decided to eliminate all Jews from their teaching posts and to change university policies. This brought about a generally unstable climate and, in fact, something of a judicial scandal, since the action was unique. The practice was not yet operative elsewhere in Germany,[40] although it soon would be.

Möllendorf's situation became more and more precarious. The philologist Wolfgang Schadewaldt demanded that Möllendorf retire so that Heidegger could be elected to the post. Schadewaldt was an active collaborator in the indoctrination courses directed by Helmut Haubold and Heinz Riedel (the theorist of racism), even appropriating Heidegger's original socialist terminology.[41] Gerhard Ritter[42] and Hugo Ott[43] claim that there is evidence that Schadewaldt played an important role in Heidegger's election, and even that they worked together.[44] In view of the situation, Möllendorf called for an extraordinary plenary session to be held April 21, 1933, during which Heidegger and the new University Senate were to be elected.[45] Ott notes the lack of solidarity in the Freiburger Centrist Party favoring Möllendorf and Bender.[46]

On April 24, Kerber, who was in the meantime named mayor, wrote in a deliberately simplistic way that the election of Heidegger as "Führer of the university" was part of the general "training" program and showed that the teaching corps was actively working to further the National Socialist revolution. Links between Heidegger and Kerber were strong and remained so until Heidegger relinquished the rectorship. Together with the student Führer Heinrich von zur Mühlen, Kerber and Heidegger sent a telegram of support to Hitler when he won the plebiscite.[47] Heidegger also worked with Kerber to find positions for the unemployed, possibly helping Kerber with an indoctrination plan. In 1937, Heidegger published an article, "Ways to Language," in the annual *Land of the Alemanni: A Book on the Traditions and Mission of the People,* edited by Kerber.[48] In 1942, Kerber was made an honorary senator of the university.[49] We may add that, according to documents at the Berlin Document Center, Kerber had been a member of the National Socialist Party since 1930. He was also in the SS (no. 309080), promoted to SS-Obersturmbannfürher[50] by Heinrich Himmler. After receiving his deaths-head ring *(Totenkopfring)*, insignia of the SS, on September 18, 1942, Kerber wrote to Himmler to thank him for this distinction and to say that he would guard it with his life.[51]

When Heidegger took over the rectorate, he had not yet made clear his political intentions and would not do so until formally designated Führer by the university. After the region of Baden was brought into line, and with the promulgation on October 1, 1933, of the university's new con-

stitution, Heidegger became Führer of the university by the application
of the Führer principle, a juridical act quite independent of the earlier
election, that made the election meaningless. Now he had the power to
name the chancellor, dean, and senators.[52]

We see Heidegger's political intentions most clearly in the changes he
made in the governing group when he replaced Möllendorf. There were
a number of professors who worked with Heidegger as the elected rector,
who were definitely not members of the new regime. These included the
theologian Sauer, who was elected adjunct rector, J. Bilz, also a Catholic
theologian, and Walter Eucken, who was Heidegger's principal opponent
at Freiburg.[53] Those whom Heidegger himself chose, with the exception
of Sauer, Möllendorf, and the geologist Soergel, were all members of the
Nazi Party or active collaborators. Heidegger named Professor Julius
Wilser, a member of the Gau Baden,[54] chancellor. Wilser was known for
his pioneer work on the use of geological technology in war[55] and the
potential exploitation of conquered lands. He had worked with Karl
Haushofer, the editor of *Geopolitik*.[56] Professors Wolfgang Schadewaldt,
Nicolas Hilling (in the Gau Baden, no. 4026344),[57] and Erik Wolf were
named deans. Later we will discuss Wolf (Gau Baden, no. 4715792), who
was one of Heidegger's most faithful workers and dean of the law faculty.[58] The senators Heidegger named were Professor Eduard Rehn in
surgery (NSDAP Gau Baden, no. 3126323),[59] Professor Georg Stieler in
philosophy (NSDAP Gau Baden, no. 2910169),[60] Dr. Wilhelm Felgenträger in Roman law (NSDAP Gau Baden, no. 5438497),[61] Professor Hans
Mortensen (NSDAP Gau Baden, no. 3289669),[62] who was also a member
of the National Socialist Committee for Higher Education and who was
known for his radical views on annexation,[63] Professor Kurt Bauch (NSDAP
Gau Baden, no. 2896282),[64] and Dr. Otto Risse (NSDAP, no. 3109698).[65]
Our source indicates that all these appointees remained faithful party
members until 1945.

We should mention one other colleague of Heidegger's. Hans Spemann was a biologist of renown who would receive the Nobel Prize in
1935. He was not a member of the NSDAP. His relationship with Heidegger seems to have begun before the thirties. In a letter dated February 24, 1929, Heidegger alluded to the urgent need for an "effective
model for a conception of the world" *(Weltbild)*, which Spemann could
create. At the time that Heidegger was giving a speech at Bremen in
October 1930, H. W. Petzet mentioned in an article the work Heidegger
and Spemann were doing about relationships between biology and philosophy.[66] In 1937, *Land of the Alemanni*, edited by Kerber, carried an
article by Heidegger on Franco-German relations that we will examine

later, and at the same time he published an article by Spemann called "The Supranational Significance of Science." In it, he refutes racist relativism applied to the exact sciences but stresses its importance in the human sciences. In another article, titled "Science in the Service of the Nation,"[67] Spemann takes the side of "our Führer" and "the government of the Reich, which has called us, scientific investigators, to struggle for the material independence of Germany. . . . Success will not be long in coming. . . . The researcher's work shows how the people are spiritually rooted in the land from which comes material existence, bread to nourish them, wool and cloth to clothe them, and iron for their weapons." Thus, science understands not only the world of technology but also "medicine and racial health." "The grandeur of the people comes not only from reason but from feelings, since reason is limited to categorization. . . . The old ought not disapprove because the new renaissance of the temple and the faith is what keeps the world alive. . . . Heroes are the elected who show the people the path to follow. . . . I beg benediction for our Führer." Heidegger fulfilled his task as Führer of the university by surrounding himself with collaborators of this sort.

Before examining the most significant aspects of Heidegger's actions (at least those that are known), we must carefully study two essential texts: the speech in honor of Albert Leo Schlageter and the Rector's Address.

The homage to Albert Leo Schlageter

The speech that Martin Heidegger gave in honor of Albert Leo Schlageter (1894–1923) is revealing for several reasons. First of all, it gives us biographical insight into Heidegger's background, since Schlageter's course of instruction seems to have been much like Heidegger's. Politically, as a speech from the new rector, it distinctly contributed to the actual atmosphere created by Nazi propaganda that set the stage for the storm troopers' hooliganism in the first years of the "movement" during the Weimar period and, above all, later, during Hitler's seizure of power.

Every year on May 26 there were festivities in Baden to honor Schlageter. Schlageter had taken part in World War I as a volunteer, interrupting his university studies for this purpose, and had become an officer. Following the German defeat, and after briefly resuming his studies, he became attached to the volunteer corps that had emerged after World War I that were actively engaged in attacking French and Belgian occupation troops in the Rhineland. The corps was compared to the "Lützowschen Schwarzen Schare" in the National Socialists' biased reports. The corps' assaults, in agreement with the Nazi image of the enemy, were concerned to repel "Communism, Bolshevism, separatism, and Polish insurrections." Because of an attempted attack on a rail line, Schlageter was apprehended, tried, and condemned to death. On May 26, 1923, he was summarily shot in Düsseldorf. His body may have been removed from a Düsseldorf mortuary and placed in an unmarked field by Viktor Lutze. In 1933, Lutze became a member of Göring's Prussian Privy Council. After Ernst Röhm's assassination he became Röhm's successor as chief of staff of the SA and was regarded, next to Reichsführer Himmler (SS) and Korpsführer Hühnlein (NSKK), among the most important operatives of the NSDAP organization.

Just as Martin Heidegger and Schlageter were fellow students at the Konstanz *lycée* (which was renamed "Schlageter's Gymnasium" in 1936), so too were they students at the secondary school in Saint Conrad and at the Bertholds Gymnasium in Freiburg. The parallels between the two go even further.

In a series including work by Hitler, Goebbels, and other prominent National Socialists, letters by Schlageter were published under the title "Germany Must Live" ("Deutschland muss leben"). In one addressed to his spiritual advisor at Saint Conrad, Dr. Mathäus Lang (who was prefect during Heidegger's stay there and, after 1907, rector), he explains his participation in the war as being essentially religiously motivated. He describes the dangers of the war and also the considerable fascination he felt for the young soldiers: "The main thing with them is that one regularly has a clean scarf and constantly keeps a clean slate with God. The war taught me how to pray and in fact to pray powerfully and devoutly." In another letter, of April 25, 1915, he communicates his decision to become a priest after the war, a decision that was assisted by a "call from the Holy Spirit and the Mother of God." In a letter of April 17, 1916, also to Dr. Lang, he grieves over the death of Albert Eckert, who had been at Saint Conrad's at the same time: "Albert Eckert has found the holy death of a hero; the war claims only the best and ablest fellows— that we may live on—who are almost unworthy of grace, who are almost put to shame."[68] Schlageter was an active member of the important Catholic student group Falkenstein, whose central association published a book exclusively dedicted to him in 1932.[69]

The cult surrounding Schlageter soon became a thematic center for agitation and propaganda among the extreme right, especially among the National Socialist students. The tenth anniversary of his death was the occasion for numerous events reported in detail by the liberal-bourgeois press.[70] In 1933, Schlageter was declared the first National Socialist German soldier and was thereby, like Hans Maikowsky and Horst Wessel, elevated as a cult figure by state doctrine. The popular playwright Hanns Johst composed a piece for the theater titled *Schlageter* that was staged in Schlageter's and Heidegger's school in Konstanz. It reached an audience of 35,000 in 1935 and 80,000 in 1943.

During Pentecost in 1933 there took place in Schlageter's home province a demonstration to honor him in which more than a thousand people participated, including Heidegger as rector, Mayor Kerber of Freiburg, the leader of the SA in Baden Ludin, and Prince Wilhelm of Prussia, representing the Reich. On May 26 the area commander Robert Wagner dedicated a monument to Schlageter on Mount Zugspitze.[71] The *Frankfurter Zeitung* gave the following description of Heidegger's speech: "Schlageter realized, among other things, [according to Heidegger] the most difficult and the greatest death. The rector exhorted the students to allow the severity and purity in which Schlageter had suffered to course through them and to preserve it and carry it with them into the German universities and among their comrades." Shortly before, the *Frankfurter Zeitung* had expressed views on the occupation of the Ruhr district that were in principle like Schlageter's.[72]

The *Völkischer Beobachter* of May 30, 1933, carried a report on the ceremony in Freiburg. According to its account, after Heidegger's speech, the thousand present raised their arms in silence to the memory of Schlageter. Heidegger gave the speech on the front steps of the main entrance to the university. The text had a systematic meaning, because at critical points it followed the lines of the analytic of Dasein in *Being and Time*, which derived from the early ideological resources of the "movement." Heidegger, who now more than ever had definitively distanced himself from the Church, did not mention at all the religious motives that had guided Schlageter's life. This suited the character of the event, which had been organized by a fanatical wing of the Nazis that excluded any connection to the Catholic youth groups, although the latter did everything to prove their preference for heroic and national objectives, which they wanted to integrate with Catholicism.

Heidegger's speech to honor Schlageter began in the following way:

We wish to honor this death and dwell a moment upon it, in order to understand something about our own lives.

Schlageter died the *most difficult* death, not on the front as a leader of an infantry battalion, not under the pressure of attack or

in a dogged defensive—no, he died *defenseless* in front of French
rifles.

But he stood tall and bore the worst of it.

However, even this would still have been borne in a final
rejoicing if there had been a victory through struggle and the
greatness of a waking nation had been enflamed.

Instead there is darkness, humiliation, and treason.

He needed to achieve greatness in the most difficult conditions.
He alone must convey to the soul of the people the image of their
future awakening to honor and greatness, in order to die in
faith.[73]

In *Being and Time,* death was the *"ownmost, non-relational, unsurpassable
possibility."*[74] Dasein could thus experience its "ownmost" potential-for-
being as a perfect "imminence" *(Bevorstand).* Dasein could then decide to
have an understanding of itself through a relationship with its *own* death.
The meaning of the existential/ontological structure of death was "found"
in the "opening of a horizon" onto finitude, and, through that, onto temporality, in which Being is revealed. Yet, just as, in *Being and Time,* the
explicit investigation of death in its authentic[75] and inauthentic[76] vari-
eties was developed, it became clear that (despite reference to the collective and authentic forms of Dasein in the forms of heroes) the account
lacked a detailed foundation, although, in *Being and Time,* Heidegger did
speak expressly of tradition, heritage, the community of the people, and
struggle as the decisive moments in an understanding of collective Dasein. What was really needed to complete *Being and Time* emerges in the
speech honoring Schlageter. There Heidegger attempts to reconcile individual as well as collective Dasein with the possibility of achieving an
authentic potential-for-being. The constitutive signs of death as "ownmost, non-relational, not-to-be-surpassed possibility" are now joined by
further distinctions. Precisely because it was "non-relational," Schlageter's
death was "the most difficult" and "the greatest": Schlageter became a
model for life (for "our life"). The death of young students, similarly "the
greatest" and "the most difficult," must be accepted with struggle, without those actions through which authentic Dasein is defined. Here, new
criteria are seamlessly attached to the theory of *Being and Time;* the speech
serves to feature the distinction of Dasein so that it would be discovered
through National Socialism. Death would not have dealt with Schlageter
so cruelly if it had come upon him as the leader of a troop in an attack
or if he had experienced death in a vigorous defensive or even after a
victory—after the awakening "of the people to their greatness and honor."

The absence of just these conditions accounts for Schlageter's distinction, for it was he alone who, without help, began the work that was to be realized by the National Socialists in 1933. Heidegger saw personified in Schlageter's death the fate of the German people following the end of World War I. This accords with the polemic of the extreme right and especially of the National Socialists against Gustav Stresemann's Ruhr-Politik. Heidegger also believed, in accord with the tale that German politicians had betrayed Germany in World War I, that the people had been betrayed by their countrymen, and so stood before an "imminent uprising." Heidegger was convinced that the student avant-garde, the "living generation," stood at the head of such an uprising.

Not only did the concept of death find a new twist in the speech on Schlageter; Heidegger's interpretation of the "people" and the "world" was reformulated:

> Where does this *hardness of will* come from that permeates this heaviness? Where does the *purity of heart* come from, the greatness and remoteness that the soul conceives?
>
> Freiburg students! German students! Live and know when, on your journeys and walks, you set foot on the mountains, the forests, and the valleys of the Black Forest, the home of these heroes: the substructure of stone and granite is the mountain where the young farmer's son grew up. For a long time it has produced this hardness of will.
>
> The autumn sun of the Black Forest bathes its mountain ranges and stretches of woods in magnificent purity. It has nourished this purity of heart for a long time.[77]

For the Heidegger of *Being and Time*, the precinct in which Dasein is utterly its own being and exists for-itself was the "world" *(Welt)*. By contrast, Schlageter conceived the world as "homeland" *(Heimat)*, *his* homeland. Heidegger added to this notion an association to national and local wills, and he linked his insight regarding the "world" to that of "dwelling" *(Raum)*—that is, that exact analogy of "time" *(Zeit)* that (from the time of his earliest idealism) before 1927 had never managed to take a concrete form. So the occasion afforded an opportunity to form just such an understanding of history. With this understanding he drew out essential features of the homeland (the *soil [Boden]* of the fatherland, the *mountains, woods,* and *valleys,* the *light [Licht]*) a reality he shared with his listeners and in which the Dasein of the hero would become paradigmatic and would gain its distinctive characteristics from a common homeland

and a common origin. "Defenseless before those rifles the inner vision of the hero rises over the muzzles, toward the day and the mountains of his homeland, so that, transfixed on the land of the Alemanni, he prepares to die for the German people and his country."[78]

The German people as a nation were not a beloved political structure for Heidegger. Agreeing with the then popular notion of regionalism developed by Josef Nadler—to the effect that the German people had their real roots and inspiration in the south and that they gradually spread to the north, Heidegger claimed that homeland is the place of birth, the point of mediation between individual and nation, a necessary condition of nationhood. Supposedly Schlageter died looking upon his homeland. He died for the German people and his country (*Reich*). This enabled Heidegger to make Schlageter's death a symbol of what was to come, of what was impending. Philosophical thought became the call:

> With a strong will and a pure heart Albert Leo Schlageter met his difficult and great death.
> Freiburg students, let the power of the mountains of this hero's home stream in your wills!
> Freiburg students, let the power of the autumn sun of this hero's valleys light up your hearts!
> Preserve both in you, and carry both, the strong will and the purity of heart, into the German university and to your comrades.[79]

In *Being and Time* conscience is conceived to be an exercise of Dasein itself, through which the "call" *(Ruf)* is received so that it may choose its own authenticity. The "call" corresponds to a "capacity-for-hearing." "Hearing" involves the possibility of authentic Dasein's choice by means of a decision.[80] Through Schlageter's example Heidegger seems to have overcome the irresolute quality of his 1927 descriptions. He not only reveals here a detailed and concrete model for Dasein that renders a resolute decision possible; he also makes clear the (heroic and patriotic) modalities of such a decision. He too, as the one who formulated the "call," was to become politically explicit. At that time his standard was so objective that he was able to form a precise criterion by which the German people were able to guide themselves. The fatherland, the foundation of nation and state, became a new totality that offered the goal and source of the real decision and capability of the German people to choose themselves.

When, in *Being and Time*, the "call" comes "in the mode of silence,"[81] an authentic Dasein is said to become aware of an anonymous *(anonymisierenden)* collectivity; hence, since the possibility of collective authenticity falls within its grasp, the "call" may be made loud without fear of falling prey to the idle chatter of inauthenticity. What was only an imprecise call in *Being and Time* (which appeals to no one) is now articulated as a call that a people and its past are tied to. They *are* thus brought to Being in an exemplary way: they are brought to it by its leader and heroes. The call that had been certified only out of the "uncanny" *(Unheimlichkeit)* in 1927 was now an explicit exhortation to "greatness" in struggle:

> Schlageter stood here and went about as a Freiburg student.
> But he was not here for long. He *needed* to go to the Baltic, he *needed* to go to Silesia, he *needed* to go to the Ruhr.
> He was obliged not to evade his destiny so that he could die the most difficult and the greatest death with a strong will and a pure heart.
> We honor the hero and silently raise our hands to salute him.[82]

The places for which Heidegger said Schlageter was *bound* are those areas in which the volunteer corps were thought to be active: the Baltic, Upper Silesia, the Ruhr. That he was *obliged* to act made him an example for Heidegger. Of course, the homage to Schlageter was greeted with the Nazi salute.

In his speech and during his tenure as rector Heidegger promoted the cult around Schlageter. He not only supported the student initiative to establish the National Schlageter Brotherhood (the Völkische Kameradschaft Schlageter) in the university[83] but also recommended once more to the students in a matriculation ceremony that same year that Schlageter should be a model:

> This city, his land and nationality, are dominated by and steeped in the Black Forest. Under the imperative of the new German reality for German students, the Black Forest has also changed its nature; it is no longer only a winter sports region, an area for walks and summer vacations. We now see in the Black Forest the mountains of the homeland, the forests of the homeland, the valleys of the homeland of Albert Leo Schlageter.

After these remarks Heidegger, in his capacity as rector, instructed a member of the student body, representing all the others, to become familiar with Adolf Hitler's initiatives.[84]

It is not accidental that the names Schlageter, Hitler, and Heidegger should appear together in this matriculation ceremony. In Hitler's *Mein Kampf* Schlageter's name appears at the very beginning.[85] In another place, where Hitler remembers his time as a young soldier in World War I, he speaks of war as of a unique and superior reality and of a decision that can only be made through a confrontation with death (the potentiality-for-death *[Sterbenkönnen]*), which is also the source of the ground for authentic Dasein, which depends on permanent and heroic decisions. He describes the impatience of the younger soldiers taking part in the war and goes on:

> And then comes a damp, cold night in Flanders through which
> we silently marched and as the day began to break out of the
> mist an iron torrent suddenly hissed over our heads, coming
> towards us, and in sharp crackles the small bullets fired between
> our lines, the wet ground was stirred up; before the small cloud was
> dissolved there roared out from two hundred throats against the
> first messages of death the first hurrahs. And then it began to
> rattle and roar, to sing and to howl, and with feverish eyes drawn
> toward the front, faster and faster, until suddenly over red fields
> and hedgerows, off in the distance, the battle began, the
> struggle of man against man. Out in the distance, however, the
> clang of a song reached our ears and came closer and closer,
> springing from one company to the next, and there in our own
> ranks, where death was taking its toll, there the song reached us
> and we let it ring out more: Deutschland, Deutschland über alles,
> über alles in der Welt!
>
> After four days we turned back. Even our step had now
> changed. Seventeen-year-old boys seemed like men. The volunteers
> of the List regiment may not have learned how to fight correctly;
> but we learned what it was like to die like old soldiers.

From the first vivid, enthusiastic experience there followed a long war that dissolved their fear and terror:

> So it goes from year to year. Once the romance of battle begins,
> the grayness soon sets in. Enthusiasm gradually cools down,
> and exuberant joy is choked out by the fear of death. Then came
> the time when everyone struggles with conflicting urges toward
> self-preservation and reminders of duty. Even I was not
> spared the struggle. Whenever death stalked the chase, one felt an

incipient revolt against an ambiguous something, worrying over the weak body before you, and finally one was left only with the cowardice that, under such a solitary mask, tries to ensnare you.

A severe agitation and warning then begins, and only the last remains of conscience can settle matters. The more this voice is heard, which reminds one to take care, the louder and more urgently it attracts us, making the conflict keener, until finally after a long inner struggle the sense of duty carries one on to victory. By the winter of 1915/16 this battle had been decided for me. Finally the power of the will had gained complete mastery. I could for the first time make an assault with joy and laughter; so I became calm and resolute. That's what endured. Destiny could now proceed to make its final test, without my nerves cracking or my mind breaking down.   .

Out of a young volunteer had come an old soldier.[86]

Here Heidegger actualizes his fundamental ontology through the then current political themes of popular and nationalistic war memories. The effects of this "thinking" are echoed in the "philosophical war correspondence" of his students Otto Friedrich Bollnow and H. Mörchen in the *Blätter für Deutsche Philosophie.*[87]

Still, Heidegger's contribution to the militarization of the universities was not by any means limited to his apologetic for Schlageter. The discussion of his Rector's Address (which follows) and of his speech "The University in the New Reich," which he gave before the student body at Heidelberg, will clarify this further.

9   The Rector's Address: its assumptions and its effects

On May 27, 1933, the ceremonial transfer of the rector's office took place at which Heidegger gave his speech "The Self-Determination of the German University" ("Die Selbstbehauptung der Universität"). According to press reports,[1] numerous students joined the celebration, as did the minister of culture, education, and justice, Dr. Wacker, the rector of the University of Heidelberg, Professor Dr. Willy Andreas, the rector of the Technical University of Karlsruhe, Professor Dr. Kluge, the archbishop of Freiburg, Dr. Conrad Gröber, Mayor Kerber, and the general of the artillery, von Gallwitz, as well as representatives of the bureaucracy of the Reich, of the cultural administration, and of the religious community in Baden. Also present were people from the SA with swastika flags and delegations from the leading student organizations. The installation was accompanied by music from Johannes Brahms (Academic Festival Overture), "Deutschlandlied," the Horst Wessel song, and Richard Wagner's "Huldigungs-Marsch." The festivities were broadcast by Freiburg Radio.[2]

Heidegger's Rector's Address should be examined from three perspectives: with regard to National Socialism's ideas about reforming university politics, with regard to its intellectual and political status, and with regard to its effect upon the public. With respect to the first issue, the speech clearly expressed National Socialist opinions about the reformation of the universities, and indeed it represented an effort to influence these opinions. For the regime had just begun to consolidate its power and to develop a general political program. The general meaning of university politics in Germany and the importance that the National Socialists attributed to it, the acts of violence by the students to "revolutionize" the universities, the active participation of the party and its sub-organizations during the discussions, the passive and distrustful position of the majority of the professors, who saw their privileges threatened by the politicization of the university—all these factors made the "university as a part of the front" a problem area for the political leaders of the NSDAP.

The situation was complicated by the fact that the party and its ideologues had not constructed a definitive reform model for university politics that would allow them to pursue systematic actions. In Aaron Kleinberger's opinion, the National Socialists basically did not succeed in formulating a workable plan for reforming the universities and therefore left the matters of university control and scholarly research to the power rivalries and intrigues of individuals or small groups.[3] Also National Socialism was, ideologically and politically, far from building a unity. This source of uncertainty produced a certain vacuum in which several plans came into conflict, each seeking to claim leadership of the reform movement. There were at least two main approaches to university reform, reflecting the political alternatives facing the Nazi regime up to July 1934.

One approach assumed that the National Socialist "revolution" had been successful in seizing control of the party and was secure in its control of the state apparatus. According to this belief, the main task now consisted in consolidating the revolution within society; it was now necessary to start reorganizing the basic structures of social, economic, political, and cultural life and to avoid destabilizing matters. This opinion was expressed, for example, in the models for university reform proposed by Alfred Bäumler and Ernst Krieck. Despite some difference of opinion, they agreed that the reform of the universities should be dictated by the goals of the National Socialist state.

Like the other rival proposals, Bäumler planned to politicize the universities and thus eliminate their autonomy. The peculiarity of his plan consisted in establishing "men's houses" at the universities in order to exclude the female-liberal element from institutions of higher education and to militarize educational life.[4] Bäumler represented the interests of Alfred Rosenberg, whose office oversaw the preservation of National Socialist Party doctrine.

The position of Ernst Krieck, the most highly regarded pedagogue of National Socialism, was presented in the speech he gave when he assumed office as rector of the University of Frankfurt on May 23, 1933. Like Heidegger, he stressed the new political and revolutionary role of the students and their soldierly comportment. But, in contrast to Heidegger, Krieck insisted on the importance of the "scientific monk" as well as the professional focus of scientific education during the reform of the universities.[5] He formulated a reform plan that stressed the independence of each discipline and the elimination of hierarchial structures among the disciplines.[6] This emphasis resulted in the need for a unifying orientation in which the sciences would operate autonomously; a common world view and service to the people was to unite them. The universities were to orient themselves to the professional demands their graduates encountered.[7] Krieck headed a group organized around the periodical *Volk im Werden*, published in Frankfurt, which strove for a leading role in shaping the National Socialist politics of culture. Friction with Rosenberg's office was inevitable, especially because of the periodical's competition with the monthly National Socialist periodical *(Nationalsozialistische Monatshefte)* published by Rosenberg's office.[8]

Representative of the second kind of approach to university reform was the circle around Ernst Röhm and his SA. In the university field his most important source of power consisted in the total control of the National Socialist student community. For the circle around Röhm, Hitler's taking office in the government was the signal for the complete reorganization of German society, in order to introduce a truly "national socialistic revolution." To him, control of the state apparatus was only the beginning of the process ("the second revolution") that would transform Germany with respect to fundamentals, supposedly distorted by liberalism, internationalism, and Judaism. This extreme reform model advocated a complete renewal of the conception of the sciences (in teaching and research) for the universities and meant a substantial shift in procedures and work at the universities, especially as it affected the relationship between students and professors. The most important leader and spokesman for this kind of university reform was Martin Heidegger.

W. D. Gudopp was correct in pointing out Heidegger's close relationship to SA positions and in showing that his Rector's Address contained not only terminology borrowed from Moeller van den Brucks, a representative of the conservative revolution ("the young force") but also terminology taken from the Strasser brothers, who belonged to the "left" wing of the NSDAP.[9] Certain typical themes appear right at the beginning of the Rector's Address:

> The assumption of the office of rector is an obligation to the
> *spiritual* leadership of this university. The allegiance of teachers
> and students awakens and gains strength only from its true and
> common roots in the spirit of the German university. But this

spirit achieves clarity, distinction, and power only and above all when the leaders *[Führer]* are first led themselves—led by the relentlessness of that spiritual order that expresses its history through the fate of the German nation.[10]

Heidegger pointed to a superpersonal principle—"the fate of the German nation" *(Volk)*—that through its movement explains and determines the action of those subordinate to it. Obedience and individual action are organized through this transcendental occasion, in the presence of which privileges disappear and which ranks agents according to the credit they gain in regard to that decisive mission. The renewal of the German university is the expression of a new way of thinking that points beyond democratic self-administration:

Are we aware of this spiritual mission? Whether we are or not, the question remains inevitable: are we, teachers and students of this university, truly rooted in the spirit of the German university? Has this essence *[Wesen]* real power to put a stamp onto our existence *[Dasein]*? Only if we wholeheartedly *want* this spirit. But who wishes to doubt that? Generally, one sees the dominant spiritual character of a university in its "self-determination"; that shall remain intact. Yet—have we really considered what this claim to self-determination requires from us?

Self-determination means: confronting ourselves with the task and resolving for ourselves the way and manner of its realization in order, precisely, to be what we ought to be. But then do we know *who we ourselves are,* this body of teachers and students of the highest school of the German people? Can we know that at all without the most constant and the most rigorous *self-examination?*[11]

And Heidegger continues:

The self-determination of the German university is the original common will to its essence. The German university is valued by us as the loftiest school that educates the leaders and the guards of the fate of the German nation through and from the power of science. To will the essence of the German university is to will that science to be informed by the historical spiritual mission of the German people. Science and German fate must *above all* gain power in the will to essence *[Wesenswillen]*. This will be accomplished *only* when we—teachers and students—*first* expose science to its innermost necessity, and *second* stand fast with our German fate in the hour of its greatest need.[12]

The university seems transformed into a community of leaders molded by "discipline" into a school that produces the guardians of the community, a nation that knows itself to be in "its" own land. Knowledge about the spirit creates a mission of philosophical reflection. Understanding the spirit is nothing but understanding the "originary" *(Ursprünge)*. According to Heidegger, the first presupposition is fulfilled "if we submit ourselves again to the power of the very beginnings of our spiritual-historical existence. This beginning *(Anfang)* is the beginning of Greek philosophy. There for the first time Western man rises up against *being-in-its-totality (Seiende-im-Ganzen)* through the power of its native speech, questions and understands itself as the being that it is. All science is philosophy whether or not it knows it. All science remains connected to that philosophical beginning. It wins the power of its being from it, provided that power has evolved from that beginning."[13]

There is no need to consider this essence from a theoretical view. Behind it there stands a people who—thanks to their abilities—demonstrate an impulse for spiritual development. Here for the first time Heidegger expresses a conviction he held until the end of his life. He is persuaded that the origins of Western man lie in that transcendental system of coordinates of unique spiritual power that extends from Greece to Germany. Thus, he argues sympathetically for the genuine National Socialist idea voiced by Hitler: "The struggle that rages today is for very substantial goals: a culture is fighting for its existence, a culture that involves thousands of years of development and that embraces Greece and Germany together."[14] In Heidegger's vision theory was for the Greeks the highest form of *energeia*. It was not concerned with "assimilating practice to theory, but the other way around. Theory is to be understood as the highest realization of true practice. To the Greeks, science is not a mere 'property of culture,' but the decisive inner medium of the entire *Dasein* of a people and state."[15] For Heidegger the spiritual task is one of facing one's own essence, not in a mere struggle in which the agent acts in accord with determinate nation-oriented vision, but, more than that, in a heroic battle, a battle in which spiritual effort becomes real only where the totality of what is being sought is never attainable. "All knowledge about things is handed over to the superpower of fate and gives out before it."[16] With this heroic and definite overcoming of the antinomy of theory and practice, Heidegger legitimates his thesis about the historical and political-transcendental praxis as *energeia*. Philosophy creates sciences because it founds the historical-transcendental ("spiritual") existence of *certain* peoples. Far from presenting himself as a candidate for the position of state philosopher, Heidegger here assigns to philosophy (his own philosophy of course) the task of instituting a new German reality. The relation between past, present, and future affecting the effort to grasp one's own essence corresponds to the very structure of temporality and historicity that Heidegger had described in *Being and Time:*

> That is the original essence of science. But does not this beginning lie back two and a half thousand years in the past? Has the program of human actions not also altered science? Surely! The subsequent Christian-theological interpretation of the world, as much as the later mathematical-technical thinking of modern times, has distanced science from its origins in time and topic. However, the beginning *(Anfang)* has not been overcome or reduced to nothing. For, provided that the original Greek science is something great, the *beginning (Anfang)* of this greatness remains its *greatest* quality. The essence of science could not ever be emptied or misused as it is today, despite all consequences and the efforts of "international organizations," if the greatness of the beginning *(Anfang)* did not still exist. The beginning remains with us. It does not lie *behind* us as the past that is long gone, but is still *before* us. As the greatest, the beginning will outlast everything that is still to come. It will discard us as well. The beginning has penetrated to our own future; it is standing there over us as the distant degree, instructing us to recover its greatness once again.
>
> Only when we resolutely submit to this distant call to win back the greatness of this beginning, only then will science become the innermost necessity of our existence. Otherwise, it turns out to be an accidental encounter, or the low-grade satisfaction of the bland pursuit of knowledge.
>
> But if we submit ourselves to the distant call of the beginning, then science must become the basic event of our spiritual-national existence.[17]

Thus, Heidegger excludes the possibility that the central question in conversations between men (like that in "international organizations") could be discussed and solved. He finally comes rather close to Rosenberg's and

Chamberlain's thesis—that spirit speaks through race, that the protection of blood and soil is the precondition for the formation and spread of the spiritual life of a people:

> If we want the essence of science in the sense of *questioning, exposed resoluteness in the midst of insecurity of being-as-a-whole*, then *this* very will for the essence of our people *[Wesenswille]* creates in its world an innermost and most external danger, that is to say, its own true *spiritual* world. For "spirit" is neither empty analysis, nor the noncommittal game of wits, nor the boundless activity of producing rational analyses, nor world reason. Spirit is originally in tune with a knowing decisiveness regarding the essence of Being. The *spiritual* world of a people is not the superstructure of a culture, nor is it merely an arsenal for usable knowledge and values; it is the force of the deepest preservation of its powers of earth and blood, the power of the innermost excitement and most profound shock *(Erschütterung)* of its existence. A spiritual world alone bestows greatness on a nation, for it forces it to the ultimate decision as to whether the will to greatness or a tolerance for decline will become the law for our nation's future history.[18]

The racist implications of this line of thought have been revealed by Rainer Marten:

> As soon as the bourgeois self-valuation of race and nation appears as the ideology of the noblest spirit along with its universal claims, then race and nation are primarily understood in terms of the spirit and no longer just in biological terms. Of course, the German to whom thoughts of nation and blood, earth and language, family standing and roots, are attributed in this most excellent way, does not live by spirit alone.

Since for Heidegger "the *spiritual* world of a people is *not* the superstructure of a culture" but "the strength of the deepest preservation of its powers of earth and blood," Marten concludes: "The spirit, although universal, actually belongs to its German blood, and to its own German homeland."[19]

On this basis Heidegger thought he could structure his ideas about the transformation of the university: the most extreme part of the student body should become the historical subject of this process. He postulates a model of political action in which rector and Führer are united on the basis of a union of transcendental consciousness and historical movement. This, of course, required the cessation of academic freedom and the subordination of the lecturers to the machinations of the Nazi students and the SA for the purpose of Social Darwinist selection:

> If we desire this essence of science, the teachers of the university really must move on to the most exposed positions of danger in a context of constant world insecurity. If they stand tall there—that is, if in the intimacy of the risky nature of everything there develops a communal sense of questioning and a socially oriented discourse—then they will become strong enough for leadership. The decisive element of leadership lies not in merely moving forward; it is rather the power to go it alone, not out of stubbornness and the wish to dominate, but out of the deepest determination and the widest sense of obligation. Such a power establishes a bond with the essential, selects the best, arouses the real loyalty of those who manifest a fresh courage. But we do not have to arouse those followers. German students are already marching. They are looking for those leaders who will help them raise their own destiny *[Bestimmung]* to the level of wise and fundamental truth and to place that destiny in the clear light of productive German thought and work.
>
> A will to realize the essence *[Wesen]* of the university is born out of the resoluteness of the German student to stand firm in the most extreme crisis facing the German destiny. This will is a true will, as long as, through their new entitlement, the German students place themselves under the law of their own essence and thereby define their essence. To give oneself a law is the highest freedom. That much-talked-about "academic freedom" has been expelled from the university, because it is not genuine; it is only negative. It means no more than taking it easy, being arbitrary in one's intentions and inclinations, taking license in everything. The concept of the German student's freedom is now restored to its truth. From that freedom will flourish our students' sense of future obligation and service.[20]

Heidegger puts the activities of the students in the context of three "obligations." This is the high point of his contribution to the discussion of the reform of university work:

The first obligation is to the community of the people. It commits us to cooperation concerning the efforts, abilities, and aspirations of all classes and all members of the nation. This obligation will henceforth be secured and take root in students' Dasein through *work service [Arbeitsdienst]*.

The second obligation is to the honor and fate of the nation in the midst of other peoples. It requires mustering everyone to be ready right up to the last ounce, secure in knowledge and ability, fortified by discipline. In the future this obligation will encompass and permeate all student existence as *military service [Wehrdienst]*.

The students' third obligation is to the spiritual mission of the German nation. Our nation realizes its own fate by risking its history in the arena of world power in which all human existence is affected and by continually fighting for its own spiritual world. Thus exposed to the precariousness of its own existence, this nation will become a spiritual nation. It demands of itself and its leaders and guardians the hardest clarity of the highest, broadest, and richest knowledge. A young student who dares to enter manhood early and who applies his will to the future fate of the nation essentially commits himself to the service of this knowledge. This *service to knowledge [Wissendienst]* may no longer provide the lackluster and expedient training that leads to a "distinguished" profession. Inasmuch as the politician and teacher, the doctor and judge, the pastor and architect, mean to follow the destiny of the nation and state *[völkisch-staatliche Dasein]* and to guard and hone it in the setting of those world powers that shape human existence, these professions and the preparatory training they involve are placed in the hands of service to knowledge. It is not knowledge that services the professions, but the other way around: the professions create and administer that highest and most essential knowledge of the nation concerned with its total existence. But to us this knowledge is not a merely quietistic cognizance of spirit and values itself, but an awareness of that greatest danger for our own existence, posed by the superior powers of being *[Übermacht des Seienden]*. The very uncertainty of being drives the nation from work and fight and compels it to form a state in which the professions must contribute.

The three obligations—that inform the nation of the very fate of the state in its spiritual mission—are *equally primordial* as far as the German essence is concerned. The three resulting services—work service, military service, and service to knowledge— are equally necessary and of equal rank.[21]

With these hints, Heidegger went well beyond official views of National Socialist goals, since the so-called organic hierarchy of the Führer-led state *(Führerstaates)* planned for work service and military service. To add the idea of service to knowledge meant (besides reducing knowledge to the level of work and the military) declaring science to be one of the highest obligations of the National Socialist state. With his doctrine of the three obligations, Heidegger turned most of all to the students. The teachers were called upon to be at the cutting edge, and the students called them to this. According to Heidegger, the conflicts that were bound to arise between an active avant-garde and the old indecisive lecturers should serve to regulate the common life of the university, now understood to be a revolutionary process:

> The will to essence *[Wesenswille]* of our teachers must wake up and develop in accord with the plain discipline due the essence of science. The will to essence *[Wesenswille]* of the students has to force itself to the highest clarity and discipline of knowledge, and it has to integrate the joint knowledge of the nation and its state into the essence of science in a demanding and determined way. Both wills have to prepare themselves separately for the struggle. All aptitudes for willing and thinking, all powers of the heart, all capabilities of the body, must be developed in struggle, intensified in struggle, and preserved as struggle.
> We choose the deliberate struggle of those questioning souls who affirm with Carl von Clausewitz: "I withdraw from the frivolous hope of a salvation by the hand of chance."[22]

Heidegger is quite forthright in his insinuations here: The university appears to him as an ideological battlefield in the historical context. Struggle is the law of all action; it is best, therefore, to have a dominant cadre of extremist Nazi students. To talk about Clausewitz in this context signals a distinct recourse to the militaristic heart of the myth of the "German movement" and of the "nationalist *[völkischen]* uprising" that had animated the Prussian wars.[23] It is an appeal to the young National Socialist lecturers and especially to the students to rise up against traditional ("reactionary") forces.

To appeal to Clausewitz has a special purpose, for the cited sentence is not from his main work, *On War* (1832–1834; new ed., 1935) but from his military and political notes, the *Three Confessions (Drei Bekenntnisse).*[24] This text contains the "War Party's Agenda" *(Programm der Kreigspartei)* of Prussia in 1812 that, as Heinrich von Treitschke said, "made every German heart shiver."[25] Clausewitz' confession was praised by the Nazis as a "holy declaration of the revolt," and its author was extolled as the "secret German prophet,"[26] "the most German among the Germans." The *Three Confessions* disputed Prussia's decision to lay down its weapons and to make arrangements with Napoleon after the defeats at Jena and Auerstedt and to sign, as Friedrich Meinecke expressed it in 1906, a "treaty of submission" with France.[27] Clausewitz withdrew from a government that abandoned its sovereignty and made a radical decision: in 1812, together with other Prussian officers, he joined the Russian-German Legion and became its general staff-officer.[28] The preparation for the national "uprising" of 1812 already had racist overtones. At the invitation of Achim von Arnim, Clausewitz had been meeting regularly with Heinrich von Kleist, Clemens Brentano, Adam Müller, Johann G. Fichte, and Friedrich Carl von Savigny in the Christian-German Tablesociety, whose statutes contained "Aryan legislation" that prevented the participation of Jews in the society.[29] Traces of this anti-Jewish Christian tradition can also be found in his remarks during his departure from Berlin. On his way to Russia he stayed in Poland for a short time. From there, he wrote: "The entire Polish life exists as if it were tied and patched together with ropes and rags. Filthy German Jews, who swarm in the dirt and misery like vermin, are the patricians of this country."[30]

For Heidegger, too, the defense of German identity was preeminent, so that the reform of the university was tantamount to deciding to save that identity. Heidegger affirmed this view before assuming the office of rector: in his discussion with "reactionary" colleagues in the Association of German Universities, the citation from Clausewitz also appears. The "reactionary" traditionalism of these fellows was to be prevented from insinuating itself into the state apparatus and from vocally opposing the revolution, because otherwise nothing basic would change.[31]

It is unclear where Heidegger got the citation from, and it will remain unclear as long as Heidegger's personal library remains closed. One can only speculate. The sentence Heidegger quotes appears in the article "Clausewitz in 1812" on the front page of the magazine *Deutschlands Erneuerung*, published by Georg von Below and H. Stuart Chamberlain.[32] After 1921, Rosenberg worked on the magazine too. After 1926 it appeared with the supplement "Race and the People" ("Volk und Rasse"), which contained, among other things, contributions by Eugen Fischer and G. K. Günther. If it could be proven that Heidegger did use this magazine as a source, the connection would be made to the Vaterlandspartei, whose most important representative was Georg von Below, Heidegger's former teacher in Freiburg, and who deemed the German capitulation at the end of World War I a betrayal.

In 1933 the quotation from Clausewitz had a clear meaning. In chapter 15 of Hitler's *Mein Kampf* ("Self-defense as a Right") there is also a reference to Clausewitz' text in order to denounce the November 18 truce as a betrayal and a kind of politics that "according to human foresight could only lead to complete submission." "The fall of Carthage is the most terrible example of such a slow execution of a nation brought about through its own fault."[33] Hitler's reference is reminiscent of certain central themes in Heidegger's Rector's Address (history as a struggle and as the site of the threat to succumb to fate). As a heroic alternative to "cowardly submission," the very demise of freedom facilitates, "after a bloody and honorable struggle, a rebirth of the nation. It is the very seed of life from which a new tree will certainly someday take root."[34]

Inside the university, too, the position Heidegger, like Clausewitz, took was based on the politics of struggle:

> But the struggling community of teachers and students will only then transform the German university into a site of spiritual legislation, and create in it a center for the strongest concentration of highest service to the nation in its state, when they form their being in a simpler, harder, and more unassuming way than do all other citizens. All leaders have to acknowledge the particular power of their followers. But following entails resistance. This spiritual antagonism between leading and following should neither be blurred nor extinguished.
>
> The struggle alone keeps that antagonism alive and instills a basic mood into teachers and students out of which a limiting self-affirmation *[Selbstbehauptung]* empowers a resolute self-reflection *[Selbstbesinnung]* to achieve a genuine self-discipline *[Selbstverwaltung]*.[35]

The new university appears here as the center of a new society out of which the spiritual law of the nation will be born.

At the end of his Rector's Address Heidegger asks the rhetorical question: "Do we want the essence of the German university or not?" And he immediately replies:

> It is entirely up to us whether and how extensively we mean to make a fundamental effort toward self-reflection and self-determination, and not just incidentally, or whether—with the best intention—we just mean to change old institutions and add new ones. Nobody will prevent us from doing that.

Furthermore, nobody will ask us what we want or don't want—
if the spiritual power of the West breaks down and cracks at the
seams, if that worn-out, make-believe culture collapses, expends all
its powers in confusion, and smothers in its own lunacy.

Whether or not this happens depends only on our decision to
remain a spiritual and historical nation—or to decide that we don't
want to be ourselves anymore. Everyone decides this, even and
especially when he avoids making the decision.

But we do want our nation to fulfill its historic mission.

We long to be ourselves. For the young and youngest power of
our nation is already reaching out to us and has already *decided.*

But we can only completely understand the glory and greatness
of this uprising if we carry in us that deep and ample level-
headedness of which the old Greek wisdom spoke the words:

"All greatness stands firm in the storm . . ." (Plato, *Politeia*
497d, 9).

Whenever Germany's fate rested on a decision leading a spiritual-po-
litical and revolutionary reformation, then the very fate of the world lay
in German hands. In an apocalyptic vision of the universe that must in-
evitably lose its own center if the Germans do not fix it upon a new foundation, Heidegger's "call" resembles an entreaty, an urgent appeal, just
like Abraham a Sancta Clara's when Abraham warned the Viennese of
the abyss signified by the Turks, the Jews, and the plague. The slogans
of the SA echo in this appeal: "Today Germany belongs to us, tomorrow
the entire world!" "The world recuperates in accord with the German
essence."

Heidegger's Rector's Address was one of many given by the new National Socialist rectors at their respective universities. Each speech expressed parts of rival projects that, of course, remained on the whole
rather vague. Although it would be appropriate to reconstruct them all
in their entirety, doing so would far exceed the terms of reference of this
essay. I will, therefore, limit myself to examining the reception of Heidegger's speech after the publication of the second edition in 1934 in
Breslau. (The 1933 first edition was distributed only in Freiburg.) Contrary to what Heidegger says in his postscript, "The Rectorate, 1933/34:
Facts and Reflections" ("Das Rektorat, 1933/34: Tatsachen und Gedanken"), which he wrote in 1945 according to the information given by the
editor, its reception both among officials and well-known followers of the
Nazi regime was quite friendly and surely much more favorable than any
other rector's address at the time. Not only did the local press, the *Frei-*

burger Zeitung, report it; the central organ of the party, the *Völkischer Beobachter*, took a stand in an editorial on Heidegger's three obligations.[36] All the commentators valued Heidegger's speech as a significant contribution to the renewal of the German university. The official newspaper of the National Socialist students remarked that of all the numerous writings on that subject only the speeches of Heidegger and the works of Adolf Rein and Hans Heyse were worth mentioning.[37] A few months later the same newspaper rescinded its positive judgment about Rein and seriously reproached H. Freyer and J. W. Mannhardt.[38] For the students, only Heidegger and Bäumler counted as far as the National Socialist reformation of the universities was concerned. If one takes note of the fact that those two authors are recommended in the official bibliography of the party,[39] which also lists Heidegger's speech, one can appreciate the importance the German students attributed to Heidegger's text.[40] In December 1933 their organ featured an essay by the student leader Albert Holfelder, "The 'Political University' and Science," which not only adapted positions from Heidegger's Rector's Address but even imitated Heidegger's characteristic style.[41] The same occurred (though on a higher level) in a commentary prepared by the historian Richard Harder, who at that time was occupied with a plan for a party university devised by Rosenberg. Harder, an SA member since 1933, praised Heidegger's speech: "A battle speech, a thoughtful appeal, a determined and forceful and timely affirmation; a serious conception of the university and science, an expression of true simplicity, firm will, profound fearlessness: a truly political manifesto by the leading philosopher of our day."[42] According to H. W. Petzet,[43] the relationship between Heidegger and Harder continued after 1945 through the Bavarian Academy of Fine Arts, of which Harder was a member and where Heidegger gave a speech in March 1950. Even the magazine *Volk im Werden*, led by Ernst Krieck, who would soon become one of Heidegger's most formidable opponents, published in 1934(!) an article by Heinrich Bornkamm celebrating Heidegger's speech as an excellent contribution to the revolutionary transformation of the university: "Out of the voluminous literature dealing with the reform of the universities of our day, Heidegger's Rector's Address in Freiburg offers, as far as I can see, the most significant beginnings. . . . I would like therefore . . . to use it as an example."[44] Erich Rothacker, professor at the University of Bonn, commented in a similar manner; he also honored the speeches of Rein, Mannhardt, and Köttgen.[45]

The unofficial press also saw in Heidegger's speech one of the "classic texts" of National Socialist university reform. It was praised, for example, by Hermann Herrigel in the *Deutsche Zeitschrift*,[46] and an editorial in the

Rheinisch-Westfälische Zeitung (Essen) remarked that Heidegger's speech
"for the first time treated the integration of the university into the state
as a whole from the standpoint of the individual. This speech . . . addresses those active German men, teachers and students of the universities, whose courage and united will will affect the future university of the
German nation in its German state."[47] A commentator from the upper-
class *Berliner Börsenzeitung*, too, welcomed Heidegger's contribution, though
in a moderate manner: "There are probably few rector's speeches that
exercised such a bewitching and compelling effect."[48] The *Zeitspiegel* in
Leipzig and *Das deutsche Wort: Der literarischen Welt, neue Folge* made similar comments.[49] It must be borne in mind that *Das deutsche Wort*, which
gave Heidegger credit for coordinating the different National Socialist
opinions about the reforms of the university, was published on June 20,
1936, a long time after Heidegger's "break" with official politics.[50] A decisive approval of the "much-noticed speech" of the "well-known philosopher" appeared in the *Stuttgarter Neues Tageblatt*, which also stressed the
ideological correspondence of Heidegger's speech with the statements of
State Commissioner Prof. Dr. Bebermayer that had been published by
the same newspaper in its morning edition.[51] Also, *Unitas*, a magazine of
the Catholic students, spoke of a "much-noticed speech" that drew attention to itself with the "proclamation of a new spiritual mission to the old
university," thus making the German university a "mirror of the German
spirit."[52]

The organs critical of the regime registered the fact that the Rector's
Address agreed with the general positions of the NSDAP in important
respects. One of these organs was *Die Hilfe: Zeitschrift für Politik, Wirtschaft
und geistige Bewegung*,[53] which in a thorough article, "Military Service of
the Mind" ("Wehrdienst des Geistes"), pointed to the militant character
of Heidegger's ideas, which placed service to knowledge on the same level
as work and military service. This is remarkable because it shows that
readers at that time were able to recognize that Heidegger had made a
special contribution to the National Socialist doctrine. This is contrary to
the philosopher's later claims, in 1945 and in the posthumously published
interview by *Der Spiegel*, to the effect that he had given primary importance to the "knowledge service." On August 6, 1933, the *Neue Zürcher
Zeitung* published an article by Hans Barth that said: "Heidegger's speech,
after three or four readings, remains the expression of an abysmal and
destructive nihilism that cannot be canceled by its affirmation of the blood
and earth of a nation."[54]

Of special philosophical interest are the reactions of Eduard Baumgarten and Benedetto Croce. Baumgarten, a former student of Heideg-

ger's in Freiburg, was politically denounced by Heidegger shortly after-wards. He wrote: "A mystical transubstantiation is taking place in Heidegger: the 'whole' *[das 'Ganze']* that now overtakes the questioner at this juncture and breaks into this impotent state of his knowledge is not metaphysically *[ontologisch]* interpreted by Heidegger as the 'nihilistic nothing' *['nichtende Nichts']* as in former times, but now appears 'ontically' *[ontisch]* as an actual solid 'being' *[Seiendes]*, quite simple and direct: in fact, it appears as the factical event of the German revolution."[55] Bene-detto Croce, who was very critical, complained about the fact that "Prof. Heidegger wants philosophy and science, at least for the Germans, to be nothing more than a German matter for the well-being of the German nation." And: "Today, all of a sudden, one falls into the abyss of the falsest historicism, which negates history, which it crudely and material-istically conceives as the assertion of ethnocentrism and racism, celebrat-ing the glory of wolves and foxes, lions and jackals, lacking in genuine humanity. . . . Thus, one offers oneself to political service. This is with-out doubt a prostitution of philosophy."[56] Schneeberger has published the correspondence between Croce and Karl Vossler about Heidegger. In Croce's letter of September 9, 1933, we read:

Finally, I have read Heidegger's speech through. It is at once stupid and obsequious. I am not surprised about the success that his philosophy will have for a while: the empty and general pronouncement is always successful. But it produces nothing. I believe he will not have any effect politically: but he deprives philosophy of its honor, and that also means a slight to politics, at least for the future.[57]

In 1936 the renowned Jewish *Monatsschrift für Geschichte und Wissen-schaft des Judentums* (an organ of the Society to Promote the Study of Judaism) also wrote about Heidegger's speech:

To Heidegger, knowledge does not mean "the quietistic cognizance of substantiality and values itself, but the sharpest threat to existence amidst the overwhelming power of being. The uncertainty of Being overall forces a nation away from work and struggle, and forces it into its state, to which the professions belong" (the "Self-Determination"—"Selbstbehauptung"—speech, p. 17). Thus, the memory and repetition of the historical fate as the basis of the self remains the only danger to Being-one's-self. Heroic nationalism, "cooperative knowledge of the nation," is the ultimate meaning of

life for Heidegger. This barrier against the kingdom of values and
its transcendental roots in God is threatening to naturalize
National Socialism together with the affirmation of historical fate
and to reduce the freedom of Being-one's-self to an *amor fati.*[58]

Shortly before the outbreak of the war in 1938, official magazines attributed an important role in the ideological battle of the National Socialists to Heidegger and his Rector's Address. For example, the *Kieler
Blätter* mentioned Heidegger in direct connection with Krieck, Heyse, and
Bäumler:

> Like Bäumler, Martin Heidegger, in his Rector's Address,
> develops the essence of science out of the notion of an active
> heroic attitude in the sense of a "questioning attitude," standing
> firm and open amidst the uncertainties of being as a whole. If
> science is desirable in this sense, then to the basic question of
> whether the German university has "true power to put a stamp on
> our existence" Heidegger has already provided an affirmative
> answer. Heidegger has placed the task of overcoming the barriers
> facing this undertaking in the hands of a special student group
> *[Fachschaftsarbeit].*[59]

The meaning of the Rector's Address cannot be measured by its immediate effect alone. As a declaration in principle, it also had a programmatic function for Heidegger's political and scientific activity during and
after his tenure as rector.

10 Martin Heidegger's activities as rector

Among the first measures Heidegger took as rector of Freiburg, on May 9, 1933, was to send a telegram to Robert Wagner when Wagner was named Reichsstatthalter of the region of Baden: "I am happy about your nomination as Reichsstatthalter of Baden and I salute the Führer of the province of the fatherland with a fighting 'Sieg Heil!' "[1] Still, we need to analyze his actions in regard to general political matters as well as the individual acts themselves. To do so exhaustively, we would have had to consult the documents held in the university archives, which are currently inaccessible and will probably remain so for some time. Using documents from other sources, I have been able to form an approximate but significant first outline. Heidegger's politics during the rectorship will be examined in the light of the three following problems: the role of students as the avant-garde of the National Socialist revolution; the new organization of the university; the new relationship of the university to the German people and their state.

When he spoke about students as the principal agents of change, Heidegger was not thinking of all students; his appeal was rather to those radical and combative ones who would know how to further the struggle to found the new university. On May 6, 1933, those student members of groups with permission to practice dueling celebrated the rescinding of Weimar's prohibition. The revocation was hailed throughout the country. The next day, *Der Alemanne* of Freiburg carried an article about the ceremonies:[2] After singing the hymn "The God Who Made Iron Grow Does Not Want Slaves," the leader of the Waffenring told the assembly that the rescinding of the prohibition "was an event of historic proportions" and that the presence of representatives of the state, the region, and the university was proof of that. Dueling is meant "to waken the most noble spiritual and bodily qualities, and, when practiced "with all the proper violence," it leads to self-mastery. "Thanks to it the student develops courage, autonomy, aggression, and the joy of knowing how to use arms, and he thereby protects himself from arrogance and other social deviations." After this speech, the chief of police of Freiburg spoke. Finally Heidegger spoke as representative of the university; according to *Der Alemanne*, he spoke on "the moral values of dueling."

The student groups that dueled *(schlagende Verbindung)* dated from before the time of National Socialism and had as members the most reactionary and violent students.[3] Very popular among the nationalists, members of these groups in their student years were now well-known members of the regime. For a young man with military traditions, it was an honor to bear a dueling scar on one's face, which showed courage and active participation in such groups. Photographs of leaders of the regime published at the time, with biographies, in the *Führer-Lexikon,* confirm this.[4] Wolfgang Kreutzberger has exhaustively analyzed the nature and development of the dueling custom in his work on the political development of Freiburg students before the last war.[5]

But if these students had the support of Heidegger, others were at least victims of his indifference under very dangerous circumstances. For a long time persecution of Jewish students was an integral part of the life of the extreme right-wing Freiburg students, who were in the majority. In addition to the Aryan clause in their rules forbidding membership to "Jews and persons of color," these right-wing groups also incorporated, from the 1920's on, rules made by other student groups throughout the Reich.[6] An example is provided by the case of Ghibbelinia, studied by Erich Stern.[7] After a long and intense campaign of boycotting and persecution and after being ousted from the central association of student groups at Freiburg, this Jewish group decided to dissolve in 1925. A review of Jewish student groups has amassed a large number of documents that reveal the strong anti-semitism in the student movements between the wars.[8] Freiburg Jewish students later grouped themselves around the Neo-Friburgia association. This does not seem to have changed the situation, for attacks on this group increased and came to a head when the Nazis took power. The Jewish group was dissolved April 20, 1933, but this did not stop the SA students from taking over their offices and examining their documents. After the house was closed, students belonging to other groups decided to guard the house against further attacks. The

Jewish students were able to prove that the attack on their house had not been carried out by order of the prosecutor or the police. For this reason, they took their complaint to the rector, giving him the facts and relevant documentation. On June 28, 1933, there was another attack, larger and more violent than the first one; the house was damaged and papers were stolen. The *Karlsruher Zeitung* of June 29 gave the following information:

> Before the news that the Jewish student group (whose house was in the hands of SA students) wanted to continue its activities, some demonstrations by Freiburg students had already taken place. About 100 of them were together in front of the house of the Jewish association, demanding that it be closed and the student members be put in prison. Six Jews were arrested by the SS, and the house remained in the control of the SA, who raised the swastika flag.

Faced with these events, on July 11, 1933, the city prosecutor sent an official note to the rector asking for particulars. The student Führer, in a letter dated July 25, as well as the rector, in a letter dated August 1, refused to concern themselves further with the matter, stating that the attacking crowd included non-students.[9]

Heidegger took a similar stance toward all non-Nazi students. In 1932, National Socialist students provoked a struggle during elections to renew the AStA (the student association), which was already under Nazi control. The National Socialist students were angry about rules prohibiting propaganda by political parties in the campaign, which prevented them from making the elections a time for demonstrations. The rector's decision to intervene made the National Socialist students violent. In an article in *Der Alemanne* the students claimed their rights under the higher interests of the party when in conflict with mere corporate order.[10] The students of the opposition, who belonged to socialist, republican, Centrist, and Catholic groups, made an appeal to the tribunal of elections. Since this board was controlled by the Nazis, the request was denied. Elections held with no opposition were easily won by the National Socialist group. The opposition disputed the outcome and sent a letter to the minister at Karlsruhe appealing the breaking of the rules and asking that the AStA be dissolved so that the university not become an anarchic arena of political struggles.[11] When the National Socialist regime took power, all discussion ended. Heidegger wrote rather abruptly to the new minister on June 22, 1933, to say that he had stopped discussion: "The whole question of dissolving the AStA is no longer pertinent, given the events, and is to be considered closed."[12] Seven days later the new student leaders wrote to the director, Eugen Fehrle, asking that reorganization of the various specialized student groups in the university *(Fachschaften)* be studied and adopted during a meeting that would take place at the village of Todtnauberg,[13] where Heidegger had a villa in which he held meetings for reflection and indoctrination.

During the first weeks of Heidegger's rectorate, the National Socialist students made their first "sweepings" of the bookstores and held an *auto da-fé* of their gleanings. The Kampfbund for German culture of Freiburg joined the student group and held its public book-burning during the first week of May 1933.[14] The one the students planned for June 1933 was called because of rain.[15] Mayor Kerber announced June 22 as "the happy ending of the clean-up operation."[16] Heidegger said in his *Spiegel* interview that he had forbidden student "excesses" as well as anti-semitic pronouncements at the university. (Now would be an excellent time for all those holding the pertinent documents that could confirm these claims to make them available.) The ceremonial book-burnings at Freiburg, even if they had taken place "in private," were only the local versions of the *autos-da-fé* held in Berlin under the direction of students as part of their "actions against anti-German sentiment" *(Wider den undeutschen Geist)*.

We can read about the Berlin ceremony in the Freiburg newspaper, *Breisgauer Zeitung*, on May 12, 1933: "The ceremony 'against anti-German sentiment' was celebrated after a march in which the majority of the students were dressed in their SA uniforms and carried swastika flags." The new professor of political education at the University of Berlin, Alfred Bäumler, gave the first speech. Next the students assembled at Hegel Square; "then, marching in close order and carrying torches," they went toward the Student Union, where a great many had already assembled. Next the columns moved to the Opera Square, where students had made a bonfire with their torches. While the crowd cheered, books were passed around, and about twenty thousand were thrown into the flames. The high point of the ceremony were Goebbels' words, "Here we see crumbling the spiritual basis of the November Republic, but from the ashes will be born the new spirit, victorious. For this reason, do not see only a symbol of decadence in the flames, but rather the symbol of renaissance."[17] Whether or not Heidegger participated in such barbarism, it still remains true that the same Berlin student leadership that organized it had, only a few days before, cheered Heidegger's nomination as rector of Freiburg as the first step in bringing the German universities into the fold of National Socialism.[18]

In his political activity with students at Freiburg, Heidegger operated on two fronts: writing articles for the student paper, and encouraging and directing a vast program of political action from the Office of the Rector, especially concerned with work camps. In addition, there were speeches here and there on important occasions. Among them, we note his short talk during a mass meeting of students and teachers gathered to hear the radio replay of Hitler's speech to the Reichstag announcing that Germany would resign its membership in the League of Nations. Heidegger spoke in these terms:

> After these words by our Chancellor, other peoples may choose the way they will. *We*, we have already decided. We, we will march down the most arduous road, the road imposed by our responsibility before history. We, we already know what that requires: BE PREPARED FOR EXTREME SITUATIONS and REMAIN COMRADES TO THE END. All of us, then: to work. And may each of our tasks during this semester, small or large, be set under the sign of this decision and this devotion to comradeship.[19]

The students of Freiburg celebrated the traditional Solstice holiday on June 25, 1933. Since World War I, the day had become a day of protest against the constraints of the Treaty of Versailles. During sports competitions, speakers recalled those who had died in combat, in imitation of the ancient Greek practice. The Nazi students organized the day, giving it their well-known dramaturgical and liturgical turn.[20] The final act, during which Heidegger spoke, had been preceded by a long military march through the town and then to the sports stadium, in front of which was a large fire. In silence, before the fire, the students heard the words of their Führer:

> Solstice Feast of 1933! The days pass by. They grow shorter. But in us grows the courage to pierce the approaching shadows. Let us never be blind to the struggle. Instruct us, flames, enlighten us. Show us the road from which one does not return! Let the flames leap, let hearts burn.[21]

All those studies that attempt to minimize Heidegger's compromise with National Socialism or those wanting to see a deeper and more "metaphysical" meaning in Heidegger show signs of a systematic unawareness of the texts where Heidegger speaks to us about his Nazi faith, tied to the person of Adolf Hitler. The mystique under which so many millions of Germans lived was also the lot of Heidegger. Karl Jaspers' evidence is revealing. Jaspers asked Heidegger during a conversation in June 1933, "How do you think a man as coarse as Hitler can govern Germany?" Heidegger answered, "Culture is of no importance. Look at his marvellous hands!"[22] This is exactly the feeling Heidegger tried to infuse in an article in the student newspaper in November 1933, where he transforms the very person of Hitler into the spirit of the new revolutionary, making the Führer a principle of existence:

German students,
The National Socialist revolution rings in the total collapse of our German existence *[Dasein]*.

It is incumbent on you to stay with this process *[Geschehen]*, those of you who always want to press on further, those who are always ready, those who are hardened, those who never cease developing.

Your will to know seeks contact with the essential, the simple, the great.

You are restless to seek out what assails you, what presses hard against you, what engages you from afar.

Be harsh and authentic in your needs.

Remain clear and certain in your refusal. Do not turn hard-won knowledge into an egoistic and arrogant possession *[eitlen Selbstbesitz]*. Keep it as the original indispensable possession of the man on whom devolves the role of chief *[des führerischen Menschen]* among the callings of the people of the state. You can no longer be only those who "hear." You must participate in knowledge, and in the creation of the future university of the German spirit. Each of you must first prove your gifts and your privileges and justify them. This is to be achieved by the power deriving from consecrating yourselves in combative fashion *[des kämpferischen Einsatzes]* to the struggle the people lead in their own name.

The faithfulness of your will to follow (of all of you together) must be strengthened day by day, hour by hour. In you there must unceasingly develop the courage of your sacrifice for the salvation *[Rettung]* of the essence of our people *[Volk]* within their state *[Staat]* and for the elevation of its innermost force.

Do not let principles and "ideas" be the rules of your existence.

The Führer himself, and he alone, is the German reality of today, and of the future, and of its law. Learn to know always more deeply. Starting now each thing demands decision and every action, responsibility.

Heil Hitler! Rector Martin Heidegger.[23]

To bring his students to the point of spiritual development that would allow them to "revolutionize" the university first, and next to offer a model for the most radical transformation of German society ("the complete overthrowing of our German existence"), Heidegger had to establish in addition to his articles and speeches a practical administration able to transform the structures of the university. Among the measures brought in during his rectorship were: the expulsion of all Jews on the teaching staff; a questionnaire for each teacher showing racial origin;[24] the new rights of students;[25] the obligatory oath for all teachers concerning the purity of their race;[26] the obligation to use the Nazi salute at the beginning and end of each class;[27] the organization of the University Department of Racial Matters, to be directed by the SS, who were responsible for organizing courses to be taught by a specialist from the Institute of Racial Purity in Berlin, directed by Professor Eugen Fischer;[28] obligatory work service;[29] economic help for student members of the SA and the SS, or other military groups, and refusal of aid to Jewish and Marxist students;[30] the obligation to attend classes on racial theory, military science, and German culture.[31]

A case of political denunciation

In the context of Rector Heidegger's administrative measures, and with an eye to determining how radical Heidegger was in fulfilling the task of "revolutionizing" his university, it pays to examine certain documents uncovered by Hugo Ott.[32] As rector of Freiburg, Heidegger informed Dr. Fehrle, the man concerned with university questions at the Ministry in Karlsruhe, that there were documents deeply implicating Professor of Chemistry Hermann Staudinger, a world-famous specialist who would later receive the Nobel Prize. Using the information sent by Heidegger, Fehrle denounced Staudinger the next day to the Freiburg police. The Gestapo at Karlsruhe took charge of the confidential dossier, called "Action Sternheim." The documents Heidegger referred to spoke of rumors to the effect that, during World War I, when Staudinger was a professor at Zürich, he had exchanged pacifist remarks with some colleagues who shared such opinions and who did not hide their opposition to German militarism. What the Gestapo was able to glean from the German consulate in Zürich was enough for the Karlsruhe Ministry to bring Staudinger to trial.

Heidegger was contacted by the Ministry on February 6, 1934, and asked to work quickly, "since any application of para. 4 of the law . . . must be made before March 31, 1934, the statutory limit." Heidegger answered four days later with a typed report containing many errors, clearly produced by a novice typist. According to Hugo Ott, this report is on the letterhead of the rectorate, but without any registering number. In it Heidegger says that he takes responsibility for the Gestapo's charges, adding a personal judgment that amounted to a condemnation:

> These facts demand the application of para. 4 of the law.
> Realizing that they have been known by the German public since
> 1925–26, the time of Staudinger's appointment to the University
> of Freiburg, the reputation of the university is at stake, and
> measures must be taken. All the more necessary because
> Staudinger is lukewarm about national recovery. Rather than
> offering him retirement, we must think of dismissal. Heil Hitler.
> Heidegger.

In answer to Heidegger's suggestions, the Baden Ministry asked the state minister, in a report of February 22, 1934, to remove Staudinger from public service.

Although Staudinger tried to have the charges reduced during his questioning, his situation became intolerable as the monstrous character of the measures taken against him became more and more evident. Consequently, for purely tactical reasons and fearing international repercussions, were all the facts to become known, first Mayor Kerber and then Heidegger himself intervened to have Staudinger not actually dismissed but directed "only" to take retirement. A letter was sent to the Ministry on March 5, 1934, again on letterhead, but with no number ("it is a good bet that there is no copy of this letter in the documents held in the archives"—Hugo Ott). Heidegger added at the end: "However it turns out, we need hardly add that this changes nothing about the thing itself. We simply want to avoid complications from abroad." As Ott says, the epilogue to the story is grotesque, and Staudinger was spared no humiliation. The Ministry obliged him to request resignation "on his own initiative." After holding the request for six months, the Ministry finally agreed not to act on it, "unless in the future there would be reasons to accept it." After time had passed, and "no reason" arose, Staudinger was given permission to retire.

We must note that Heidegger's attitude toward the persecution of his Jewish colleagues certainly had ambiguous nuances, especially for two professors—Georg von Hevesy, a specialist in chemistry of international repute (Nobel Prize, 1943), and Fränkel in classical philology, who had a similar reputation. In the general archives at Karlsruhe,[33] there is a letter from Heidegger to the ministerial counsel Fehrle, dated July 12, 1933, where Heidegger defends these two academics, saying they ought not be taken out of public service. Heidegger emphasizes their prestige in their disciplines around the world, adding that "these are Jews of worth" *(Sie seien edle Juden von vorbildlichem Charakter)*. He argues that absolute exclusion of Jews would bring a strong backlash from abroad and would hurt the renown of German science in powerful intellectual circles. He also emphasizes that the defense of particular cases ought in no way be considered as contrary to the general orders concerning Jews in teaching. Rather, he assumes this attitude, all the while "fully conscious of the need to apply the law unconditionally in the reorganization of the public service." He must consider, however, the grave consequences this disbarring could have "on the need to reinforce throughout the world the prestige of German science, for the new Reich and for its mission."[34]

Students and workers

The administrative changes adopted by Heidegger were completed by a series of measures intended to make adjustments in the lives of the students, whose habits up to 1933 were to live an easy life with no thought other than professional and material success, concerns now judged decadent and individualistic. The eagerness with which Heidegger took on this task in a university where the students were almost entirely from the middle and working classes is certainly a sign of his decision to impose the nationalist program in its most radical populist variant. Wolfgang Kreutzberger has brought out clearly how the social origins of the Freiburg students worked against the rector's decision. The actual participation of the students in voluntary work was in fact of little account. The majority of those attached to this service belonged to the least favored classes and frequently demanded as a condition of their participation that the work details have some connection with their professional training. At the same time, they refused to do any "nasty work." Most often those who "volunteered" were moved more by anti-internationalist ideas and

National Socialist convictions than by any identification with the working classes.[35]

Heidegger saw in this transformation of student life—which would be attained thanks to its concrete links with the world of work—the accomplishment of one of the points of the SA program. This is clearly stated in his speech of November 26, 1933, "The German Student as Worker," delivered during registration. The ceremony and the speech were broadcast and elicited much commentary on the radio at Frankfurt, Freiburg, Trier, Cologne, Stuttgart, and Mühlacker.[36] The new student does not become a student (of the state), Heidegger says, simply by the fact of his entry into the university, nor by other connections thereby made with the state, but by his integration through "work service, with the SA." "The new German student proceeds through work service; he is in the SA."[37] The true sense of the service to knowledge is to integrate the student into the "workers' front." It is only by becoming a "worker" that the student can authentically become tied to the state, "because the National Socialist state is a workers' state" *(Arbeiterstaat)*.[38] This speech, in fact a statement of principles, finds its complement in the article "The Appeal to Work Service," published by the student paper on January 23, 1934.[39] This article was printed alongside another one that defended the book-burning organized by the immediate political superiors of those editing the *Deutsche Studentenzeitung*. The fires lit to burn books "written by Jews are fires against intellectual delinquents; they will not burn out until the last of their writings will become ashes, until the last of the parasites who wrote them will be interned in a work camp, and when these beasts will be clean and shaven."[40]

Heidegger's article is meaningful in political-historical and philosophical terms. According to the spirit of the variant National Socialism he is defending, Heidegger develops and transforms a series of themes that he had treated in a general and abstract manner in *Being and Time:*

> The new educational mode of our German youth proceeds through work service.
> Such service affords a basic experience of toughness, of closeness to earth and tools, of the rigor and severity of the most simple physical work, and thereby of what is most essential within the group.[41]

In this way Heidegger reconsiders the relationship between existence *(Dasein)* and world *(Welt)* by linking them in terms of one's proximity to the earth at the same time he finds a new way of explaining the meaning of "tool" *(Zeug, Zuhandenes)* and the data of immediate experience *(Vorhandenes)*. When Heidegger affirmed in *Being and Time* that the tool as such would disappear precisely in order to become efficient, he had to specify its nature within a form of inauthentic existence. The possibility of an authentic "use" of tools, not developed in *Being and Time*, now appears to be grounded in that cognitive and transcendental act that is public service. The same thing results from concretely experiencing the world, here understood as acting through contact with the land. In the same way, abstract notions of being-with *(Mit-sein, Mit-dasein)* were to be reformulated in a community of people whose qualities go beyond the limitations of a historically indeterminate sense of prudence *(Fürsorge):*

> Such a service brings the basic experience *[Grunderfahrung]* of a daily experience firmly ruled by the discipline of work in an army camp.
> Such a service brings the basic experience of purification *[Klärung]*, and of daily solidarity as a test of backgrounds according to different callings and social levels *[ständischen Herkunft]* and in accord with the responsibility of each of us beginning with the connection we all share with the same [Aryan] people *[volkhafte Zusammengehörigkeit]*.
> Such a service secures the basic experience of the origin of all authentic comradeship that comes from the demands of great common danger, or from the ties that never cease to be strengthened in a task that is larger than can be measured and that has nothing to do with mere enthusiastic reciprocal exchange or with the muddle-headed inhibitions of isolated persons who decide to sleep and eat and sing under the same roof.[42]

Developing what he had said about community in the speech on Schlageter, which at one time was construed precisely in terms of the relationship between people and hero, Heidegger here offers the authentic variant of being-with *(Mit-sein)* as the sharing of an action directed toward a common "cause," and then ties it to genuine "comradeship." When he claims that this comradeship is essentially due to a structure of the state, it is clear that the social frame able to receive that formation is none other than the characteristic order of fascist society and work. Heidegger refines the notion by adding that the social construct deriving from working in common determines meaning because it is exposed "to a great common danger," which virtually makes a society a heroic community.

The SA variant is clarified next, when Heidegger says that work service for the student youth is something qualitatively superior to any form of economic production established by a state program for such renewal.

We must think beyond the already visible action of work service and come to understand that what is being prepared here is a complete remodeling *[Umprägung]* of German existence by an awakened youth. Little by little, we shall find at the very heart of the university a new basic attitude regarding the toil of knowledge *[wissenschaftliche Arbeit]*. In doing so, we shall find the notion of "intellect" and "intellectual work" with which until now the "cultured man" has lived, and which his delegates still want to save for their own professional and social ranks—that is, the notion of "intellectual workers"—disappear completely. It will be only at that point that we will learn that all work is, as such, intellectual. Animals and those content simply to live from day to day are not capable of work, for they lack the essential experience required— the thoughtful commitment *[der entscheidungsmässige Einsatz]* that a mission offers, the power of decision and of resolve *[Standhalten]* once the mission has been decided, that, in a word, brings *freedom,* that is to say, brings *spirit.*

So-called "intellectual work" is not called such because it is concerned with "high spiritual matters"; rather it becomes so only because it leads us more deeply and sympathetically into the imperious necessity felt by a people and because it is more knowingly and immediately hemmed in by the harsh dangers of human existence.

There exists but a single "vital level," a single social living body *[Lebensstand]* rooted in the bedrock of a people and building freely within its historical will, whose imprint is preshaped by the German National Socialist *Party* movement of *work.*

Work service calls!

The inert, the comfortable ones, the lukewarm "will go" into work service because failing to go there will perhaps compromise their chances on exams or for professional possibilities. The strong, those that nothing breaks, those who decide their existence from the exciting secret of a new future for our [Aryan] people, are proud that others demand tough things of them, for this is the moment when they rise to the harshest demands, for which there is neither salary nor recompense, but only the "gift of happiness" *[Beglückung]* at being ready for sacrifice and service within the most profound necessities of German existence *[deutschen Seins].*[43]

Certainly more original, even though always within the radical populist option, is the initiative Heidegger took to connect student work and the program for social rehabilitation begun by Mayor Kerber, which created a "living bridge" between the university and the workers that had no equal among the initiatives of any of the other rectors of the time. In fact, work service was not new with the Nazis, but was rather an old idea begun in many universities involving the youth movement *(Jugendbewegung)*. This service had now been taken over by the state and offered various options. However, to build a "living bridge" under the auspices of the university and in concert with the revolutionary "base" was a true innovation. In addition, it not only intended students to leave the classrooms but also workers to come into the university itself for courses of indoctrination.

We must see this in context. The province of Baden, and especially Freiburg, until the end of the Weimar Republic, was economically and socially in a catastrophic situation.[44] As elsewhere in Germany, a very large number of people were without work and lived in misery. After the party took power, quick and effective solutions were needed. Putting together large projects able to alleviate the situation became a special program of Freiburg's Mayor Kerber. He encouraged the creation of jobs for some of the inhabitants, as well as giving training to those out of work, and transferred the unemployed to the countryside to increase the number of peasants in the province.[45] Thanks to this political move, there was a substantial reduction in the number of unemployed and in the pressure on social workers.[46] The university participated broadly in the Freiburg Plan, not only by sending students (and some academics) to places where the program was working but also by bringing a number of unemployed workers into the university in order to prepare them ideologically.

Recognizing the need and the possibility of helping workers in general, and the unemployed especially, to see the path of the "new society" and of "German socialism," the *Freiburger Zeitung* of January 24, 1934, emphasized the participation of students in these efforts. The students ("workers of the mind"), who at the time of taking power were the avantgarde engaged in violent combat in the streets and in spreading National Socialist ideas in the country—"take on today responsibility for the political education of manual workers."[47] The central organ of German students, *Der deutsche Student,* in its January 1934 issue, echoed the program. The article was titled "The University Transforms Itself into a University of the People" and affirmed:

> Under the protection of Professor Heidegger, rector of the University of Freiburg, Freiburg students and the Department of Work accepted an important accord whereby the university and a group of students will assume over the winter semester *the political education of a large number of the unemployed of Freiburg.* The lessons are to be given by National Socialist forces of the student world and the university. This agreement means a great step in the struggle for the renewal of the university, and the work will be directed by Dr. [Helmut] Haubold.[48]

The administrative decision that organized the courses was called the "Circle for the Political Education of the People," and its first group of lectures had the title "German Socialism." The courses first set up for the avant-garde were given by Professors Erik Wolf ("Socialism and the Law"), Maximilian Beck ("Socialism and the Economy"), Hans Mortensen ("Socialism and the Countryside"), Kurt Bauch ("Socialism and Art"), the civil servant Walter Müller-Guiscard ("Socialism and Public Assistance"), and Dr. Helmut Haubold ("Socialism and Work Service").[49] We note here that Haubold was named by the National Socialist student Führer, Dr. Oskar Stäbel,[50] chair of work service and the work camps of the southern group of the Association of Students (NSDStB). In mid-May of the same year, Stäbel and the students of Freiburg asked for authorization from the Ministry and the faculty for Haubold to lead a course on "Work Camp and Work Service" and asked for the assistant at the Psychiatric Clinic, Dr. Heinz Riedel, to talk on "The Problems of the Racial Question."[51] These authorizations were granted in December 1933.[52] Haubold, a physician like Riedel, was a member of the SS-Physicians and, according to a document at the Berlin Document Center, worked on a vaccination program in the concentration camps.[53]

A speech by Heidegger marked the solemn opening of the political education courses for workers included in Mayor Kerber's program. The speech was given in the university auditorium for hundreds of workers on October 30, 1933:

> German countrymen! German workers!
> As rector, I welcome you warmly to this house. My greeting also means the beginning of our work in common. We begin

immediately by recognizing this unparalleled event, which has never before occurred, that you, workers of the city of Freiburg, now in a state of emergency, that you join us in this great auditorium of the university.

What does this fact mean?

As a result of broad measures taken by the city of Freiburg, and by a new action by the services of allocation of work, you have been brought here to find work and earnings. In this way you enjoy a state privilege along with others in the city without resources. This privilege also entails obligation.

Your duty is to appreciate the work allocations and to take up the responsibility for paid work, as the Führer of our new state demands. For the allocation of work is not simply alleviation of the harshest disasters, it is not merely the elimination of inner discouragement, if not actual despair, allocation of work is not simply a way to lighten what oppresses and burdens us—allocation of work is in fact at the same time a way to build and to edify *[Aufbau und Bau]* within the new future of our people.

Allocation of work ought in the first instance to enable our unemployed and penniless compatriots to live in the state and for the state, and thereby for the whole of the people *[das Volksganze]*. Our fellow citizens who succeed in finding work ought to learn from this that they are not rejected, not allowed to drop out, that they are part of the proper order of the people and that each service and each attainment holds a value that can be seen in other services and other gains. This experience ought to give them a true sense of their own dignity and of the true support of their fellow citizens *[Volksgenossen]*, which yields true surety and is the source of true decision.[54]

Then Heidegger continued by explaining the social structure manifested in "fellowship," that is, the corporate, fascist organization of society:

Our goal is to become strong through our fully useful existence as German citizens in the German community of the people. *[Zu einem volkgültigen Dasein als Volkgenosse in der deutschen Volkgemeinschaft.]*

For this we must know our position as members of this people;

We must know how this people comes together and how it renews itself in this composition;

We must know what is happening to help the German people in this National Socialist state;

We must know through what harsh struggle this new reality has been conquered and created;

We must know the meaning of the future health *[Gesundung]* of the body of the people and what this demands of each of us alone;

We must know to what state urbanization has brought German men and how they must be brought back to the earth and to the countryside, thanks to land division *[Siedlung];*

We must know the meaning of the fact that 18 million Germans belong to the people but are not part of the Reich because they live beyond its borders.

Every worker of our German people must know why and to what end he is where he is. It is only through this living and ever-present knowledge that their lives are rooted in the totality of the people and in the destiny of the [Aryan] people. Allocation of work necessarily implies that this knowledge be acquired *[Beschaffung dieses Wissens]* as your right, but also because it is your duty to demand this knowledge, to acquire it with whatever difficulty.

And here are your younger fellow citizens of the university standing ready to dispense this knowledge. These students have decided to contribute so that this knowledge may live in you, so that it may be used and strengthened and never become dormant. They themselves stand ready here, not like upper-class "snobs," but as fellow citizens *[Volksgenossen]* who know their duty.

They stand ready not as "learned people," not facing a social gap, not even a lower social level, but as comrades. They are ready to listen to your questions, your troubles, your misery, your doubts, ready to consider them from beginning to end and clarify them together in this common work, offering solutions, decisions. What does it mean that you are assembled here in the university auditorium?

This fact becomes a sign of the new common will that can throw a *living bridge* between the worker of "brawn" and the worker of "brains." This will to build a bridge across is no longer today an intention without action, and why not? Because our whole German reality has been changed by the National Socialist state, with the consequence that our whole manner of thinking and seeing *[Vorstellen]* and our concept ought to change.

What we have until now understood in the words "knowledge" and "science" has taken on another meaning.

What we have meant until now by the words "worker" and "work" has earned another meaning.

This speech is reminiscent of Heidegger's 1910 article on Abraham a Sancta Clara. Heidegger speaks here of the "health of the body of the people," which derives from Hitler's assumption of power, which in turn implies a mystical order in the community of the people. This renews the demagogical magician's conceptual trick that belongs to the National Socialist goal of eliminating social differences and contradictions, and then of eliminating the political organizations that had acknowledged those differences in order to combat them. The transubstantiation of *thought* into *work* and of *work* into *thought* refers us back to the more general plan to erase real social differences by dissolving them in mystifying notions of nation and people. All this is done, of course, without adversely affecting the model of fascist organization in which each is said to receive what he is due:

If all of you there know how to become a people who "know," you will not be served crumbs or the tatters of any sort of "general culture," certainly not as a charity after the act. There is much more: *Knowledge* is to be wakened in you, in such a way that you, each one in his work group and his work place, *you can be German men, clear and resolute.*

To know and to possess knowledge, as National Socialism understands these words, does not divide classes, but relates and unites fellow citizens and professional groups in the one great will of the state.

Just as the words "knowledge" and "sincere" have new meaning and a new sound, so also do the words "worker" and "work." The "worker" is not what Marxism wants him to be, a simple object of exploitation. The body of workers is not the class of the disinherited advancing toward the general class struggle. Work is no longer simply production of goods for others. Work is no longer simply the way to be paid. On the contrary:

For us "Work" designates every action and every orderly activity that is the personal responsibility of each of us, in the group and the state, which then becomes the service of the people.

This is why the will to build a living bridge among us, as

among you, can no longer remain an empty wish, without issue. This will to find work is a true acquisition of knowledge; this will ought to be for us the innermost certainty and never a wavering belief. For with this will, we are only following the eminent *[überragend]* will of our Führer. To be among those who follow him means in fact: to want untiringly and unshakeably that the German people find again their native unity *[gewachsene Einheit]*, their simple dignity and their true strength, and how as a workers' state Germany can recover its life and grandeur. For the man of this extraordinary will, a triple "Sieg Heil!"

The Rudolf Stadelmann papers in the federal archives in Koblenz contain part of the correspondence between Stadelmann and Heidegger. Two letters from Heidegger and one from Stadelmann from this time speak of the structure and the nature of the Nazi indoctrination camps for teachers and students, and about Heidegger's participation and the function he gave them. In Heidegger's letter of October 11, 1933, he indicates to the young teacher that the camps are places where political confrontation is put to the test. "For everyone the camp holds perils. . . . Today we are to learn some tough things. . . . We must not avoid these situations. On the contrary, when they do not arise by themselves, we must seek them out and create them." The motto is, "We must harden ourselves deliberately." The letter in which Heidegger refers to confronting the attitude and tendency he expected to find in Stadelmann received a response from Stadelmann himself dated the 16th of the same month. It brings out clearly the submissive attitude of subordinates in front of their Führer, and the domination of the Führer over his collaborators, an attitude that recalls exactly the kind of organization found in the bundist Youth Movement (to be examined later) and whose Adult Circles *(Mannerhäuser)* proposed by Bäumler were the ideological model. Stadelmann writes Heidegger:

> Probably no one came through the tests of the camp with a perfect score. However, we all returned from them convinced that the revolution has not yet reached its term but that the goal of the revolution in the university is the SA student. . . . This student will eliminate both forms of students still existing today: the simple student as well as the SA student who came to the university as a dilettante. The goal is evident: all those who search ought to march together.

Indicating Heidegger's value as a guide, Stadelmann adds: "They have a Führer who leads them and brings them to this goal, and they are his partisans" *(Gefolgschaft)*. At the same time that he alludes to the factional struggles ("the activists who came from Kiel" and the "radicals"), Stadelmann shows his unconditional attachment to the political direction Heidegger had taken, reproaching him with a certain ambiguity in the face of the splinter groups. "Never before had he seemed so clear as today, at Todtnauberg, when I belonged to the revolutionary party, and in no way to the opposition, nor to the observers playing with rhetoric. I observed the discipline." Heidegger's response, dated October 23, 1933, clarifies several points. Above all, it shows the feverish activity of Heidegger at that time ("I've just arrived from the Bebenhausen camp") and at the same time the complete similarity of his attitude and Stadelmann's. This whole affair contradicts completely what Heidegger wrote in his attempt at rehabilitation.[55] Not only did the Heidegger faction directed by Dr. Stein (a confederate of Krieck's) show its respect for Heidegger, but, faced with Heidegger's threat to close the camp, Stein "begged him insistently to continue the work of indoctrination and to do it as he saw fit, taking into account above all that those who came from elsewhere had no one to lead them." Heidegger, however, wrote that Stein gave a talk at the camp, a talk on race and the racial principle, but that Stein's mission was to see the camp fail, as Krieck had told him to do.[56]

Lessons on "The Fundamental Questions of Philosophy" during the summer semester, 1933

Heidegger's course on "The Fundamental Questions of Philosophy" is certainly the most important contribution among the texts we have examined up to now. The original text, although extant, is not accessible at this time. The quotations offered here are from notes taken during the course and are in the archives of Helene Weiss. Although they do not have the strict accuracy of citation, we use them for their great interest, but with a certain caution.

The class began with a reflective statement on student experiences early in the National Socialist revolution:

The student youth seized the importance of the historical moment that the German people experienced in the space of a few weeks. What was in the process of becoming? The German people found itself and also found at its head a great commandment *[Führung]*. Thanks to this, the people, now returned to itself, created its own state. The people shaping itself in its state grew and raised itself to be its own nation. This nation accepted the destiny of its people. And such a people conquered its spiritual mission, surrounded by other peoples, and forged its history. But this process was a vast movement with distant repercussions moving toward the difficult dawning of a still obscure future. To encourage this, the German youth has today begun to march. It responds to its vocation. And here is what that means: It is moved by the will to find a discipline and an education that will bring it to maturity and strength so that it can assume the role of spiritual and political guide, which it guards for the generation to come and which will be invested by the people at the determined moment for the state, in the midst of the peoples of the world. Every grand and authentic commandment is moved by the force of a fundamentally hidden destiny *[Bestimmung]*. And its will, finally, will be nothing other than the political and spiritual mission of a people. It is the knowledge relating to this mission that is to be wakened, rooted in the heart and will of the people and of each and all that constitute it.

And next:

Such a knowledge *[Wissen]* is not obtained by knowing the present political situation of the people, a knowledge admittedly indispensable but not decisive. The knowledge relating to the political and spiritual mission of the German people is a knowledge tied to its future, and this knowledge of the future does not coincide with a prophetic knowledge of what will come to be some day.

It is not just an anticipation of the knowledge of what future generations, one day, will experience as their present. Happily, such a prophetic knowledge is closed to us because it would sap, would strangle, all action. The knowledge related to this mission is a demanding knowledge. It is the demanding knowledge of what is necessary, before everything merely possible and taking precedence over everything else, so that a people can raise themselves to the spiritual grandeur that is theirs. Be exigent, go to war, venerate—these three things together constitute that single great anguish that must drive us to become our own destiny. We are, to the extent that we demand, that we go to battle, that we venerate, that we continue in that direction. We are, to the extent that we seek ourselves. And we seek ourselves to the extent that we question who we are. Who is this people, what is their history, and what is the process at the depth of their being *[Sein]*?

Heidegger gave a certain precision to the point of that question, without breaking out of the categories found in *Being and Time,* by making it concrete in historical and transcendental terms. Because he was dealing here, as in 1927, with a question that went beyond the mere *what (was)* to the *who (wer)* that question cannot be understood within the terms of inauthenticity:

> Such an interrogation *[Frage]* is not idle conjecture, nor simple curiosity about events we face, but a spiritual commitment *[Einsatz]* at the highest level, an essential questioning. With such questioning, we live our destiny, we expose ourselves to the obscure necessity of our history. This questioning through which a people lives its destiny, affirms it in the face of danger and threat, exposes it to risk, which is the grandeur of its mission—this questioning is its philosophizing, its philosophy. Philosophy is the question of the law and structure of our being. We want to make of philosophy a reality to the extent that we ask the question. We initiate this question to the extent that we risk ourselves on the fundamental question of philosophy.

The objectives attributed to philosophy in *Being and Time* have changed, but it is not simply that philosophy is now made more concrete. If, in 1927, Heidegger understood being-in-the-world, existence, as a sort of space within which can arise that which is to be questioned, namely, being, and if this space included the possibility of authentic being, in both an individual and collective sense, now, in 1933, and finally without questioning it (i.e., without questioning being), without ceding its place to any other object, it has a different status and a different nature: it is not to be understood epistemologically, but ontologically, and, perhaps, as the context in which being is, and is identified by Heidegger with, the German people. It is in itself that the German people is to ask the philosophical question, using those guides who lead it to the philosophical plane, because the people itself has become this question and its object. In the classrooms, in "the highest school of the people," something ought to be forthcoming—that is, the most decisive process of the history of the German people—because it is within these walls that we are to answer the question of who this people is. Having claimed that the very structure

and meaning of the fundamental question of philosophy have been decided at the first beginnings of philosophy itself, Heidegger continues to
analyze the necessary conditions so that this question can *from now on*
appear in its own guise:

What is not decided, on the other hand, and deliberately could
not be, is the question of knowing if we ourselves are always
prepared and strong enough to find the way to this fundamental
question. What is not decided is knowing what will become of us if
ever we lack the stature to be worthy of the grandeur and the
unique character of this question. We must be driven by such an
urgency that we find again this fundamental question *[Grundfrage]*.
One thing is clear: We will never really get to this fundamental
question, as question, if we are not drawn to it by true
urgency and authentic necessity. This urgency must draw us so
that we will be great enough to pose the question. . . . When and
where is this fundamental question of philosophy decided, and
from there, what is its proper essence? This was when the Greek
people whose ethnic stock *[Stammesart]* and language have a
common origin with our own, the Germans', began to create
through its great poets and thinkers a unique and new form of
the historical existence of man. What began then, perdures. It is a
simple fact that until now this commitment has not been solid.
This beginning remains always and loses nothing of the
beginning. This beginning of the spiritual and historical existence
of Western man still exists; it remains like a commandment from
afar and powerfully anticipates the destiny of Western man like a
commandment—as we know—to which German destiny is
bound. Now we are faced with the question of knowing whether
we will the spiritual grandeur of our people, whether we have the
tenacious will to assume a great spiritual mission among the
nations.

We are asked if we are learning through our experience and if
we understand that the present moment of German destiny marks
our existence in the most extreme and greatest urgency, to the
point where this moment puts us before the decision of willing to
create a spiritual universe or not, for the development of our
people and of our state. If we do not want it, and if we are
incapable of exercising it, then some barbarism coming from
elsewhere will sweep us away, and we will have finally lost our
function as a people who create history.

The task of assuming the National Socialist revolution imposes on Heidegger, however, a concrete political option within the movement itself:

An opinion is current that we must raise and spiritualize the National Socialist revolution. I ask the question: Using what spirit *[Geist]*? Where is the spirit to be found? Do we yet know what this spirit is? We have been convinced for a long time that the mind is empty shrewdness, the nonchalant play of subtlety, an activity of the understanding without limits, which is bent on dissecting, on decomposing. The mind therefore would be so-called universal Reasoning, whereas spirit is breath, wind, tempest, commitment, resolve. Today we have no need to spiritualize the great movement of our people. Spirit is already there. But today, as in all historical moments, spirit is still in chains, deprived of its already fashioned universe. If we want it to succeed at this moment, if we must create this spiritual universe, not in one day, not in a year, not even in a decade, but perhaps within a century, then we must find the will to begin to create, to stand in line to wage this second combat of our intellectual confrontation with all the spiritual history of our own past. To do this, we must first learn to understand and to seize the present moment, beyond all the obscurity that past history drags in, heavy and insurmountable. We must learn to understand this historical moment and to know that it is sufficiently grand and rich in power for us to be able to risk ourselves by again connecting with the authentic beginning of our historical beginning, carried by the unique will to create a spiritual future for our people and assure them a vocation among other peoples.

Later, when he analyzes the founding work of the Greeks, and especially the work of Heraclitus, Heidegger translates fragment 53: "War is the father of all beings and reigns over things. It lets us see certain things, the Gods, other beings like humans, some as slaves, others as free." The note adds: "This is why, when Heraclitus said that combat is the father of all things, he was speaking of combat not only as origin but also as authority—An original Greek thought!"

Heidegger adds: "To understand these fragments truly, we must have a different consciousness of the existence of Man and of a people from what we had until just last year"—that is, before the National Socialist takeover.

11   Heidegger and university politics in the Third Reich

The "combat" *(Waffengang)* Heidegger was alluding to in his remarks on Heraclitus was not limited to Freiburg, for its objective was to create a model that could transform the whole society. Heidegger had also used the term "combat" when he answered Fehrle's congratulations, sent from the Ministry to Karlsruhe when Heidegger joined the party. Heidegger said that the question was one of "conquering the world of educated and learned men to steer them to new objectives and new ideas of the nation."[1]

Just as he had done at Freiburg, Heidegger began his political work at the national level by seeking first an alliance with the students and their help. He turned to the headquarters of the Studentenschaft. Immediately after his election to the rectorship—that is, on April 24, 1933—he wrote Georg Plötner, director of the Department of Sciences and Political Education (based in Berlin), evidently a friend, to propose a day of study to bring together all the Führers of the science section of the Deutsche Studentenschaft.[2] This organization was the bastion of the SA; its most important chief, Dr. Oskar Stäbel, was a man from the south like Heidegger. His adjunct was Heinz Zähringen. Its organ was the *Deutsche Studentenschaft: Akademische Korrespondenz*, which, along with its staff, had no political role before 1934. The leadership of the Studentenschaft was, as we saw above, the group responsible for the book-burnings throughout the Reich.

The letters back and forth to organize the conference tell us much about the politics of the group. In his first letter, Plötner informed Heidegger about the program and the participation of Bäumler and Krieck.[3] In the next letter, he outlined the political situation in Berlin, most of all the attacks by the reactionary press, particularly the *Deutsche Zeitung*, against the organization and its publication.[4] The situation Plötner was referring to was that the newspaper, which after 1930 took a rigid position on "German nationalism,"[5] published on April 27, 1933, a circular for internal distribution in which the Deutsche Studentenschaft gave instructions on the art of espionage and denunciation of professors, asking for lists of Jews, Communists, or those guilty of insulting the national Führers or the national military draft or German soldiers during World War I. In addition, the students were to draw up a list of those professors "whose methods included liberal ideas or especially pacifist doctrines, that is, those who ought not be allowed to remain as teachers of German students in a national state. These cases were to be detailed, giving sources (writings, remarks during classes, and so on)." These lists were needed to begin the student boycotts against professors "whose expulsion by the state could not be achieved immediately."[6]

In the third letter (June 1, 1933),[7] Plötner told Heidegger about his contacts with the Freiburg teacher Rudolf Stadelmann, with Dr. Rath and Dr. Haupt (of the Ministry of Education and Culture in Berlin), and with Dr. Holfelder, so that they also could attend the meeting. Heidegger confirmed his participation in a telegram (June 3)[8] and in a letter (July 9),[9] where he repeats his confidence in Plötner, inviting him to join the others at the meeting he would lead at Todtnauberg.

The days of study and indoctrination finally took place at Berlin on June 10 and 11. Heidegger gave a paper titled "Teaching and Research." Alfred Bäumler spoke on "Schools and Departments in the New University," Dr. Walther Voigtländer on "Construction of the New Primary School," and Plötner on "Construction and Tasks of the Science Department."[10] Like Heidegger's other political activities, his contribution here proves the inaccuracy of his later claims that he never had contact with official events of the National Socialist Party.[11]

Speeches at Heidelberg and Kiel: Heidegger and the corporate associations of university professors

In addition to his initiative in training the student Führers, Heidegger took several other actions to transform other universities and associations of professors. Some of the first activities were his speeches at Heidelberg and Kiel, where the Association of Students invited him. At

Heidelberg, where he spoke first, on June 30, 1933, he delivered a speech on "The University in the New Reich." This speech was part of the student program. Just before Heidegger's talk, Dr. Walter Gross, chief of the NSDAP's Department of Racial Purity, spoke on "Medicine and the People," and some days later the most important jurist of the Third Reich, Carl Schmitt, spoke on "The New State of Law."[12] In passing, we should note that it was Heidegger who invited Carl Schmitt to join the National Socialist movement, in a letter dated April 22, 1933, located in Schmitt's personal archives.[13] Participation in the Heidelberg conferences gave strong support for student actions, especially at that university, where there was heated discussion about the legality of reforms in university life in the region of Baden, as we noted above.

The text of Heidegger's speech was not published in its entirety, but the Heidelberg student paper *Neueste Nachrichten* printed some important parts of it on July 1, 1933.[14] According to this text, Heidegger was deeply upset by the situation in the German universities. Although Germany is in the midst of a revolution, he says, one could ask if the universities are aware of it. Heidegger has to answer in the negative, standing solidly on ideas of the radical group. Measures taken by that time appeared grossly inadequate to him, even though campaigns for expelling Jewish teachers, discrimination against Jewish students and other opponents, and, finally, the Führer principle that reformed studies and university leadership were already in place and actively pursued.

Heidegger was fully aware of what his demands called for: changes in administration could only be the prologue for the "existential" transformation of men and institutions. For this reason, Heidegger says in his talk, everything done so far is but a "prelude to the true combat"; the single real blow struck against the system is the creation of work camps because their institution opens up the possibility of real change in life style. Promoting the struggle by taking actions parallel and supplementary to traditional university practices, Heidegger warns against the danger that the German university could "receive a mortal blow, killing the last remnants of an educating force," and recommends on the other hand that after its renewal the university be integrated into the community of the people and indissolubly united to the state so as to avoid this loss.[15]

None of this could become reality unless the universities transform themselves into true communities, beyond their style of research (which has lost sight of any bounds and fools itself into believing in the so-called idea of the international progress of science), as well as their style of teaching (which replaces true instruction by a fetishism of regulations). The proper action, Heidegger says, is to follow "a tough struggle to the end in the spirit of National Socialism, which will not be drowned by Christian and humanist notions." If we do want to grasp the new reality, "it won't do to put a little political coloring on things" while still using an outmoded concept of science, even if somewhat aided by a small dose of anthropology.[16] True transformation presupposes that we are all aware of the "urgency" *(Not)* of the situation.[17] Alluding directly to elements inside and outside the party that were complaining about the excess time taken from studies for days of indoctrination by the SA and attendant paramilitary activities, Heidegger claims that one must not see this training as a waste of time, but rather as the students' answer to the state appeal for participation in the struggle.[18] "There is never danger in work for the State. Danger comes only from indifference and resistance! Only the force that opens on the true road, not on ordinary terms, is the true one." Listing his rivals as those suspected of "indifference" or those "who offer resistance," Heidegger states that the new studies ought to represent "a risk and not a refuge for cowards. Those not able to win in combat ought to die."[19] "The new spirit is to be prepared to persevere because the struggle for the bastions to educate the Führers will last for a long time. It will be carried on by the new Reich, to which the people's chancellor, Adolf Hitler, will give a new reality. . . . The struggle that is beginning is the struggle for the new Teacher and the new Führer of the university."[20]

Invited by the extremist students, Heidegger was strongly in support of the violent struggle that Heidelberg students were leading to remove Rector Willy Andreas, who had until then survived the attempts to bring the Baden universities into line. Memoirs by the historian Gerd Tellenbach, who taught at Heidelberg, support this interpretation. "One student was turned into a fanatic by the agitating speech and said to another that, after what had just been said, Andreas ought to be shot in the head."[21] Rector Heidegger came to the conference in special dress. While the professors and teachers came to the talk in their usual long pants, and the students came in their somber costume or their uniforms, Heidegger was dressed in knickers and an open shirt such as worn by the Völkische in the Black Forest and in Bavaria.[22]

Judging by the press, Heidegger gave the same speech at Kiel as he had at Heidelberg, with some important variants. Heidegger made the changes because the previous rector, Scheel, had now been replaced by Lothar Wolf.[23] According to the Kiel newspapers that printed comments on the talk, Heidegger apparently eliminated everything negative about Lothar Wolf's administration, which, at Heidelberg, had served to destabilize Andreas. Unlike Andreas, with whose leadership Heidegger had differed, Wolf was an active adherent of National Socialism and a principal ally of Heidegger's. In his writings, Wolf[24] speaks against those who attempt to keep a private space in the midst of a people's revolution.[25] The central faculty in the "political university" cannot be theology ("for those studies there are convents"), but philosophy. It alone is able to unite the sciences. To ground these claims, Wolf often cited Heidegger's Rector's Address.[26] Later, Wolf was to participate with Heidegger at the inauguration of National Socialist organizations of professors to replace the associations that had not yet come into line, and he would send many teachers and students from Kiel to attend the indoctrination classes that Heidegger held at Todtnauberg. Hermann Heimpel reported about these courses that "for some months, about a year, Heidegger believed that, in the triumph of the revolution, his own philosophy also triumphed. . . . He then invited student Führers to his chalet at Todtnauberg, but he refused access to those disagreeing with him. Such was the situation in 1933. . . . I never took Heidegger for a National Socialist, and when he called one of his colleagues 'a Jew,' it was as if he had denied himself."[27] About the Kiel speech, the *Norddeutsche Rundschau,* on July 15, 1933, wrote that Heidegger explained and enlarged what he had said in his Rector's Address.[28]

Heidegger's speech on the university in the National Socialist state

The speech Rector Heidegger gave at Tübingen on November 30, 1933, again witnesses to his activities at other universities. The event was organized by the local NSDAP, the Kampfbund (an organization begun before 1933 by Alfred Rosenberg to bring together pro-Nazi scientists and propagandists), and university students. There was coverage by the local press, and the *Neues Tübinger Tagblatt,* on November 30, 1933, printed an invitation to the speech:

The name Heidegger is a sign. There are few professors who care as much as he does about National Socialism and who defend it in such a total and radical way. In the past, the name Heidegger meant something only in the special world of philosophy. . . . Today it is at the very heart of teaching. His text on "The Self-Determination of the German University" was not well known for some time. Today no one who wants to meditate on the essence

and the will of National Socialism can be unaware of it. Heidegger
is one to point the way. . . . He has personally assumed the
leadership of the House of Comradeship for Students of Freiburg,
and he is trying to make soldiers of those who are depositories of
learning. . . . There emanates from him a force that engages all
who know him. His incisive and profound teaching leads us
beyond the superficial and the ephemeral to the truly essential for
German self-realization. He lets us see directly the total meaning
of our national surge *[völkischer Ausbruch]* and its consequences for
university teachers. Someone who participated in the camp
[Lager] led by Heidegger this fall said: "When Heidegger speaks,
the fog that used to be there disappears." This was the impression
of those at the camp. . . . Today at Tübingen we have been
visited by a veritable combatant from the front line, a man who
was invited to show the manly objectives of the German reality of
the future and who as a scientist is here to describe the work of
German science in the future. He has declared a state of war and
is calling for an offensive. Let us hope that all those respond
who still wait and doubt, and hope that he may turn them around.
Anyone concerned with the changes in the universities under the
new Reich must come to know Heidegger. Anyone loving the
tempest and danger must listen to Heidegger![29]

The speech itself and the demonstration were reported in the *Neues
Tübinger Tagblatt* and the *Tübinger Chronik* on December 1, 1933. Many
teachers, students, and dignitaries from the Ministry of Culture at Wür-
tenberg attended. The *Tübinger Chronik* printed the complete text, a text
until now unknown.
    Heidegger began:

The university is the advanced school of science whose task is to
transmit scientific doctrine based on scientific research to achieve a
scientific education. In its relationship with the state, the
university functions as an organ of public law. W. von Humboldt,
who was among the founders of the University of Berlin in
1809, a university that has remained until today a model
university, gave on that occasion its currently held meaning. In a
scientific report, Humboldt wrote that, in relationships between
the university and the state, the state ought never to lose sight of
the fact that the state remains an obstacle for the university and
that, therefore, it must not become embroiled in its work. The

university would work much better without the state. On the other hand, the state must procure the needed funds for the university. Humboldt described the university in three ways:

1. It is defined from the point of view of the teachers and the researchers.

2. Research is dominant, not teaching. Teaching is to be grounded in research.

3. The university is an advanced school, a community of students and teachers.[30]

Heidegger's analysis of the relationship between the university and the state is pursued in the spirit of the National Socialist revolution; the revolution develops the choice that until then had been openly defended only by the radical faction of the SA and the students depending on it. To understand the rest of the speech, we must keep in mind this beginning:

> In the meantime, the revolution has taken place in our country. The state has been transformed. This was not a revolution achieved by a power already existing in the state or by a political party. The National Socialist revolution meant rather the radical upheaval of the whole German existence, which also touched the university. How does the university present itself in the new state? The new student is no longer a bourgeois who hangs around the university; he goes through work service; he is a member of the SA or of the SS; he practices sports of all kinds. All this will soon bring a new harmony. The new teachers make plans for the university; they edit brochures on the new idea of science; they speak of the political student, of political faculties; there are courses on the "science of the people" *[Volkskunde]* and on work service. But all that is still only old wine in new bottles. In the best of cases, it is not more than a purely surface application of certain results of this revolution, while fundamentally everything is still stuck in its habitual inertia.
>
> But what ought it still to bring us? According to the very words of the Führer, the revolution has reached its end and has become evolution. Evolution is to replace revolution. Yet, at the university, *not only has the revolution failed to attain its goal, but in fact it has not really even begun.* And if, in the meaning the Führer has given it, we are at the stage of evolution, this evolution can be accomplished only by means of the struggle within the struggle.

Revolution in German universities has nothing to do with shifts on the surface. The National Socialist revolution is and will become the complete remaking of men, students, and young teachers of tomorrow. This cannot happen outside the new reality, but only if we are immersed in this reality, only if we live it. The only ones able to live it are those whose spirit is disposed to receive it; not the simple spectators, who perhaps are content to read National Socialist literature to find out about new ways of speaking, but only the active participants, for revolutionary reality is not something already in existence *[Vorhandenes]*; by its essence it is something still developing, still gestating. The nature of this reality demands that we consider it quite differently from the way we consider mere facts. First of all, we must ask ourselves questions about the new reality, ask ourselves if we truly are within it and how we are to behave within it. To do this, we must tear off the choker of traditional forms and appearances at the university. These forms and appearances will no longer be anything but a provisional frame. We must also guard ourselves from precipitous changes, for the forms are determined by our actions within this community. Our actions are an "ought-to-be," and they are determined by what we are and who we are. Our own being is determined by what we become in this new reality, and what we become because of taking the risk, what we come to realize. It is clear to us that forms and appearances have meaning only to the extent they come from the living activity of humans themselves.

Heidegger asks a triple question based on these principles:

1. What is the new reality? The Germans are becoming a historical people: not that they have not had a long and eventful history already, but to have a history does not mean to be historical. To be historical is to know that as a total people history is neither past nor present, but is that act of questioning that is born from the movement of the future that erupts into the present. The future does not consist in what is not; it is part of every decision which is made with full consciousness and through which a people seeks to grasp itself. To be historical means to be by knowing; it is a way to liberate what the past necessarily conceals, the forces that engage us and that become the great carriers of change. This knowledge is the state itself. The state is

the structure that wakens, and that unites, and when we submit to it, we put ourselves into it as a totality. Forces, nature, history, art, technical advances, economics, the state itself, are affirmed by the noble struggle. In this way, we see that what makes the people sure, clear, and strong becomes tangible. The tangible character of these powers is the measure of Truth. To become historical is to act within these great powers of existence that are placed in the state. Doing this, the people lay claim to the right to possess the state, to know what it is in itself and the great powers of its existence. This process is an inexorable movement, almost violent, one of the great necessities to which the human heart submits. It is only through the state that it is possible to raise ourselves to glory. We are in the power of this imperious force for the sake of a new reality. We are seeking those who understand this new force so as to execute its commandments. It can only be a question of those who are not yet worn out, those who by the roots of their being and their existence become one with the people, those who feel in themselves the elan toward the future, the need to begin by assault *[Stürm]*. And these are the German young people. They possess the certainty of their own being. Authentic youth acts by necessity, and they know they are commited to a grand scheme. It is in view of this scheme that a new knowledge is to be realized.

Heidegger turns then to consider the situation of the new student:

2. How does the new student relate within this new reality? By definition, the student is to begin by learning: here we touch a danger often denounced, which is to take students too seriously, to attribute too much importance to them. They say we must avoid this, for the aptitudes of today's students are too primitive, which is not to imply that their knowledge is considerably less than the knowledge of the professors. But being primitive means having the elan and interior forces just where things really start; to be primitive means to be impelled by inner forces. It is precisely because the new students are primitive that they are called to bring before us the new right to know. They demand of their teachers information on nature, philosophy, art, the state, and so on. Ought they take note only of what has been taught in the past? They will not be content with what teachers give them incidentally as results of personal opinions. Without letting themselves be detoured, tenaciously, the new students will attempt

to impose the people's right to know in their state. In this assault, the young people are obeying their own will, which is for them a sure guide. Those who find themselves wherever youth is under attack come together with youth and with their will. This obedience under common attack is the origin of the new comradeship, and not the reverse, with comradeship being the origin of obedience. This true comradeship educates the Führers, who are more ready to act because they endure better and they make more sacrifices. Comradeship takes each one beyond himself. We know young men, and the firmness of the lines of their faces, the brutality *[Rücksichtlosigkeit]* of their speech, their resolve of steel. This student no longer studies in the traditional way. He is always moving. This student becomes a worker.

This is how Heidegger ties student and work by an essential link in which we are to understand what is specifically National Socialism both in the "new student" and in the new state:

Has the student not always been a worker? Today we speak of those who work with their heads and those who work with their hands. The term "worker" designates here a vast collective; it is a concession given to comrades of the people who are commonly called workers (i.e., skilled workers). With the new German reality, the essence of work and workers has also changed. "Worker" is not a corporate notion, a cultural notion. "Work" is an ambiguous word: on the one hand it means the act of accomplishing, and on the other it means the result. All human behavior is work. The essential part does not reside in the act of accomplishing, nor in the result, but in what is there truly being produced. Man as worker enters the struggle with all that is available, thus producing the affirmation of the powers of nature, art, state, and so on. Understood in this way, the essence of work determines the existence of Germans and, no doubt, the general existence of humans on earth. Our existence begins to be transformed into another form of being. The National Socialist state is the state of work because the new student knows that he is charged with bringing to its goal the political demands of knowledge. This is why he is the "worker." *The new student studies because he is a "worker" and his studies are called today development of the will so as to consolidate this knowledge of the people in virtue of which they will become a historical being in the state.* After a decade, perhaps after a generation, this new type of student will dominate the university. Then this student will have done his duty and will be in the front line of the new teachers.

For Heidegger, this is why the revolutionary impulses of the students would be the first factor to use in transforming the German university. And it is precisely from this impulse that he wants to understand the "new teacher." The "new teacher," who is basically the student of today, is described as follows:

3. *How does the new teacher act in the new German reality?* The new demands for knowledge are imposed on all sides for those who have eyes to see and ears to hear. This demand for knowledge consists at the same time in the will to teach and to seek masters worthy of this will to learn. But the truth is that present academic teaching is characterized by a lack of goals, and allows the students to just skimp on the exams. Corresponding to this lack of academic goals is the abyss in which we have fallen. It is called "international progress," but it is these two factors that have brought us to the powerlessness in which the German universities have wallowed for decades, a helplessness also in the face of the world, which has been running in that direction. This is why during the Conference of Universities last year, people complained about the swelling population of the universities, which hinders its functioning. The reality is the contrary: it is the failure of the universities that has brought on the overpopulation.

This has brought an inevitable shock to the new German reality. The fact is that we always drag out the old ghosts according to which the university risks falling into barbarism, instead of seeing the other danger, which is to prevent, knowingly or not, the new demands for knowledge from being fruitful. It is not enough to greet the new order. It is rather a question of choosing one or the other, of deciding to put ourselves under the authority of the new reality or of disappearing together with a world now in decline. If our closest experience with this new reality makes us choose it, only then will we have begun the struggle, our confrontation with this demand for the knowledge that emanates from youth. . . . Every desire for knowledge takes the form of a question, and it is a question for us who need to bring this knowledge to fruition to know in advance what importance we give to true questioning. Posing questions is not a mere play of curiosity, an obstinate desire to be right at any price. The courage needed to ask questions is in itself a more noble response than any specious answer, more noble than any artificial system of thought. Questions are posed in opposition to those who hold the power and can bring those who hold the power closer to the essence of everything. Asking questions is always marching ahead, sounding the future. It is the fundamental attitude, the gift of true teaching.

The complementary relationship between learning and teaching in a "revolutionary" manner gives birth to attitudes that redefine for Heidegger the relationship between the student and the sciences, on the one hand, and the university and the state, on the other:

In this confrontation with the demands of knowledge we find again the first notion of what the final goal of teaching is and the corresponding attitude of the learner. To teach is to allow the other to learn; it is to encourage learning. To learn is not to receive and to store given knowledge. To learn is not to receive, but fundamentally to give oneself to the self. In the act of learning I give myself fully to me, I give myself to that basic self that I know already and that I guard closely. *To learn is to give yourself to yourself, grounded on that original possession of your existence like a member of a people* (völkisches Dasein), *and being conscious of yourself as a coholder of the truth of the people in its state.* To teach is to bring the pupil to ask questions that indicate he necessarily understands his knowledge; teaching is letting those who want to know how to rise toward the powers of existence of the people so they can collect their stimulating forces; teaching is to become sure of the essential view toward being; it is learning to neglect the non-essential. *It is only through this kind of relation between teachers and learners—that is, in a close-knit community—that science can come to life.* It is what is worthy of learning that makes the decision of where to place the limits of knowledge. Teaching in this way will be quite naturally implicated in the new task incumbent on students, which is to develop and clarify the new demands of knowledge. The teacher becomes in this way the worker. Teacher and student find themselves side by side in the same attack. Submission to chief and comrade arises naturally, just like the comradeship between teachers. The former type of coexistence, "collegiality," will disappear as something negative. By obedience, teachers and learners are integrated with the state, and the new way of being is developed as a reality within which the relationship with the state takes on another character. We can no longer speak, however, of the relation with the state because the university itself has become state, an element of development of the state. In this way we see the disappearance of the character that the university has worn until now, an empty isle in an empty state.

Heidegger made some veiled criticisms of Hitler's claim that the reality would follow closely after the revolution and that then only a quantitative development (an evolution) would be needed, criticisms he expressed again when characterizing the general situation at the beginning of the National Socialist "offensive":

We, men of today, we are at the heart of the struggle for the new reality. We are but a transition, an offering. As participants in this combat we ought to be able to count on a strong generation, which no longer thinks of itself, but which unites with the basic being of the people. It is not a struggle for persons and colleagues, any more than it is for empty and extraneous things, nor for vague feelings. Every true struggle brings within itself the permanent traits on the faces of the combatants and their task. Only the struggle develops true laws according to which things are attained. The struggle we wish for is the heart-to-heart struggle, man to man.

The presence of the Kampfbund and the local NSDAP proves that this time Heidegger was supported not simply by Nazi students.

Heidegger and the Association of German Universities

Heidegger's involvement with "revolutionizing" the German universities, of course, was not restricted to this end. In cooperation with the German student community and other National Socialist rectors and professors he systematically coordinated efforts designed to change the structure and composition of German universities and the Congress of Rectors. The first meeting of the Congress following Heidegger's election took place on June 8, 1933. Like other rectors, Heidegger saw in this meeting a chance to radicalize the Congress and the Association of German Universities.

But both institutions had already brought themselves into line *(gleichschaltet)*, either because they feared such a radicalization or because of their own convictions. Indeed, on March 5, 1933, three hundred professors and lecturers signed an appeal for Hitler's election and supported National Socialism. And, on April 3, the Association of German Universities protested angrily against campaigns by foreign countries intended to discredit Hitler's government. By April 12, 1933, the Congress of Rectors had decided to establish a commission to review its organization vis-à-vis the new state. On April 22, the leadership of the Association of German Universities made an official statement that contained the following: "The rebirth of the German universities and the rise of the new German Reich means the fulfillment of the desires of the universities of our homeland and the confirmation of their always deeply felt hopes." Just as the professors had supported the founding of the Reich by Bismarck, had vocally supported World War I with jingoistic statements, and had rejected international recriminations against Germany, so they now took part in this "rebirth" of Germany. The April 22 statement says: "We do not construe freedom of research as a sort of homelessness of the spirit or as a blind relativism but rather as an expression of the ancient German freedom of spirit that continues building the world of German science informed by its ethical responsibility for the truth." Tradition ("old, dignified forms")—that is, "self-government by the rector, senate, and faculties"—should be preserved. But: "We are also committed to reform: Reinstating the old system of selection according to nobility of mind and character. . . . There lies our spiritual will to serve. We mean to consider new forms of national education—like work service, settlement schools, military-style physical education, protection of the border lands. . . . These are matters for the whole nation." The statement ends with a plea for respect for the work of the university as an institution that would enable coexistence but at the same time would acknowledge the legitimacy of the regime. The statement was signed by Professors Tillmann (Bonn), Fröhlich (Halle), Schlink (Darmstadt), von Köhler (Tübingen), Bumke (Munich), Spranger (Berlin), Nägel (Dresden), Solger (Berlin), Schleicher (Aachen), and Fels (Munich).[31] Through these measures both governing bodies linked up with the old traditions.

The Association of German Universities had been founded in 1920 as an organization of professors intended to "counterbalance the new political situation."[32] It defended without reservation the reconstruction of

Germany. Its "self-coordination" *(Selbstgleichschaltung)* began with a declaration on March 21 that preceded the one cited above.[33]

Facing a threat of further radicalization, the leadership of the Association requested a meeting with Hitler in order to explain their program and at the same time to express their recognition of his regime. The meeting was approved and planned for May 12, 1933.[34] According to the available sources, it seems that Hugo Bruckmann (National Socialist member of the Reich Parliament, editor of the works of Wölfflin and H. Stuart Chamberlain, and official NSDAP representative of the Kampfbund for German Culture)[35] used his influence to get the Association its meeting. In a letter of May 10, Bruckmann informed State Secretary Hans Lammers about a meeting that had taken place in his apartment during which Professor Bumke let it be known that the Association intended to cooperate with the government. The point of the meeting in the Reich Chancellery was to make the declaration of this intention explicit. At the same time, the government would take the opportunity to express its wishes for a reform of the Association's leadership. Except for Professors Spranger and Nägel, the current representatives would remain in their positions. Apparently, Tillmann, a Catholic theologian, was an opponent of the Centrist Party. The other board members could not be trusted. After the planned meeting was confirmed, Tillmann once again expressed his thanks and took his leave.

The meeting, however, did not take place. Surprisingly, the leadership of the Society of German Students together with the rectors of the universities of Freiburg, Kiel, Rostock, Cologne, and Frankfurt intervened and asked Hitler to postpone the meeting at least until the "unification" of the Association was completed. On May 18, the Society of German Students sent a telegram to Hitler calling the Association of German Universities an institution unworthy of the Führer's attention. They claimed it had repeatedly demonstrated its hostility toward the Society, which "has always stood in the front lines in the battle against the non-German spirit." On the same day, the rector of Kiel, Lothar Wolf, also criticized the hostile position of the Association toward the Society and demanded that the meeting with Hitler be canceled. On May 20, Heidegger sent the following telegram to Hitler: "To the Chancellor of the Reich, Reich Chancellery, Berlin. I beg you most devotedly to postpone the planned meeting with the leadership of the Association of German Universities until such time as the Association's leadership has been fully organized in the spirit of cooperation especially needed now. Heidegger, Rector of the University of Freiburg/Breisgau." In similar telegrams, Rectors Schulze (Rostock), Naendrup (Cologne), Horrman (Technische Hochschule Braunschweig), and Krieck (Frankfurt) also spoke in favor of postponing the meeting.

Subsequently, without giving any reasons, Lammers told Tillmann in an official communication (repeated in a separate letter to Bruckmann) that the reception had been postponed. In a telegram dated May 20, and in a letter to Hitler dated two days later, in which he attributed responsibility for the attacks against the Society of German Students to Eduard Spranger, Tillmann protested:

> If Herr Prof. Spranger intended certain phrases in his April 22 appeal to apply to the Student Society, this is his personal opinion, which the leadership of the Association of Universities has . . . nothing to do with. If we had considered it possible that one could expect an attack against the Society of German Students or even against the national government in this declaration, the appeal would not have been approved and published. Rather, the appeal was intended to express our willingness to cooperate in the rebuilding of our state. . . . With respectful devotion, Tillmann.

There is no evidence that the letter was answered. At the Association's extraordinary conference on June 1, 1933, a new board was elected.

In referring to the "Spranger case" in his letter, Tillmann was alluding to the dispute between the rector of the University of Berlin, Professor Kohlrausch, and the students who were organizing book-burnings at that time. Spranger had declared the student's excesses unworthy of the new Germany, seeing in them a deviation from the otherwise ethically valuable Führer principle. In a public declaration, Spranger also protested that he had not been consulted before arrangements were completed for a new chair in political pedagogy instituted by Minister Bernhard Rust. He ended the letter by letting it be known that he was vacating his position on the board of the Association of German Universities.[36]

The contemporary documents show that Heidegger's assertions before the Denazification Court at Freiburg that had to judge his behavior after the end of World War II are at least questionable. In front of this body, Heidegger warned against a misinterpretation of his telegram to Hitler. In no way had he understood the unification to mean that the universities needed to adopt official doctrine. Rather, his concern was for a "spiritual renewal" based on National Socialism. Unfortunately, in the introduction to his account of the matter, K. A. Moehling records only where Heidegger's telegram to Hitler is mentioned for the first time. The telegram is no more than a small part of the documentation from the denazification proceedings that ended in Heidegger's suspension from the university.

The Congress of Rectors that took place on June 8, 1933, declared its solidarity with the Association of German Universities insofar as it, too, stated clearly that it wanted to take part in the meeting that was to take place with Hitler. Immediately thereafter, those prominent in National Socialism left the conference in protest. Heidegger was in this group, along with Krieck, Wolf, and Friedrich Neumann (Göttingen). There are several letters concerning this meeting in the state archives at Potsdam that Ernst Krieck and Lothar Wolf wrote to Professor Achelis at the Council of Ministries on June 18, 1933 and to the permanent secretary in the Ministry, Gerullis, on June 6, 1933.[37] They prove that the rectors of the universities of Kiel, Frankfurt, and Göttingen had threatened to withdraw their universities from the Association in order to create additional pressure in favor of a "true unification" *(Gleichschaltung)* (a point that goes beyond what Ott reports about their intentions).

Heidegger, Krieck, and the creation of the KADH

Before this partial and momentary defeat, and because they had predicted it, Heidegger had quietly begun to organize with Ernst Krieck, Friedrich Neumann, Lothar Wolf, and several other professors a kind of association with the goal of regrouping those professors and rectors who were committed to a National Socialist renewal of the universities. Its goal was certainly to intervene in the Congress of Rectors and to attain power, when circumstances were favorable. This organization was called the Political-Cultural Community of German University Professors (KADH, *Kulturpolitische Arbeitsgemeinschaft Deutscher Hochschullehrer*). At its inaugural assembly, which took place May 3, 1933, Ernst Krieck seems to have taken the initiative.

By drawing on the documentation about the Community,[38] we can deduce that Heidegger had first been invited to be part of the founding group. In one of his letters, dated April 22, Heidegger shows his "disappointment that some faithful colleagues like Bäumler at Dresden and Heyse at Königsberg were not among the first group." In a second letter, Heidegger acknowledged receipt of a letter and expressed thanks for the Community's proposed bylaws and the list of members. He repeated his suggestion that Bäumler and Heyse be invited and expressed some difficulty in accepting Hammer as a "person to be trusted" in the Community at Freiburg: "Although he is a faithful National Socialist worker in the sense that he is certainly attached to the undertaking, his teaching activity is only tangential." Heidegger proposed that documentation be sent to Professors Mortensen, Wilser, and Winterfeld (these men were to become part of his own rectoral group). He insisted on not recruiting colleagues who lacked the needed scientific qualification, "no matter what their" militant National Socialist commitment.[39]

Nineteen professors participated in the constituent assembly. By April 22, 1933, the organization had 123 ordinary members. This included professors and teachers and Georg Plötner, who represented the students. Among them were Bauch (Freiburg), Oskar Becker (Bonn), Heidegger (Freiburg), Jaensch (Marburg), Kirchner (Frankfurt), Klausing (Frankfurt/Marburg), Krieck (Heidelberg), Petersen (Kiel), Mannhardt (Marburg), Rein (Hamburg), Neumann (Göttingen), Panzer (Heidelberg), Erich Rothacker (Bonn), and Lothar Wolf (Kiel), along with teacher Rudolf Stadelmann (Freiburg), and Ministerial Counselor Fehrle (Karlsruhe).[40] The fact that Bäumler was not among this group, in spite of Heidegger's insistence, may be due to his strong ties with Alfred Rosenberg, who never got along with Krieck.[41]

The act of constituting the group attests to the will of the individuals to fix their political lines clearly and in distinction from other organizations. Their goal was not to promote the professional interests of the group but "to form a small circle of trusted people, an activist avant-garde" to resolve university problems. During the first meeting, one group insisted on administrative questions (Hertzberg and Grebe); others like Krieck, Walz, Panzer, and Klausing called for the formation of a small avant-garde, an activist homogeneous group; Heidegger called for ways of increasing membership, but asked that the discussion of the notion of science be deferred until the next meeting. The assembly charged members Mannhardt, Dahm, Klausing, and Heidegger to give a report at the next meeting.

The founding members included Professors Grahe (Frankfurt), Grebe (Frankfurt), Hasse (Frankfurt), Heidegger (Freiburg), Henkel (Frankfurt), Hertzberg (Marburg), Jaensch (Marburg), Jantzen (Frankfurt), Klausing (Marburg), Krieck (Frankfurt), Küchner (Giessen), Kuhn (Giessen), Mannhardt (Marburg), Rothacker (Bonn), Schaffstein (Göttingen), Schmidt (Frankfurt), Walz (Marburg), Wiskemann (Marburg), and Zeiss (Frankfurt). They also approved the bylaws. Out of thirteen signatures, nine came from Frankfurt, indicating that the Community had in Ernst Krieck, rector of that university, the mover of the group. Krieck's instructions were designed to direct the work of "confidential individuals" in their universities. In this document, Krieck carries the title of president of the directing council of the Community.[42]

During the meeting of March 1933, the directors were still Küchner, Klausing, Krieck, Pfannenstiel, and Walz. Heidegger was designated as "confidential representative" for Freiburg (he was not yet rector). It is quite possible that Heidegger's call for more members and his wish to include Bäumler and Heyse indicated his hope for a change in power relationships within the group.

The bylaws began with a declaration of commitment to the wakening of the German people, who "searching for their proper identity would start a new chapter of their history. They want to create their own vital and essential order so as to realize their mission among other peoples of the world." Universities ought to be shaped according to this fundamental criterion:

> German universities are to have German characteristics. . . .
> Scientific knowledge has a living relationship with the character,
> history, situation, and task of the *people*. Thus, knowledge is called
> upon to forge the action, attitude, and development of the
> people in order to direct them. . . . The freedom of academic
> research and teaching is essentially grounded in the character of
> the *researcher* and the *teacher*. These are joined together by their
> relationships with the totality of the people, with their manner of
> being, with their tasks *[völkische Art und Aufgabe]*. . . . German
> universities ought to be integrated into the vast movement of the
> renewal of the consciousness of the people *[völkisches Bewusstein]*
> inside and outside the Reich. . . . Anyone who would deny
> harmony with the people *[völkische Bedingheit]* or who would not
> see in them an unspoiled condition, in particular concerning
> university work, has no place in these ranks.

The Community claimed it was independent of any political party. Only German-born university teachers *(Volksdeutsche)* could be members. The bylaws were unanimously accepted.

From letters sent by Heidegger to Kirchner and Krieck (April 4 and 8), we can learn something about his activities within the group and something of their political significance. Heidegger insisted that the discussion of science be deferred. The meeting of April 23 had a program on "Research and Teaching." In the letter to Kirchner, Heidegger explained that, rather than give a speech, he preferred to see the young members take the initiative to express their wishes and needs. His task would then have been to redirect this discussion to fundamental questions and encourage a dialogue on the different sciences. But while preparing this suggestion, he recognized that it would only be possible at a later time. This is why he renewed his proposition to organize an open meeting for several days during which this theme, "decisive for the clarification and consolidation of our society," could be treated. He then decided not to give the expected speech, adding that at this time what was needed was an effort to pull together methods of action and to organize proper ways to work in other universities.[43]

Although the minutes of subsequent meetings are unfortunately not extant, it is possible to deduce that the later break with Krieck began around these problems, and surely around rivalry for power in this group. The event that began the definite break will be discussed later. Whatever it was, Krieck and Heidegger were not always at odds. Their differences, certainly considerable but hardly disabling, did not keep them from working together at this time on political convictions that coincided absolutely. The Community had only a brief life, but as a definite political attempt, it expressed National Socialist plans within the German universities early in the regime, clarifying Heidegger's political practice at that time. Later, when all such groups, all such teaching groups, were linked within the Association of National Socialist Professors, which was directed from the central government, they were left, as we have seen, without a political base.

12 Support for Hitler and conflicts with Krieck

The Demonstration of German Science for Adolf Hitler

Heidegger's political activities to "revolutionize" the university include his participation in what was called the Demonstration of German Science, which took place at Leipzig in November 1933, initiated by Gauobmann Arthur Göpfert from Saxony, Führer of the Association of National Socialist Professors (NSLB). The colloquium was organized to support science in Hitler's government, that is, to support the most famous German scientists. The fire at the Reichstag on February 27, 1933, had given Hitler the excuse to publish the next day a decree suspending all constitutional rights and also giving him direct control over all the provinces of the Reich. In spite of the deployment of Nazi forces, the March elections gave Hitler only 44 percent of the vote. And although he was already assured power in the provinces by being named Reichsstatthalter, it was clear that Hitler still needed to consolidate his power. For this reason he called for a plebiscite to take place November 12, 1933.

The Nazi Party called on all its forces, among them certainly the universities. At the solemn ceremony organized by Göpfert, we find Professor Eugen Fischer, rector of Berlin University, Professor Arthur Golf, rector of Leipzig, Martin Heidegger, rector of Freiburg, Freidrich Neumann, rector of Göttingen, Eberhardt Schmidt, rector of Hamburg, and Professors Hirsch, Pinder (Munich), and Sauerbruch (Berlin). Guido

Schneeberger[1] was the first to collect information about this celebration and about Heidegger's having participated in it.

Heidegger's speech began:

> Teachers and fellow Germans!
> German compatriots!
> The German people have been called to cast a vote for the Führer, but the Führer asks nothing from the people; rather he is giving the people the most immediate possibility of a free decision, the noblest one—that is, to know if the entire people want their own existence or if they do not want it. Tomorrow the people decide nothing less than their own future.
> It is quite impossible to compare this vote with the series of electoral acts that have taken place up to now. What is unique in this vote is the simple grandeur of the decision *[Entscheidung]* to be achieved. The implacable character of the simple and the ultimate tolerates neither wavering nor hesitation. This ultimate decision goes right to the farthest limits of our people. And what is this frontier? It consists of the original demand *[Urforderung]* of all Being, whose own essence it preserves and nourishes. And so a barrier has been raised between what we can expect from a people and what we cannot. By that fundamental law of honor, the German people keep the dignity and fixed purpose of their lives. The will to assume one's own responsibilities is not just the fundamental law *[Grundgesetz]* of the structure *[Erwirkung]* of its National Socialist state. Starting from this will to assume one's own responsibilities, the work of every social level *[Stand]*, whether in large things or small, is consigned to the place and the rank of its fixed purpose, the same necessity that makes all equal. The work of skilled workers and their classes *[Stande]* support and complete the living edifice *[Gefüge]* of the state. Again it is work that renews its link with the earth *[Bodenständigkeit]*, and work that determines this state as a reality of the people within the field of all the essential forces of human existence.

To analyze the relationship between Führer and people, Heidegger uses certain fundamental notions from *Being and Time,* but rather than construing the phenomenon of "resolute decision" in terms of individual existence, Heidegger holds that it is the people facing itself that makes the choice: to elect itself or reject itself. For Heidegger, given all the political and philosophical forms fascism can assume, this possibility to choose does not have its origin in the people itself but in the transcendental and constitutive mediation that the Führer provides here. Certainly for Heidegger, the "people" is all the more "sacred" because it is from this origin that the figure of the Führer emerges. But it is only in giving birth to its guide *(Führer)* that the people has the objective possibility of recognizing itself in him and attaining its own identity; there is of course the other equally essential possibility of not recognizing the Führer and thereby denying him. The people in itself can never be the "sufficient" cause of its own existence. It is only thanks to the Führer, and through him, that the people can be what it is to be, an active "subject" in the process of its own realization.

Now changed into an absolute subject, the Führer makes no requests, but, on the contrary, grants possibilities. The possibility of attaining an authentic existence is rooted, according to *Being and Time*, in the possibility of choosing an autonomous mode of existence, one beyond conventions. This is also the case with collective existence, which corresponds to living within the parameters of its tradition. Mediation between the possibility of conforming to tradition and the possibility of choosing oneself in the person of the Führer, and mediation between *Being and Time* and the Leipzig speech, now derive from the transcendental exaltation of the "hero" *(Helden)*, a generic word that Heidegger had not yet found in 1927. In 1933, he found this "hero." In the November 3 article cited above, Heidegger was proposing to the students that they replace their ideas and principles by the vigor and will of Hitler. This notion has now been perfected. Not only is the Führer the "criterion" of this choice; he has become the agent of historical possibility itself. After the vote in favor of the Führer, when the "people" opted for itself in the person of Adolf Hitler, the possibility of developing its own authentic existence was open to it. The means the people had at their disposal was work, work that is to be developed in the Führer's state. But, here again, Heidegger went beyond what could be seen as the model for a simple dictatorship. What is particularly Nazi in this notion is that for him the totality of all workers will be organized into corporations. For Heidegger, the work of the corporations is the support of the living structure of the state—the support, not the subject.

It is not ambition, nor desire for fame *[Ruhmsucht]*, it is not blind egoism, nor thirst for power, that made the Führer quit the League of Nations, but it was his single and clear will to take responsibility on himself by assuming and becoming master of the

destiny of our people. This does not mean a turning away from
the community of peoples, but rather the contrary, because our
people places itself under the essential law of human existence,
the law that every people must first follow, if it wants to remain a
people.

It is truly from this communal way of following in the same
direction when faced with the unconditional responsibility for
oneself, taken by oneself, and only then, that the possibility of
taking oneself and each other seriously can grow, so that,
now already beyond, we gain an affirmative *[bejahen]* with regard
to the community. The will for a true community of the people is
as distant from worldly friendship, which is committed to nothing,
and which is based on nothing, as it is from the power of blind
violence. This will acts beyond that opposition, and creates
independence and solidarity of peoples and states. What happens
within such a will? Is it a return to barbarism? No! It is a turning away
from all empty material exchange and from secret actions, and
finding the simple and noble need to act in a responsible way for
the self. Is it moving toward illegality? No! It is an act of faith in
the inalienable autonomy of every people. Is it the denial of the
creativity of a spiritual people? Is it the destruction of its historic
tradition? No! It is the eruption of a purified youth finding its
roots *[in ihre Wurzeln zurückwachsenden Jugend]*. This youth's will
for the state makes the people strong for itself and respectful of
all true works.

Heidegger answered the attacks against Hitler's Germany in the League
of Nations, its violations of the most elementary human rights, especially
the violence of its anti-semitism,[2] by replacing world fraternity based on
the solidarity of the human race with the relationship of each people with
itself.

Heidegger then treated the question of truth:

What even is this then? The people again find the truth of
their will to be *[Daseinswille]*, for truth is the evidence of what makes
a people safe, luminous, and strong in its actions and knowledge.
From this truth has come the will to know *[Wissenwollen]*. And this
will to know limits claims to knowledge. This is the beginning of
mapping our frontiers, within whose limits an authentic questioning
and research are to be grounded and are to construct its proofs.
It is from this origin that knowledge is born. It is riveted to the

heart of the necessary authenticity of the existence of the Aryan people *[völkisches Dasein]*, responsible for itself. By this fact, knowledge is made subservient to such a necessity, as also is the educating function, which wants to know in order to be able to transmit this knowledge. To know means for us: dominating things with full consciousness and the resolve to act.

We have detached ourselves from the idolatry of thought without roots and power. Finally we see the goals of philosophy put into service. We are sure that harsh clarity and the certainty that asks simple questions that retain the essence of being will return. The original courage of growing or dying when we are faced with being, this is the most profound impulse *[Beweggrund]* of the questioning of knowledge that comes from the authenticity of the [Aryan] people *[das Fragen einer völkischen Wissenschaft]*.

Later Arthur Göpfert, Gauobmann from Saxony, supported the publication of a volume containing all the speeches given during the Leipzig ceremony. The book was to include as introduction the "Appeal to All the Educated Men of the World," a manifesto approved during the ceremony that was to be sent to all foreign universities and governments. The preparations leading to this publication and Heidegger's role in them can be constructed from documents in the archives of the Foreign Office at Bonn,[3] which also contain the text of the "Appeal to All the Educated Men of the World."

Göpfert planned to make this a deluxe edition and raised the money for it by writing all the rectors to ask for financial help. Heidegger immediately composed a letter for all the deans to ask for their contribution and contributions from their faculties. Heidegger's letter of December 13, 1933, took almost verbatim the text of Göpfert's circular and emphasized the interest shown by Goebbels' Ministry of Propaganda in the Leipzig demonstration. "It is to be held in our memories like a historical piece of German science, and its meaning must be placed at the service of foreign politics. The Ministry of Propaganda is happy about the measures taken to exploit it in this way and asks us to hurry." Advising the deans that the text would be in German, English, French, Italian, and Spanish for foreign consumption, he added that it was to be a witness to the *whole* of German science. Heidegger asked that the "Appeal to All the Educated Men of the World" be signed by as many scientists as possible. "So as to avoid the thought that some of the signatures were not genuine, each volume should carry also a facsimile page of original signatures." To cover the costs (approximately 10,000 marks), Heidegger asked for contributions from the universities according to their prestige. At the end of his letter, Heidegger included a sentence from Göpfert's circular: "We certainly need no reminder that no non-Aryan names will appear among the signatures" *(Es bedarf keines besonderen Hinweises, dass Nichtarier auf dem Unterschriftenblatt nicht erscheinen sollen).*

Gerhard Ritter and Walter Eucken brought complaints against Heidegger's action in a letter (December 23, 1933) to Ministerial Director Stieve of the Foreign Office. They stated that Heidegger's letter had brought trouble to "many colleagues, even though it would be an honor for all of us and a joy to give witness before the whole world of our esteem for the new German state, but only if we agreed that this was truly useful for Germany." Ritter and Eucken protested that they were being asked to sign their names to a document they had not yet seen. In particular, they argued against the exclusion of non-Aryan professors, even those protected by law. "If names so well-known throughout the world, as Husserl, or Lenel, the best German romanist, were not on the list from Freiburg, the effort would lose all credibility with the world. This sort of document might well produce just the reverse of the effect desired." They added that they did not know who was behind the effort, whether the Foreign Office was aware of it, and what its judgment might be. "Since the request for signatures has gone ahead rapidly, the question ought to be examined carefully."

Among the documents in the Foreign Office is a letter sent on February 8, 1934, by the Ministry of the Interior to Fischer, Führer of the Association of University Professors and Rector of Wurzburg, asking him for information on the demonstration at Leipzig and the expected publication. The answer, dated February 12, summarizes the facts and includes Göpfert's circular. In the archives of the Ministries of Interior and Propaganda at the Federal Archives in Koblenz, I could find no more correspondence on this matter. In spite of isolated attempts by Ritter and Eucken, we can suppose that the project was not stopped by any official action. The publication appeared, and more than one thousand teachers and German universities subscribed. In spite of his opposition to Heidegger and his membership in dissident circles, which led to his imprisonment in 1944, Ritter was a convinced partisan of Greater Germany. In 1938, he hailed the invasion of Austria and the making of a "great and powerful Germany" as the definite realization of the permanent hope of all Germans.[4]

Heidegger is called to the universities of Berlin and Munich

Documents concerning the process that led to Heidegger's nomination for the chair at Berlin are scarce.[5] Steps to designate a successor for Professor H. Maier began with the meeting on March 16, 1933, of a committee composed of Professors Max Dessoir, Nicolai Hartmann, Eduard Spranger, Alfred Bäumler, Köhler, Vierkandt, von Laue, Eberhardt Schmidt, Werner Jaeger, Oncken, Petersen, Max Planck, Stumpf, and Wechsler. The dean recommended the teacher von Rintelen; Bäumler spoke for Professor Bahrdt at the University of Basilea. Only Professor Paul Hoffmann recommended Heidegger as the sole person worthy of being considered, even though his philosophical method was questionable. According to the available documents, the committee did not recommend Heidegger to the Ministry as Maier's replacement. The aversion of the Berlin professors to Heidegger can be explained by their recollection that in 1930 the Ministry had tried to name Heidegger to a chair in their university, before he took the rectorship at Freiburg. Only Bäumler and Petersen, both members of the SS,[6] could have supported him.

We do not know whether the committee ranked the three candidates, but they said that the deliberations ended with a new ministerial fiat. On September 7, 1933, the Ministry sent the following laconic note to the faculty: "I am informing the faculty that I have named Professor Martin Heidegger (Freiburg) to the chair of philosophy at Berlin for the winter semester. Offering the chair to Heidegger fits well with the workings of university reform and is indispensable for reasons of state." Minister Bernhard Rust and Secretary of State Wilhelm Stuckart signed the letter. Before this was received, the dean had told the committee that the Ministry favored Heidegger.[7] The fact that they designated Heidegger and justified it in such terms gives some idea of the relationship between the philosopher and the Nazi authorities and his prestige during the National Socialist reform of the universities. The fact that in Berlin this reform was being fueled by the students helps us understand the context of the offer. As in 1930, Heidegger refused the appointment. Later we will examine his refusal more fully, but for the moment, we must be aware of problems that arose between Heidegger's notions and the politics of the regime.

Bäumler's archives, kept by his widow, contain an important document written by Bäumler about Heidegger, dated September 22, 1933. (The complete text of the letter, according to Mrs. Bäumler, will be published by Guido Schneeberger.)[8] Given the dates, we can presume that Bäumler wrote the letter at the same time Heidegger was offered the chair at Berlin. Its importance is even greater because Bäumler was a powerful figure in the Science Department of Alfred Rosenberg. It appears that, until then, Heidegger was on good terms with the Science Department. Bäumler wrote:

> Heidegger is the most important German philosopher since Dilthey. In a systematic as well as historical way, Heidegger has revolutionized the questions to be asked in philosophical research. The appearance of his book *Being and Time* has propelled philosophical thought into a new era (in preparation for some time). Every current philosophical work must carry a critique of this book, favorable or not. As for his system, Heidegger's work consists in reexamining and completing what since Dilthey has commonly been called the philosophy of life *[Lebensphilosophie]*. With unequaled subtlety Heidegger has built a radical position that has stripped traditional, formal logic of its power and prestige, at the same time that it replaces it with an ontology that treats subjects at one and the same time as both thinking and acting in the world. . . . The derivation of the notion of ordinary time that is the summit of *Being and Time* is a contribution without equal in the literature.

Departing from the ways other ideologues criticized Heidegger's notion of "care" *(Sorge)*, Bäumler wrote in 1933:

> When he characterized existence as "care," Heidegger influenced present-day philosophy in the most profound way. . . . In my estimation, bringing to light such a phenomenon is the equal of those rare and remarkable discoveries in the history of humanity. . . . As for history, Heidegger's contribution is equally extraordinary. The breadth of his historical vision is unequaled by anyone today. . . . And when Heidegger seems to be working in arbitrary ways in his historical analyses, he does so with the privilege we grant philosophical geniuses.

Unlike the scanty documentation on the Berlin offer, the events that led to offering Heidegger the chair of philosophy at Munich can be reconstructed in detail.[9] This chair had belonged to Professor Richard Hönigswald, who had been dismissed because of his Jewish origins. According to the first of the documents bearing on the matter, Professor Sauter of Vienna had formally inquired of Minister of Bavarian Culture Schemm whether there was a chance he could obtain the chair. In fact, Sauter was among the candidates. He was the protégé of the Benedictine abbot Schachleitner, a Catholic monk who was known for his enthusiastic ties to National Socialism and who was for some time used by the Nazis to promote a militant Nazi Catholicism. Despite his connections, however, Sauter's candidacy was considered only after Heidegger had refused the post.

The ministers' preferences seem to have been clear from the start. On September 20, 1933, Ministerial Counselor Müller told his colleague Fehrle, minister at Karlsruhe, that Schemm wished to propose Heidegger for the chair. Müller asked Fehrle if he objected. According to the letter, Schemm's decision was based on earlier conversations with Heidegger. Heidegger must have already been informed, because in a letter of September 4, 1933, he thanked the civil servant Einhauser for Schemm's proposal:

It was only yesterday evening when I returned after a brief stay in the Black Forest that I found your important news. This morning I received an offer from the Prussian minister of education for the post at Berlin "with a special political mission." I did not commit myself. What I do know is that, when I put personal reasons aside for the moment, I know I ought to decide to work at the task that lets me best serve the work of Adolf Hitler. I will keep you informed.[10]

The file that includes this letter ends with a remark by the minister of employment, who expressed his conviction that Heidegger must go to Munich: "He is willing and the students are in favor of it." In a letter of September 23, after again thanking the ministerial counselor for the offer and observing that he now had more information about other functions he would be responsible for in addition to holding the chair, Heidegger said what he thought of the plan in distinctly political terms:

The situation created by the new university constitution makes the decision of knowing where best to deploy one's forces a very difficult one. It is important for me to know if they simply want me to accept the vacant chair, or if I am to take on the broad responsibility of restructuring the university. With my deepest regards, and Heil Hitler. Yours, Martin Heidegger.

On September 26, while working at his regular duties, Schemm wrote to the expert on racial matters at the Ministry of the Interior at Berlin to inquire about Heidegger's Aryan ancestry. The answer was received in Munich on November 7. "Professor Heidegger, born at Messkirch September 26, 1889, is Aryan. I have examined the records as far back as his great-grandparents and can state that all were Catholic and of Aryan origin. Professor Heidegger is therefore Aryan."[11]

Then, on September 27, the faculty sent their list of candidates to Minister Schemm. They began by saying that after serious considerations that especially took into account the status of the University of Munich and the qualifications of the candidates, the committee had agreed not to propose the name of Heidegger, "even though he is one of the most respected and best-known German philosophers, abroad as well as at home." After alluding to Heidegger's academic career, to the fact that he was part of Husserl's school, and to his personal contribution to those studies (his book *Being and Time*), the faculty added that this book, "which has had great influence among the young, is more a profession of faith in the foundations from which the strong personality of Heidegger philosophizes than a methodically constructed metaphysics that could be discussed. Perhaps it will be able to be discussed, when it is completed, but right now that is impossible. His smaller essays are even more tentative."

As for his work in the history of philosophy, they felt that this area was certainly slighted: "The best specialists do not hesitate to note that the historical aspects are the weakest parts of his writings." In practical philosophy, in spite of what one could say on a first reading, Heidegger had made a contribution, but "in his last rector's speech philosophy tends in practice to disappear like pure consciousness and dissolve into an aporetic of endless questioning. At this time, we are unable to determine if what lies behind that position is a deep skepticism regarding questions of knowledge or a new positivism. This is what we have to say for now; the rest depends on Heidegger's future development. In any case, one ought not to be silent about certain themes of the philosophy of 'care' *[Sorge]*, which, like anguish, could lead to truly paralyzing effects. In his general positions we find a fragile relationship with the state as well as anti-Christian tendencies that cannot be denied. . . . The effects of his philosophy could be more inspiring than educating. Youths could easily be intoxicated by his ecstatic language instead of concentrating on the content of his philosophy, accessible only with difficulty."

The three candidates proposed by the committee were Nicolai Hartmann, Friedrich Brunstäd, and Erich Rothacker. While emphasizing the philosophical merits of Hartmann, the faculty also praised his fight against

Communism, helpful "in national life," as well as the theological training
of Brunstäd. Rothacker they praised as "one of the masters in the area
of the philosophy of German culture."

The records do not give us the names of the committee members, but
by examining the philosophical faculty of Munich, we can discern that
the majority were conservative and Catholic. Besides the dean, Alexander
von Müller (at this time allied with the Institute of Nazi History, directed
by Walter Frank), the faculty included Joseph Geyser, philosopher and
priest (the same one who in 1917 held the chair at Freiburg that Heidegger wanted), Alexander Pfänder (a strict disciple of Husserl), Karl Vossler, Aloys Fischer, Richard Pauli, and Kurt Huber, all Catholics and tied
to Geyser.[12] Later Huber was to become the spiritual mentor of the Catholic resistance movement, the White Rose, directed by Hans and Sophie
Scholl, Catholic students at Munich, who were executed when their activities were discovered. We can suppose that one of Heidegger's rare partisans (we do not know if he was part of the committee) was Kurt Schilling, who went to Prague as professor after the Nazi occupation of
Czechoslovakia and who gave courses on Heidegger as late as 1943. And
certainly he would also have been supported by W. Pinder, who had been
at the demonstration with Heidegger at Leipzig.

In spite of the strong opposition of the faculty, communication between the Ministry and Heidegger continued. In a letter of September
29, 1933, the Ministry let Heidegger know that Schemm needed Heidegger to join him in working to complete university reform and that he
would be pleased if they could meet soon to discuss it. The official request arrived October 1, 1933, and asked him to begin his duties with
the winter semester 1933/34. The Ministry informed the press the same
day. This information included comments alluding to the fact that this
appointment was made in opposition to the will of the faculty: "The faculty was strongly interested in Heidegger, one of the best representatives
of German philosophy abroad. There were also reservations, but they did
not oppose the nomination because the minister had already made the
choice of Heidegger."[13] Heidegger answered the official letter on October 11, 1933: "Just today I was informed of my nomination to the Munich chair. The day before receiving it, I had left for a hike with the students in the mountains."[14] A note of October 20 indicates Heidegger's
visit to the Bavarian minister to determine the conditions of the post.
Thus do we learn that he had refused the offer from Berlin. "Professor
Heidegger is certainly interested in the Munich offer, wanting especially
to take an active part in the National Socialist forces at the university."

It was at this time that, through Professor Lothar Tirala, Schemm learned about some confidential information on Heidegger assembled by the close friend of Krieck's at Marburg, Professor Erich Jaensch. Tirala had been a gynecologist at Brünn until 1933, when he became professor of racial health at Munich. Because of strong criticism about his scientific competency and his professional ethics, he was relieved of his post in July 1934. In 1939 he was also relieved of his post as director of the Institute of Racial Purity. At the Berlin Document Center there is a wealth of information on Tirala, which notes that he was a protégé of Eva Chamberlain-Wagner. Jaensch's denunciation of Heidegger was unusually violent. He called Heidegger "a dangerous schizophrenic," and called his writings incomprehensible, just "psycho-pathological documents." It was essential to denounce once and for all this "German talmudist," so admired by his Jewish followers. It is "typical that the Avocassiero-talmudic thought of Jews is felt to be so close to Heidegger's philosophy. In fact he owes his fame to Jewish propaganda. . . . It is a scandal that Jewish doctors themselves bastardize medicine by using Heidegger's terminology. But in fact the language is in total harmony with the rabbinic way of thinking, which would want to make natural science a kind of Talmudic exegesis. . . . In the bottomless depths of their madness, fools admire each other."[15] In a cover letter attached to this document, which does not give the name of the recipient, Jaensch expressed his formal opposition to Heidegger's nomination to Munich, making it clear that he had also been in contact with Berlin. He added:

> The responsible authorities ought to know that if they appoint such a dangerous schizophrenic as Führer of universities, and if they give him the exercise of decisive influence, then all educated Germany—professors, students, young and retired—ought to be united in opposition to the situation, as would every healthy person who is subjected to a schizophrenic. Heidegger is an opportunist of the worst stamp.

Jaensch sent the letter to Krieck, asking him to use it with great care. However, Schemm at Munich (as well as Rust at Berlin) did not change his ideas about Heidegger. His first wish was to place Heidegger in the chair taken from Hönigswald, as we saw in the official offer noted above. It was only Heidegger's final refusal that brought him to reopen the file and propose the following list: Geissler, Herrigel (Erlangen), Krieck (Frankfurt), Sauter (Vienna), and Schultz (Görlitz).

Heidegger sent his refusal to Schemm on January 15, 1934:

Given that the question of my retaining the rectorate is still unresolved, and that my work in progress would be put in abeyance, I must decide to remain at Freiburg. I keep the strongest hope that there will be a proper successor. . . . Thanking you again for the confidence expressed by your offer, I remain at your disposal. Heil Hitler. Yours, Martin Heidegger.

Attacks from Ernst Krieck and his faction

Jaensch's violent denunciation of Heidegger is in the usual style of the ideological discussions of the Nazi period, but it also marks the beginning of the offensive by Krieck's group against Heidegger. These attacks bore mostly on the "language" of the philosopher, and Heidegger must have been aware of the moves. It is in fact difficult not to see something more than chance in the appearance of an article at this time by his associate J. Harms praising the language of Heidegger as "the language of a German philosophical master."[16] This article was followed by another by R. Deinhardt, with yet more praise.[17] The first article provoked a violent reaction from Krieck. In an article published in 1934 in *Volk im Werden*, Krieck said that Heidegger "could not write in German because he could not think in German."[18] A short while later, he published another article strongly attacking the essential link Hans Naumann saw between Heidegger's thought and German mythological thought. Naumann had in fact written a chapter in his book[19] showing the parallelism between German mythology and essential themes in Heidegger's *Being and Time* and had come to the conclusion that Heideggerian philosophy was the contemporary expression best adapted to convey the spirit that animated the earlier mythology. Opposed to Naumann and calling him irresponsible, Krieck accused Heidegger of opportunism and of wanting to bring the German people into "the saving arms of the Church," of nihilism, and of working secretly for the destruction of the National Socialist movement.[20] I have not been able to verify whether Heidegger and Naumann were friends, but, whatever the case, Naumann's dithyrambs really upset Krieck. In fact, even if in 1938 Naumann would have trouble with Rosenberg's office because of his sympathy with the "Barth case," up to 1934 he had the reputation of being a "hard-liner." As rector of Bonn, Naumann had spoken during the book-burnings,[21] and was one of the most noted German scholars in the area of Nazi Germanistics and ethnology.[22]

Krieck's offensive against Heidegger had a much greater significance.

Krieck, a Swabian like Heidegger, was an old NSDAP member and had been asked by Alfred Rosenberg in 1931 to give talks to the Kampfbund for German Culture *(Kampfbund für Deutsche Kultur)* at Potsdam. Krieck taught in the secondary school system; he had been criticized by Minister Adolf Grimme and forced to quit his Kampfbund activities, which drew from the press strong reactions against Grimme. After joining the Nazi Party in 1932, Krieck had had to give up his civil service job. On May 1, 1933, he was given the chair in pedagogy at Frankfurt, and in July of that year, he took the professorship vacated by Max Scheler. During the summer semester, he took over the rectorate. In 1934, he became the representative *(Obmann)* of the National Socialist science department in the State Association *(Reichsverband)* of German Universities. After a meeting with Hitler in January 1934, Krieck was offered the chair of philosophy and pedagogy that Heinrich Rickert had occupied at Heidelberg. Krieck closely supported the work of Nazi cells in the industrial quarter of Mannheim, as well as the work service that was to transform the university into a "University of the People." In 1934, he was clearly tied to the Röhm group and claimed that the Student Association was a "Socialist University." His strong influence on Wacker, minister of Baden education, his collaborator Fehrle, and their bureaucratic apparatus allowed him to go through the 1934 crisis without serious losses. Beginning that same year, Krieck joined the political police, the SS; in 1938, he became Obersturmbannführer.[23]

One can imagine that at this time some of Heidegger's colleagues in the Rector's Office had difficulties because of his radicalization of the movement and their own ideas of managing the university. Using the available documents, we can trace the relationship of Heidegger and Hans Spemann as it appears in two letters from the philosopher to the academician dated May 5 and September 13, 1933.[24] From what we can find in his writings, Heidegger was trying to minimize the difficulties Spemann had suffered from Nazi students or colleagues. Heidegger even suggested that he might send "immediately a denunciation to the Ministry." He ended with "I sincerely hope that you overcome everything harsh and difficult that these changing times necessarily bring, and that you will keep the strength of your personality as teacher and researcher." Unlike other letters written by Heidegger at this time, the "Heil Hitler" is absent from the closing. Spemann had received a Nobel Prize, yet was not a favorite of the regime. Some years later, his younger son would marry a Jewish scientist from Budapest, and they would leave for the United States.

13 The city and the country: the return to the fatherland as a political theme

It was at this time that three texts of Martin Heidegger's appeared that indicate important changes in his acceptance of National Socialism. First was the letter to the *Freiburger Zeitung* of January 6, 1934, and then an article in the *Freiburger Studentenzeitung*, January 23, and another article titled "Why We Choose to Remain in the Province." These were prepared and published before Heidegger had decided to refuse the offers from Berlin and Munich, and in them we find his strong accent on the patriotic choices offered him by National Socialism. In the letter to the Freiburg newspaper on its one-hundred-fiftieth anniversary, entitled "Preface for the University,"[1] Heidegger said that "the more the individual states become directly a part of the National Socialist state, the more we ought to waken and protect, without fail, the popular, the autochthonic ways *(Volkstum)* of the regions. Only in this way will all the people be able to develop the diversity of forces that together can create the state." The article in the *Studentenzeitung* is even more clear:

> Here at the frontier of the southwest, how far does the political will of the Germans extend? Are we as lofty, are we on the same level, as those in the northeast? Are we directing our creative forces to that end *[Geschehen]*? Or along with the rest of the West ought we to sink slowly with the setting sun?
> Here is the decision we must take to enable us to engage the

political needs of the future, those suitable for the people of our land.

This question arises as we work to succeed in training the untamed forces of the Germanic soul, in tearing it away from all middle-class vestiges and from its careless indifference toward the state, so as to give it the will to rejoin all the others under the will of the National Socialist state.[2]

What is new is that, without abandoning his National Socialist ideals, Heidegger is able to treat Germany's situation as a play of forces, like an arena in which the "nationalities" ("the individual states") are engaged, all equal, in competing to build the central state together. He picks up the traditional "south" German ideology according to which the south is the source and the driving force of the nation's culture. He wants to concentrate and focus local forces as a counter-balance to "the will of Germans to displace the political center toward the northeast," that is, toward Berlin. That Heidegger speaks in this way, that he reactivates north-south differences, proves that he has changed his understanding of the immediate political crisis. But if the first two writings pose the question of north and south, the third one, "Why We Choose to Remain in the Province," is even more radical and explicit, concentrating on the opposition between "city" and "country."

Heidegger tried to focus these words as the fulcrum for the political debates of the time, since he wrote them to be broadcast on the radio, to be brought to the consciousness of the greatest number of people, thanks to a means of communication that then had a prestige it has since lost. Listening to the actual voice of the Führer was an event, as when Heidegger and his students came together in the stadium for the live broadcast of the Reichstag speech. Even the German word for transmitter (*Sender, Sendung* = dispatch) carries this meaning. The Freiburg National Socialist newspaper, *Der Alemanne,* gave quite a bit of space to the broadcast. On March 7, 1934, the paper asked its readers to listen to it.[3] The broadcast was important, and the transmitter was hooked up to a series of radios to send it to all of southern Germany.[4] Heidegger's access to these broadcasting facilities confirms the philosopher's fame and influence throughout the region.

It was not, however, a simple provincialism that lay behind these formulations but rather the consciousness that certain contradictions were developing among the various factions of the movement. One indication of the changes brewing was the choice of Ernst Krieck and others like him for important functions. The return to the province that Heidegger chose looks very like a strategic retreat when we consider the coming troubles he must have known were heating up. When we consider the general crisis that three months later would eliminate Röhm's faction as well as the political "apparatus" Heidegger had been able to count on at the national level, we may assume that the submerged political ferment was felt even at Freiburg.

The text of Heidegger's speech is usually handled as literature or as cultural criticism. We are faced with bucolic prose that derives from a reactionary and irrational provincialism.[5] But in the description and analysis of the world around him, Heidegger reduces and destroys all the elements of a bucolic world. He first evokes the environment (as a visitor or sightseer might find it) and then he evokes a sense of "work." The first part is a pure and simple panorama of nature, which for Heidegger is just a moment in his universe of work, in fact the result of this very "work." Beneath the natural and daily world, there is the act of work, which makes this a "universe of work." It is only by understanding this connection that we can go beyond the apparently bucolic world and see the close continuity of the text with the other things he was publishing at the time. The chalet (Todtnauberg) became a place of *retreat* (in the traditional sense); in the same way this text is nothing less than a break in the spiritual élan that was carrying Heidegger forward before he resigned from the rectorship. The chalet had been and still remained his own "place of work," but also of course the place where he often held meetings on political indoctrination, a kind of secularized temple that some called "Freiburger National Socialism." Students would come like pilgrims to Todtnauberg, and teachers and professors also came to reflect at the source as a way of coordinating their efforts. Heidegger's thought started with perspectives uniting science and philosophy, student action in the service of work, the party as the National Socialist Party of workers, the state as the state of the German people, and the latter as the people of work. The very simplicity of the chalet with its asceticism recalls the monastery. This emphasis on "work" is precisely characteristic of the populist nature of Nazism. But at the same time that he affirms or suggests this general option, Heidegger's text reveals a change of emphasis. At the beginning of his rectorate, in the speech in honor of Schlageter, Heidegger had called for an understanding of nature as the fatherland of a hero creating a political plan for a new state; but now, without abandoning his penchant for that state and his own plans, he comes back to what he believed was the productive basis of the authentic National Socialist state and of true political action: one's local land and the work that makes it what it is. This is why his thought does not shift here as it did in May 1933 from the fatherland (Black Forest) to the hero (Schlageter), but turns instead from the daily pace of professional and political life to its transcendental origin. Heidegger wants to describe his work as comparable to the peasant's work:

> Philosophical work does not develop over time without revealing a pattern. It has its place right alongside the work of peasants. When the young peasant starts toward his farm, down the perilous slope with his sledge loaded with heavy beech logs, without slowing down, when the shepherd with slow and dreamy step urges his sheep to the uplands, when the peasant in his shed prepares the endless shingles for his roof, then do they and I work *in the same way*. The immediate connection with the peasant world finds here its roots.

By indicating the value of peasant work, Heidegger is using certain notions all Nazis shared and which were part of the plan:

> We cannot speak too strongly of the need to keep the peasant class healthy as the foundation of the whole nation. Many of our present ills are simply the result of a falsified relationship between urban and rural life. A solid group of peasants, both smallholders and comfortable ones, has always been the best safeguard against the social difficulties we know today. It is also the only way to ensure that the country will have the bread it needs in a closed economy. Commerce and industry then lose their dominant and unhealthy position and are united with the general national economy, where needs are made equal.[6]

But we also need to see what was original in Heidegger's contribution to these ideas. He spoke against another concern: the Germans' desire to shift the political center to the northeast. And since this displacement brought power to the large cities (especially Berlin), Heidegger fought to prove that spiritual and political impetus was not simply in the provinces but was actually found in the countryside. Heidegger tried to support the revolutionary movement in the local fatherlands as a way of opposing the bureaucratization of the states, which was moving steadily forward under the direction of the institutional faction. His criticism of the urban world, while finding value in the peasant world, encompassed a precise political plan:

The city dweller thinks that he's "part of the people" when he
deigns to spend an evening talking with peasants. When I sit with
peasants in the evening for a moment of rest, next to the fire, *most
of the time we do not talk at all.* We smoke our pipes in *silence.* Now
and then there's a remark about cutting timber, or that last night
the marten got into the henhouse, or that probably tomorrow the
cow will drop a calf. . . . The close connection of my work with
the Black Forest and those who live there comes from secular
roots in the land of Swabians and Alemanni, and nothing
can replace this.

The city dweller is at most "stimulated" by what he usually calls
a day in the country. For me, however, all my work is guided and
supported by the world of mountains and the peasants living there.
At the present time my work there is interrupted for rather long
periods because of negotiations, traveling to give talks, discussions,
and even my teaching down here. But as soon as I go back up
there, during the first hours at the chalet, the whole universe of
ancient questions invades me, and they even retain the same shape
as when I left them. . . .

City people are often puzzled by my long, monotonous
isolation in the mountains among peasants. It is not, however, an
isolation, but a *solitude.* In large cities a man can easily be more
isolated than anywhere else. But there he can never be alone. We
know that solitude has the absolutely original power not to *isolate*
us, but rather to *throw* all of existence into the spacious proximity
of the essence of all things *[des Wesens aller Dinge].*

Down here, we can become a celebrity by sleight of hand, by
the power of the press. It is even the surest road to let our
best will be *misinterpreted* and to drop radically and quickly into
oblivion.

Peasant remembrance, on the contrary, gives witness to simple
fidelity, proven and unflinching. Lately an old peasant woman
up there reached the time of her death. She would talk often and
readily with me, and on these occasions, she would tell old stories
about the village. She kept in her powerful and vivid peasant
language many old words and proverbs that had dropped from
the living language and that the youth of the village could no
longer understand. Still last year, when I was living alone in the
chalet this *eighty-three*-year-old peasant woman several times
climbed the rather steep slope to come see me. She would say that
she wanted to make sure I was still there and that "some people"

had not come by unexpectedly to rob me. She spent the night
of her death talking with family members. Then again, about a
half-hour before her death, she told them to greet "the Professor."
Such a remembrance is incomparably more valuable than the most
able reporting in a world-famous journal on my supposed
philosophy.

It is in this way that Heidegger's discourse brings us to the critical
moment when he must answer the University of Berlin, accepting or rejecting their offer. Studying the process that led to the nomination shows
that, as in 1930, the offer was based on a ministerial mandate that was
clearly in opposition to the preferences of the faculty. One basic reason
for Heidegger's refusal was his unwillingness to accept a professorship
that had not followed the usual university process, an act that could stain
his reputation. Heidegger could explain the refusal of the Berlin faculty
to accept him because it was a conservative world, traditionalist and reactionary, one he had to surpass. But this would not let him forget the
clear opposition to his person, an opposition that was being pointedly
repeated. Rust's proposal included the mission to accomplish some "special political work," thanks to the absolute support of the Ministry. Berlin
could certainly open a chair for Heidegger, letting him then appear to
be *the* philosopher of the Third Reich. The Ministry said that its nomination was made for "state reasons." In other circumstances and at another time, this could have led Heidegger to make a break. But faced
with the swift events that were moving toward consolidation of the bureaucracy, and because of the dominant conservative forces in education,
the change seemed risky, even though Heidegger could have counted on
the strong support of the Berlin students, who were controlled by the SA
faction. Faced with signs of the impending storm, it was reasonable and
prudent to stay safe in his own place. Although the process leading to
the Berlin offer was taking place at the same time as the Munich offer,
Heidegger mentioned in his speech only his rejection of the Berlin offer.
The final exhortation does not lack a certain charm:

Lately I received *a second offer from the University of Berlin.* When
something like this occurs, I leave the town to return to my chalet.
I listen to what the mountains and forests say. This is how I
happened to visit an old friend, a peasant seventy-five years old.
He read about the Berlin affair in the newspaper. What is he
going to say? He looks deeply into my eyes with his clear eyes,

keeping his mouth tightly closed, puts his loyal hand on my shoulder and almost imperceptibly *shakes* his head. This means *absolutely No.*[7]

The official organ of the National Socialist Party, *Völkischer Beobachter,* thought it necessary to explain Heidegger's refusal in these terms: "We have it from a trusted source that the reason is to be found simply in the philosopher's decision to remain at Freiburg."[8] The *Deutsche Studentenzeitung* of Munich told its readers much the same thing.[9]

14 The end of the rectorate

Although Heidegger decided to remain at Freiburg, he stayed nonetheless busy, and even so had little effect on the course of events. The opposing nationalist faction regrouped to become a homogeneous front, which, in spite of internal dissension, led the final fight against the populist sector to upset an already unstable equilibrium of forces. Some weeks after the violent purge of June and July 1934, Oskar Stäbel, the student Reichsführer, and his whole group were relieved of their functions. The student movement then came under the control of Rudolf Hess, Röhm's greatest enemy. But before these events, we find the same contradictions at Freiburg that would break out at the national level.

After some persuasion, the associations of Catholic students, especially those who dueled, joined the "national revolution" in January 1934. To make this move effective, these associations eliminated their rules about religious practice. Forschbach and Hank, Führers of the major Catholic groups, signed an accord with Stäbel that brought all the other small Catholic student groups into line,[1] an important tactical move. By getting rid of the religious-practice rule, the Catholic groups could then join the youth movement run by the party and the state and avoid being eliminated. Stäbel accepted the move because his policy was violently anticlerical, and he had always wanted to suppress the religious groups.

The first assault was the temporary suspension of the Catholic club Ripuaria and its Freiburg branch. The suspension was carried out by order of Dr. Forschbach, Führer of the Catholic groups, who had an understanding with the most extreme sectors of the Nazi student movement.[2] The suspension took place the first week of February 1934 but was countermanded by Stäbel, who allowed Ripuaria to pursue its activities after dropping the religious rule.[3] This action alienated the entire extremist faction at Freiburg, whose student Führer, Heinrich von zur Mühlen, had accepted the suspension heartily. These events were felt by the rector because von zur Mühlen had been one of the principal supporters of Heidegger's political actions. Von zur Mühlen and Mayor Kerber had joined Heidegger in sending Hitler the telegram promising the unconditional support of the town, teachers, and students.[4] Heidegger had also supported von zur Mühlen in organizing the National Schlageter Brotherhood.[5] And in November 1933, Heidegger had pressured Stäbel to replace A. Künzel, a former SS member, with von zur Mühlen.[6]

Thus, Stäbel's action was a harsh blow to Heidegger because he too had been among his unconditional comrades. Moreover, such orders came certainly not from the Reichsführer, but from much higher. Finally, this was a breach of the concordat between the Vatican and the Hitler regime that, since it effectively neutralized the Catholic Church, guaranteed Germany non-interference during a period of serious instability. Since the radical anti-clericalism of the SA faction threatened the stability of the state, and not only its relations with the Roman Church, as we will see later, Stäbel's actions were certainly imposed from above, since they went against his personal convictions. Heidegger wrote asking him to revoke the permission for Ripuaria to continue its activities in the Reich and especially in Freiburg:

Freiburg, February 6, 1934.
The Rector of the Alberts-Ludwig University to the Reichsführer of German students.
Dear Mr. Stäbel,
I have been informed today by the press that the suspension of the Catholic group Ripuaria has been canceled. This action has forced Mr. von zur Mühlen, local student Führer, to resign. We must in no way allow this clear Catholic victory to continue, especially in this region. *A greater damage to the work already done could not be imagined.*
For several years, I have been aware of the local situation and the forces at work here in their smallest details. I am aware that I did not act after your telephone call and your letter requesting this suspension, but, *on the other hand, I had reason to believe that you wanted the suspension.* This is why I vouch *unconditionally [unbedingt]* for the actions of the student Führer. I beg you in this instance to reinstate von zur Mühlen.
There are different ways of analyzing the elimination of the

religious rule. This is because we *misconstrue* the tactics of the Catholic Church. Some day this error will be costly for us. Heil Hitler! Yours, Heidegger.[7]

Heidegger's anger is even more understandable when we consider that some weeks earlier he had been part of a demonstration in favor of the suspension of all Catholic student groups, where all the active leaders called for such action. The leader of the Catholic groups said:

> The old ideal of all the groups is now finally a reality. All students ought to be together in service and with the SA. The time for battles in the streets and individual action is gone. And in addition, since the groups and the corporations do not in fact act this way, it is correct to ask if they have the right to exist.[8]

The *Freiburger Zeitung* of January 29, 1934, wrote about this meeting:

> After singing the Song of the Germans and the Horst Wessel song, the rector of the University of Freiburg, Professor Heidegger, spoke. He indicated that we could not engage in political action in the absolute but that it was grasped only in some immediate actual moment. The meaning of the word "engaged" *[Einsatz]* comes from this perception. This is why our universities must bring political work into the educational process. The spiritual and political combat at this southeastern rim of the Reich can be led in the right direction when the youth movement *[Jungmannschaft]* understands that it is our duty to plant the living will of the state in the national traditions *[Volkstum]* of our Alemannic province.[9]

Heidegger's virulent anti-Catholicism may surprise us at first. The feeling probably owes something to his early childhood experiences, possibly the persecution of his family at Messkirch during the religious struggles when he became a victim because of his father's professional connection with the Church.

But there are also other reasons for this aversion. Heidegger devoted all his intellectual energy and human resources to helping the Nazi revolution succeed by developing positions that were based on his most original ideas (the way, for instance, he made the people sacred), and thus the Church's ambiguous opposition, its diplomatic tactics, but especially its "revisionism," made it his mortal enemy. If Heidegger's fight to bring the universities within the terms of the party line by using a student base had come into conflict with general student indifference, the problem posed by the Catholic students was certainly more complex. Wolfgang Kreutzberger indicates in his book that 44 percent of Freiburg University students were Catholic, a significantly larger percentage than at other universities.[10] In addition, they belonged for the most part to groups organized under religious auspices. Kreutzberger also notes that 70 percent of the Catholic students participated in organizations,[11] and that, in spite of their anti-liberal and anti-republican ideas and their extreme nationalism and general indifference to the political situation, they would not become active in a movement that was increasingly anti-clerical.[12] Nevertheless, and as proof of Heidegger's radicalism, there was no attempt during the years 1933–1934 to block the Church in the student world. In Freiburg, as throughout the Reich, most saw the concordat as a call for more collaboration because it gave legitimacy to Hitler's government. Many Catholic theologians as well thought that nationalism would restore the "idea of the Reich" as basically Catholic in its origin and would therefore offer the Church the chance to become influential "from within."[13] The general Catholic student body in these early years was clearly favorable to National Socialism. The articles published in the Catholic student review *Academia* speak openly on the subject. There were articles on Schlageter, one written by an SS officer[14] called "Essence and Tasks of the SA and the SS," another on "Catholic Groups Add the Führer Principle to Their Constitutions,"[15] and a series of strongly anti-semitic articles.[16]

At Freiburg, because of his relationship to Heidegger, we must consider the role of Archbishop Conrad Gröber, as well as Engelbert Krebs, a radically conservative priest. Krebs had been a spiritual advisor of Heidegger's during his first years at Freiburg, and it was he who had celebrated his marriage in 1917 and also tried to get Heidegger the chair of theology. During World War I, as we saw above, Krebs was strongly pro-German. When Hitler took power, Krebs saw him as a gift of Providence and called for active collaboration from the students.[17] Yet at the same time Krebs held intransigent positions that brought him under secret police surveillance. In his text *The Original Church and Judaism (Urkirche und Judentum),*[18] he criticized anti-semitism harshly, as much in its "racist" forms as in its religious and "spiritualist" forms. Krebs's papers kept in the Berlin Document Center tell us that he was watched by the Gestapo very early and was forbidden to speak in public.

To complete the group, we must briefly examine Oskar Stäbel, student Reichsführer. Like Heidegger, he was from the south, a man the rector

trusted. One senses this in the letter Heidegger wrote him about the Ripuaria conflict. We have spoken also of their plan to name von zur Mühlen
as the Freiburg student Führer. In the SA, Stäbel was a close friend of
Röhm's in the SA, whom Röhm named Reichsführer and covered with
decorations. Röhm sent him at Christmas 1933 the "dagger of honor,"
engraved on one side with "Everything for Germany" and on the other,
"As sign of our warm friendship. Ernst Röhm."[19] When the SA were
given the charge of indoctrination in the universities, Stäbel and Röhm
were the principals.[20] After Röhm's assassination, Stäbel showed his usual
opportunism by sending Hitler proof of his faithfulness, trying to save
himself, and added a plan to "depoliticize" the universities as the new
powers understood that term.[21] During the period we are examining,
Stäbel's political activities were exactly the same as Röhm's. Otto Strasser,
the brother of Gregor Strasser, was one of the high officials assassinated
in 1934 and, like his brother, was one of the important ideologues of the
"socialist" faction. In his memoirs Otto Strasser wrote about Stäbel and
the destruction of the student movement:

> After the SA came the students' turn. Dr. Stäbel and the engineer
> Zähringen were hated by the reactionaries. It was they who had
> held to the adage "The enemy is to the right!" Both were turned
> out. Stäbel was put in prison and replaced by Andreas Feickert, a
> weak, docile, and insignificant man who at once ended the fight
> against the reactionary student groups.[22]

If we are to understand the nature of the political environment from
which Heidegger was to resign, we ought first to describe what was happening before the SA crisis and then explain the SA's indoctrination in
the universities and finally the brutal break that led to their fall. The SA
first appeared as the "shock troops" of the NSDAP. Tactically, Hitler
thought of them as a sort of army of the party before any civil war, and
strategically as a new social element. They were an instrument of power,
combining military and police functions within a modern state and per-
formed "jobs" of psychological and physical intimidation.[23] Even though
from the beginning the Nazi Party tried to make an absolute separation
between politics and the military, and therefore between the party and
the militarized activists (SA), it was the SA that in fact was most active,
chiefly in the small towns of the provinces.[24] The SA clearly adopted the
violent and brutal style of what they thought was "proletarian."[25] The
name SA (Assault Section) was given them after the first street fight in

Munich on November 4, 1921, and from that time on, they developed the most refined terrorist tactics.[26]

Röhm's importance was decisive when the NSDAP was founded. As a military man, Röhm used his personal influence and his access to arms depots to build an armed infrastructural support for the new organization. From this time on, Röhm dreamed of a populist and military variant of Nazism ("German socialism") in which he and his men (SA-Männer) would play decisive roles. The French occupation of the Ruhr allowed him to retaliate on the French from "bases" coordinated by the SA. Although they often worked together, Hitler never accepted the SA as his only bodyguards. From the beginning he had a personal guard commanded by Himmler, which developed into the SS.[27] After the failure of the attempted coup d'état of November 8, 1923, when Hitler spent time in prison, he tried to give the party more of a civilian quality, an action with which Röhm disagreed, but one that increased the role of the SS in the party. The SA acquired another role in 1926 that was due to the increase of social conflict and hence to street riots.[28] Next, the SA became the "political educators" as well as the "physical trainers." The educational and indoctrination programs set up next in the universities were improvised, rather elementary, and heavy, dull, and repetitive.[29] The SA were also responsible for discipline within the party.[30]

For a long time Ernst Röhm was the "second man" inside the NSDAP, and he owed some of his power to the fact that until the day of his assassination there were 170,000 men under his direct orders, men who controlled a mass of about 4 million, some in batallions within different organizations that would later become professional army forces.[31] This element, along with the political, economic, and cultural programs that foresaw reforms that threatened to destabilize social life, formed an alliance of extremely diverse sectors and tendencies. This broad alliance pressured Hitler and even threatened a coup d'état.

We know this alliance was dominated by large capital. This development brought to power what Röhm called "the reaction," which then gave hegemony to the controlling groups of the Nazi Party: Herman Göring, Fritz Thyssen, and later Joseph Goebbels. All this opened a road that, after Germany's shift to a war economy in 1936, would bring about World War II in 1939. Historical research has shown that the populist tendencies of the NSDAP were hardly socialist and that the most important leaders kept in close touch with the great capitalists. Ch. Bloch and others have explained that, after Otto Strasser left the NSDAP in 1930, there was no longer any Nazi "left faction." The enormous influence of large capital, especially from Thyssen, an active member of the party from 1931, who gave direct financial help to Gregor Strasser's SA, proves clearly that a leftist National Socialism was only a notion, having no reality.[32]

But this violent elimination of populist tendencies also marked a period of qualitative changes, above all concerning the ideological definition of Nazism. When Hitler and the party took over the government, some thought this meant that they had only to consolidate matters; but, for the "revolutionary" faction, things were quite different. In June 1933, Röhm wrote:

> There has been a great victory, but not *the* true victory. In the new Germany, gray and disciplined batallions of the revolution are forming, side by side with the armed forces. They are alongside, but not part of them. . . . The Führer and chancellor has need of them as a powerful tool able to bring about the great work of renovation in Germany. The SA and SS are the essential pillars of National Socialism of the future. . . . Some bourgeois critics contest this, whether as allies of our clearest enemy or even as members of the movement who carry the swastika banner but who will never grasp the meaning of the German revolution. They think national recovery is the German revolution. . . . To those sitting in the easy chairs of the administration we say that the goal is still distant, not yet gained. . . . Now is the end of the national revolution and also the beginning of the National Socialist revolution.[33]

With their control of the indoctrination process, the SA held the decisive role until 1933. In their national program, they set themselves the goal of "breaking the universities' chains" by imposing wide obligatory programs of ideological action, which included courses in political education and also times when students and teachers were given physical training in military and sports activities.[34] Without these courses, students were forbidden to take their exams. The data U. D. Adam has collected describing the situation at Tübingen gives us an idea of what was happening at all the universities. For the summer semester of 1934, the SA program included a general course once a week, firing practice and political education once a month. There were also weekly meetings—Thursday afternoons and evenings and Saturday afternoons. Then there were required weeks of training (May 15–27), and four Sundays as well.[35] The demands were sufficiently heavy to force serious changes in studies and to draw complaints from students who tried to avoid the SA courses. Things became strained and the Ministry of Education at Berlin was upset.[36] Teachers and professors added their voices of protest, triggering student demonstrations that forced a reduction of the time demanded by the SA.[37] It was only in July 1934, with Röhm's assassination and the complete revision of the SA, that the crisis in the universities ended. The first ministerial measure was in fact to exempt all degree candidates from SA and SS service. By the end of 1935, SA service was a minor concern in the universities.[38]

The revision of the political line and the institutions of the party were officially announced to the Conference of the Reich at Nurenberg in November 1934. During the Conference, the students had an unusual meeting where Minister Bernhard Rust and Hitler's representative Rudolf Hess, who had control of the student organization, explained to the students the changes made. Hess's speech is explicit and announces political choices radically opposed to those Heidegger had defended. That Hess spoke on that occasion had clear political implications: he was one of the great adversaries of the SA and an outspoken enemy of Röhm.[39]

Hess began by stating that he was speaking officially, in the name of the state and the party. Trying to make them believe that he was in a position to understand the students' feelings, Hess recalled in a patronizing way his student years at Munich, his early contacts with Hitler, and the struggles of the time. And while emphasizing how valuable the intense work with the movement was for him, he had to say that "with passing time, this activity was not very helpful for my own studies":

> I tell you this because I know that you and the young men you instruct—particularly after the coup—have had to live painfully with the rather mixed situation of wanting and having to study while thinking of your future and also of party work, especially SA demands. Students have accomplished these tasks, perhaps by stretching their efforts beyond what they thought was needed. . . . I know that during this first period great things have been done. I know also that frequently we have asked students to contribute a lot of time that has really hurt their serious studies. And I know that once in a while we all sin: the political organizations calling for this or that demonstration, the SA insisting again and again on elementary exercises, the student organizations that have bored students with their speeches and evenings of supposed political education, offering damned little education. . . . But don't be someone who holds old grudges. Take heart by telling yourselves that all that was in the past, and especially tell that to those students for whom you are responsible.

From now on, we will make things clear: students will find out what is truly valuable in political education and will have the time to develop their minds in new ways. Time to learn to think, which is not as easy as you suppose, time to work with your head and dig to find solutions. . . . If you have in the past cursed institutions that have been stealing your time, in the future you won't even remember it.[40]

The shift was radical and total, and the political force driving it was exactly what Heidegger considered the greatest danger, what he had railed against in the Heidelberg speech as treason toward the state and had even seen as "resisting" the "revolution." For Heidegger, who was in total accord with Röhm—who agreed that Röhm's becoming involved in the bureaucratic state and helping it to function was in fact just the first step in the complete transformation of German life, who agreed that the university provided the political and social setting for the new revolution to come—this tactical shift meant a strategic abandonment. Georg Picht, a contemporary and friend of Heidegger's, reports that the philosopher's students "embodied the notion that the true revolution was to begin in the university and that the present time (1933–1934) was just a prelude."[41] The shift adopted by the political administration brutally interrupted this prelude. Heidegger expressed his ideas: "As for me, at the beginning of 1934, the meaning of my resignation was clear. It became absolutely clear after June 30 of the same year. Anyone who accepted the post of leading the university after that date would know who his confreres were."[42] June 30, 1934, was the date when they finally succeeded in eliminating Röhm and the SA administration by claiming that they were preparing a coup d'état.

The facts leading to Heidegger's resignation from the rectorate have been well detailed by Hugo Ott in the second part of his work, although he makes no reference to the general political and ideological situation, nor offers any explanation of the Ripuaria crisis. This serious confrontation with the central authorities of the party was exactly comparable with the general national situation. Ott contradicts the version of the facts given by Heidegger in 1945 about "those who conspired against everything that was National Socialism" and especially about the so-called conspiracy tied to the authorities at Karlsruhe. Ott believes that the trigger was Heidegger's struggle with the Law School faculty. We can deduce the actual political situation from Ott's facts: the Law School was run by Erik Wolf, who was close to Heidegger, but within the school were opponents like Walter Eucken, von Bieberstein, and von Schwerin who played important roles and who had brought into question the legal basis that Heidegger used to institute paramilitary exercises during the summer semester of 1934. In other words, it was a fight over the legal status of the SA in the university. Before this conflict, there had been another one. On December 7, 1933, Erik Wolf had offered his resignation as dean to Heidegger following complaints from his faculty. Based on the Führer principle, Heidegger refused the resignation, because in the new university constitution, Wolf's post depended, not on the will of the faculty, but on the decision of the rector. Heidegger gave Wolf his complete support. In his letter to the other deans, he used the same arguments, noting that university reform went beyond administrative arguments and was devoted to essentials.[43]

Complaints continued from Wolf's colleagues until Minister Wacker suggested to Heidegger on April 12, 1934, that it would be best to name another dean at the end of the summer semester. Heidegger said that, at the end of the winter semester 1933/34, he was called to Karlsruhe, where Fehrle asked him to request Wolf's resignation as well as the resignation of von Möllendorf, dean of medicine. Heidegger claimed that he had opposed the request formally, and had offered his own resignation. The document Ott found in the archives of Karlsruhe indicates Heidegger's faulty memory. The letter from Heidegger is dated from the time when, according to Heidegger, the situation had been nullified by his own resignation. The letter suggests also the possibility of a change of dean for the law faculty after the end of the next semester. But the official letter from the Ministry also informs us that the provincial authority *counted* on Heidegger to keep his post and to accomplish the change in question.

Heidegger immediately told his close associates (the chancellor and the five deans) about his resignation at a meeting on April 23, 1934. Before this, there had been a problem concerning Adolf Lampe, the economist, who was a possible replacement for Karl Diehl. Heidegger and Wolf were violently opposed to him. This is the context in which Heidegger sent his last official letter to the ministry of Baden, April 23, 1934.[44] We note also that Adolf Lampe was among Heidegger's most determined adversaries. With Gerhard Ritter and other professors at Freiburg, Lampe was part of the tribunal after the war that examined the charges by which Heidegger was suspended from the University of Freiburg.

Ott has also shown that Heidegger's claims that the National Socialist newspaper of Baden, *Der Alemanne,* had praised the naming of Professor Kern to the rectorate as the "first National Socialist rector of the University of Freiburg" are false.[45] The issue of the newspaper of April 30, 1934, limited itself to acknowledging the ministerial decision under the title "Change of Rectors at the University"; in the ministerial text, Heidegger was thanked for his work.[46]

It seems that the decision to resign was Heidegger's. Yet, if we can speak of an intrigue opened by the Ministry and the conservative forces at the university, we can then note that their actions encouraged the move. A populist National Socialist to the bitter end, a "revolutionary," a rebel against any compromise with the need to respect the rhythm of political development by "stages," Heidegger was a danger as much for the Nazi political leadership as for the conservatives. The conservatives saw him as a threat to the university structure in which their functions were fairly secure. For the political leadership he was a danger because his revolutionary moves threw into question all the alliances and plans still necessary, at a time the fundamental question to be faced was one of how to consolidate power. The pact of the "old" with the "new" was denounced in Heidegger's text of 1945[47] because of what Heidegger took to be untenable political reasons, which were thus not compatible with his own radical ideas of National Socialism. Thus, there were several different reasons for getting rid of Heidegger, and Heidegger's relations with the two camps were different. While the open hostility of the conservatives never ceased, Heidegger's links with the party and the party leadership, and even with his own associates, were of an entirely different sort. By his resignation, Heidegger made it possible for the University of Freiburg to return to "normal." This is precisely what, from the conservative point of view, Professor Constantin von Dietze said, recalling the situation at that time: "At the University of Freiburg, a certain calm returned after Heidegger's departure."[48]

III

After the rectorate:
from 1934 to the
posthumously published
interview

15 The Academy and the professors of the Reich

The declaration of August 1934

Martin Heidegger ascribed his failed attempt to revolutionize the University of Freiburg to the political leadership of the university because he found its decision to be false to what he held to be "the inner truth and the grandeur of National Socialism." This failure did not make him alter his allegiance to the Nazi "idea" and the broad politics and strategies of the regime, as his active membership until 1945 proves. His positions after the "break," after his resignation from the rectorate, were meant to show this too. We must construe his attitude toward Hitler and the Nazi movement in the same spirit, for Heidegger always acknowledged these to be the guiding powers of German society.

At the death of Field Marshal and President Paul von Hindenburg, ·Hitler decided to combine the functions of chancellor and president of the Reich and called for a plebiscite to confirm this decision on August 19, 1934. Because of the political importance of the measure, there was a general mobilization of all the forces tied to Nazism, including of course those of the scientific and cultural world. The *Völkischer Beobachter,* as well as the most important German newspapers, carried a declaration signed by eminent people in culture and science. The declaration, which included Heidegger's signature, consisted of the following text:

> On August 19, the German people are once again called on to make a weighty decision for the future. The decision of the government to bring together in the person of Hitler the

functions of both chancellor and president of the Reich has brought an end to the anguish of many Germans lately as they held vigil over the now dead field marshal and president of the Reich. We the signatories, representatives of German science, and many whom we have contacted who work in the world of science, firmly believe that under his leadership science will receive the support it needs to fulfill the high mission incumbent on it for the reconstruction of the nation.

The importance of the issue, both abroad and for interior politics, demands that the German people once again give proof of a unity and spirit of decision in their search for freedom and honor by professing their faith in Adolf Hitler. The signatories, representatives of German science, answer the call given to the German people by the government of the Reich so that the decision can be made on August 19.[1]

Signing this document were Professors Nicolai Hartmann, Eugen Fischer (Berlin), Erich Jaensch (Marburg), Carl Schmitt (Berlin), W. Sombart (Berlin), Trendelenburg (Berlin), Karl Haushofer (Munich), Krüger (Greifswald), Martius (Göttingen), K. A. von Müller (Munich), Petersen (Berlin), Panzer (Heidelberg), and others. Taking on the functions of both posts, chief of government and chief of state, gave Hitler consider-able scope: with Hindenburg dead, there was no longer any authority able to offer "national" guarantees (even though such guarantees were only theoretical), leaving the way open to extreme totalitariansim. More-over, the situation allowed Hitler to compel the armed forces to swear their fidelity to him. In this way, his power was consolidated. Finally, the disappearance of national guarantees served as the juridical basis for Hit-ler's racial laws *(Nürnburger Gesetze)*, which in 1935 stripped Jews of all their rights as citizens.

Heidegger and the Academy of Professors of the Reich

In a text of 1945, Heidegger claimed that persons accepting official posts in the universities after June 30, 1934, knew the people they were joining.[2] This claim can be turned against him because later he be-came part of far-reaching projects of the Ministry of Education at Berlin, and he even tried to become director of the project that was to organize the Academy of Professors of the German Reich *(Dozentenakademie des Deutschen Reiches)*.

In their study *The Third Reich and Its Thinkers*[3] Josef Wulf and Léon Poliakov published a letter from Dr. Gross, chief of the Association of German Physicians and of the Department of Racial Purity of the NSDAP, to Thilo von Trotha, chief of the party's Department of Exterior Relations. We find in the letter a reference to Heidegger as a serious candidate for the presidency of the Academy, with mention of the dangers this could bring, at least for the political line of Krieck and Jaensch. Gross asked Thilo von Trotha to inform Rosenberg immediately. Wulf and Poliakov do not give the date of this letter, which makes it difficult to put it into context. I was able to find the original letter, which was written February 26, 1934, in the archives of the Center for Contemporary Jewish Documentation at Paris. I also found a large number of documents at the Zentrales Staatsarchiv at Merseburg that enabled me to reconstruct the essential facts.

Gross's letter runs as follows:

> Dear Comrade Trotha!
>
> My attention has often been drawn to Heidegger's activities at Freiburg. At present he has succeeded in making himself known to a large group as the National Socialist philosopher.
>
> Having personally no way of making a judgment of Heidegger, a while ago I asked for information from Jaensch at Marburg (you met him when you visited Rosenberg at Munich). He sent me a totally negative report prepared by Krieck, who had taken the same attitude toward him as I did.
>
> This means that Heidegger could be a serious candidate for director of the Academy of Prussian Professors. I would be grateful if you would inform Rosenberg of this so that, should he not be aware of it, he can decide whether to take a hand in this clearly dangerous affair.

Rosenberg implied later, in a letter of March 6, 1934, to Minister Rust, that supplementary information about Heidegger was lacking and that he had received several warnings about him from different sections of the party. He recommended that Rust discover what he could.[4]

This project to create an academy was already a familiar one, reported in an article by W. Rudolf in *Der deutsche Student*, February 1934.[5] The Prussian Academy of Professors was charged with enlisting the teaching bodies of the universities of Cologne, Halle, Marburg, Königsberg, Giessen, Kiel, Breslau, Münster, Bonn, Berlin, Frankfurt am Main, and Greifswald and with extending its scope to the whole Reich. The idea of the Academy was tied to the reorganization of the teaching body—that is, to all the new full professors—according to the provisions adopted on October 11, 1933, by the Ministry of Sciences and Education.

This move organized all the teachers, assistants, and professors (those not civil servants) in the faculty *(Dozentenschaft)* of each university, while the Prussian faculty at Berlin was to bring together local organizations. The goal was to exercise political, ideological, and administrative control over the group of young "academicians" who would later have the functions of full professor. The new law granted teaching rights in universities (the *venia legendi* after a habilitation) only to those completing their political indoctrination classes. According to the law, this new legislation removed from the faculties their traditional rights to grant the *venia legendi*, which was now held only by the Ministry.[6] The Prussian Academy of Professors was to be the supreme executive arbiter, with control over the whole Reich.

The Ministry charged Secretary of State Wilhelm Stuckart with organizing the Academy. Stuckart was an important figure in the party, the one who had pushed the nomination of Heidegger to Berlin in 1933, and was known to be tough. He held, among other things, the position of honorary president of the Society for Racial Purity in Vienna, and he was first president of the German Association for Racial Purity.[7] From 1922 he had been a member of the NSDAP and had been in the SS since 1936. He had received several honors (the Totenkopfring, the Julleuchter, the Ehrenwinkel with star, and the SS Honor of the Dagger), and in 1944 he reached the rank of Obergruppenführer of the SS. His correspondence with Hitler and Himmler is found in the archives of the Berlin Document Center. As a jurist he devoted his most important work to legal questions relating to education and to the administration of occupied countries, for which he established a juridical basis. In the book of essays given to Himmler (Darmstadt, 1935) on his fortieth birthday, Stuckart published "Centralized Power, Decentralization, and Unified Administration" ("Zentralgewalt, Dezentralization und Verwaltungseinheit").[8] In educational law, his most important book is *National Socialist Legal Training (Nationalsozialistische Rechtserziehung* [Frankfurt, 1935]).[9] For the law governing occupied lands, his work is *Total War and Administration (Der totale Krieg und die Verwaltung* [1943]).[10] He was part of the Wannsee meeting where plans were begun for the extermination of all European Jewry on an industrial scale, and, in 1935, Stuckart had already helped draft the "racial laws." The Nurenberg Court found him guilty as a war criminal and sentenced him to four years in prison.[11]

Stuckart began to organize the Academy of Professors of the Reich in a letter of August 18 sent to Heidegger, G. A. Walz (rector at Breslau), Werner Studenkowski, Otto Reche, Friedrich Klausing, Friedrich Neumann (rector at Göttingen), Lothar Wolf (rector at Kiel), and Hans Heyse (Königsberg). Stuckart proposed a comprehensive plan and asked his correspondents to send him their plans for organizing the Academy.[12] These were militant professors of a certain eminence, which explains his confidence in them. On the other hand, Stuckart's request for their help for such a wide-ranging political action emphasizes their importance. We can get an impression of them from their party cards in the Berlin Document Center.[13]

G. A. Walz had been a member of the party since 1931. As a professor at the Law School at Marburg, he had received his *venia legendi* in 1927. He began his career as full professor in October 1933 at Breslau, and in December, he was named rector.

Werner Studenkowski became a party member as early as 1925. He was the student Führer at Leipzig, and in 1926 he was named official party orator. He was director of the Berlin section of the NSDAP from 1927 to 1928. In 1934, he was Gauamtsleiter for political education in Saxony and director of the Department for Adult Education of the NSDAP. He held similar posts at Leipzig and the Technical School at Dresden. He was also editor of the review *Die Vorposten*.

Otto Reche was a professor of anthropology and ethnology and director of the Institute of Racial Sciences and Populations, and also director of the State Institute of Populations at Leipzig. He was the author of *Races of the German People* (1933), director of the *Zeitschrift für Rassenphysiologie (Review of Racial Physiology)*, and first president of the German Society for Research on Blood-types. Along with others, he was the founder of the extremist Völkisch-Soziale Party in 1918 and, while a professor at Vienna, published *The Hereditary Factor (Racial Purity) and Its Importance for Our People (Erbgesundheitspflege [Rassenhygiene] und ihre Bedeutung für unser Volk)* [1928]). At the time Stuckart wrote him, Reche was working at the Department of Race at Dresden. In his correspondence with the SS at Prague, located in the Berlin Document Center, we find that as a jurist he had asked to take part in the racial research being done in the camps in occupied Czechoslovakia.

Friedrich Klausing was part of Ernst Krieck's circle. He was an active participant in the review *Volk im Werden* and coeditor with Krieck of the series *Die Deutsche Hochschule* (Marburg, 1933). In March 1935 he was dean of the Law School at Marburg, and from 1944 the rector of the University of Prague. When it was confirmed that his son had participated in the attempt on Hitler's life in July 1944 (in von Stauffenberg's group), Klausing committed suicide.[14]

In the "Proposals for the Internal Structure of the Academy of Professors" (probably Stuckart's text), it was stipulated that the Academy not repeat any functions of existing academies (the French Academy or the Prussian Academy of Sciences). It "was to be the center of an intellectual organization of work, in the best sense of the word." Even before the whole structure was put into place, the Academy had to create a group of permanent teaching members. The Academy had the responsibility "to groom young professors as educators and men of science within the spirit of National Socialism" in order to prepare future generations of German professors. On the scientific level, it was recognized that there was a need to develop a more comprehensive picture of the world, and the Academy was expected to reorganize scientific research in this direction. Its program would therefore include courses directed toward new generations of university students in each scientific specialty. In addition to the director of courses and the teaching body, there would be a director of physical education and cultural education (rhetoric, singing, and theater). At first, students would be selected for their intellectual, spiritual, and physical abilities. This selection would promote those able to become true National Socialist Führers. There should be no more than forty to start. The teaching available at the Academy ought to guarantee the highest level of doctrinal education and a rigorous preparation so that these future professors would be able to handle the problems of university reform. Without relying simply on the criteria of their specialties, they must secure the foundations of the new university and National Socialist science.

The courses would be divided into three areas. The first was to study the situation and development of universities during the past 150 years—their historical evolution and the National Socialist concept of the university in contrast to that of liberalism and objective science. The second was to be concerned with links between pedagogy and the direction of the masses *(Führung)*, with the history of pedagogy as it related to the history of culture, with special attention to the analyses authored by Alfred Rosenberg. The third section was to treat notions of the new university, the political university, and notions of socialism, of reform, and of the university revolution.

Among the faculty, there must be a philosopher, a pedagogue, a physician, and a jurist. The scientific courses must take into account the relationship between the disciplines and the needs of the people and the state.

In the part of the text called "Life at the Academy of Professors," it was made clear that through the session the director of courses, professors, and participants were to become a "tight community of life at the heart of the Academy." The daily rhythm of the community was to tie together activity and repose, intellectual and physical work, physical and artistic efforts. Physical activity was not to consist solely of gymnastics but was to include endurance training (road building, agricultural work, and horticulture), and everything relating to work service. Intellectual work was to be facilitated by a library, which would include periodicals. One clear part of the plan was to teach oratory. The organizers wanted to train future teachers who had firm and clear principles and who would be able to win in any debate.

The Academy was to have a permanent director chosen by the minister of education and sciences. Future professors were to be recruited by the Ministry and the National Socialist organization of teachers. The plan also foresaw that the Academy would become the definitive judge for the transformation of the universities and for the planning for professional ranks throughout the Reich and would be a center for the development of teaching and research. It was to retain this role when the future German university would emerge as "a true National Socialist university."

The documents at Merseburg do not state how many professors actually sent their own plans to Stuckart. But we can say that plans were sent by Wolf and Heyse (in collaboration), Neumann, Reche, and Heidegger. There is among the documents a fifth one whose author cannot be determined. Heidegger's plan is six pages long (Stuckart's is only five) and notable for its precise, concrete proposals. He expresses a pedagogical notion that is original and meticulously conceived.

In the letter accompanying his plan (August 28, 1934), Heidegger wrote to Stuckart: "In response to your request, I shall send you my opinions on the organization of the Academy. Every point of your plans on which I offer no comment is one I agree with. With German greetings and a Heil Hitler! Yours, Martin Heidegger." The accompanying text begins with the objectives:

1. The creation of the school for professors is to be determined by its objectives: to educate professors with the will and the ability to develop the German university of the future.

2. The education of the professor must have as its goal:

a. To waken and strengthen an *educative* attitude (since, here, the professor is not a researcher communicating the results of his own research and that of others).

b. To rethink traditional *science* in terms of the strengths of National Socialism.

c. To understand effectively that tomorrow's university is a *community of educative life* based on a homogeneous notion of the world *[geschlossene Weltanschauung]*.

Describing a pedagogical model based on the example of the educator more than on content, Heidegger continues:

3. This triple task can be accomplished only in a frame where the educative attitude, the transformation of science, and the community of life are achieved as *an examplary reality*. Inadequate and even harmful are simple courses "on" objective science, "on" the university and university reform. This is why:

4. Not courses, but a true school. This means that students working in common with professors must prepare their *future* work as educators. As a permanent institution, the school is to develop a specific spirit (in its vision of things, its attitude, its criteria of values) and create a tradition that inspires and engages the students beyond their stay at the school. Nothing is more long-lasting in education than the implicit influences of atmosphere.

The school of professors is to be a permanent institution. For it will not be superseded even when the future teachers will be educated at the National Socialist school or by the Hitler Youth. Even in these cases the specific task of the university professor is ultimately not different from the specific tasks of other groups of professors who work within the structure of ordinary "education."

5. The school is a community of learners. The *vita communis* of professors and students is maintained by the rigor of the order of the day and by the simplicity of its life, by the natural alternation of scientific work, recreation, concentration, martial games, physical work, walks, sports, and celebrations.

The school is not therefore a camp. In all cases it ought to allow *personal* work and the individual preparation of students and teachers. What is achieved *for* the community can be achieved only *in* and *by* the community, but there must also be time for real solitude and concentration.

6. Character of the director and professors. Their attitudes, their will, and their ability are more important than any planning

and organization of the school. The director and professors are to exercise their influence through what they are and not through what they teach.

a. Given their specific task, they are to be National Socialist members. It is not enough that they be politically safe, responsible representatives of their disciplines, but they must also be National Socialist in spirit, able to prepare for the revolution of science starting from notions of science itself.

b. The director and professors (at least the important group) must be able to devote themselves exclusively to this task. The work of education demands total commitment and cannot be achieved superficially; thus it must even form the most important part of vacation time.

c. At first the professors will come from different universities. Their academic origin, language, notions will be different. To coordinate action, there must be continuing and collective preparation during as well as before terms.

To eliminate any possibility of bureaucratic inertia, Heidegger proposes that "the choice of the first director and first professors not be permanent. But barring obvious ineptitude, they ought not be changed too rapidly. They ought to be able to benefit from a fairly long period to gain experience, to correct their inadequacies, and to grow into their task."

There must be communication between the Academy and general university life:

d. The director and professors are to be informed about the permanence of the objectives and the direction of the whole educational system, in particular concerning the universities. In fact, if the teaching offered by liberal arts departments is to be directed to the education of teachers and not of philologists, the school for professors also ought to give the new generation of liberal arts teachers a living image of the future university, just as the evolution of the professional world of physicians and lawyers ought to have their occasional university retreat.

Heidegger then gives a concrete account of the essential form that the education of educators ought to have:

7. The *fundamental character of the education* to be offered by the school for professors is as follows: The students will have concrete experience for their future profession by handling responsible

tasks (such as directing debates, defending basic questions in their own disciplines, developing a clear defense of spiritual tasks and fundamental political questions). As for the structuring of the courses, keeping them to essentials, making them lively and striking, the students will learn by the example of their teachers, as well as from the content, which will be tied to the objectives of the school. By the same methods they will learn to defend their opinions in dialogues, to hold a *disputatio*, to know how to listen, to grasp essentials, to reason with clarity, to respect the direction of the question and the sequence of arguments. University seminars today and for a long time have gone beyond the acceptable limits of laxity, viz. the inability to think, the lack of ready speech and handling of concepts. This situation can be remedied only by renewing the teaching of university teachers.

To avoid having professors too dependent on their own university, Heidegger suggests that the Academy not be situated near existing universities. He also has some precise ideas about structuring the physical life of the professors. Some of his ideas, such as the *vita communis* and the *disputatio*, remind us of monastic life.

> 9. There must be: classrooms, small rooms for group discussions, a refectory with a lectern, a room for communal festivities and for artistic life, dormitories for the students. We must also have personal work space where one or two students can study. The director and professors whose work will extend beyond the ordinary work days will have their own small quarters.
>
> 10. The library is essential, really the school's analogue of the peasant's plow. We would also need a reading room for periodical literature. All the guests of the school would have free access to *everything* in the library. All must participate in ordering books for it, thereby learning to form true and reflective judgments on books to be made available. Nothing indicates better the ruin of present academic life than today's literary criticism.

Concerning the number of students and their selection, Heidegger suggests:

> The number of members ought never to go beyond forty. If we take the principle of accepting as students those who have already received the habilitation, the selecting functions of the school

would be limited to refusing those it considers not competent. Those with the habilitation have already been selected by their own professors. And who can guarantee that teachers will not err in their selection of the best students for the future? For this reason we ought to see that older students, even those with the doctorate, become part of the school. It is very possible that we will find among this group new strength awakened during the process of teaching, strength that in the universities as we know them could have been mischanneled and lost. Given the large number of candidates and therefore the difficulties of selection, we should have local teachers' organizations make the first selection according to special fields. . . . Those with the habilitation ought to be willing after two years of teaching to go through another series of courses at the school, as well as refresher seminars, even if, or especially if, they have been promoted.

Heidegger gives other criteria before defining the schedule to be followed in the school: "No course would be shorter than three months. When are they to be offered? This question is to be answered by recognizing that the director and professors must not lose contact with the university population; on the contrary, they should live with their students, especially the young ones, in a close community."

Heidegger gives only a single criticism of the proposal sent by Wilhelm Stuckart—the tendency to limit the activity of the school (Heidegger speaks of a "school" rather than of an "academy") by having only a series of general courses. On the one hand, these courses would work against the need for quality. On the other, they would run "the risk of underestimating the difficulties of organizing the sciences":

To reduce, and later to eliminate, the excessive importance of an "Americanized" sort of scientific activity, the sciences must be organized so that they can be developed according to their own needs. This has never taken place and never will do so without the decisive influence of individuals. This in no way means the reign of schools and tendencies, but rather the need for combat [Kampf], which is "the father of all things," in the intellectual domain, and perhaps more necessary here than elsewhere.

Heidegger's concern with the Academy of Professors and its direction (which he expected to assume) seems to have been in concert with the concerns of Lothar Wolf and Hans Heyse, rectors respectively of Kiel and Königsberg. Wilhelm Stuckart indicated his general satisfaction with these responses even though he had asked in the pamphlet that the matter "be held in close confidence." In fact, in his letter of April 18, 1934, Stuckart advised Dr. J. D. Achelis, the ministerial counsel at Berlin, that he had asked Heidegger, Wolf, and Neumann to draw up a plan for the Academy and to send a list of individuals who could be considered for the teaching body. It is clear that this collective effort for the project was never accomplished, since Wolf (with Heyse) as well as Heidegger and Neumann sent their own plans. Before Neumann sent his to Stuckart, on August 11, 1934, Neumann had drawn up another, more detailed plan, now held in the archives of the University of Göttingen. This plan, which Neumann sent on May 8, 1934, had many details in common with the provisional one sent by Stuckart to Heidegger at the beginning. We can surmise that Stuckart used it.

The documents held at Merseburg indicate that the general plans received the endorsement of the ministerial authorities. The Academy of Professors was offered a restored villa at Kiel to begin its activities.

In April 1934, Stuckart invited the Amt Rosenberg to participate in a conference. Alfred Bäumler, a close collaborator of Rosenberg's, had been asked to teach a course for the teachers selected for the first semester. Following this favor, Rosenberg seems to have approved the project.

Eight courses were given: The first two took place at Kiel on April 9–22 and April 23–May 6, 1934. The third was also given at Kiel on August 6–September 20, 1934, directed by Bäumler. Ernst Krieck directed the fourth course (August 6–September 20). Professor von Arnim did the sixth (September 17–October 6). The last two were given by Professors Gleispach and Heyse and were held respectively October 2–20 and October 16–November 3, 1934. The documents I have used do not indicate what happened to the Academy of Professors. It is quite possible that these plans to centralize the training of professors came to naught. Many such plans came to the same end because of frequent intrigues between professors and Nazi functionaries responsible for university reform. The Academy of Professors of the Reich seems to have given way to organizations of professors at each university, therefore lacking the coordination Stuckart had hoped for. We can perhaps attribute the failure of the project to Stuckart's removal from the Ministry. Volker Losemann has studied the structure and functions of these separate academies.[15]

It seems that Heidegger had a real chance to become director of an institution that would oversee the selection of new university teachers, and thereby have a hand in controlling university life in the Reich. We have two reasons to believe this: first, the feverish actions of Krieck's faction to see that Heidegger not receive the post and, second, the important role played by Heidegger and his friends (Wolf, Neumann, and Heyse). We can add to this the influence Heidegger had with the Ministry of Education and Sciences. We can confirm this by the fact that Heidegger and his allies were solicited by Secretary of State Stuckart at the very time the chair at Berlin fell vacant.

All this explains Krieck's immediate and violent reaction. Among the documents located at Merseburg are letters from Krieck to Erich Jaensch showing clear concern.[16] One of February 14, 1934, says:

> I have confirmed rumors that say that Heidegger may receive the post of director of the Academy of Professors, which would put him in control of a whole generation of Prussian professors. This would be a great concern. I beg you for a report on this man, on his behavior, his philosophy, his use of the German language, so that I can send it to the highest levels of the party.

Krieck suggested to Jaensch that the report also be sent to Munich. Jaensch sent the report directly to the Ministry, to a subordinate (Dr. Schwalm). The report went through channels and was eventually received by Dr. Bagheer, the ministerial counselor, on February 23, 1934. This is the report I cited earlier in explaining Heidegger's refusal of the chair at Munich.

In the report, Jaensch noted: "Yesterday I received a letter from Krieck saying that Heidegger had directed spiritual exercises at the monastery of Beuron (yet he said to others that he wanted to write a book against Christianity)." Krieck's reference was to a speech Heidegger had made on the *Confessions of Saint Augustine* (no doubt an intentional distortion of the facts) delivered to the monks at Beuron. The original text remains in the archives at Beuron and is not available. After the speech, the monks were chastised by Archbishop Gröber of Freiburg, an act that angered Heidegger.

The report also included Jaensch's conclusions based on his having observed the reactions of a student reading sentences of Heidegger's terminology. (Jaensch was then professor of psychology at Marburg.) His impression was that the student could only "suggest" what he had understood, without being able to give coherent explanations.

Also with the report was a letter from Jaensch's brother Walter Jaensch, professor of medicine at Berlin, who gave his comments on a speech about Heidegger's philosophy delivered at Berlin. The speech was read with respect and earnestness, said Jaensch, but it was clear that no one had understood a thing. The speaker himself, a "psychological Jew," did his best to explain the fundamental questions, but failed:

> After a pause, I could not refrain from telling the audience that in my estimation we were faced with ideas produced by a sick soul, and that the Heideggerian variant of existential philosophy was only schizophrenic babblings, banalities with an appearance of depth, which could come only from a sickened mind. The Jewish speaker told me next: "Doctor, I agree with you. But these days it is extremely dangerous to disagree with Heidegger. People say that Heidegger is the greatest thinker of our time and is the National Socialist philosopher. Listen to them singing (as the SS walked by outside singing); if things were not as they are and if I were not Jewish, I would speak differently. Today it is dangerous to oppose Heidegger!"

Jaensch said in this twenty-three-page report, which was compiled to block Heidegger from becoming director of the Academy:

> If Heidegger were to have decisive influence on the formation and selection of the new generations of university teaching, this would mean putting in the universities and intellectual life the descendants of Jews who still drag along among us. . . . Heidegger's ideas, or ideas deriving from Heidegger (for the plague is being propagated), go beyond the common swindlers of the past. These ideas have become pathologic swindling. . . . Now we are threatened by an intellectual plague that could become a mass psychosis.

Jaensch emphasized the danger of Heidegger's "revolutionary ardor." Heidegger had joined National Socialism simply because of his innate penchant for revolution, period. "Well-informed sources say that he fears the day when revolution among us would cease. I am certain that this 'pure revolutionary' would then no longer be on our side, but would be a turncoat."

Jaensch concluded his report with a list of names for director of the Academy: the first name was that of Krieck, whom he claimed was the only one worthy of holding the post.

This letter and report (Schwalm notes that no one had requested it) drew a harsh reaction from Achelis, the ministerial counselor, making clear the Ministry's support for Heidegger. Achelis strongly criticized Jaensch's procedures and asked him to abstain from such mediation in the future, warning him that failure to heed these warnings could bring disciplinary actions.

It seems, therefore, that the failure of the plan itself, and not a hostile attitude on the part of the Ministry, explains why Heidegger was not given the post of director of the Academy.

Heidegger and the Academy of German Law

The Ernst Krieck papers located at the regional archives at Karlsruhe contain a paragraph from the *Frankfurter Zeitung* of May 4, 1934, referring to the formation of the Committee for the Philosophy of Law at the Academy of German Law. The inaugural session of this committee, which took place in May 1934, at the Nietzsche archives at Weimar, was attended by the founder and president of the Committee, Dr. Hans Frank, Reichsjustizkommissar, and representatives of the National Socialist administration and intelligentsia. Also present were Professor Emge (Jena), Counselor Kisch (Munich), Reichsleiter Alfred Rosenberg, Ministerial Director Nicolai, and State Counselor Schmidt. Among the professors on the Committee were Heidegger (Freiburg), Rothacker and Naumann (Bonn), Hans Freyer (Leipzig), Baron von Uexküll (Hamburg), Geheimrat Stammler (Berlin), Binder (Göttingen), Geheimrat Heymann (Berlin), Erich Jung (Marburg), Bruns (Berlin), and Dr. Mikorey (Munich). It is interesting to see that, according to notes held in the archives, Krieck intended to allude to the Committee for the Philosophy of Law in a draft of a commentary for his review, *Volk im Werden*, where he comments ironically on the news in the *Frankfurter Zeitung* and expresses the weak hope that the lessons that Rosenberg was going to give would have some effective bearing on the plan of the doctrine. Krieck's commentary did not, however, appear in the review.

The *Frankfurter Zeitung* article also notes that the Committee's goal was to become the highest arbiter of doctrine and theory of the Academy of German Law and would design the new German law as a substitute for Roman law and any other "foreign" law. The Committee was "to be founded on the philosophical notion of the community of the people, of National Socialism as a historical event, of German law, and the question of racial law and the right to life."[17] Here is how, in his initial speech, Rosenberg defined his doctrinal approach to the new law: "Justice is what the Aryan man deems just. Unjust is what he so deems." Rosenberg explained further the process by which such a conviction was to be supported, and its apogee achieved in Nazi Germany.

To understand the significance of Heidegger's presence on the Committee that was formed by the Reichsjustizkommissar, we must briefly describe the Academy of German Law. At first, it was a corporation of public law in Bavaria, with its seat at Munich. By the law of July 11, 1934, it was transformed into an institution of the Reich falling under the jurisdiction of the Ministry of Internal Justice. After 1934 it was directed by Hans Frank. Frank was one of the key figures in Hitler's Germany, and was executed as a war criminal at Nurenberg in 1946. He had seen the need to form the Academy of German Law and had himself selected the members of the Committee for the Philosophy of Law, among them Heidegger. The *Frankfurter Zeitung* of May 5, 1934, informed its readers of Frank's inaugural speech:

> He linked his important speech to Nietzsche, the prophet of authoritarian feeling who saved our people during World War I and who has also provided us with a position of authority among the Aryan youth. "We," said Frank, "we wish to define the social doctrine of National Socialism by scientific reliance on notions of race, state, Führer, blood, authority, faith, land, and idealism. All this can be accomplished through a serious formulation of German law achieved by the leaders among the people. The first work of the Committee for the Philosophy of Law was therefore to avoid carefully any philosophy of law that derived from non-German dogma. Ours must be founded on the people and not on a social base separated from the people. . . . Therefore, this must be a German law, not a foreign one. . . . It ought therefore to serve the collectivity and not the individual, but at the same time it must be a *law of lords,* not of *slaves.* . . . We will redefine the notion of the National Socialist state, starting from the unity and purity of German manhood; it will be formalized and realized through law and in accord with the Führer principle. . . . These are the principles that govern this first meeting of the Committee. . . . To this extent it must be understood as a fighting committee."

It is in the same terms that the *Berliner Tageblatt* of May 4, 1934, announced the creation of the Committee, with the title: "The philosophy of law as a firearm."[18] Using this same terminology, the newspaper mentioned the press conference Frank held for foreign reporters the day before. It explained the role of the Academy of German Law: its duty was to formulate the new German law beginning with National Socialist doctrine. It was in this context that the Academy and its Committee for the Philosophy of Law were called on to play a fundamental role in the new Nazi state.

A later speech by Frank in a hall at the University of Munich covered by the party newspaper, *Völkischer Beobachter*, on June 28, 1934, gave the principles and clearly indicated the political importance of the institution. One can find a complete collection of this newspaper with complementary documents in the annual of the Academy.[19] Because of the scarcity of sources (documents on the Academy kept at Munich in the Hauptstaatsarchiv were mostly destroyed), I have been unable to verify Heidegger's later participation on the Committee. The report of the inaugural meeting (to be found in the Goethe and Schiller Archives at Weimar) indicates Heidegger's participation without giving details.

Heidegger and the Advanced School for German Politics

Under the title "Political Education for Students," the *Völkischer Beobachter* (Berlin edition) wrote on May 9, 1934:

An accord has been signed by the Advanced School for German Politics *[Deutsche Hochschule für Politik]*, the university, and the High Office for Political Training *[Hauptamt für politische Erziegung]* that beginning with the summer semester 1934 students at the University of Berlin may participate during their first three semesters in the important conferences organized by the chair of the Academy of the Advanced School for German Politics. Those who delivered papers: the ministerial director, Dr. Gütt of the Ministry of the Interior of the Reich, Professor Heidegger, rector of Freiburg, Dietrich Klagges, minister president of Braunschweig, Bernhard Köhler, president of the Committee for Political Economy of the Reich of the NSDAP, Dr. Jahnke, ministerial counsellor of the Ministry of the Reich for Popular Education and Propaganda, and the vice-chancellor, Franz von Papen. The chair of the Academy of German Law will be inaugurated May 16 at the Advanced School for German Politics by a speech by the Reichsjustizkommissar, Minister of State Dr. Frank. Other speakers will include: Dr. Bruns, director of the Institute for

Public International Law, Secretary of State Dr. Freisler of the Ministry of Prussian Justice, Professor Carl Schmitt, and Counselor Schraut of the Ministry of Justice of the Reich.

It seems that Heidegger's participation as speaker at the Advanced School for Politics was due to his work with the Committee for the Philosophy of Law of the Academy of German Law. But Heidegger had additional reasons for participating in the German Advanced School. Not only did he want to take on all these activities *after* resigning from Freiburg (there is no mention of him as rector); his participation was also consonant with his work involving student indoctrination and with the possibility of his forming a school for leaders in the party and the state. All of this was done in collaboration with political figures of all sorts, including Alfred Rosenberg. This is how we must understand the allusion in the *Berliner Tageblatt* of May 5, 1934, to the fact that Heidegger was no longer rector of Freiburg.

From its formation in 1920 until 1934, the Advanced School for Politics at Berlin was under the aegis of the Ministry of Prussian Culture. As part of the National Socialist program of reorganization *(Gleichschaltung)*, it was controlled by Goebbels' Ministry of Popular Culture and Propaganda. According to information in the Geheim archives at Berlin (where we find the documentation on the German Advanced School), it was founded in 1920 through the efforts of industrialists and important financiers as a way to encourage teaching and research in political science. Ernst Jäckh, Otto Suhr, and Theodor Heuss were among the most prominent members. In 1933, they were relieved of their functions. Even as early as the Weimar government, there was an anti-democratic faction in the leadership headed by O. Spann; so when Hitler took control Spann's faction transformed the institution into a true school for political aspirants. This was why the highest civil servants began their political education in an educational framework controlled by Goebbels' ministry.

We can imagine what the studies were at the Advanced School for German Politics by looking at the list of speakers. During the summer semester of 1933, Goebbels, Secretary of State Walter Funk, Alfred Bäumler, and Eugen Fischer were among the speakers. During the following semester, speakers included the ministerial director Rudolf Buttmann, Dr. Otto Dietrich, chief of the Press Department of the NSDAP, Dr. Walter Gross, director of the Department for Racial Purity of the NSDAP, and Alfred Rosenberg, followed by Heidegger and Vice-Chancellor von Papen. Heidegger was one of the speakers during the winter semester of 1933/34, along with Hitler's representative Rudolf Hess, Ministers Goebbels, Göring, Walther Darré, Alfred Rosenberg, and Baldur von Schirach. The programs of the 1935 semester also showed Heidegger and these same Nazi officials, as well as Ernst Krieck. Beginning with 1936, the programs indicate special speakers, but without giving names.

In its teaching programs, the Advanced School defined its functioning as being "to serve in education and research on all political questions." There was a seminar department, a university department, the archives, and the library. The seminar courses (first level, two semesters; second level, three semesters) treated "essential questions regarding National Socialism's conception of the world," and the students were taught the fundamentals of politics. Students attained the seminar level after spending six weeks writing a paper and taking four written exams and one oral exam. Afterwards, they spent three semesters in the university department, which offered scientific education in specialties. This process led to a diploma.[20]

Heidegger as informer

In his academic and political activities Heidegger always showed particular concern for young people, especially for young professors. His growing popularity in the 1920s was linked to his sincere interest in these "living forces." In his eyes, there were two essential conditions to be met: faithfulness to National Socialism and good academic qualifications. Heidegger explicitly underscored the complementarity of these criteria, as much in making out his plans for the Academy as in his discussions about the University Study Group *(Arbeitsgemeinschaft)* organized by Krieck. For Heidegger, politics in the strict sense was an autonomous reality. He even went to the point of debasing himself by making accusations against certain people, accusations of the same sort Jaensch and Krieck had directed against him. Heidegger adopted a rather different attitude when he dealt with National Socialist academics and when he dealt with dissidents. As examples, we offer here the cases of Eduard Baumgarten and Rudolf Stadelmann.

The papers Baumgarten left after his death contain a slanderous denunciation that Heidegger made against him. Baumgarten had begun his career at the University of Wisconsin (Madison) as professor of philosophy. He then returned to Freiburg to obtain his habilitation with work on John Dewey, directed by Heidegger. Heidegger and Baumgarten were friends, as were their families; the Heideggers were godparents of Baumgarten's son, and the two families were neighbors. But the relationship on the philosophical plane was clearly strained. Baumgarten was strongly influenced by American pragmatism and was attacked by Heidegger as well as by intemperate disciples of Heidegger's in his seminars. According to Wilhelm Schoeppe,[21] Baumgarten's son-in-law, these differences came to a head in one of Heidegger's seminars on Kant's philosophy. The relationship was broken for good, and Baumgarten was reduced to teaching American culture and philosophy, mostly pragmatism.

The quality of Baumgarten's courses was such that the University of Göttingen reconsidered his status and asked the Ministry to give him the title of professor with the habilitation and allow him to give exams.[22] Heidegger chose exactly this time to intervene from Freiburg. He sent a confidential political report to the National Socialist organization of professors at Göttingen, fiercely attacking the faculty's proposal. The report was as follows:

> By family and spiritual attitudes, Dr. Baumgarten comes from that liberal-democratic circle of intellectuals gathered around Max Weber. During his time here, he was everything but a National Socialist. It surprises me that he is teaching at Göttingen. I cannot imagine on what academic basis he has earned his habilitation. After disappointing me, he became closely tied to the *Jew* Fränkel, who had been active at Göttingen and was later expelled. I suppose Baumgarten found some protection by this shift in affiliation. I deem it impossible to bring Baumgarten into the SA as well as to bring him into the teaching body. Baumgarten is a gifted speaker. In his philosophy, however, I think he is pompous and without solid and true knowledge. This judgment comes from my experience with him for two years. In the meantime, has there been a change in his political attitude? I am unaware of it. His stay in the United States, during which he was Americanized, no doubt allowed him to learn much about the country and its inhabitants. But I have solid reasons to doubt the sureness of his political instincts and his judgment.[23]

Heidegger sent this document[24] to the Führer of professors at Göttingen, Dr. Vogel, who put it in the archives with the notice: "not usable, filled with hatred."[25]

The document is of considerable importance for what it reveals of Heidegger's connections with the party after 1934. In fact, although Vogel put the letter aside in 1933, the case was reopened by his successor, Dr. Blume, who decided to question again Baumgarten's presence at Göttingen. Sending Heidegger's slanderous report to Berlin (probably at the same time other similar reports were sent) had immediate results. Baumgarten was immediately relieved of his work, his salary was stopped, and moves were made to expel him from Germany to the United States. The official decision was sent to him April 12, 1935.[26] Thanks to the intervention of friends who told him that it was Heidegger who had denounced him, Baumgarten went to the Ministry at Berlin on September 17, 1935, and obtained a cancelation of the sanctions taken against him.

In unpublished biographical notes, Baumgarten says that he later wrote Heidegger for an explanation. His letter seems to have been answered by a citation from Aeschylus. Baumgarten continued his career and years later became a professor at Göttingen.

Heidegger's report in 1935 in favor of the candidacy of Rudolf Stadelmann for the chair of history in the philosophy faculty, also at Göttingen, was of an entirely different kind. Stadelmann had made the rank of professor at Freiburg. His inaugural speech, on "The Historical Consciousness of a Nation,"[27] was delivered before Rector Heidegger, professors, teachers, and students on November 9, 1933. In it he claimed, among other things, that Hitler's coming to power and the attainment of his external political plans had restored to Germany "its character of a great and feared people, traits it had previously lost."[28] Among Stadelmann's important works is also an article on Hippolyte Taine and the French right,[29] a piece on the essence of German revolutions,[30] and an article on the struggle for the Saar.[31] Stadelmann had worked as a teacher together with Heidegger for the celebration of the Solstice. On that occasion he had given the official speech extolling Bismarck's glory, and citing his words: "I would never have any friends if I did not also have enemies."[32]

In his report of July 1, 1935, Heidegger wrote:

> I have known Stadelmann since 1928, the date of his habilitation. Since that time, he has gone through an extraordinary development. He is the opposite of instability and inconstancy. He is a true Swabian, obstinate with a hard head. We can expect on his part some collisions, especially with people not his equal. Stadelmann has never practiced science by conjecture. Above all he is a strong fellow, in my estimation the best of the young professors specializing in the early medieval period. We can't afford the luxury of losing the sharpest intellectuals in our disciplines. I would immediately propose Stadelmann for the chair in history, with the conviction that such a responsibility would bring him to

surpass himself and would give him definite assurance. Stadelmann is one of those who have the ability to transform their discipline by going to the source of things, instead of merely using the teachings of the past. With a collegial salutation, and a Heil Hitler! Yours, Martin Heidegger."[33]

It would surely, however, be unjust to think that Heidegger would give his assent to candidates on uniquely political criteria. On the contrary, his radical and austere adherence to the National Socialist line drove him to a particular rigor when it was a question of university people in the NSDAP. To illustrate this attitude, we may cite a third case, that of Professor Arnold Ruge, presented for the chair of philosophy at Heidelberg. In his report of December 18, 1933, after disqualifying Ruge for inadequate competence, Heidegger added:

As long as National Socialism considers effectiveness as the necessary condition for the election of Führers and responsible leaders, there is no way to offer a chair of philosophy to Mr. Ruge. To offer him a post in any university of the region of Baden would clearly be scandalous. For me it would be absolutely intolerable to have him as a colleague.[34]

16 Heidegger and the state ideological apparatus

The chair at Göttingen

After the Ministry sent out a request on October 12, 1935, for candidates for the chair left vacant by Georg Misch, the philosophy faculty of the University of Göttingen sent in a list of three names: Martin Heidegger at the top, Professor Glockner (Giessen), and G. Krüger (Marburg). During the deliberations of the nomination committee, Professors Hermann Nohl, Friedrich Neumann, and Theodor Lipps proposed Heidegger. Teachers Josef König and Otto Friedrich Bollnow were consulted by the committee and were also in favor of Heidegger. In his report of September 30, 1935, Hans Plischke, dean of the faculty, justified their preference for Heidegger: "The faculty gives the name of Heidegger (Freiburg) first. In this way we would have the privilege of welcoming at the same time one of the first figures in contemporary German philosophy, a professor who knows how to encourage philosophical questions, and a thinker ready to work in the direction of the National Socialist concept of the world."

The Ministry did not respond immediately, but eventually the dean advised the committee that the Ministry had rejected the faculty proposals and had expressed its wish that Hans Heyse of Königsberg be nominated. On February 27, 1936, the faculty substituted Heyse's name for that of Krüger on the list. Then, on May 13, they decided to propose Heyse as Misch's replacement. Heyse took his post for the winter semester 1936/37.[1]

Certainly the preference the Ministry expressed must have troubled Heidegger. Misch was the most eminent disciple of Dilthey, and to replace him they had indicated a preference for Heyse, whose National Socialist philosophy was nothing more than a simplification of Heidegger's philosophy, the work of a subordinate. In his article "The New Idea of Science and the German University," for example, Heyse had taken almost verbatim Heidegger's ideas on "existence" and the importance of the Greeks.[2] We are certainly far from the time when Heidegger was able to press Krieck to invite Heyse and Bäumler as "safe colleagues" for the Political-Cultural Community of German University Professors.

Heidegger would probably never have relinquished his chair at Freiburg for the one at Göttingen. The Ministry's choice, however, no doubt made him think that "the principle of achievement" had already begun to lose its effectiveness in decisions made by the regime. This Misch incident would, in fact, be a sign of a growing tendency: until now (including the Weimar years) Heidegger had been imposed by the Ministry on particular faculties, even against their inclinations; from now on, faculties would offer Heidegger posts, and the Ministry would reject his candidacy.

We must not suppose there is any sort of "resistance" to be found in the behavior of the faculties, nor a change in Heidegger that turned him into an adversary of National Socialism and the state. Still, the facts must be mentioned and assessed.

The Ministry's preference for the rector of Königsberg reflects Heyse's growing influence in the movement. This influence is marked especially in his active participation in the Academy of Professors of the Reich. A short time after assuming his duties, Heyse organized and directed the Academy of Professors at Göttingen, beginning with a personal plan that would replace the one that Rector Friedrich Neumann had begun in 1934.[3] He was quickly named Führer of the delegation to the International Philosophical Conference in Paris (1937), and Heidegger was dropped to second place, where he continued to work for the political orientation of the delegation.

The fact that the ministerial authorities preferred Heyse to Heidegger shows no explicit animosity for Heidegger. In fact, in 1936, the Ministry at Berlin asked the rector of Freiburg to name Heidegger as dean of the faculty of philosophy. This confirms that good relations continued between the Ministry and Heidegger, or at least that Heidegger was not considered unreliable.

The "Introduction to Metaphysics" lectures (1935)

The "Introduction to Metaphysics" lectures ("Einführung in die Metaphysik") were preceded in 1934/35 by lectures on Hölderlin. This fact in itself is significant because Heidegger's increasing preoccupation with the work of Hölderlin, which would become important for his later development, began with a discussion of the philosophical and political problems of National Socialism.

At a central point in the lectures on Hölderlin Heidegger says:

> The truth of a nation is the revelation of its Being in the whole *[des Seins im Ganzen]*, according to which its sustaining, shaping, and commanding forces receive their respective stations and achieve their unanimity. The truth of a nation is that revelation of Being out of which the nation knows what it wants historically by wanting *itself [es sich will]*, by wanting to be itself. . . . The truth of the existence of a people is originally given by the poet, yet the Being of beings *[Sein des Seienden]*, revealed as such, is conceived and ordained as *Seyn [Sein =* Being] and is only then disclosed by the thinker. And *Seyn [Sein]* conceived as such is fixed as the first and ultimate concern of existing things—that is, as the *definite [be-stimmte]* historical reality it is, by bringing the nation to itself as a nation. This the creator of the state accomplishes by founding the state conformably with its very essence *[Wesen]*. But this entire process has its own intrinsic time and therefore its own chronological order; the powers of poetry, of thinking, of the creation of the state, are effective forward and backward and, in general, are not calculable by any means. For a long time they can go unnoticed and though they exist without a bridge between them they still affect one other, each depending on the various developments in the power of poetry, of thinking, and of statecraft, each functioning within a distinct, important circle of the public.[4]

By aligning this with his own view, Heidegger argues that a fundamental change has taken place, but that this change has not yet found a way of manifesting itself:

> The preparation for the truth that should someday emerge *[ereignen]* does not happen overnight and on request but requires many human lives and even "generations"; this long time remains

closed off to all those who are beset by boredom and have no awareness of their own boredom. This long time, however, allows the truth, the self-manifestation of *Seyn [Sein]*, will come to pass *[ereignen]*. . . . It is in such a metaphysical predicament that the poet stands.[5]

The course "Introduction to Metaphysics" was given in the summer semester of 1935. Its main subject is the thematizing of history or, if you will, a reflection on the role of philosophy (which Heidegger understood as "metaphysics" at this time) as the very constituting of history. Whereas in his earlier works Heidegger had insisted on connecting history and philosophy, he now tries to represent history in its dynamic movement, a movement that from its origin has formed a model for the present and the future. In this way, Heidegger took up again the issues that had been occupying his attention (even in their immediate political contingencies), but now from a new perspective—now with the purpose of indicating the fundamental difference between the very essence *(Wesen)* of the German nation and whatever particular historical form that essence may take. This distinction enables Heidegger to judge the identity achieved by National Socialism in relation to its own origin. Therefore, he insists on the difference between the standard view of philosophy and that view that hopes to transform philosophy into an effective instrument for actually drafting a new society:

> With such expectations and demands, the capability and essence of philosophy is . . . overstrained. This overexertion appears mostly in the form of a criticism of philosophy. One says, for example, "Because metaphysics has not participated in the preparation of a revolution, it is to be rejected." This is just as smart as if somebody claimed that, because one cannot fly on a carpenter's bench, one should get rid of it.[6]

That Heidegger does not attribute any immediate efficacy to philosophy does not mean that he intended to deny its historical possibilities. He tries rather to transcendentalize them historically:

> What, according to its essence, philosophy can and must be is this: an intellectual disclosure of the channels and modes of knowledge that decides questions of scale and rank and through which, in the historical world *[geschichtlich-geistigen Welt]*, a nation comes to understand and consummate its own existence, that

knowledge that attacks and threatens and compels all questioning and calculating. . . . The essence of philosophy doesn't mean making things easier; it means making them harder. And not just casually, because the nature of its message seems strange or even crazy to the average mind. Rather, the real function of philosophy is to make historical existence and existence itself more challenging. By making things, actual things, more difficult, it gives them back their weight [their being—*Sein*]. And why is this the case? Because increase in difficulty is one of the basic conditions for the emergence of everything great, by which we estimate the fate of a historical nation and, above all, assess its works and achievements. But fate is present only where a true knowledge of things governs existence. However, the channels of that knowledge are opened through philosophy.[7]

According to Heidegger, official ideologists have missed this point. They were incapable of understanding how and where the problems really lie. They failed to realize that talk about "nothing" *(Nichts)* is something completely different from the phenomenon "disintegration" *(Zersetzung),* which has "undermined every culture and every affirmative belief." They thought pure nihilism to be "what both ignores the basic law of thinking and destroys the will to construct and believe."[8] In Heidegger's judgment, the danger that threatened was exemplified by the situation that Europe now found itself in:

This Europe, in wicked blindness always on the point of doing itself in, today lies in a pincers between Russia on one side and America on the other. Metaphysically conceived, Russia and America are the same. They are both driven by the mad rush of unbridled technology and the endless organization of the average man. When the last corner of the globe has been conquered by technology and has finally become exploitable, when each and every event at each and every place at each and every point of time has become easily accessible, when one can simultaneously "experience" an attempt to murder a king in France and a symphonic concert in Tokyo, when time is nothing but speed, immediacy, simultaneity, and when time as history has disappeared from the life of all nations, when the boxer is valued as the great man of the nation, when the mass meetings of millions are a triumph—then, yes, like a ghost, the spectre of the question will haunt us: What for?—Where to?—and What now?[9]

This cultural criticism, joined to a profound aversion for all forms of democracy, was completed by the appraisal of Germany as the only "center" or medium that could produce universal salvation:

> We are caught between claws. Our nation, caught in the middle, experiences that most direct pressure from them. We are the nation with the most neighbors, hence the most endangered, and along with all that we are the most metaphysical people. But from that very condition, of which we are certain, this nation will form its own fate, if, *in itself [in sich selbst]*, it creates a response, a possibility of a response, and grasps its tradition in a creative way. All this entails that this nation must assert itself as historical, must place itself within the history of the West, at the center of its own future, in the original sphere of the very power of being *[der Mächte des Seins]*. Only if the important decisions about Europe do not lead down the path to destruction, only then can its destiny be drawn, from this center, through the development of new historical *spiritual [geistiger]* powers.[10]

By readapting the ultranationalist and imperialist ideology that had been formulated by German professors before World War I in order to justify the politics of aggression, Heidegger establishes continuity between that epoch and fascism. The German nation, as Europe's "center," as metaphysical and therefore *as* an *especially* an endangered nation, as the elevated authority, should decide about the fate of all nations in just the way it has decided about itself. The centrifugal movement with which technology has spread across the planet demands a counter centripetal force in the direction of the metaphysical nation as the stabilizing center. In the heart of that center there arises the "question of being" *(die Seinsfrage)* through which it vindicated itself. "Therefore, we pose the question about being *(Sein)* in the context of Europe's fate, in which, also, the fate of the entire earth is being decided and in which, for Europe, our own historical existence has shown itself to be the critical center."[11]

This extreme nationalism, which has been aptly criticized by Robert Minder,[12] must be understood in terms of Heidegger's ties to National Socialism and in terms of the "critique" Heidegger was preparing in order to present National Socialism in a favorable light. What Germany had lived through from the moment its National Socialist leadership had departed from the right way seemed to Heidegger analogous to what had transpired in the nineteenth century, and seemed similarly to be the source of present evils and dangers. The event that "one refers to readily and succinctly as the 'collapse of German idealism' " did not have any of these features. "For it was not German idealism that collapsed; it was the era that was not strong enough to match the stature, the breadth, and the originality of that spiritual world."[13] "Existence *[Dasein]* began to slip into a world lacking the depth out of which whatever is essential *[das Wesentliche]* comes to, and returns to, man. . . . The predominant dimension became one of mere expansion and number. . . . In Russia and America this culminated in the excess of the perpetually uniform and apathetic until the quantitative is converted into its own sort of quality."[14] "From now on, the predominance of a mean of indifference is no longer something insignificant or dull; it is the gathering of that which aggressively destroys and deems a lie every worldly spiritual station and thing. This is the gathering of what we call the demoniacal (in the sense of what is maliciously destructive). There are many different symptoms of this rise of the demoniacal in line with the growing helplessness and insecurity of Europe. One of these signs is the stripping away of the spirit's power of interpretation, a condition in which we find ourselves today."[15]

Heidegger, here, makes a connection in context and form to the Manichean sermon of his fellow German, Abraham a Sancta Clara, who wanted to make the people of Vienna aware of the meaning of the plague, which he believed was caused by the Jews, and further appealed to them to "wake up" to the threat of the Turks. Heidegger integrates this attitude into National Socialism's world view. Hitler, too, had developed a strange demonology, and not only in regard to the Jews. To him, the originators of Marxism, "this sickness of the nations," were "true devils . . . , for only in the brain of a monster—not a human being—can . . . the plan for an organization take on significant form, the activity of which must necessarily lead to the final collapse of culture, and therefore to the devastation of the world. In that case, resistance remains our only salvation, a final struggle that uses every weapon in order to capture the mind and understanding and will of man, regardless of whose fate will be blessed in the tipping of the scales."[16]

The battle that had to be fought from the "center," the crusade that would cover the whole planet and destroy the apocalyptic enemy, had to be carefully planned. It was essential to sharpen the most important weapon in this battle, the "mind," because it was there that everything would be decided, and because one of the symptoms of the demoniac reign consists in the distortion of the true activity of the mind. Arguing from this premise, Heidegger formulates his "critique" of National Socialism in a thoroughly unique way. The "reinterpretation of mind as *intelligence*" seems to Heidegger especially despicable: it reduces mind "to the role of a tool in the service of something that can be taught and that one can learn how to handle."[17]

This reinterpretation had appeared in three forms. In Marxism, intelligence was put to the service of "regulating and controlling the conditions of material production"; in positivism, it was restricted to the "thorough ordering and explaining of everything that already exists and is already established"; and in that version of National Socialism that had gone astray, mind and spirit were reduced to mere intelligence "in the organizational guidance of the life of the multitude and the race of the nation." Heidegger's characterization of these three ways of debasing the concept of the mind seems well formed and exact. Yet, though he identifies the first two (Marxism and positivism) by their proper names, he merely complains about a developmental mistake in the third. It is obvious at once that here, too, Heidegger is distinctly concerned to affirm the "inner truth and greatness" of the National Socialist movement:[18]

> If one conceives of the mind as intelligence, as Marxism has done
> in the most extreme way, then, in opposing that view, it is entirely
> justified to say that the mind—that is, intelligence—must, in the
> functional order of life, be subordinated to efficient bodily health
> and character.

As opposed to Marxism and positivism, the very embodiment of the demoniac, even that form of National Socialism that has deviated from the right path is acting quite "correctly" in the sense that it defends the mind. On Heidegger's view, National Socialism's mistake does not lie in having embarked on a struggle conducted under the sign of racism, but in having been guided by inadequate principles. For "every true power and beauty of the body, every security and boldness of the sword, also every authenticity and cleverness of the mind, are rooted in the spirit and find enhancement and decline only in the respective power and impotence of the spirit. It is the principal and dominant element, the first and the last, not just an indispensable third."[19]

The "justness" of the racist or warlike alternative *can* and must therefore become reality. This may seem impossible to the two forces behind the pincer movement ranged against Germany—that is, Marxism and postivism—but, according to Heidegger's judgment, it is possible, indeed even necessary, for the third variation, National Socialism. The important difference in what Heidegger had said in his lecture "The Fundamental Questions of Philosophy" ("Die Grundfragen der Philosophie")—that is, that the revolution did not need spiritualization—and what he is saying now is that, now, spiritualization is necessary because its object, National Socialism, is about to risk losing essential attributes.

Heidegger is by no means alone in claiming to found racism and aggression in the "spirit" ("every true power and beauty of the body, every security and boldness of the sword"). Hitler, too, posits the spiritualization of the sword:

> Can one destroy spiritual ideas with the sword? Can conceptions
> of the world be combatted with raw violence? I have asked myself
> this question many times. . . . Conceptions and ideas, whether
> true or false, that have a certain spiritual basis, can, only at a
> certain point of time in their development, be broken by means of
> technical power when physical weapons are themselves also the
> bearers of an inspiring new idea, an idea or world view. . . . The
> use of violence alone, lacking the motive power of a spiritually
> fundamental conception, can never destroy an idea or its spread
> except in the form of a complete extermination of a tradition
> down to its last supporter. But this essentially means eliminating
> such a state from the context of politically significant power, often
> for an indefinite time, possibly even forever, because such a
> blood sacrifice, as we know from experience, affects the best part
> of a nation. Since any such action lacking a spiritual basis hardly
> seems morally justified, it prods the more valued stock of a nation
> to protest. But such a protest has the effect of appropriating the
> spiritual values of the victimized but still unjustified movement.
> This may happen simply because of a sense of opposing any
> attempt to crush an idea by brutal violence alone.

Therefore, Hitler sees the only solution in the coordintion of the "sword" and "spirit":

> The very first precondition for a kind of battle with the weapons
> of cold violence is and will be steadfastness. . . . The very first
> condition for success lies in the perpetual, steady use of violence
> alone. But this persistence is always only the result of a certain
> spiritual conviction. All violence that does not issue from a firm
> spiritual foundation will be unstable and insecure.[20]

The false mediation of spirit and action that seems to be the greatest danger for the "center" and the "movement," according to Heidegger, is also reflected in the university:

Science, which is particularly important to us at the university, obviously reflects the condition of the last decades, which remains unchanged even today despite many a purging. If, now, two apparently different conceptions of science seem to oppose one another—science as technical, practical professional knowledge, and science as a cultural value in itself—then they are moving *both in the same* path of destruction toward a misunderstanding and an emasculation of the power of the spirit. They differ only in that the technical and practical conception of science can, as a special branch of science, claim the advantage of the open and clear sort of logical consistency favored in current circumstances, whereas the allegedly reactionary interpretation of science construed as a distinct cultural value, which is again becoming popular, tries with its usual unconscious hypocrisy to cover up the impotence of the spirit. This confusion could extend so far that the technical view of science could actually concede that science was also a cultural value, so that each reading could understand the other's in the same stupid way. If one wants to identify the combination of the special branches of science after the style of the teaching and research universities, it will be in name only, with no genuinely unifying or binding spiritual power.[21]

From this perspective Heidegger's lectures were not simply an event determined administratively by a schedule, an "intellectual" address with philosophy as its "subject"; rather they aimed at "actualizing" *(verwirklichen)* the "spirit" as historically transcendental authority. This rescue attempt was rooted in a return to origins, to the beginning of Western philosophy among the Greeks. It concerned a kind of deliverance, because the approach to this source had been closed off. In the origins of their thinking the Greeks understood being as *physis:*

This basic Greek word for that which exists *[das Seiende]* is usually translated as "nature." One uses the Latin translation "natura," which actually means "to be born," "birth." But, with this Latin translation, the original content of the Greek word *physis* is already altered; the actual philosophical power of the name is destroyed. This is not only true for the Latin translation of *this* word, but also for the translation of the rest of the Greek philosophical language into the Roman. This act of translating Greek into Latin is hardly random or harmless but the first phase in perpetuating the isolation and alienation of the original essence of Greek philosophy. The Roman translation became decisive for Christianity and the Christian Middle Ages. This survives in modern philosophy, which moves in a world of medieval ideas and then creates those common conceptions and terms that one still uses today to make the beginnings of Western philosophy comprehensible.[22]

Already in the manner of his criticism of Descartes' philosophy in *Being and Time*, we see signs of Heidegger's massive reservations about the so-called "Latin" or "Roman." Such features are typical of a tradition for which Abraham a Sancta Clara is exemplary. From his earliest alliance with National Socialism, Heidegger displayed a radical xenophobia toward the Latin that gradually became characteristic of his thinking, although he did find, at the time of "On the Essence of Reasons" ("Über das Wesen des Grundes," 1929), a phenomenologically acceptable concept of the *kosmos* in John the Evangelist, which was then developed further in the exegesis of the world by Augustine and Thomas Aquinas.[23] Heidegger's xenophobia was not abstract or directed merely at philosophical concepts. For him, philosophy and language do not represent isolated spheres but rather, constitutive moments of human existence. Heidegger was convinced that "nations" realized themselves nowhere more soundly than in their philosophy and language.

National Socialism had pushed this view to its most extreme consequences. For National Socialism, the Greek and German axis rests at the center of a universal culture. Alfred Bäumler argues very much in this way against Jules Romains in his essay "The Dialectic of Europe" ("Die Dialektik Europas"):

We differentiate between the Roman culture and the Roman tradition that we have been thrown in contact with historically and the freely chosen relationship we have with the Greek spirit, but we do not consider that relationship less important than the other contact. We are aware not only that the Greek world has been transmitted to us by Roman tradition but that we keep recovering it independently in ever-new ways. Luther, who translated from the Greek original and not from the Vulgate, Winckelmann, who exprienced Greek marble by touching it, Goethe, who found Homer once again in the Storm and Stress movement, Hölderlin, who freed Pindar, and Nietzsche, who rediscovered the Dionysian tragedy—these are some of the many disclosures of the Greek essence that have been made without the mediation of the Latin culture, even against it. Indeed, these discoveries issued solely from the substance of our own essence.[24]

Heidegger takes on the battle to free the "origin" from being dragged down by the Roman:

> Precisely because we dare to assume the arduous task of demolishing a world that has grown old and rebuilding it in a truly new—that is, historical—way, we must be aware of the tradition. We must know more, more rigorously and more bindingly than all earlier eras and upheavals that preceded us. Only the most radical historical knowledge lets us face the unusual nature of our mission and keeps us from succumbing to mere reconstruction and uninspired imitation.[25]

There is something titanic about the attempt to meet the demands of this mission: "We . . . now skip over this whole process of distortion and decline and seek agian to conquer the undestroyed naming power of language and word."[26] Objectively, the possibilities for accomplishing this are already given: "The fact that the formation of Western grammar originated in the Greek consciousness of the *Greek* language gives the process its entire meaning. For the Greek language (seen in terms of its possibilities for thinking) is, next to the German, at once the most powerful and the most spiritual."[27]

The most important guide for regaining this origin is, according to Heidegger, Heraclitus. With him, it can be grasped that from the beginning of battle *(polemos)* has formed the ontological bridge between *physis* and truth *(aletheia)*. If we admit the equivalence of *polemos* and *logos,* the original dynamics of "being" should become obvious:

> The battle that is intended here is original battle, because it enables those in combat to appear as such for the first time: it is not a mere assault on what is already present-at-hand *[Vorhanden].* The battle sketches and then develops for the first time the un- heard-of, the un-spoken, and the un-thought. This battle is then fought by the creators—the poets and the thinkers and the statesmen. They throw all their works against that overwhelming power and with that they exorcise *[bannen]* the world opened in this way. It is with these works first that the power of *physis* comes to presence. Being only now begins to be as such. This world in

the making is true history. Such battle not only allows the first emergence *[entstehen]* of things, but it alone preserves whatever exists in its constancy *[Ständigkeit]*. Where the battle stops, "being" does not disappear, but the world turns away.[28]

Heraclitus' concept of *polemos* forms the ontological foundation for the fascists' idea of social stratification, of discrimination among people, and of the radical disavowal of human solidarity. "Strife *[Auseinandersetzung]* is the progenitor of everything [that exists at present=*Anwesenden*], but also the ruling preserver of everything. For it lets some appear as gods, others as humans, some as servants and some as free men":[29]

> But those who do not grasp the *logos* "are not capable of hearing or saying" (Fragment 19). They are not capable of erecting their existence *[Dasein]* in the Being of beings *[Sein des Seienden]*. Only those capable of this—the poet and the thinker—have control over the word. The others just stagger around in the circle of their stubbornness and ignorance. They simply accept what crosses their path, what flatters them, and what is familiar to them. They are like dogs: "for dogs bark at those they don't know" (Fragment 97). They are asses: "asses prefer chaff to gold" (Fragment 9).[30]

Heraclitus' hatred for the masses, his high regard for those who have rank as well as power, and the fact that he figuratively talks about the inauthentic as dogs and asses "belongs essentially to Greek existence. If one today is all too enthusiastic about the *polis* of the Greeks, one should not suppress this side; otherwise the concept of the *polis* will easily become vapid and sentimental. What is established according to rank is the stronger. . . . Because existence is *logos, harmonia, aletheia, physis, phainesthai*, it does not manifest itself in just any way. The truth is not meant for everyone, only for the strong."[31]

All this paves the way for putting the Greek *polis* on the same level as the stratified society of National Socialism, that society that is the state is the work of "the strong":

> The *polis* is the historical place, the there *[Da]*, in which, *out of* which, and *for* which history happens. The gods, temples, priests, festivities, games, poets, thinkers, rulers, the council of the elders, the congregation of the nation, the army and ships, all belong to this historical place. All this does not first belong to the *polis;* it is not political merely because it enters into a relationship with a

statesman, a leader of the army, or affairs of state. Rather, all these people and things first are political when in the original historical place, for example, insofar as poets *only* then are really poets, thinkers *only* then are really thinkers, priests *only* then are really priests, the rulers *only* then are really rulers. But "are" *[sind]* means "requiring effective authority and power *[Gewalt-tätige Gewalt]* and looming over historical existence as doers and creators." Being prominent in this historical place, they simultaneously become an *Apolis*, without a city or state, a-lone *[Ein-same]*, un-canny, *[Un-heimliche]*, with no way out of the middle of being-in-the-whole *[Seienden im Ganzen]*. At the same time, they are without rules and limits, without structure and connections, because *as* creators they are obliged to establish all these things first.[32]

The "Introduction to Metaphysics" thus becomes the "Introduction to Politics," in the sense that politics becomes transcendentalized without weakening its innate power.

The thesis that this text of Heidegger's marks the beginning of his break with National Socialism and that his break had been inevitable, insofar as Heidegger did not want to relinquish his line of thought, appears to be quite dubious.[33] Alexander Schwan promotes this view. His view that Heidegger stopped marching with the National Socialists because he had recognized the totalitarian nature of their ideology does not correspond with his other claim that Heidegger still supported the totalitarian state in 1935.[34] For in the "Introduction to Metaphysics," Heidegger justified the same sort of state that he defended in 1933/34, indeed, a state treated as the central power of a society formed in terms of *corporate* "social standings" wherein the execution of political power was exclusively attributed to the statesmen—exactly as in fascism. Schwan also thinks that Heidegger conceived of the "historical nation" as the primary social category. Since this nation would gain its unity through the state (as a nation in a state), Heidegger had imagined the nation as a "work" of the state, as an abstraction, indeed an a-historical "self-activation of truth" *(sich-ins-Werk-Setzen der Wahrheit)*.[35] But Heidegger never doubted the fundamental, indeed sacralizing character of the speech of the German people, even if he supposedly claimed at this time the equivalence of the state and the nation in this "enterprise" *(Werk)*. For in this idea of the "enterprise" Heidegger did not lose sight of the *historical* approach to the problem. Even in 1935 he wanted to develop the state out of the nation, just as in 1934 he had demanded of the nation that it find *itself* in the state and in the leader *(Führer)*.

When the text "Introduction to Metaphysics" was published in 1953, the question arose whether or not it was identical with the 1935 lectures. In this regard, the main point of interest was a certain sentence that Heidegger claimed to have written but not to have read. In that sentence, the movement of thought of the entire lecture series appears to come together in a formula that illustrates its political connotations in an exemplary way. After having alluded to the reduction of the concept of spirit to an instrumentalized role in a philosophy of values and unities, pointing out thereby where National Socialism had gone astray, Heidegger went on to say: "All this is called philosophy. What today is presented as the philosophy of National Socialism, but has nothing to do with the inner truth and greatness of this movement (namely the meeting of planetary-determined technology and modern man), takes its fish catch *[Fischzüge]* from these muddied waters of 'values' and 'unities.' "[36]

Heidegger later claimed not to have read out the words in parentheses in the original text.[37] In saying this, he wanted to suggest a criticism of National Socialist philosophy, of the political leadership, and thus of National Socialism itself. Clearly, it should be asked whether the intended criticism of the National Socialist philosophers and the political leadership had not been made in the name of that very form of National Socialism that had been betrayed in 1934 and only freed by Heidegger himself in the *polemos* of his lectures. Even if the words in parentheses were in the original text, that does not make for a qualitative change in the preceding argument of the lectures. National Socialism itself strove for "a match between a planetary-determined technology and modern man" because Heidegger, above all, recognized in National Socialism the power and possibility of achieving such a union. It concerned a power and efficacy that Marxism and positivism lacked because they were the agents of evil.

In 1987, Rainer Marten reported on Heidegger's behavior during the preparation of the new edition of "Introduction to Metaphysics":

The three of us recommended to him concerning the printing of the lecture course in 1953 that, because of our fear of its effect on the public, he alter the phrase "with the inner truth and greatness of National Socialism" in the expression "what today is being presented as the philosophy of National Socialism, but has nothing at all to do with the inner truth and greatness of National Socialism." He chose to change the second "National Socialism" to "movement" and inserted after this the parenthetical statement: "(namely the meeting of planetary-determined technology and modern man)." But around 1935 the vision of a National Socialism perverted by some technological abuse of things did not exist for Heidegger at all. At that time the unpleasant essence of technology was still attributed to non-German sources. Heidegger quite literally says in an earlier section of the same lecture course: "Russia and America are both . . . the same; the same wretched mad rush of unbridled technology and the same unbounded organization of the average human being." No, this "famous" expression clearly speaks essentially in favor of fascism, which is philosophically recognized as sincere and good and proves by itself that subsequent self-interpretations are lies.[38]

An article by Elfride Heidegger-Petri

It is important to take note the fact, unknown until now, that Elfride Heidegger-Petri, Heidegger's wife, helped in his fight to reform the university system. In 1935, she published a polemical article on the need to bring young women into the universities, calling on notions analogous to those her husband had used in the Rector's Address. This article, "Thoughts of a Mother on the Higher Education of Young Women," was published in the review *Deutsche Mädchenbildung: Zeitschrift für das gesamte höhere Mädchenschulwesen*, edited by Karl Stracke.[39]

Karl Stracke was the director of the Goethe-Gymnasium at Dortmund and professor of mathematics and physics. A Protestant and a well-known educator, he had received by this time numerous decorations, among them the Ritterkreuz.[40] He had been a member of the National Socialist Party since 1937 although he was not engaged in any particular political activity.[41] Until 1933, the review had clearly followed a strong nationalist (*deutschnational*) line, after which it adopted an unconditional National Socialist direction.

The second issue of 1935 contains an article by Dr. Elisabeth Meyn von Westenholz on "Higher Education for Young Women as a Stimulus for National Unity."[42] In the sixth issue of 1935, there is a work by H. Wendt, "Other Writings on National Socialism and the Woman Question."[43] In the seventh issue (1935) is an article by H. Voigts, "Traits of Students and Observations on Hereditary Biology."[44] In the eighth issue (also 1935), there are interesting articles by Alma Langenbach, "The New Type of German Woman,"[45] and Edith Ullbrich, "Biological Thought in Teaching the Lutheran Religion in Advanced Studies."[46]

The article by Elfride Heidegger-Petri generally fits into the National Socialist notion of woman as Hitler had formulated it in his speech given at the Congress of Women held at Nurenberg on September 8, 1934.[47] The work of the chief of the women's organization of the party, Gertrud Scholtz-Klink, is similar.[48]

Certain original notions bearing on a much-debated issue invite closer study, since Nazism accords men gifts superior to those of women. The contribution of Elfride Heidegger-Petri is important given the status of women in National Socialism. But here we are solely concerned with how her work supports and parallels her husband's positions.

First, in the university world Martin Heidegger had assigned an avant-garde role to student groups. Heidegger-Petri, in a similar spirit, takes up the defense of a group considered distinctly less important by the conservative parts of the society, by prominent National Socialists, and by the very structure of the party. She sets out to defend the right of women to take an active part in university life as well as in society at large and in the revolution.

The point of departure for her reflections conforms closely to the credo of National Socialism:

> Every era like our own that tries to create a new world view must ask itself what the goal and direction of education for subsequent generations should be. The old goal of modern humanism, the education of the free person, is not sufficiently modern. Beyond the singular "I" exists the "we"; beyond the needs of individuals exists the needs of the community of the people.[49]

Elfride Heidegger-Petri applies these notions to the specific situation of women:

> Our understanding struggles to go beyond the fatal error of believing in the equality of all human beings and tries to recognize the diversity of peoples and races; at the same time, it correctly and pointedly confirms the fundamental difference between the sexes. The question of how to develop an educational plan for the coming generations recognizes from the beginning an immediate difference in our ways of considering the education of young men and women.[50]

For Heidegger-Petri, however, there is no reason to establish a difference in the programs of studies, for the primary school has already divided boys and girls. She favors the same similar secondary education for all girls, whether they then go into university studies or to professional schools. Any division would harm "the true community of the people, the most precious but also the most threatened of the gifts given to the people by our great Führer,"[51] and also contradicts the general principle according to which "every German woman must become both mother and comrade of the people":

> The honorific name of "comrade of the people" that the Führer, in his speech, gave to German women is opposed to any inclination to discriminate against women. If we want to go beyond a pamphleteer's interpretation of these principles and give a name to the essential, we must say that being a woman is not to be a slave, that maternity is in no way a sentimental affair. To reduce this to a simple physiological state means to lower woman to the rank of female. To be woman and mother means to attain spiritual values. Woman is not a comrade of the people unless she goes beyond the narrow frame of the family to be also the comrade of her husband in his struggle to make the life of the German people a reality; not only is she a comrade of the people as mistress of the household performing her specific tasks as guardian of the principal richness of the people; woman is a comrade of the people only when she becomes the bearer and guardian of the precious racial heritage of our Germanness and as authentic teacher of her children by giving them the chance to become future agents of our national destiny. Finally, she is comrade of the people only when, when the fated moment arrives, she is ready as a German woman to submit or to undertake any sacrifice for the survival of the fatherland.[52]

From these principles, Heidegger-Petri deduces the essential objectives of women's education: waken and educate the abilities of women to become woman and mother; "communicate and reinforce the conviction that all members of the people are united through the fundamental links of race, custom, history, and the economy of their society"; educate girls in an appreciation of their own bodies with a view to becoming mothers; prepare them as women for their professional life, whether at the hearth, in scientific activity, or in the workplace.[53] It is only when all girls share the same education that their future connection with the community of the people can be guaranteed. "If the military spirit of soldiers transforms young men into comrades, to be woman and mother creates the unity of women."[54]

For Elfride Heidegger-Petri the reforms of 1908 and 1925 that envisaged the reorganization of secondary education for women failed precisely because they ignored the specifics of women's condition, in addition to the errors contained in the education programs for young men.[55] The new plans also highlighted important weaknesses and dangerous errors in execution. Because the development of women's education was taking place in the large cities, the majority of the new women at the universities were being recruited from the cities—that is, from sectors "that are not culturally and racially the best."[56] The number of subjects studied also needed to be reduced, without sacrificing rigorous and solid theoretical education. This certainly was not impossible, she argued, because the idea that practical education is not a stimulant for theoretical education is an error based on "the general prejudice according to which it is not possible to attain something spiritual by practical means." It is also an error and a prejudice to think that practical activity is not spiritual and to claim that it is very different from "science in the strict sense."[57]

Without ignoring women's specific characteristics, women must be allowed access to advanced studies. By insisting on the need to encourage those women not living in the large cities to elect to continue their studies, Elfride Heidegger-Petri was taking up her husband's programs. She was doing the same thing when she argued with National Socialist pedagogues who were opposed to allowing women in higher education. The allusion to alternatives that Alfred Bäumler had proposed is clear:

> Our people situated here at the heart of Europe need sufficient strength, talent, and the spirit of sacrifice in order to affirm ourselves. Closing once again the doors of higher education to women would make them second-class citizens. The injustice that has been corrected for the working class may thus be corrected as well for the women of the people. Moreover, that error would harm the prestige and the organic growth of our culture. Old and young, man and woman, city and country, all must be able to participate. As long as the universities mean to be the bearer of our culture, the educator of our people, and the bastion of corporate leadership, it ought in principle to be accessible to all the people.[58]

Elfride Heidegger-Petri also criticizes Krieck's alternative, which tended to turn the universities into specialized schools *(Fachschulen)*: "If it were to be this way, advanced studies for women would be no more than an appendix to the education given to young men." According to Heidegger-Petri, Germans had patterned themselves too slavishly on Anglo-Saxon practices. But when one thinks about the "needs imposed by German spiritual life," these practices do not correspond to reality. For if the people want to make the family the authentic source of national strength *(völkische Kraft)*, and if to that end children must be recognized to be the most precious possession of our nation, then we must accord wives and mothers the best education possible, the education offered to our leaders, a university education. To be blunt, it is essential not to forget that "this leadership group is formed exclusively of those recognized for their character and qualifications."[59]

Heidegger-Petri also deduces from this the urgent need to open professional work to women. Women had shown their abilities in the past twenty years, by becoming part of the community of the people as physicians, judges, social workers, with a competence clearly at the level of men. In this way they had proved themselves capable of undertaking tasks men could not take on. Neither social work nor the education of girls can be really effective without the participation of women as specialists and professors. This becomes quite clear when, as we say, "the best education is built on a good example":[60]

> Those who have had the chance to study girls from all walks of life, in the schools, in the National Socialist Association for Girls, or in the service of women's work, understand the source of their spiritual and intellectual strength, that original and lively strength that is now struggling for education. We must not ignore them, and certainly we must not deliberately put them aside. On the contrary, we must create for them the genuine possibility for an education and for their integration into social life.[61]

The work of Elfride Heidegger-Petri must be connected to the debates on reforming education and the structure of political work for women within the party. Conventional opinion tended to limit women's activities strictly and to restrict women to their own organization, the National Socialist Women's Force *(Frauenschaft)*[62] which had been from its inception until 1934 in favor of the Röhm faction and the SA. The issue of July 15, 1932, of the *Nationalsozialistische-Frauenwarte* (the official organ of the National Socialist Frauenschaft) printed an appeal to German women written by one of that faction (Gregor Strasser). The issues of July 15 and October 1 carried articles about Strasser and his political work.[63] The doctrinal line of the review was radical, as we can see from some article titles—for example: "Reflections on the Sterilization Law" by Dr. Schwab,[64]

"Contribution to the Racial Problem" (not signed),[65] and "Frauenschaft and Racial Purity" by Professor Stämmler.[66]

The women's organizations Elfride Heidegger-Petri mentions proclaimed in its statutes and declaration of principle:

> We are struggling for the conservation of the Aryan race, therefore also to free national life from all foreign racial influence. The spirit must be German, German also our language, German our law, and German our culture. . . . We are struggling by word and deed, using every means at our disposal against the Jewish-Marxist spirit. We want to make our vital and national will a rampart against the destruction menacing us from pacifism and Communist bolshevism. We support the development of social conscience and the task of social service.[67]

The same year Elfride Heidegger-Petri applauded the work of the Frauenschaft saw the promulgation of racial laws and the increase of violent persecutions against German citizens of Jewish descent, especially in Freiburg. The women's Nazi organization participated actively in this work:

> In 1935, the leader *[Führerin]* of the National Socialist Frauenschaft at Freiburg called on all German women of the city to boycott Jewish stores. When the Jewish businessmen dropped prices to get rid of their goods, the Nazi commandos tried to block entry to their stores, provoking violent reactions. During the summer of 1935, Jews were banned from public baths and threatened in the press with harsh reprisals should they try to break this interdict.[68]

This was just the beginning. On November 9, 1938, the synagogue at Freiburg was burned by the SA and the SS, who dragged the rabbi from bed to help them destroy his synagogue. It was demanded that the Freiburg Jewish community pay the costs of cleaning up the ruins of the building.[69] More than one hundred members of this community were murdered at Dachau.[70]

Persecutions against Jews had begun in 1933 with the boycott of Jewish businesses, also of physicians, lawyers, and professors, organized by the SA and the National Socialist students. Coordination was important and extended to the whole Reich.[71] Karl Jaspers recalls these acts in a letter to Heidegger of July 24, 1952, linking the suffering of the Jewish people to the suffering of his own wife: "When she learned from the

Völkischer Beobachter the news of the boycott, my wife began to weep, as one can weep when we see the world crumbling at our feet, and you, you were content to say: "At times it does us good to weep" *[es tut gut, einmal zu weinen].*[72]

Jaspers also reports that Heidegger had warned him then to be careful of the dangers of "the Jewish international."[73]

On several occasions, Heidegger denied having been anti-semitic,[74] invoking in his favor that he had helped Professors von Hevesy and Tannhauser, as well as his student Helene Weiss. Discussion of this question, begun with great vigor by François Fédier, could be carried on more objectively if the correspondence between Jaspers and Heidegger were published, or at least opened to the public.

What is available is a citation that makes reference to an ideological constant in the philosopher's attitude. The citation comes from a responsible source, from the work of a disciple and friend of Heidegger, H. W. Petzet, in a work carefully reviewed by Elfride Heidegger-Petri.[75] Petzet says: "If he found any sort of city life repugnant, and if everything about city life seemed strange to him, this was even more true of the worldly spirit of those Jewish circles that dominated the great cities of the West."[76]

The attitude of the regime toward Heidegger around 1936

Heidegger's critical attitude toward such high-ranking Nazis as Alfred Rosenberg and Ernst Krieck does not seem to have attracted the hostility of the regime. It was at this time (1935–1936), for example, that the Ministry of Education and Sciences at Berlin used the slanderous report that Heidegger had written in 1933 about Eduard Baumgarten. The fact that the Ministry accepted Heidegger without hesitation as part of the system of informers on which such reports were based clearly indicates what the authorities thought about his orthodoxy.[77]

The same ministry also showed its sympathy for Heidegger by proposing to the rector that he appoint Heidegger dean of the faculty of philosophy. This fact, which clarifies retrospectively circumstances that could have been the basis for Heidegger's resignation in 1933, provoked a response from the Office of the Rector at Freiburg. On May 18, the rector answered the Ministry:

I must speak against the nomination of Heidegger as dean. During his rectorate, Heidegger lost the confidence of his colleagues. The administration of the region of Baden also had troubles with him, and he was led to resign. For me, working alongside Heidegger in such a confidential situation would be impossible. He relieved me of my function as dean of the law faculty, replacing me by Erik Wolf. As for his ability to hold the post of dean, should it be necessary, I ask you to speak with Professor Eckhardt. Anyway, I doubt that after his experiences as rector he would accept the post of dean.[78]

Contrary to Heidegger's claims in 1945, that his Rector's Address was strongly attacked, especially among the teachers,[79] the speech was reprinted in 1937 for the third time and five thousand copies were printed,[80] and this during a time when every publication was subject to rigorous censorship. Heidegger could not have been unaware of this edition. On April 27, 1937, he wrote to Madame Maria Lietzmann, sending a copy of this third edition with a dedication, as well as an author's copy of the essay on Hölderlin.[81] This third edition is also noted in the *Gesamtverzeichnis des deutschsprachigen Schrifttums* for 1911–1965.[82] The first edition was issued by the library of the University of Freiburg. The second and third were published by Korn at Breslau.

As for the publication of "Hölderlin and the Essence of Poetry," here again we cannot accept what Heidegger said about it later in his *Spiegel* interview.[83] On April 2, 1935, Heidegger delivered the original text at the Italian Institute of German Studies at Rome, which was under the control of Mussolini's government. The speech was sponsored by the Italian authorities and also by the Ministry of Foreign Relations of the Reich. The Institute was housed at the villa Sciarra-Wurts and funded by the Italians to strengthen the cultural relations between the two countries, all part of an attempt to cope with the demands of the time.

Heidegger's speech was on the program of the Institute for 1935. The annual series was opened on January 10, 1935, by Hans Carossa, who read from his poetry. Carossa received the Goethe medal from the city of Frankfurt in 1938, and in 1941 he was made president of the Union of European Writers, an association begun by Goebbels for the task of coordinating cultural propaganda abroad.[84] Although Carossa is usually considered a dissident writer (he refused to become a member of the Chamber of Writers for personal reasons), his work was given a very warm official sanction. His poems were printed in party reviews,[85] and in 1942 The Amt Rosenberg gave one of his books to Hitler as a birthday present.[86]

The next speech ("Cultura e storia nelle fluttuazioni ambientali del loro svolgimento") was given by Karl Haushofer. Haushofer was professor of geopolitics at Munich, and one of the important theoreticians of the ideology of "vital space."

In addition to Haushofer's speech, there were also speeches by Magnus Olsen, professor at Olso ("Roma e l'antica poesia nordica"), and Heinrich von Srbik, professor of ancient and modern history at Vienna ("Liberalismo e democratizia in Germania fino al 1848"). Von Srbik was later named by Minister Rust as president of the Pangermanic Historical Commission. After 1935, he was a member, in Vienna, of the Institute of the Reich for the New Germany, directed by Walter Frank.[87] In 1943, under the government of Reichsstatthalter Baldur von Schirach and thanks to his donations, von Srbik was instrumental as a member of the Academy of Sciences at Vienna in publishing the works of Abraham a Sancta Clara.

Other speakers on the program were Hans Heyse ("Kant e l'antichità classica"), Carl Schmitt ("Il problema teorico dell' unità statale nei suoi tre elementi teorici costitutivi"), Karl Löwith ("Lettura e interpretazione di Nietzsche"), C. Antoni ("La formazione storica del Reich"), and D. Cantimori ("Le dottrine politiche del nazional-socialismo").[88] The invitation sent to Heidegger was signed by the official philosopher of the fascist regime, Giovanni Gentile.[89] Heidegger's participation in the series was approved by the Ministry of Foreign Relations, which sent Heidegger the official notification. This document is located in the archives of the Foreign Office (*Auswärtiges Amt*) at Bonn.[90] Moreover, we can suppose that at this time and through his participation at the Italian Institute of German Studies, Heidegger established personal ties, directly and indirectly, with people in Mussolini's government. Some years later, with help from Il Duce, who contacted Goebbels, Heidegger was able to publish his "Plato's Doctrine of Truth," which Rosenberg tried to veto, in the *Annual* edited by his disciple Ernesto Grassi.

Heidegger's speech was published as "Hölderlin and the Essence of Poetry" in the journal *Das innere Reich* (1937). This journal was begun by special governmental permission at a time when there was a ban on new journals. The first issue (April 1934), defines its purpose:

> Our work is not meant just for German readers, but for all those beyond our borders who are ready to recognize that, in spite of those who have fled our land, our best thinkers have not abandoned our people; on the contrary, in National Socialist Germany, there has recently been created a space for the best Germans, those who belong to the central Reich [*Innere Reich*].[91]

We must note that the journal was suspended for a time in 1936. Heidegger published his work in the first issue after the suspension.[92]

The article was well received. The review *Die Neue Literatur* (Leipzig) noted in February 1937 that Heidegger had dedicated his work to Hölderlin's editor, Hellingrath, who "died in combat," and that Heidegger had presented Hölderlin correctly.[93] The review *Blätter für Deutsche Philosophie*, directed by the National Socialist philosopher Heinz Heimsoeth, also complimented Heidegger in 1939 for having understood Hölderlin from the point of view of the German people by presenting him as the "poet of poets."[94]

Heidegger's claim in his 1945 writing that his work had been violently criticized by the Hitler Youth journal, *Wille und Macht*, is inaccurate, to say the least. In the March 15, 1937, issue, the author of the criticism, Dr. W. Konitzer, claimed only that "our youth are more likely to understand Hölderlin than Professor Heidegger," without however denying "that Heidegger shows in the last paragraphs that he understood how to approach the power of the poet's language, and how to adjust his own voice to that of Hölderlin. This is how Heidegger finally discovered how to reveal the true Hölderlin."[95]

Nonetheless, Heidegger's pride was hurt. In a letter to Benno Mascher, a reader for the review *Das Innere Reich*, he said: "The claim of the famous gentleman at *Wille und Macht*, according to whom my article on Hölderlin is quite foreign for our youth, shows clearly that we must not expect much from such Germans. A former member of the SS-Führer who knows Marburg society informs me that Dr. K. was still a Social Democrat in 1933."[96] Note Heidegger's confidence in this former member of the SS-Führer who denounced his former comrade in the Hitler Youth.

To illustrate the relationships Heidegger kept around 1936 with Nazi organs and publicists, it is important to refer to documents kept in the Berlin Document Center, where we find information on Heidegger's later participation with the review *Das Volk*, edited by Adolf Ehrt and Wolfgang Nufer.[97] Nufer had been a member of the SS since 1935 and had been in the NSDAP since 1932. At the beginning of 1936, he was named administrator for the Freiburg theater. Adolf Ehrt had also been a member of the NSDAP since 1932, and of the SA since 1933. Beginning in 1934, he was editor of the *Völkischer Beobachter* and also wrote *The Armed Rebellion (Bewaffnete Aufstand* [Berlin, 1933]) and *The Jew as Delinquent (Der Jude als Verbrecher* [1937]), which had a preface by Julius Streicher. The first title of the review was *Völkische Kultur*. This is the name recommended to Nazi members in Unger's catalogue.[98]

We learn from a letter sent by the board of the review to the Ministry of Education and Sciences on May 2, 1936, that the decision of the directors of *Das Volk* to ask Heidegger to join them was not new. The letter asked for information on Heidegger, "on his work and personality." The Ministry answered on June 3, 1936, including no criticism of the philosopher and refusing information "for reasons of principle." Wolfgang Nufer began to live and work in Freiburg in 1936; so it seems that the decision to ask for Heidegger's participation was due to his relationship with Nufer, or at least to Nufer's confidence in Heidegger's ideological position. The fact that *Das Volk* intended to invite Heidegger indicates that at this time, in spite of his "critical" attitude, he was still publishing in journals as orthodox as Nufer and Ehrt's.

Another proof of the confidence that the Ministry of Education and Sciences had in Heidegger can be seen in the attempts to reorganize (in a political sense) the Kant Society *(Kant-Gesellschaft)* and the crisis of this famous philosophical society in 1933. In the Central State Archives at Merseburg, there is a series of documents illustrating especially the Amt Rosenberg's efforts to reform the Kant Society by changing the leadership.

According to documents kept in the archives of the University of Halle (home of the Kant Society), once the statutes were amended, the president, Paul Menzer, was relieved of his functions following strong official pressure. Professor Hans Heyse, the key person in the change, became head of the Society and of *Kant-Studien*. Then, after the leadership had undergone a number of other changes leading to Heyse's resignation, Dr. Martin Löpelmann became the ministerial member of the board. Until 1934, Eduard Spranger was, along with Löpelmann and Menzer, part of the editorship. On October 10, 1934, Löpelmann gave up his functions at the demand of the NSDAP.[99] In a letter from the Amt Rosenberg to Alfred Bäumler, located in the Institute for Contemporary History *(Institut für Zeitgeschichte)* at Munich,[100] it is clear that Rosenberg was not in agreement with the ideological bent of the Kant Society, and that Löpelmann was to resign.[101]

On October 10, Löpelmann addressed his resignation to the Ministry, the controlling body of the Kant Society.[102] Analyzing the documents leaves no doubt that Bäumler's decision to assume power ran into opposition, even within the Society.

In the meantime, a Kant Society was created abroad, directed by Professors Liebert (Belgrade) and Kuhn (an émigré in Holland). Husserl (Freiburg) and Driesch had agreed to be members. This was arranged without official sanction. It was the Kant Society itself (or a member of the board) who offered this compromising information. It was addressed to Schäfer in the NSDAP Department of Foreign Relations on December 18, 1935.[103] In a letter of July 24, 1936, Hans Heyse spoke to Schäfer about his difficulties as president of the Society and editor of *Kant-Studien* in trying to turn both of these organs into instruments of Nazi cultural and scientific propaganda. Heyse accepted both posts in July 1935, as Alfred Rosenberg had asked him to do. He also asked for more funds and permission to transform the Society along NSDAP lines.[104]

At this time the Ministry of Education and Sciences intervened to designate Governmental Counselor Frey as the one to reorganize the Kant Society. According to Bäumler's report, located in the Institute for Contemporary History at Munich, Frey proposed a "rapid and unimpeachable change" of leadership, with Heidegger as president, Löpelmann (Berlin) as vice-president, and Koellreuter (Munich) and Metzner (Union of Writers of the Reich) as third and fourth vice-presidents. Frey also proposed Stieve and Gauss (from the Ministry of Foreign Affairs) as members of the board. Posts were held also for philosophers from Japan, America, the Netherlands, England, and France, with the agreement of the Ministry of Foreign Affairs. Frey's proposal included also members from the Union of Writers, and from Rosenberg's Office.[105]

The letter from the Amt Rosenberg to Bäumler showed clearly its disagreement with the ministerial list (without giving names) and claimed they needed Bäumler as president, if possible—a proposal that Frey later accepted.

The note to Bäumler in February 24, 1937, is the only document giving information on the development of this crisis. It notes the resignation of Heyse (February 8, 1937) from his post and from the Society.[106]

The journal *Kant-Studien* began publishing again in 1942/43, with Hans Heyse once again as editor. Heidegger had been a member of the Kant Society since 1916 while a professor at Freiburg. The struggle over the change of leadership shows the internal contradictions and the factional struggles between Rosenberg and Heidegger.

Writings: "Origin of the Work of Art" and "Ways to Language"

Heidegger's philosophical and political-philosophical orientation at this time can be seen more systematically in his works "The Origin of the Work of Art" ("Der Ursprung des Kunstwerks") and "Ways to Language" ("Wege zur Aussprache"). Heidegger made two drafts of his essays on art. The first draft was for a speech given to the Society for

Science and Art at Freiburg on November 13, 1935, and was offered again at the invitation of the students of Zurich University. The final text was published in *Holzwege* and includes three speeches to the Freien Deutschen Hochstift at Frankfurt in 1936, on November 17 and 24 and December 4.[107]

In these papers a new conceptual element appears, which Heidegger now uses to explain the essence of the work of art. The philosopher conceives the work of art as "truth embodied in the work" *(Sich-im-Werk-setzen)*. The notion developed here by Heidegger has a more general application beyond the arts: it means to explain also the origin of the state, as the framework in which the being of what is, as well as the inquiry being gives rise to, is formed. The political reference is Heidegger's characteristic way of "revolutionizing" the conception of the state and society as site of a primal struggle, with history supplying their dynamic source. "When a world opens up, a historical humanity is called to victory or to defeat, to benediction or to malediction, to domination or to servitude."[108]

In this reflection we see the introduction of another ideological constant: The subject in which truth appears, truth embodied in the work, is the people. The categories of earth, of world, and those things that flow from them are grounded in the act by which a "historic people" constitutes itself, makes truth concrete, makes it an artwork. Thus Heidegger interprets his own work as a moment in the struggle of the German people for its own identity: "Are we, in our being-there, historically at the source? Do we know—that is, do we bring our attention to the essence of the origin?—or rather, in our attitude toward art, are we not calling for more than academic knowledge of the past?"[109]

For Heidegger, the subject he has in mind is a kind of eminent figure, a transcendental, historical judge who speaks from within the people and its traditions and becomes the examplar of future action: Hölderlin. "For this alternative and its resolution, he is a sign that does not lie. Hölderlin, the poet of the work from which Germans still need to be released, has named it when he said: 'With great labor is released/What remains near to the origin, the site.' "[110] For Heidegger, to turn politics into aesthetics means to spiritualize politics. In this move Heidegger encounters a spiritual Führer. Hölderlin, or at least Heidegger's Hölderlin, does not replace Hitler but becomes the supreme exemplar that allows Heidegger to unite political and spiritual activity. In the 1934 course, Heidegger emphasized Hölderlin's essential role, historically as well as politically and philosophically. Hölderlin is invoked at a crucial point in the philosopher's evolution, in his text on the work of art. This role will be even more important during World War II. The new category elaborated by Heidegger ("the truth embodied in the work") is adapted to allow us to analyze the history of a people and its real alternatives: this seems to be an essential element of the spiritualization that Heidegger wanted to impose on the movement.

This category was only formulated in 1936. Therefore it cannot be used to understand all the "political ontology" that Heidegger developed during the Third Reich. Alexander Schwan tries in vain to apply it in a broad way.[111] It would be incorrect to explicate early theoretical propositions by means of categories that only appear later.[112] On the other hand, Heidegger never rested until he subordinated every conceptualization to that originary event, the formation of the German people, which he treated as the ultimate paradigm.

Later we will see more exactly the role Heidegger attributed to Hölderlin, and especially the essential link tying Hölderlin to the Swabian fatherland, his native region as well as Heidegger's. Here, it is important to emphasize that Heidegger tried to render the historical moment spiritual as a way of expressing his explicit will to establish his reflection on what he called "the earth." It is in this spirit that Heidegger published his "Ways to Language," which appeared in 1937 in a collection edited by Kerber, the mayor of Freiburg:[113] *Land of the Alemmani: Book on the Fatherland and Its Mission.* By examining Heidegger's article as part of his collection of documents,[114] Guido Schneeberger has brought attention to this work, which was later included in the *Collected Works.* We looked at the political attitudes of Kerber earlier, but it is good to recall here that in 1937 he was a member of the SS at Freiburg and that some months later he was promoted by SS-Reichsführer Himmler to SS-Sturmbannführer.[115]

Kerber situates the doctrinal context of the work clearly in his article "People, Culture, and Town." The book is to be part of the "spiritual movement" that made National Socialism possible by putting an end to the frightful state of German culture before January 30, 1933. "A nation alienated within its own race, bereft of freedom, is not able to develop a creative cultural life of its own."[116] Freed by the revolution, "there surged from all sides and in all the arts new creative forces" that could use the newly discovered German spirit, could "obey the peremptory needs of racial blood," and could give new form and contour to the people's soul.[117] The freedom achieved by the new Germany is unique: "Germany alone possesses an office of culture *[Kulturkammer]* that works to guard the freedom of the creative forces of the spiritual culture."[118]

By linking the work of the town to that of the state, Kerber used his

book as an effort to promote autochthonous forces. Germany is different
from other countries in that it is not a single racial unit nor a culture with
a single voice; it does not have a unique center that guides and unites the
whole life of the country, as does a capital city, and assigns the provinces
a secondary and subordinate role:

> These countrysides surrounding us have always been able to
> develop in us a distinctly German life that reflects its own nature,
> its history and character, always in constant contact with the earth.
> This is why, along with the peculiar liveliness and decentralization
> of German culture, there is always to be found the rich variety of
> the German native, wherever this culture grows. . . .
> German culture has always been a people's culture. Even in its
> darkest times, it has been original. For even if the damage caused
> by liberal civilization and Jewish alienation has been great, no
> one has ever succeeded in taking the earth from German culture,
> nor the links that connect the two, nor has anyone turned the
> provinces into deserts by imposing a foreign spirit on the
> pavements of our great cities. . . .
> The southwest area also has a task given by destiny, that is to
> struggle in its own ways, given its geography and its countryside,
> for the very existence of its people, its ideas, its Führer, to
> struggle with all the forces it can draw from its "alemannic" being.
> . . . The town of Freiburg, situated at the heart of the alemannic
> country, plays a central role owing to its cultural importance. The
> essential political and cultural character of the southwest Reich has
> ancient traditions. Yet its mission is not based only on its past and
> its traditions, but finds its dynamism in the living present, whose
> strength and will and assurance indicate the direction of
> Germany's future. The autochthonous people of the upper Rhine
> understand better than ever its historical and cultural and political
> task. Recent events have given it a new meaning. Freiburg has
> become a pioneer town. It is the central point of the Reich, yet is
> bounded by three countries.

Kerber then shows the immediate political objective of his *Annual:*

The political question of the upper Rhine has been clearly settled
by our Führer. There is no longer a question about that. But what
does remain, and always will, as our particular task is the
conservation of the essence, the type, the very wealth of our

autochthonous element, linked to the land and entrusted to us, and the need to offer once again to the whole of the German being the sources of its distinctive strength.[119]

What was needed was a dialogue with France in this region in order to promote peace and mutual understanding. Hitler's troops had entered the Rhine zone and occupied it, contrary to certain clauses of the Versailles Treaty. The Locarno Pact had provided for such an eventuality by prescribing military actions against Germany, but Italy had already given its word not to intervene. England kept its distance from France, which after some hesitation capitulated in turn.[120] From that moment, Hitler's government had to accept the task of maintaining peace and consolidating the conquered land. Kerber's role in his *Annual* is precisely to support this effort intellectually. This is also why he requested and obtained the collaboration of four Frenchmen so as to give an appearance of an international exchange. Henri Lichtenberger, a Sorbonne professor, contributed an article "Goethe and France";[121] Professor Jean-Edouard Spenlé, rector of Dijon, contributed "Nietzsche, Spiritual Mediator between France and Germany";[122] and Alphonse de Chateaubriant wrote "How I See Führer Adolf Hitler."[123] The most elegant article was by Dr. Joseph M. Maitre, leader of the French Frontkämpferabordnung-1937 (frontlines delegation), who contributed "The Fighters at Freiburg im Breisgau."[124] In it the author describes and praises the friendly relations of former fighters on both sides of the Rhine.

Chateaubriant's article is unique. We offer an excerpt here as it was reprinted in the book titled *La Gerbe des forces* (Grasset, 1937):

> Often on a Sunday around Berchtesgaden, the crowd comes around, stretches out its right hand, and sings songs of joy. And he [Hitler] answers. His face appears in the light from the sun of the mountains, as if he were part of them, as if he were an emanation of their light. I believe that physiognomic analysis of his face reveals four essential characteristics: by the striking height of his temple, a high idealism; by the structure of his nose, tough and searching, a remarkably shrewd intuition; by the distance of the nostril from the ear, a lion's power, and it is this that goes so well with Dr. Goebbels' words: "He possesses an unbeatable vitality, with nerves of steel, and he is of a stature to meet any situation and is never broken by any crisis." The fourth characteristic is his immense goodness.
>
> Yes, Hitler is good. Watch him among school children, watch

him leaning over the tomb of those he loved. He is immensely good, I repeat: good with the perfect conviction that this scandalous claim will not stop the delicious, incomparable grapes from maturing on the slopes of Beaugency.[125]

Kerber's *Annual* meant to engage in dialogue, but not at the expense of his cherished principles. Because of Spenlé's extremism, Kerber thought he had to object:

> Nietzsche's thought is so original that it can never be understood as a synthesis of the existence of north and south. The importance of his thought lies precisely in the fact that it recognizes that the historical misery of the West has reached such extremes that there is no mere synthesis by which to resolve it, that only the most creative decisions could be effective.[126]

Kerber's criticism was meant to be an interpretation of the dialogue between different minds of "the two cultural nations." From this perspective, Kerber praises Heidegger's formulation in the article of this latest *Annual*.[127]

In fact, "Ways to Language"[128] is a perfect example of what Heidegger understood by *polemos*—a combat from which the truth emerges and which ought to be a dialogue, come what may. Peoples come to being in the persons of their spiritual leaders. Once the rules of the game are posed, the only thing remaining is to determine for the French people and the German people what its "most specific character" is or could be, from which dialogue and renewal are to grow.

Otto Pöggeler wants to see in this invitation to a dialogue between peoples a will to go beyond National Socialist positions.[129] But Heidegger is really reaffirming here no more than the principles that guided his speech in support of Germany's resignation from the League of Nations, applying them to the realm of the spiritual, now become an essential concern. The essential subjects for reflection and study are nature and history, but the reflections of the two peoples on these subjects are qualitatively different. While the French think (inadequately) about what nature is, thus giving the Germans a reason to think about it correctly, the Germans alone have been able to comprehend the essential domain, history. Modern knowledge about nature, its use, and its mastery rests essentially on the mathematical mode of thinking that we owe to the French thinker René Descartes.[130] But Descartes' thought is opposed by that of Leibniz, "one of the most German of all the German thinkers,"[131] who took a direction contrary to Descartes' and who posed questions that remain timely. As for the other domain of being, history, things are even clearer. In Western history, we must thank the poets and thinkers of German idealism who for the first time introduced a metaphysical understanding of the essence of history.[132]

Kerber's book and Heidegger's article in it were mentioned by the regime's reviews. *Die Neue Literatur* (Leipzig) in its April 4, 1938, issue, published a commentary, which called the book "an exemplary collective work, virile in manner on the courageous and combative consciousness of the German bastion of the upper Rhine, and on the difficulty of linking culture and peoples."[133] The review *Die Buchbesprechung* echoed similar sentiments.[134] The welcome Kerber's *Annual* received in the National Socialist German-speaking areas of Switzerland shows clearly that the goal of this *Annual* was to spread National Socialist thought. The *Schweizer Nationale Hefte* was sorry there was no comparable publication among the "alemannic" Swiss. It emphasized the work's contributions made "by the most illustrious persons of present *Alemannentum* (alemmanism) that showed the importance of the bridgehead of the constructed in the western Reich and gave readers an image of the mission of Alemannentum." The praise given in the article by J. Schaffner ("Rund um die alemannische Kulturtagung") reveals that the interests served by this review were openly favorable to the Reich's annexation of Switzerland's German regions.[135]

The philosophical congresses at Prague (1934) and at Paris (1937)

The International Philosophical Conferences that were held at this time illustrate Heidegger's relationship with National Socialism and reflect how the institutions worked.

In his postscript "The Rectorate, 1933/34" and in his *Spiegel* interview, Heidegger claimed that the Ministry kept him from participating in the Prague Conference in 1934 as well as the Paris Conference in 1937, or at least made it difficult for him to attend.[136] Here again we can prove the inexactitude of his claims. The documents I have used are in the Zentrales Staatsarchiv at Potsdam[137] and the Hoover archives at Stanford.

At the Prague Conference (September 2–7, 1934), the German delegation included Professors F. Tönnies (Kiel), Friedrich Lipsius (Leipzig), Erich Przywara, SJ (Munich), Aloys Wenzel (Munich), Willy Helpach (Heidelberg), Paul Feldkeller (Berlin), S. Frank (Berlin), I. M. Verweyen

(Bonn), Friedrich Seifert (Munich), Karl Löwith (Marburg), and Nicolai Hartmann (Berlin).[138] No documents remain of this conference. There is nothing in the archives of the Ministry of Education at Potsdam, nor in the archives at Merseburg, nor in the records of the central office of the international congresses, whose archives are at the Ministry of Foreign Affairs at Bonn. Therefore I have had to base my information about it on allusions in documents from the Paris Conference.

There is no doubt that the Ministry and the party were only minimally active in choosing the delegation, which was composed of politically neutral professors. We even see the Jesuit Przywara there. In addition, the eminent National Socialist philosophers (Krieck, Bäumler, Heidegger, Heyse, Rothacker, Rosenberg) did not attend. Both these facts indicate the bureaucracy's indifference to its makeup. And the non-Nazi philosophers took advantage of this indifference to exclude from the Conference their colleagues who were close to the regime. Otherwise, we cannot understand why Heidegger, who was at the zenith of his academic and political influence in 1933–1934, was excluded.

If, for the Prague Conference, we risk becoming entangled in conjectures, we can draw quite clear conclusions regarding the Paris Conference. In his *Spiegel* interview, Heidegger claimed that the authorities had from the start excluded him from the German group. As a result the director of the French organizing committee, Emile Bréhier, wrote Heidegger to verify the omission of his name. In his answer, Heidegger suggested that Bréhier write the Ministry of Education and Sciences. Somewhat later, "there arrived from Berlin a request that I take part in the Conference. This I refused."[139]

Documents at the Potsdam Archives tell quite a different story. In a letter sent July 14, 1937, to the rector of Freiburg, Professor Metz, Heidegger says that after he received the letter from Bréhier, he wrote to the Ministry of Education and Sciences with a concrete proposal, specifying the criteria that he felt were needed for carefully choosing the members of the German delegation in order to convey a definite sense of their orientation. This letter has not been found in the archives I have been allowed to consult. But the allusion Heidegger makes in his letter to Metz lets us reconstruct the fundamental issues: "The invitation was sent me about one year and a half ago by the president of the Conference. I sent it to the Ministry of Education, indicating that this Conference centered on the anniversary of Descartes was a conscious attack coming from the dominant liberal-democratic concept of science and that therefore we had to prepare a strong and effective German delegation." He added: "Since my proposition received no answer, I did not send the

Ministry the subsequent invitations from Paris. It is not the desires of the French leaders on this subject that are important to me, but only the initial will of the *German* authorities to have me there or not as part of the German delegation." For all these reasons, Heidegger felt that he was "unable to prepare himself in a period of only one month and a half before the date of the Conference, and to be part of a group when he himself did not know who was to be in it and who would be its director."

When he alluded to how his writings were read abroad ("my work for German philosophy"), Heidegger informed Metz that his writings had, in the meantime, been translated into many languages, including Spanish and "Argentinian." While the Conference was being prepared, and at the time Heidegger sent his combative proposal to the Ministry, the Ministry was submitting his name for dean at Freiburg. We must suppose that the Ministry had no doubt about Heidegger's right to take part in such an important Conference. It is certainly more probable that his refusal was due to personal quarrels about power. As we will see, the German delegation acted properly and conformed to the offensive rules Heidegger had defined.

The first of the documents about the Conference shows that the Ministry agreed that Hans Heyse would organize the delegation. Heyse sent a letter to the Ministry on August 4, 1936 (alluding to his earlier report of May 3) to explain the political importance of this event:

The honorary president is Henri Bergson, . . . who can pass for one of the most brilliant representatives of contemporary French thought, even though he is of Jewish origin. . . . The conference will do everything it can to show the unity of philosophy, of human thought, of the common human origin of truth, by presenting Descartes as the creator of our modern and universal thought. This assumes (implicitly and from the beginning) a notion of philosophy corresponding to the most prevalent opinion. The hope and conviction of the organizers of the Conference were to show here that the present German philosophical will was a complete denial of the great European traditions, the expression of a naturalistic particularism, a denial of rational thought underlining thereby the isolation of Germany and the role of France as the spiritual guide for Europe. [Faced with this antagonism], which deliberately obscured its political intent, Germany's only answer could be a radical opposition to the line of the 1934 Prague Conference. It is a question of *defending the intellectual will of National Socialist Germany and showing its*

practical application. Since the Conference will take place in conditions that we cannot control and since manipulation will certainly play a role, we must carefully find the most effective way to direct our combat for the German spirit. These must be the only criteria in choosing members. [The members of the delegation must bring together the conditions necessary] to express the National Socialist will, starting with the struggle against the current scientific ideology. It is a question of a spiritual struggle to defend a place in the world and the international prestige of German philosophy. It is a question of *a spiritual German offensive in European space.* The only persons who could be useful in the German cause are those who are deeply attached to the new Germany, able at the same time to participate in this combat, which will be the discussion of concrete problems of philosophy and science on an international level. . . .
Unfortunately, very few people fulfill these conditions, and not only with regard to their philosophical competence.

Heyse's proposed list included the following:

Professor Becker (Bonn) as a Descartes specialist, Heidegger (Freiburg) as a critic of Descartes, Heyse (Königsberg), Otto (Königsberg), one of the best Nietzsche scholars who could also handle aesthetics, Carl Schmitt (juridical questions), and Alfred Bäumler.

So as to guarantee unity and to have an effective offensive force, we must ask that each of those named add other proposals on which the designated Führer or the Ministry could act. . . .
The preparatory work must begin at the beginning of the winter semester 1936/37 . . . so that all the participants may be brought together again.[140]

From a later letter sent to the Ministry (April 28, 1937), we conclude that Heidegger had already told Heyse (April 24, 1937) that he would not be a participant. A ministerial note of June 8, 1937, confirms that Minister Rust tried many times to change Heidegger's stand:

I beg that you let Heidegger know that I would welcome his participation in the Conference. Should he accept the offer, I would immediately send him my consent and the sum of two hundred marks, and would name him a member of the delegation. As for

the composition of the group, for its present state, see my list of
June 8, which I sent to Heidegger. I am asking that Heidegger
change his mind and that you let me know his decision
immediately.[141]

There is no doubt that Heidegger's refusal was linked to his expressed
desire to be the Führer of the delegation; after making tactical and strategic proposals, and finding that the Ministry was still firm in their wish
to have Heyse (a follower of Heidegger), there was nothing else to do
but to send his third refusal. This refusal had nothing to do with any
attempt by the Ministry to keep him from the delegation.

The numerous documents from the Paris Conference located in the
archives of Potsdam and the Hoover Foundation allow us to reconstruct
the details of the activity and the almost military organization of the German delegation. We note in particular the report Heyse sent to the German Central Congress (*Deutsche Kongress-Zentrale*) on January 26, 1938,
and the press cuttings he sent about German émigrés at the time of the
Conference.[142] Also revealing are the documents on the intense propa-
gandist activities of Heinz Heimsoeth in the French provinces after the
Conference. Husserl, who wanted to participate in the Conference, was
treated quite differently by Minister Rust than was Heidegger. Rector
Metz claimed in a letter sent to the Ministry that there was no objection
to Husserl's participation in the Conference, but the Ministry answered
that they were opposed to his being part of the German delegation.[143]
Reasons for this refusal are to be found in an internal note of June 1,
1937:

We have information that certain émigrés want to establish an
anti-German philosophical organization. . . . Decisions related to
the necessary measures to prepare for the Conference were based
on advice from professors Mattiat, Heyse (Königsberg), and
Bäumler (Berlin). Bäumler proposed Heyse as Führer. At no time
will anyone reveal the names of those who received French
invitations whom we do not want in the delegation. Professors
Husserl and Dessoir must not receive authorization to participate.
This action is in conformity with the fair principle followed by the
Ministry, whose goal is not to allow participation by non-Aryans
in international scientific congresses. In light of the earlier
Congress, we must remember that Husserl was applauded by the
émigrés, which could be interpreted as a provocation in the face
of the German delegation. The French, for their part, did not

expect that non-Aryans would participate. This had been already determined at the embassy in Berlin, where the cultural attaché, Professor Jourdan, had been informed of the situation both by the German Academic Exchange Service (DAAD) and by the central congress.[144]

An earlier memorandum of March 19, 1937, said that "French diplomatic people were not in opposition to the measure refusing entry to Jewish philosophers who wished to participate. Accepted also was the German request not to allow the presence at Paris of elements Germany found undesirable."

The German side took the initiative in prohibiting the sale of traveler's checks to "undesirable elements" who might want to participate as private citizens.[145]

Emile Bréhier tried at the beginning to impose the following conditions: A German delegation could participate in the Conference only if it included the permanent members of the Permanent Committee of the International Philosophical Conference, that is, Bruno Bauch, Ernst Cassirer, H. Driesch, Nicolai Hartmann, N. Hoffman, and Edmund Husserl. A report sent to the ministry by Karl Epting, the director of DAAD as well as of the German University Affairs Office in France, mentions this initial demand of Bréhier's.[146]

Did Bréhier maintain this condition? What was the official French position in accepting this decision and what was the extent of the measures adopted? The question remains open. The civil servant who gave the request to Epting added, in pencil, the following names: "Bauch, yes; Cassirer, no, a Jew; Husserl, no; Driesch, no; N. Hartmann, yes."

In another memorandum also related to people who might want to participate in the German delegation (March 19, 1934), we read: "Driesch (no, leader of pacifism), Günther (no, a shameful German!), Jaspers (Bäumler says no!), Groh (no!, married to a Jew, stays out of politics), K. Löwith (non-Aryan, refused), Kuhn (non-Aryan, incompetent). The delegation ended up with a reduced list: Heyse, Bäumler, Heidegger, Nicolai Hartmann. . . . Bäumler proposed Heyse as Führer."[147]

The lectures on Nietzsche's philosophy

That Heidegger's sympathies for the general principles of National Socialism remained active up to this time is demonstrated not only in his upholding international relations as a means of struggle, which he felt was to be guided ideologically and institutionally, but in the conduct of the authorities who for the most part held him in high esteem, in spite of the fact that in many cases they denied him access to decision-making positions.

By his own admission, Heidegger's "critical" attitude became public during the year of his lectures on Nietzsche. He supposedly came to grips with National Socialism in these lectures.[148] But he also favored an ambiguous formulation, for he did not claim to have criticized National Socialism there; he merely stated that he came to terms with the historical role and function of National Socialism. The impression of that ambiguity was additionally strengthened, since Heidegger relativized the "metaphysical" meaning of National Socialism at that time, and simultaneously as well as publicly demonstrated his ties to the party and the "movement." Moreover, he remained a member in the NSDAP and began and ended his lectures with the Nazi salute. The salute, obligatory during his time as rector, was later deemed not binding by the new rector. That Heidegger continued with the ritual, that he was even eager to make its performance a matter of principle, is clear-cut proof of his political views and his entrenched totalitarianism, which carried considerable weight at this time in the regime, when repression was heightened and the German economy was transformed into a war economy rooted in the strategic alliance between business and the "SS-State" (as described by Eugen Kogon). Jaspers relates in a letter from July 24, 1952, incidents about Heidegger from this time: "Fräulein Drescher [a doctoral student of Jaspers'], who attended your lectures in 1936/37, reported on her futile attempt to advise you of the then-rector's decision that beginning every lecture with the Hitler salute was no longer considered necessary."[149]

Even if it were the case that Heidegger was in these years under the surveillance of the police, as disclosed by a student accused of being an agent for the security service who had the task of reporting everything that Heidegger expressed in his lectures,[150] this only speaks to the uncertainty that surrounded Heidegger up to 1937. That student, Hans Hancke, does not appear at all to have been an agent of the SD at the time; this is clear from his party records in the Berlin Document Center.

The lectures on Nietzsche began in 1936/37 under the title "The Will to Power as Art" ("Der Wille zur Macht als Kunst"). They continued through 1944 (and some until 1946). Heidegger read "The Eternal Recurrence of the Same" in 1937, followed in 1939 by "The Will to Power as Knowledge," in 1940 with "European Nihilism" and "Nietzsche's Metaphysics," in 1941 by "Metaphysics as a History of Being" and "Sketches on the History of Being as Metaphysics"; between 1944 and 1946 Heidegger spoke on "The Being-Historical Significance of Nihilism." The lectures were assembled and published in two volumes entitled *Nietzsche*.[151] Since it is not possible to compare the published text with the original critical manuscripts (a matter of particular importance, given the nature of these special lectures), the claim that Heidegger permitted material to be pulled from the published text must necessarily remain provisional.

If one takes Heidegger's claim seriously that the lectures on Nietzsche form the key to the questioning of National Socialism, that means that, in Heidegger's eyes, Nietzsche constituted an essential theme connected with his own coming to grips with National Socialism. The meaning and context of this theme are not difficult to make out. The ideological attack Heidegger was exposed to from the leading group surrounding Ernst Krieck repeatedly culminated in the reproach that his philosophy was nothing more than an expression of destructive nihilism, a kind of by-product of Jewish thinking that the Nazis regarded as "subversive." A reproach of this kind had tremendous consequences, not only because it brought Heidegger into open conflict with certain fundamental political directives that Hitler had formulated in *Mein Kampf*, but also because the value of those directives formed a valuable part of official political strategy. Fearful of the possibility of a general and radical opposition from the Church, Hitler tried to unsettle its hegemony in important areas of German society, while maintaining and integrating it into a "positive Christianity." So he turned against the "ever-stronger incipient struggle against the dogmatic principles of a separate Church without which in this world of men the practical continuance of religious belief is unthinkable."[152] He thought of religious nihilism as a revolt "against the general lawful foundations of the State." Since not all men are philosophers and since they know that they are not, if a suitable world view is to develop, the destruction of traditional elements of belief can be seriously pursued "only by fools and criminals."[153] Hitler called for the overcoming of religious differences. He demanded that members of the party not get tangled in religious quarrels, since it would endanger the mission of the party and the people.[154] In the situation of 1937, the hostility toward Christianity, which Heidegger brought to light in his address at the University of Heidelberg and later in connection with the suspension of the Catholic student group Ripuaria, could well have been taken as a deviation from the official political course. For it was indeed an anti-clerical maneuver, although it tolerated no radical nihilistic arguments. That Heidegger was subject to some suspicion and related political pressure at this time is clear from his lectures on Nietzsche. In this regard he reports: "Where, in the process of raising the issue of the 'Nothing' *[Nichts]*, and certainly where it is mentioned in essential connection with the doctrine

of Being *[Sein]*, one plainly means to speak of nihilism, but silently im-
parts a 'Bolshevist' tinge to the word 'nihilism,' this is not only a superficial form of thinking; it is unscrupulous demagogy."[155]

A critical engagement with Nietzsche was especially well suited for
Heidegger's indirect but also radical and polemical philosophical confrontation with the official ideology. Nietzsche was a key figure in the
effort to give the National Socialist movement a philosophical consistency. As a forerunner, Nietzsche validated the central ideological elements of National Socialism and therefore played an important role in
its cultural politics. The remark by Alfred Bäumler, Rosenberg's official
mouthpiece, that whoever says "Heil Hitler!" salutes Nietzsche's philosophy at the same time, is a telling clue.

In Heidegger's own declaration may be found the main intent of his
reflections on the philosophy of Nietzsche: understanding the essence of
nihilism and "listening to Nietzsche himself, listening with him, through
him, *and at the same time against him,*" that is, listening to Nietzsche, the
decisive forerunner of present historical events and thematizing their
concrete political implications.[156] According to Heidegger, the group of
reigning ideologies rejected two notions above all: first, they did not acknowledge that nihilism was more than a random occurrence that resulted from special circumstances in the intellectual history of the West;
and, second, they refused to acknowledge that the essence of Nietzsche's
philosophy was an answer to nihilism.

Had Heidegger still considered it possible in the "Introduction to Metaphysics" (1935) to warn the metaphysical nation *(Volk)* and its errant
leadership of a threatening danger, his lectures on Nietzsche would have
supposed that National Socialism had gone astray without being aware of
it. Now, resistance against nihilism needed more than just a battle against
"corruption" or "physiological degeneration";[157] it needed an essentially
changed spiritual disposition. Heidegger thought that Nietzsche had considered this problem in just this sense. The supposedly growing difference between the "movement" and "its inner truth and greatness"[158] formed
the basis for Heidegger's differentiation between a "true" and a "false"
National Socialism. In his ironic explanations Heidegger employed a terminology similar to the one used by Rudolf Hess in his speech at the
special conference of the NSDStB at the Nürnberger Reichsparteitag when
he censured the influence the SA exerted on the student community and
defended the exclusion of Röhm's faction. Heidegger said:

> How liberating it would be for "the" sciences, if it needed to be
> said for necessary historical reasons, that the nation and state need
> results and useful ones at that! Good, says science, but we need

peace and quiet—everyone understands and luckily we have it again. That means now that the old philosophical-metaphysical lack of suspicion can go on as it has for half a century. Hence, today's "science" is experiencing a certain expansiveness in its own way; it feels confirmed in its importance and so it feels mistakenly confirmed (as never before) in its essence as well.

Whoever thought science could sustain its essential calling only by recovering it through an originary self-*questioning* must in such a situation look a fool and destroyer of "the" sciences, for asking for such reasons produces an inner exhaustion for which we have at our disposal the revealing term "nihilism." But that spectre has now passed, thank goodness. We have peace and tranquillity again, and the students, they say, really want to work again! So the general philistinism spirit can begin anew.[159]

Heidegger's opinion at that time regarding the development of the universities and the destiny of the Germans was also clear from his letter of April 20, 1939, to Rudolf Stadelmann: "Today, perhaps more decisively than ever before, the work of the 'university' depends on the independence of the individual. For the foreseeable future there will be no change in the established forms of science. But we must prepare for a change if we want to keep the essence of the German character fit for history."[160] It is in just this context, so the objection goes, that the official philosophers have left the political leadership of the movement without any intellectual basis for acting. In doing that, they have blocked every access to thinking in general, as well as to the "true" Nietzsche and a proper reflection on the substance of nihilism. According to Heidegger, 1937 repeated what had led to the collapse of German idealism in the nineteenth century. The Germans had proved themselves incapable of meeting the challenge of the day: "Schopenhauer did not achieve his zenith because his philosophy defeated German idealism in philosophical terms, but because the Germans themselves succumbed in the face of German idealism and could not measure up to its grandeur. Their failure made Schopenhauer a great man, and consequently, seen from Schopenhauer's commonplaces, the philosophy of idealism became rather unattractive and strange and fell into oblivion."[161] Heidegger warned that Nietzsche's philosophy might, by a parallel process, also fall into oblivion.

The leadership was on the verge of destroying the special potentialities of the "metaphysical nation," of spoiling its spirit or of exposing it to history with no means of defense—that is, of exposing it to a history that could only become possible "through an exemplary and authoritative historical formation of individual nations in competition with one another."[162] It was about to trace the nation back to the banal and a-historical level of a "Negro tribe" *(Negerstamm):* "But the essence and history of Western man are characterized by the fact that knowledge and recognition belong to his basic relationship to existence in its totality *[zum Seienden im Ganzen]* and thus also to reflection in that critical sense in which the essence of Western man is determined and formed through such reflection. Because this is so, historical Western man can be overcome by thoughtlessness and lose his presence of mind, a fate that a Negro tribe *[Negerstamm]* remains protected from."[163]

The shift was clear and simple: Heidegger no longer identified his own thinking with the National Socialist spirit, but now demanded that those who had gone astray reorient themselves to Nietzsche's thought and regard themselves as protagonists of a subjectivity engraved in their nature by the will to power *(vom Willen zur Macht)*. Thus, Heidegger's "confrontation" with them developed along two lines: on the one hand, they were incapable of taking Nietzsche seriously; and on the other, in order to do just that, they would have had to understand themselves in terms of a process of development that would have reached its culmination and definite objective with Nietzsche—that is, in terms of the history of metaphysics. "Because Nietzsche's fundamental metaphysical position is marked by a sense of the end of metaphysics, it was effected by the greatest and deepest concentration, in the sense of bringing to fruition all the essential positions of Western philosophy formed since Plato and in the light of Platonism, in a thesis limited by Platonism but genuinely creative. It can continue to be such only if it is developed in all its essential powers and unfolds into all its *counter-positions*. Nietzsche's philosophy—itself looking backwards—must become forward-looking in a way that anticipates counter-positions."[164]

It was exactly in this way that Heidegger wanted his philosophy understood—as a "beginning," as a prologue of a thinking which was new but which set the archaic free again. But since, according to Heidegger, "thinking" was the transcendental objectification of a nation and since the "nation of the Greeks" had posed the transcendental question about origins in "the sharpest and most creative confrontation with the most alien and the most difficult elements," so too, now, should the overcoming of the given *(das Gegebenen)* be the work of a nation, of that ever-metaphysical nation of the Germans. Nietzsche was on the verge of this realization. He had given it a name without grasping it. Only Hölderlin had gone beyond it and thus became himself a transcendental authority. His realization was "hidden in a letter to Böhlendorff, a friend":

The letter was written on December 4, 1801, shortly before his departure for France (WW ed. Hellingrath, V 318). Here, Hölderlin, in the spirit of the Greeks, juxtaposed the "holy pathos" and "the western *Junoesque reasonableness* of the gift of representation." This opposition does not have to be understood as an indifferent historical determination. Rather, it shows itself in an immediate reflection on German fate and destiny. We must accept this hint, since Hölderlin's own knowledge could be adequately fixed only through an interpretation of his work. It would be sufficient if we could surmise from this hint that the variously labeled antithesis we know as the opposition between the Dionysian and the Apollonian, the holy passion and the portrayal of sobriety, is a kind of hidden law governing the historical determination of the German people, by which, one day, they will find themselves ready and willing to be fashioned. This opposition is not just a formula that assists us in describing "Kultur." Hölderlin and Nietzsche have, by means of this opposition, placed the question mark over the task of the Germans: to find their essence in historical fashion. Will we understand this questioning? One thing is certain: history will take its revenge on us if we do not understand it.[165]

The "distancing" of Heidegger from National Socialism ended in a "spiritual" restoration of the very fundamentals of the National Socialist world view. The further distancing from all those who had gone astray from "true" National Socialism occurred under reference to the same principle from which National Socialism originated: the claim of the ontologically founded superiority of the "German nationality." Therefore, Heidegger's position concerning the National Socialist regime could at no point in time, even after World War II, be that of a relentless critic.

Heidegger and the state
ideological apparatus
(continued): Rome and Berlin

Heidegger at Prague (1940) and at Munich (1941)

In the archives of the Munich Institute of Contemporary History is a document written by a member of Alfred Rosenberg's Science Department. The text shows the ambivalence of Heidegger's political position during the 1940s (total acceptance of the regime coupled with a rejection of its concrete politics). The report speaks of the influence of Heidegger's philosophy at the University of Prague during the German occupation and the effects of this influence in Professor Kurt Schilling's courses.

We also discover here the tight surveillance of Heidegger by the Amt Rosenberg at the same time that his philosophy was being taught by professors whose political loyalty could not be questioned. Within the limits of their power, the Rosenberg faction used surveillance and informers.[1] Rosenberg would receive these reports as minister of the Reich for the occupied Eastern areas, a post he held from 1941 to 1945.

The very strict selection of professors who were sent to the occupied territories, as well as personal facts about them, left no doubts about political loyalty. The Schilling dossier at the Berlin Document Center testifies that Schilling, a member of the NSDAP since 1933, first was professor of philosophy at Munich and then, in 1939, was chosen to hold a chair at Prague. In the report concerning the nomination of Schilling to the chair at Prague, written by Gaupersonalamtsleiter Best and Gauhauptstellenleiter Reichinger on July 20, 1939, we read: "Schilling has been a member of the NSDAP since 1933. His social attitude is irreproachable. In philosophy, he can be considered as one of the most promising scholars. He is one of the new generation of university teachers who ought to be promoted unconditionally." The letter of recommendation from Dr. E. Betzoldt, Führer of the National Socialist group of teachers at Munich, said: "For Schilling, Adolf Hitler's state has been the decisive experience."[2]

Kurt Schilling took the chair on November 11, 1939.

To understand this information, we must recall that at the time (the report is dated March 12, 1940), the ideological war could afford no weakness. The report includes lists of information about Schilling's courses and the number and nationality of the students attending them who were responsible for reporting matters treated in the courses: "There was reference to the Heideggerian concepts of *Befindlichkeit* [the atmosphere of existence], *Gestimmtheit* [also, atmosphere of existence], *Geworfenheit* [like *Faktizität*, the actuality of human existence in the world, the notion that we are subject to circumstance]." The report is important because it refers to Heidegger's principles and Schilling's use of them: "If someone wants to speak of us and our present existence, there must first be an explanation of the existential determinations of historical situations."

It speaks for itself that Heidegger's philosophy could be presented in universities in the occupied zones. This belies Heidegger's claims in 1945 that after 1938 his name was not spoken and that commentaries on his works were forbidden.[3] In fact, commentaries and editions of his works appeared frequently and were politically irreproachable. This is the case for instance with the critical remarks that appeared in the *Blätter für Deutsche Philosophie* edited by Heinz Heimsoeth. In volume 13, issues 1–2, of 1939, we find commentaries on Heidegger's essay "On the Essence of Reasons" ("Vom Wesen des Grundes") and on his Hölderlin book.[4] Bruno Bauch's critical remarks on this occasion were very favorable.[5] Heidegger's text on the hymn "Wie wenn am Feiertage"[6] was discussed in *Die Literatur*,[7] in the *Frankfurter Zeitung*,[8] and in *Scholastik*.[9]

To illustrate the attitude of the regime and its members toward Heidegger during the 1940s, we have the example of the selection process at Munich in 1941 to fill the chair open since M. Büchner's death. These documents are located in the University of Munich archives.[10]

By the act of July 15, 1942, members of committees were made known. The faculty of philosophy formed a committee to draw up a list of three names to be sent to the Ministry of Education and Sciences. The top names on the list were the rector of the University, Professor Walther Wüst, and the representative of the National Socialist teachers, Rudolf Till.

Rector Wüst had taken his post in 1941. According to papers in the Document Center at Berlin, he had been a member of the NSDAP, since 1933, and of the SS. At the end of January 1937, he was in the Reichsführung of the SS. On November 9, 1942, he was named Standartenführer of the SS.[11] His scientific specialty was "culture and Aryan linguistics."

Rudolf Till was a classical philologist and had been a member of the NSDAP since 1933 and a member of the SS. From 1938, he was SS-Führer at the Institute of the SS-Ahnenerbe (classical legacy) and director of the SS Institute for Teaching and Research on Classical Philology and on the Ancient World. At the request of the Italian SS-Ahnenerbe, he published a work on Tacitus. The publishing house wrote to the German office of publishing "that Till's writings were gobbled up by Himmler, Reichsführer of the SS, and that they were published thanks to His Excellency [Giuseppe] Bottai, Italian minister of culture."[12] At the end of the report, SS-Obersturmbannführer Sievers warned the Office that "it was not to put any book on the market before sending deluxe editions to Minister Bottai, to the German ambassador [F.] Mackensen, and a third one to Reichsführer Himmler."[13]

Later we will analyze the relations between Giuseppe Bottai and Himmler.[14] Thanks to Himmler, Heidegger published his article on Plato in Ernesto Grassi's *Annual*, in spite of Amt Rosenberg's strong opposition. This illustrates the context of the committee's work to name a successor to Büchner's chair.

The proposed list carried the names Herbert Cysarz (Munich), Hugo Dingler (Munich), Herbert Haering (Tübingen), Heidegger (Freiburg), August Faust (Breslau), and Kurt Schilling.

According to the dossier at the Berlin Document Center, August Faust had been a member of the NSDAP since 1937. The Baden leadership said about him (Karlsruhe, February 19, 1937):

From the beginning of the National Socialist revolution, he immediately became actively involved in the movement. Faust was Fachschaftsleiter of the teachers, and held the equivalent office for social questions for the Hitler Youth. His willing actions and his collaboration are recognized without exception by the acts of the party. His promotion to ordinarius professor is recommended from a political point of view.[15]

Hugo Dingler became a party member only in 1940, after Hitler had given him amnesty for his membership in Free Masonry, from which Dingler had resigned in 1927. His major book was *Max Planck and the Foundations of "Modern Theoretical Physics."* This was published by the SS-Ahnenerbe and denounces Planck "as a precursor of the destructive Jewish physics that wanted to eradicate Aryan physics."[16]

In defining the criteria of selection, the report of the committee indicated that "from the time that Adolf Hitler took power and brought a profound renaissance of spiritual life, representatives of all the sciences feel more and more intensely the need to assemble all fragmentary scientific results into an organic view of the proto-German world, which will inspire our youth and in which will be found the best tradition of the glorious history of German spirituality, making the great leap into the future."[17] Thus the committee decided to vote for Professor Cysarz, for his intellectual gifts and also because he could "open the door to a generation who after the war will flood the courses and absorb the spirit that feeds at the eternal spring of German National Socialism."[18]

Heidegger got second place. We can put this fact together with the appeal the Bavarian minister of education sent to Heidegger in 1934, which led to nothing.

Professor Dingler was in third place. We find no subsequent information about this candidacy. From what is at our disposal, the Ministry made no decision and the chair remained empty.

Heidegger's good relations with the regime are confirmed by a note held at the Berlin Document Center. In January 1944, a time when publications were curtailed or suspended because of the serious lack of paper, the Ministry granted the Klostermann publishing company a delivery of paper to print Heidegger's works.[19]

Heidegger and Il Duce

Heidegger claimed in his *Speigel* interview that the authorities forbade any commentary on "Plato's Doctrine of Truth."[20] When I tried to establish the circumstances of this publication, I found a series of documents that clarify the situation. These papers are in the archives of the Munich Institut für Zeitgeschichte.[21] They help us understand relations between Goebbels' ministry and the Science Department of Alfred Rosenberg, and Heidegger's relationship with both. This is to be understood in the framework of the links connecting Germany and fascist Italy.

When Heidegger claimed that the official press was forbidden to mention his works, he was giving but a partial view of the truth: only the Amt Rosenberg suppressed all commentary. Moreover, Heidegger remained silent on the full circumstances that enabled him to publish the essay in spite of Rosenberg's absolute opposition.

Heidegger's text on Plato was to be published in Ernesto Grassi's *Annual* titled *Spiritual Traditions (Geistige Überlieferung)*. Heidegger's article was to be in the second volume of the *Annual*. The first one had been edited by W. F. Otto and Karl Reinhardt, working with Grassi, in 1940.

In the midst of the war, W. F. Otto wrote the preface to the first volume:

> What gives a new foundation and new meaning to the study of antiquity is not only the fact that the Greek idea found its realization at this precise moment in time, as the most sublime manifestation of German life, but also (and the two are linked) in the German's new faith in their duty. When we use all our energy in the effort to renew the spirit of the ancient Greeks, we are obeying the genius of our essential being, which is for us a sacred task: we are answering the needs of our nature. We turn toward our own origins and celebrate the feast of our ancestors, our creators and founders. It is they who ought to be present here in a work that is destined to live and that affirms with all its might the renewal of that original creation.[22]

This resurgence of the Greeks is the work of Germans, and such a renaissance "could not have been possible if the German spirit had not been shaken anew by the life of the world. This return to the ancients necessarily means the creation of a new man. After bitter deceptions, this new man succeeded in hearing anew the appeal to the creative origin. If we have the courage to see in this philosophical turning the beginnings of a larger and more powerful movement, we are obliged to take the full measure of this fact: a destiny of almost two centuries separates us from the last flourishing of humanism."[23]

In despite of the distance separating the Amt Rosenberg and W. F. Otto,[24] the Amt worker Dr. Erxleben warmly welcomed the appearance of the first volume in the *Bücherkunde: Monatshefte für das deutsche Schrifttum,* the official organ in the care of Hans Hagenmeyer, director of the Department of the Führer responsible for the control of political and pedagogical education for the party. Edited by Grassi, the book was praised: "A collective work of German and Italian scholars, it is a sign of the historical force of the powers that struggle in open contest to find the true road within their own historical past. . . . The articles are based on the consciousness that the revolutions shaking the German and Italian peoples are points of departure for new roads toward the spiritual tradition of our peoples."[25]

Erxleben, in particular, points out Grassi's article ("The Beginnings of Modern Thought: The Passion and Experience of the Originary"), which shows with the greatest effect the source of the Italian spiritual movement, beginning with the Renaissance, and establishes with the greatest clarity the specific spiritual development of Italy as compared with that of Germany.

Grassi's *Annual* also received a warm welcome from the German Academy *(Deutsche Academie),* directly under Goebbels' ministry. F. Dirlmeier reviewed the book with praise as "an encounter between the Nordic and the Mediterranean. . . . Those who read the work in 1941 could see under the monumental and developing form of the book the European cosmos in its struggle against chaos. They take heart and find the certainty that at the center of this cosmos lie forces that guarantee the victory of arms and of the spirit."[26]

The collection of documents bearing on the second volume of Grassi's *Annual* show that it was Heidegger's decision to break the harmony between Goebbels' ministry and the Amt Rosenberg. Erxleben wrote to Dr. Lutz of the Ministry of Propaganda on June 17, 1942, to say that the Amt Rosenberg did not want Heidegger's work to appear in the second volume. We must thus note that Goebbels' office was in favor of the article. They were willing simply to excise one sentence of Heidegger's, which was in no way satisfactory to the Amt Rosenberg.[27]

In contradiction with his own review of Grassi's book, Rosenberg said in the letter:

> I think Professor Grassi ought to remove Heidegger's contribution from the work. His position on the important problem of humanism helps to validate the Italian claims to exist and compete with German science. By claiming that humanism can be understood either from a political or a Christian-theological point of view, Heidegger went against the position recently defended by Comrade [Wilhelm] Brachmann in the National Socialist *Monatshefte.* His position indicates strongly and insistently that for us in Germany contemporary humanism has ceased to exist and that we oppose to the contemporary humanism a political humanism. We explicitly support this position. In the present state of the discussion, Heidegger's tendency to support

Grassi's efforts to bring contemporary humanism into the German spiritual world will only bring confusion.

It seems to us that by eliminating this single sentence from the text, there has been no modification of Heidegger's views in the article. Notwithstanding the respect we hold for Heidegger's professional importance, we cannot approve the appearance of his article in Grassi's *Annual*.

At this point in the discussion, there was a unexpected discovery. An internal memorandum of July 3, 1942, at the Amt Rosenberg reads:

> Dr. Lutz of the Ministry of Propaganda has let us know by telephone that Grassi's *Annual* will appear *with* Heidegger's article. At the request of Il Duce, the Italian ambassador [Dino Odoardo] Alfieri has spoken personally to Goebbels asking that the *Annual* appear in its entirety. Dr. Lutz knows our opinion and has taken steps to see that the press will not mention Heidegger's article. At the same time, Dr. Lutz has informed us that there is a plan to publish Heidegger's complete works in Italian. We will keep you informed on developments.[28]

To understand the context of these events, let us recall the state of relations between Goebbels and the German leaders. We will then explain Heidegger's connections with Mussolini's government and the indirect influence of Mussolini on Goebbels' ministry.

To illustrate relations between the Italian fascists and the Reich government, we cite a passage from Goebbels' political diary:

> January 31, 1942 (Saturday). At noon I took part in a reception given by the Führer to honor a delegation of the Italian party that had come to Berlin to commemorate the anniversary of coming to power. . . . I had occasion to speak in detail with these gentlemen. They are a superb elite, comparable to the best of our Gauleiter. There was not one of them who did not praise the Axis. Little by little, Mussolini seems to have eliminated from the leadership of the party all those who were silently against it. The Italians made the best impression on me.[29]

To these National Socialist opinions, we add the contacts Grassi himself made with the leading Italian fascists. His confidential friend was Giuseppe Bottai, then minister of education in Mussolini's government and the author of an article in Grassi's second volume.[30] Bottai was one of the early leaders in Italian fascism. According to the *Enciclopedia Italiana Trecanni,*[31] Bottai joined the futurist movement early and was one of the founders of the Fasci italiani di combattimento (1919). As political and military chief of the party, he led one of Mussolini's three columns against Rome. Bottai's proclamations on the question are in his work *Pagine de critica fascista.*[32] At that time, Bottai became lieutenant general of the volunteer militia for national security and founded the journal *L'Epoca.* Beginning in 1923, he edited *Critica fascista* and became head of the Ministry of Corporations. Bottai offered Mussolini careful help in creating this key ministry, a pillar in the construction of the fascist state.

Bottai was also the author of the fascist statute on work, *La carta del lavoro* (1927). In 1930 he held the chair of theory of corporatist politics at the University of Pisa. In 1932, he left the Ministry of Work to become governor of Rome. In 1936, he became minister of education and culture. In the meantime he had become a renowned specialist in questions of corporatism.

Among his many works, we cite *Il fascismo e l'Italia nuova* (Rome, 1923); *Mussolini constructore d'impero* (Mantua, 1923); *L'ordinamento corporativo italiano* (Rome, 1927); *Sviluppi dell 'idea corporativa nella legislazione internationale* (Leghorn, 1928); *La construzione corporativa e il Ministero delle Corporazioni* (Milan, 1929); and *Politica e scienza economica nelle concezione corporativa* (Rome, 1930). In German, he is known for *Der korporative Staat in Italien,* published by Petrarca Haus at Cologne in 1933. While working at the Ministry of Education and Culture, he published fundamental political documents, in particular the *Fascist Constitution for Italian Schools (La carta della scuola).* His essential work on fascist reforms of education was translated in a series edited by the Kaiser Wilhelm Institute of Arts and Sciences (Rome/Vienna, 1939) with the title *Die grundlegenden Ideen der italienischen Schulreform* (no. 11). Also published in this series are works by the greatest German specialist in racial purity, Eugen Fischer, translated into Italian. Later the *Carta della Scuola* was added as *Das neue fascistische Schulstatut.*

At the time of the invasion of Abyssinia (1935–1936), Giuseppe Bottai was named first governor of Addis Ababa. He collected his memories of this time in his *Quaderno africano,* a journal of the invasion, published in Florence in 1940 and later translated into German with a prologue by Bernhard Rust (Berlin, 1940). Rust wrote that his attachment to Bottai "was not simply due to the close ties that grow between men who direct and govern in similar ways two countries united in war," but also to his qualities as a soldier. It comes out in his journal that, as a true man, he wanted to be nothing more than a "comrade among comrades, a fighter among fighters in the struggle for a common goal."[33]

When Rust was writing the prologue, he surely had in mind certain passages of Bottai's journal:

> I was at the wheel of the truck as I drove into the town, this town where tomorrow I was to be civil governor. It was already dark. Now and then, we could hear grenades exploding nearby and afar. The car lights formed a camera, taking pictures of the falling houses, the destroyed streets, the corpses in the mud swollen with rain. White shadows entered the ruined houses and slipped away. They were robbers obeying the last orders of the fleeing government: steal and destroy. Tomorrow we will establish order in this burning town, in the name of Italy and Rome.[34]

In Bottai's article in Grassi's *Annual,* we read:

> In the year 154, Aelius Aristides could already say that the word *Roman* did not mean a genealogical line, but defined a privilege, just as *imperium romanum* had not only a political meaning but also a broader and more universal sense, a kind of education *(Zucht)* that made the world submit. Triumphant in war, wise in its ways of ruling, the Romans built and lived in the place they had just conquered. They brought life where the sword had annihilated it. *Ubicumque vicit Romanus habitat.*[35]

I have pressed the description of Bottai's political nature because he was one of the key figures in the events we are analyzing.

The other important person was Ernesto Grassi. His personal and political contacts with Mussolini's ministry were so close that he was able to write the prologue for Bottai's work, *Defense of Humanism: The Spiritual Foundations of the New Studies in Italy,* published in Berlin (1941) with the title *Verteidigung des Humanismus: Die geistigen Grundlagen der neuen Studien in Italien.* What Grassi wrote in the prologue reveals the background of his humanism:[36]

> We believe the message of this book is decisively important for the future. It is not the expression of two different notions of the Italian tradition. It carries in itself premisses of the great reform in Italian studies, which the *Carta della Scuola* means to achieve.

The author of this book had the courage to give new life to
the concept of humanism, which had lost its vigor.[37]

Such was the ideological context at the time the editors planned to
have Heidegger's article appear in the *Annual.*

We can also measure the extent of the Amt Rosenberg's objections.
We must realize that Ernesto Grassi had begun his teaching career at
Freiburg as reader in Italian.[38] In 1932, he dedicated his first work to
Heidegger, *Il problema della metafisica platonica,*[39] thanking him for having
opened the doors to the ancient world. His second work, *Dell'apparire e
dell'essere,*[40] indicates his dependence on Heidegger ("the last event of
German philosophy").[41] According to the *Kürschners Lexikon* (1961),[42] Ernesto Grassi was also in 1933 a teacher at the University of Milan. According to the review *Minerva* (1934), he was reader in Italian at Freiburg. The same year he received the annual prize from the Italian
Academy. The *Kürschners Lexikon* adds that Grassi received his habilitation in 1935 at Rome and later became a professor at Pavia. In 1937, he
was named honorary professor at Freiburg and in 1938 at the University
of Berlin, where he had been since 1937. In the review *Minerva* of 1938
he is cited as member of the faculties at Freiburg and Berlin (reader in
Italian and director of a course on "Italian Philosophy and Its Relation
to German Philosophy"). At the same time we find him as professor at
the Instituto Magistrale of Pavia. In the 1950s, he was professor of philosophy at Santiago, Chile.

His work *Vom Vorrang des Logos: Das Problem der Antike in der Auseinandersetzung zwischen italienischer und deutscher Philosophie*[43] is clearly the
work of a follower. Although, according to Heidegger, it was forbidden
to use his name at this time, the publisher wrote in the preface of Grassi's
book that it was "an interpretation based on the writings of Heidegger,
and a new interpretation of Plato." Grassi's book was subsidized directly
by the Ministry of Education and Sciences of the Reich, also with a large
subsidy from the publishers Beck'schen Verlagsbuchhandlung, in spite of
the unfavorable reports from Heyse and Bäumler.[44]

To complete this picture: Dino Odoardo Alfieri, Italian ambassador at
Berlin from 1940 to 1943, had interceded with Goebbels on Il Duce's
orders to the benefit of Heidegger. This same Alfieri in 1936 was minister of propaganda in the same cabinet as Bottai, then minister of education under Mussolini.[45]

In spite of the Amt Rosenberg's determination to prevent Heidegger
from publishing and to stop the distribution of the book, things took a

surprising turn. Dr. Wilhelm Brachmann, to whom Erxleben alluded in his letter, reviewed the *Annual* and Heidegger's article in the most prestigious philosophical review in Germany, the *Kant-Studien*.[46] This review was edited by the Kant Society, directed by Heyse, in conformity with the Society's rules adopted in 1934. In his article "Contemporary Humanism,"[47] Brachmann presented Grassi's *Annual* as the expression of a group of partisans of Heidegger's philosophy: "This humanism, with ties to the problem of speech, has as source not Stefan George, as one could think at first glance, but existential philosophy as inspired by Heidegger, as we find in Grassi's contribution."[48]

Brachmann begins the discussion of Heidegger's humanism by distinguishing political humanism based on the notion of race from another humanism based on language and spiritual traditions.[49] For Brachmann these *two* forms of humanism can be found *in* the historical orientation adopted by Italy and Germany at the end of World War I. Brachmann's tone is quite measured, contrary to what Heidegger claimed in 1945. He found in the current spiritual tradition represented by Grassi and Heidegger an eminently respectable notion of the world held by Italians that could be grasped through renewed humanism.

Brachmann gives an accurate resumé of Heidegger's article. He writes with care and talent and draws attention to questions of interpretation that Heidegger left open.[50]

Brachmann was a permanent editor of the National Socialist *Monatshefte*, the Amt Rosenberg's periodical, yet he did not bend to the will of the Amt, which demanded silence about Heidegger's article. He drew up his article in careful terms and with a spirit of solidarity that can be found in diverse yet also basically united fascist positions. These facts indicate something of Mussolini's intervention in favor of Grassi's and Heidegger's group.

Wilhelm Brachmann began his studies in evangelical theology and was an evangelical pastor from 1926–1929. He became part of the Amt Rosenberg in 1937, when Alfred Rosenberg asked him to edit an important study on "German religion, past and present." In his biography for the NSDAP, he gave his evolution from Protestant theology to National Socialism and emphasized the influence exercised on his education by Heidegger's philosophy.[51]

Heidegger's text on Plato can be inscribed in what we have called the "relativizing" of National Socialism. Heidegger situated the text in the Platonic tradition in which truth is technically construed as adequation to *being*, and also in the philosophical line that affirms the being of *values*.

In this way he was attacking the deviationist version of Rosenberg, and demanding also a new foundation for thinking about the meaning of political events. In fact, the historical processes in which *values* are situated as "being and existence" was, for Heidegger, a process that Nietzsche had brought to an end. The reaction of the National Socialist *Monatshefte* could be explained in this way. But their position was not strong enough to defeat politically the pressure group that acted in favor of Heidegger with Goebbels' support. It was Goebbels who was ultimately responsible for delivering authorization for such works.

Hölderlin

The criteria that Heidegger established for the "relativizing" of National Socialism were basically not heterodox. His work on Hölderlin, published up to the end of World War II, makes this clear. Earlier in his lectures on Nietzsche he had insisted that the age of metaphysics, whose final end Nietzsche had readied, could only be overcome in the conceptual horizon opened by Hölderlin, who thereby restored the connection between the Greeks and the Germans and confronted the Germans with the necessity of developing this connection further. For Heidegger, the turn backwards to Hölderlin was an attempt to revitalize the peculiar original power of the "German essence." In his opinion, only under this sign could the question of Being be plausibly raised and renewed.

Heidegger's mystification of Hölderlin had its parallel in Heidegger's self-conscious stylization. In a formal request to the dean of the philosophy faculty at the University of Freiburg Heidegger wrote on July 17, 1943:

> I ask to be relieved of my duties, lectures, and examinations for the winter semester 1943/44 in order to complete in its final form a work I have been engaged in for years. It concerns the basic question of Western thinking, whose theme I have earmarked for the second volume of *Being and Time*. The task that stands before me is not exhausted by a mere summary or the notes of a detailed train of thought. In philosophy, as a consequence of its essential relationship with art, the very shape of thought drawn from the lay of the topic *[Sache]* belongs to the topic itself. For this shaping requires a focus and effort impossible to manage while occupied

with teaching, since this is of a different nature and demands
an attitude and way of thinking unsuited to my students.

And:

> The request I am making does not arise from a personal interest
> in the promotion of my own work, but from a knowledge of the
> historical limits of German philosophical thinking with regard
> to the future of the West.[52]

The dean, Professor Schuchardt, supported Heidegger's petition:

> Given the general esteem in which Heidegger's name is held
> today, not only in Germany but also outside the country, especially
> in Italy, Spain, and France, the completion and publication of a
> great work by him will have a significance that will reach well
> beyond the context of the discipline. It ought to bestow
> upon German spiritual life and the European intellectual world an
> impetus whose weight and productivity can be hardly
> estimated. . . . Heil Hitler! Schuchardt. Dean.[53]

The appropriate minister approved Heidegger's petition.[54]

The historical and journalistic context in which Heidegger's text "Remembrance of the Poet" ("Andenken") was published was arranged through the efforts of the authorities so that Hölderlin could be used for their cultural agitation and propaganda. The one-hundredth anniversary of Hölderlin's death in 1943 gave them the opportunity for a campaign that included more than three hundred festive occasions throughout the land.[55] The spiritual center of the fete was, of course, Tübingen. Along with the rejuvenation of the Hölderlin Society, which was supported by Goebbels,[56] new editions of Hölderlin's work began to appear in Stuttgart.[57] On the anniversary of the poet's death many wreaths were placed on his grave, including one by Hitler.[58]

"Remembrance of the Poet" appeared in a collection edited by Paul Kluckhohn (a second edition appeared in 1944) on the occasion of the celebration. The volume was financed by the university and the city government of Tübingen. In his introduction Kluckhohn reported on Hölderlin's significance:

> The spiritual discussion with the heritage of the nineteenth
> century in its ideological, scientific, and artistic transformations

and upheavals enables Germany to recall it once again. He was the poet most invoked by the youth movement; in respect to the emotional trauma of World War I, he enabled many young men to adopt a new attitude toward life and death. . . . The great political change . . . that occurred after the war had the special goal of bringing to the fore a new common life through Hölderlin's work. This political change lent greater appeal to the "minstrel of the people" and the ideal of sacrificing one's life for the fatherland. His tremendous significance is that he makes us aware of the best in the German people, and the living effect that he generates is so much greater than that of any other poet. In World War II, which we now have to fight our way through, he is still the most strengthening source of inspiration for many soldiers, just as he was in World War I. He provides inner support, he is a blessed genius. Thus the hundredth anniversary of his death, though we might find ourselves in the thick of battle, will not pass unnoticed.[59]

Josef Weinheber opened the volume with a poem "An Hölderlin, Ode":

> What is form to the Germans, what is effective in them,
> also you have conjured that up. Thus eternally bowing to you,
> off to distant shores in dreamy deliberations,
> that is the power of the Fatherland to you.
>
> You too have sensed that what we call the Fatherland
> is the West. You have totally absorbed this.
> Whether through Apollo or Christ:
> you felt our needs.
>
> Now once again there is an awakening, as you lead us,
> it is the time of the Germans. More German than ever before.
> Guide us, you genius, you see already
> how the fallen ones rejoice in you, hero![60]

Weinheber was an assistant for *Das innere Reich*, the periodical in which Heidegger's essay "Hölderlin and the Essence of Poetry" ("Hölderlin und das Wesen der Dichtung") was published.[61] Wilhelm Böhm had also contributed to the volume edited by Kluckhohn: " 'So I Thought. Before Long': The Completion of the Romance of Hyperion," a sort of potted explanation to the effect that, along with National Socialism, the glory of Hölderlin might finally become a political reality.[62] Kurt Hildebrandt

("Hyperion/Empedocles") saw in Hölderlin the realization of the essence of the German people and of the leadership principle *(Führerprincip)*, a seer and creator of a new German religion.[63] Finally, Paul Böckmann, another contributor to the volume, revealed a noteworthy ultra-nationalistic side of Hölderlin's work.[64]

Heidegger's essay centered around Hölderlin's poem "Andenken." The play in the poem's title on "remembrance" and "memory" was concretized by Heidegger in the experience of the homeland. Heidegger took the remembrance of his own origin and the dialogue with Hölderlin as the spiritual reappropriation of the homeland realizing a program that Hölderlin had offered to the Germans through which they would be able to discover their essence. In the course of making his subject sacred, Heidegger's language became more and more like that of a mythic tale, a liturgy of a new mythos. The action of "Andenken" entails a journey to a distant place in order to come to understand the homeland and its special character. On this journey "the future poet of Germany" is encountered.[65] Heidegger's references to the original text, a mere fragment, make his ideological intentions clear. The "future poet of Germany" traverses France[66] and penetrates even further into the distance. Finally, he arrives at the "source." However, against all expectations, the source does not lie in Greece[67] but in a place where National Socialism looked for the origin of the Aryan race—in India:

> But does he come any closer to the original self *[dem Eigenen]* in the outer reaches of the homeland? When he arrives in *India* is he not in the place where there is an exit from the colony leading back to the source to which he turns? Can the thought that leads him be anything but the thought of the homeland? *now however— to India*—These are confident words. In India he turns back to Germany. . . . The spiritual stream of India made the original homeland of the elders a home and established the first dwelling place. In the region of this stream the wanderer will experience the parental source *[Elterliches]* and thank them for guarding these beginnings that are now fulfilled in the German homeland.[68]

Though this serves as a beginning for the time being, it will later be necessary to search for a new principle in the axis Greece–Germany, which was already expressed in thought and poetry and could only be expressed in both together. Hölderlin establishes the concept of a transcendental dialogue when he writes in a letter: "Nothing is harder to learn than that we need national freedom. And what I believe is that the clarity of exposition is as natural to us as the fire of the heavens is to the Greeks. But the self must be as well informed as the ancients. Therefore the Greeks are indispensable to us."[69] Solely on the grounds and the means of "clarity of exposition" are the Greeks capable, as Heidegger argued, of bringing fire from the heavens to the center of their existence: "That is their basis and foundation for the *polis* as the essential abode of history determined by the Sacred. The *polis* determines 'the political.' As a result, 'the political' can never determine its own principle, or the *polis* itself, or the latter's principle."[70]

> What is *natural* to the Germans, however, is . . . *the clarity of exposition.* The ability to understand, models of planning, the construction of scaffolding and mounting, the arrangement of context and subject matter, the classification and the subdivision sweep you away. These innate abilities turn out to belong not solely to the Germans, these abilities to understand prove not necessarily apt in comprehending the unintelligible or in producing a system [of government] in the face of the unintelligible. In the stress of such bewilderment one is forced to learn what is proper to oneself and then to apply it. . . . Therefore, . . . [that is,] in the epoch of the Germans *the main trend must be to be able to encounter something [great], to have a destiny, since to be fateless . . . is our weakness.*[71]

Heidegger replaced the biological-substance ideology of National Socialism (which he believed to deviate from the right way and to miss the metaphysical dimension of politics) with a "natural," innate German essence that should now manifest itself "historically":

> What is *natural* in a historical people is first true by nature, that is to say, the ground of essence, if the natural is to become the historical of its history. Therefore, the history of a people must find itself in its ownness and dwell within it. . . . On this account, however, . . . it might yet be thus with the Germans, if we suppose that they learn to use their ownness, in which what was once foreign to them (the "fire from the heavens") surpasses even what was proper to the Greeks, if they became open so that the "opened vision exposes the brilliance" (of the heavens). It could be that for the godly a "guest house" and an institution have been given and built, which the temple of the Greeks can no longer match.[72]

With the transsubstantiation of Hölderlin into the highest "spiritual authority" and the homeland into a holy place, Heidegger did not forsake the subject of politics, as Robert Minder has assumed,[73] but transferred it to a context that he maintained was critical and, in his view, essentially spiritual.

Contemporaneous with the publication of the essays in the commemorative volume edited by Kluckhohn, likewise on the occasion of the centenary of Hölderlin's death, Heidegger delivered an address at the University of Freiburg titled "Homecoming/To Our Kin" ("Heimkunft/An die Verwandten") that was printed by V. Klostermann in 1944. The inner connection between both texts on Hölderlin is found in the fact that the "remembrance" of the journey of the "future German poet" spoke of the Aryan origins in terms of which it attempted to understand the homeland, while "the homecoming" thematized the return to the homeland, to life in its encounter with "kinfolk." This text, with Heidegger presented in the middle of the war, conveyed a feeling of joy and peace, an experience that one is capable of encountering oneself only in the homeland. It is as if Heidegger implicitly wanted to answer those who regarded his philosophy as nihilistic, restricted to the themes of dread and negation:

> According to its title, Hölderlin's poem tells of homecoming. It
> makes us think of the arrival on the soil of the homeland and the
> reunion with the country folk (or the homeland). The poem
> relates a trip over the lake "of shaded Alps" to Lindau. In the
> early part of 1801, Hölderlin, the private tutor, traveled back to
> his Swabian homeland by way of Hauptwyl near Konstanz and
> over the Bodensee.[74]

However, to reach the homeland still doesn't mean becoming aware of your essence. Whoever arrives still remains a seeker. In one of Heidegger's revisions of the original text, Hölderlin became more explicit. He even changed a second, definitive copy of the poem to read: "But the treasury, the Germanity . . . is still spared" *(Aber der Schatz, das Deutsche . . . ist noch gespart)* instead of "But the best, the discovery . . ." *(Aber das beste, der Fund . . .).*[75] What the homeland was, lay nearby, but still not quite in the sense of being found: in the sense that explicitly became history. And indeed this was so because what " 'the Fatherland looked after' has still not become the ownmost of the homeland, 'the German' that properly has his own property."[76] In Heidegger's interpretation, for Hölderlin, the homeland was the radiance that sent joy. It was that which gave space, which illuminated and united, a place in which a people makes its history, *"das Hauss."* The poet appealed to those who were able to grasp the homeland as the source of joy: the "angel of the house." "The year" was the time "of the house," the ground from which things bloomed and ended. "The earth" was the first "angel of the house"; the light that pleases was the first "angel of the year."[77] Like the "angel of the year," the "angel of the earth and the light" greeted the "indigenous," illuminated it, and allowed it to rise into the light and into time:

> Suevien, the mother, lived next to the hearth in the house. The
> hearth constantly watched over the glowing fire, which, when
> it was ignited, opened the air and the light into the serene. The
> workplace is around the hearth fire, where secret decisions will be
> forged. . . . Suevien, the voice of the mother, manifests the
> essence of the fatherland. In the vicinity of the source the
> neighborhood is created in joyousness. The ownmost and the best
> of the homeland rest there, solely in the vicinity of the source, not
> outside it. Therefore, the truth of the source is born in this
> homeland. One then leaves this place of familiar surroundings, if
> one must, only with difficulty.[78]

The vicinity of the source shows this as "secret," and the secret is not to be revealed or analyzed. " 'The treasure,' the ownmost of the homeland, 'what is German,' is saved. The vicinity of the source is a saving nearness."[79] "The elegy 'Homecoming' is not a poem about homecoming, but, as poetry, which it is, the elegy is itself the homecoming that still obtains *[ereignet]*, so long as its words ring out in the language of the Germans."[80] The word greets the Germans as that which does not come into view, although it is utterly close. At the same time, Hölderlin sang of the light and the established joy of his homeland. He translated the tragedies of Sophocles in order to indicate how the "singing of the Germans" ought to be sung. Hölderlin had thus discovered that only "the elders of our princes" and the "angel of our holy fatherland" could hear the singing.[81] The holy is manifest, although the "god" remains at a distance: "we are lacking holy names," which, to begin, are requisite. In this situation it was not possible to find a new god or to summon the already forgotten gods. In this, only the god's absence become a secret. The poet could not and should not do anything further but hope and prepare the space for a future "god." " 'The others' must first learn to reflect on the mystery of the saving vicinity."[82] Only through the word of the poet is the proximity of the homeland heard, which still does not belong to them. As they become aware of it, they become the "next of kin of the poets," whose life "far from the earth of the homeland . . . is squandered in suffering."[83] "This homecoming is the future of the historical essence of the Germans. They are the nation of poetry *and* of thought. For there must be thought in order to grasp the word of the poet. . . . Therefore, the poet turns to the others whom his own remembrance helps to grasp the poetic word that each in his own fateful way manifests in the homecoming."[84]

Parmenides and Heraclitus (1943–1944)

Heidegger's centripetal movement to the intimacy of the homeland was part of a totality. For just as the official announcements and many representatives of the academic world at that time conceived of Hölderlin as a warrior, in the same way Heidegger conducted a kind of philosophical war against what he considered the fateful development of German thinking as regards its purity. In his lecture on Parmenides he wrote as follows:

> The *original beginning* can only take place as a *first beginning* in a Western historical people of poets and thinkers. . . . Therefore, it is of value to note that this historical people, if it is ultimately a question of coming to a "victory," has already won and is unconquerable—if it is indeed the people of poets and thinkers that will remain in its essence *[Wesen]* as long as it is not threatened by invariably menacing deviations or falls victim to mistaking its own identity.[85]

What I have cited here is published in the complete works, although in this case there is some justified doubt about its agreement with the original, since, in a commentary on this edition, M. Frings has observed that Heidegger "put some finishing touches and additions" to the manuscript[86] without indicating which parts were altered and when his corrections were introduced.

In the effort to keep German thinking pure, Heidegger's evaluation of "romantic" thinking reached its high point. The occasion derives from the more precise determination of what is false and what is true. According to Heidegger, the German language suffered considerable alienation as it took over the word "false." The Grimm brothers had already taken "false" (*falsum*) for a non-German word.[87] It entered the German from the medieval *falsum*, which in turn stems from the Greek *sphallo*, which means "to bring to ruin," "to cut, to make unsteady," and therefore something that could be transformed into the opposite of truth or *aletheia*. For the development of the Latin *falsum*, the link to the "imperium" and the Imperial was essential, that is, the link to what the others dismiss. Undoubtedly alluding to the war experiences of the period, Heidegger determined that the "romantic" (Latin) version of the false "has now become the deception, the 'trick', a word that not by chance comes from the English . . . , the false is a malicious deception."[88]

The word "truth" had a similar fate according to Heidegger. The surroundings in which *aletheia* arose was destroyed by the romantic conception of the essence of truth.[89] "It is decisive that the Romanization of the world of Greek-Roman history was grasped as a *change in the essence of truth and being*."[90] The essence of *aletheia* was not only shaken, but was directly obstructed by "that immense apparatus that in a multiple 'Latin' sense has come to determine the essence of truth."[91] Romanization was a mediating factor in a degeneration that in modern times has encroached upon the entire world, and its influence has led to the decline of the essence of truth.[92] Only in the union of Greek with a purified German did it appear possible to restore the assertive power of the words "true" *(wahr)* and "false" *(falsch)* and to open the spirit for a new encounter with truth *(Wahrheit)*. In an allusion to Alfred Rosenberg's *Mythos*,[93] Heidegger claimed that a mythos must first be grounded in such an understanding of truth. Humanism, on the contrary, is unjustifiable because it is rooted in linguistic confusion. "German humanism has mixed up this uniqueness and has made Hellenism completely inaccessible. Goethe is destiny *[Verhängnis]*."[94]

The aggressiveness that characterized the lectures in the summer semester of 1942 made Heidegger's link to National Socialism clear, and even clarified his open and public support for the war unleashed by the Hitler regime. When the United States entered the war, Heidegger said to his students:

We know today that the Anglo-Saxon world of America is determined to annihilate Europe, and that means the homeland that is the beginning of the West. But the beginning is indestructible. America's entering this planetary war is not an entering into history but already constitutes the last American act of ahistoricality and self-destruction. For this act is the repudiation of what is beginning and a decision for undoing the beginning. The hidden spirit of the original in the West does not look upon this process of the self-destruction of those without beginnings with contempt, but out of the equanimity *[Gelassenheit]* of the originary *[Anfängliche]* it awaits its auspicious hour.[95]

This shows that Heidegger's intention to transcendentalize the "source" of the West was closely tied to the spiritualizing of National Socialism. From this perspective, the lectures on Heraclitus in the summer semester of 1943 and 1944—hence, immediately after the defeat of the Germans at Stalingrad—were a call to the German people to recover from this blow:

In whatever way and however the external fate of the West occurs, the most significant and specific test for the Germans still lies ahead, that test in which they perhaps will be tested by the ignorant against their will, to determine if they, the Germans, are in agreement with the truth of being, if they are strong enough in their readiness for death against the small-mindedness of the modern world in order to rescue the originary in its unpretentiousness. The danger, which the "holy heart of the people" of the West face, is not that of a decline but a danger that we, self-confused, ourselves produce and set in motion through the will of modernity. To stave off this calamity we needed to learn, in the approaching decades of the thirties and the forties, essentially how to think[96]

In view of these words, one can fully agree with W. D. Gudopp, who said: Heidegger "is a strategic thinker and wishes to be that."[97] Consequently, in the middle of the war he repeated the thesis of the transcendental German mission: "The planet is in flames. The essence of man has come apart. Only we Germans, granted that we find and protect what is 'German,' can arrive at world-historical awareness. This is not arrogance, but it is the knowledge of the necessity of an original exigency."[98]

In contrast to his later testimony, Heidegger defended Hitler's regime and its war activities between 1940 and 1944. Heidegger later claimed that the Gestapo had expanded their investigations of the Catholic members of his department, Father Schumacher, Dr. Guggenberger, and Dr. Bollinger, in connection with the mobilizing of student resistance by the Scholls, whom, they presumed, were supported in Freiburg by students attending his lectures.[99] The resistance group "The White Rose," to which Heidegger referred, was organized under the spiritual and political guidance of Professor Kurt Huber, a Catholic philosophy professor at the

University of Munich. Most of its members were killed after its discovery. In my efforts to reconstruct what happened at Freiburg in 1943 and 1944, and especially to question those people mentioned by Heidegger, I was only able to locate Dr. Heinz Bollinger. His concise judgment contradicts Heidegger's claims and throws light on the image of the philosopher among members of the student body. Confronted with the description that Heidegger committed to paper in 1945, Dr. Bollinger wrote: "During my time in Freiburg, 1938–1943, Martin Heidegger was looked upon as a Nazi; for me he was a Hitler in an academic chair." He further added: "In my interrogation by the Nazis I was never asked about my relationship with him, only about other professors."[100] In a later letter, Bollinger wrote: "No one was known to me in my resistance circle and that of the White Rose (with which I entered into contact in December of 1942) who had a relationship with Heidegger. I encountered the names of Schumacher and Guggenberger from you [Farías] for the first time."[101]

The end of the war and the beginning of *polemos*

The Freiburg daily *Badische Zeitung* reported on March 14, 1947, that "as part of the actions of political purification, Professor Heidegger has been forbidden to teach. He will no longer be a member of the University."[102]

This decree was the result of a long process of obligatory denazification of the University of Freiburg under the direction of the French occupation beginning April 25, 1945. The occupation forces were convinced that the university had played an important role in supporting National Socialism in the region. The French were eager to see denazification work thoroughly and refused to give any autonomy to the university,[103] which did what it could to protect the teachers and to avoid their expulsion and punishment by the French.[104]

By decree of the military government, at the beginning of May, Heidegger's home was confiscated as "a party house," one belonging to a "typical Nazi."[105] In spite of protests by Heidegger and his wife, the decree was upheld, and the Heidegger family had to share their home with another family.[106]

The "caretaker," an officer named by the military government to reorganize the university, named as his representatives a group of three: Professors Constantin von Dietze, Gerhard Ritter, and Adolf Lampe. These three had just been freed from a Berlin prison where they had been held since July 20, 1944 (the attempt on Hitler's life). Documents left by Lampe contain much information on Heidegger's trial, but unfortunately they are not available to researchers.

Martin Heidegger was to appear on July 23, 1945, before a commission of these three persons, later enlarged to admit Professors A. Allgeier and F. Oehlkers. Except for Lampe, the group was sympathetic to Heidegger. Ritter, in particular, claimed that Heidegger was "a resolute adversary of Nazism" from 1934.[107]

The report on Heidegger was rendered in September 1945, and was quite mild.[108] It insisted on the radical incompatibility between Nazism and Heidegger's philosophy. Yet, given Heidegger's responsibility for promoting Nazism in the university, the report ends with the recommendation to the university senate that Heidegger retire *(Emeritierung)*, maintaining his right to teach.[109]

The senate debated this on October 17, 1945, and resolved to ask the French military government to change its stand (taking into account his earlier expulsion). The senate also asked the Ministry at Karlsruhe to offer retirement to Heidegger, as he had requested.

At the beginning of 1946, Heidegger had to declare formally that he gave up his rights to teach until the university was reorganized.[110]

In spite of everything, the sentence of the senate was harsh: Heidegger was retired without the right to teach and was barred from taking part in any public activity at the university.[111] The military government refused this, increased the charges against him, and asked that his pension *(Pensionierung)* be stopped.[112] The university, especially the philosophy faculty, tried without success to soften the position of the military government.[113]

To understand this intransigence, we would have to consult the papers of the French government and the archives of Heidegger, neither at this time available.

We note here that, while these events were occurring at Freiburg, other German universities were trying to offer Heidegger a chair. At Tübingen there was a chair left vacant by Herbert Haering in November 1945.[114] On November 24, 1945, the faculty put Heidegger's name first on the list, ahead of Gerhard Krüger (Münster), in spite of strong opposition for academic and political reasons by Professors Schonfeld, Dannenbauer, Kern, and Kamke. Those in favor of Heidegger were Rudolf Stadelmann and Paul Kluckhohn, both active National Socialists, and Romano Guardini.

The faculty repaired the list: Nicolai Hartmann was placed first, Heidegger second, and then Heinrich Scholz and Gerhard Krüger.

The opposition to Heidegger came especially from Knoop and Kamke, who were against him because of his "nihilism" and because of the impression he left after his speech in November 1933 on "The University within the National Socialist State."

The text of the second report, drawn up by Stadelmann for the faculty, makes no allusion to Heidegger's political position.

The three letters sent to Rudolf Stadelmann by Heidegger, July 20, September 1, and November 30, 1945, complete and confirm the results of Hugo Ott's study of Heidegger and the process of denazification.[115] Heidegger complained about the attitude of the authorities at Freiburg, about the aggressiveness of French Resistance members, the faculty, and the faculty senate. At no time did he seem to lose confidence in his own stature: "They do not want to be shamed in the face of foreign opinion. By keeping me as a member of the university, they would show that they still recognize my spiritual power." In answer to the rector's request that he not return to teaching for a while, Heidegger wrote, "I wrote to say that for me I saw no problem in not returning to teaching just now, but the problem was to know if the German youth and the spiritual situation of Germany could wait or not. The university assumes the responsibility."

Heidegger's letters to Stadelmann show also that Heidegger (via Stadelmann) continued to exercise his influence after the war, in spite of his marginal situation, by using a structure that let him take part in choosing holders of chairs, at least at Tübingen. In these letters, Heidegger recommended his students Gadamer, Becker, Krüger, Karl Löwith, and Robert Heiss. As for the possibility of taking the chair at Tübingen, Heidegger answered on November 30, 1945, that he was skeptical. In his last letter, on January 30, 1946, he asked Stadelmann to drop the subject.

The senate and the rector of Freiburg had meanwhile asked him "not to appear at any public function of the university."

Echoes

In the posthumously published *Spiegel* interview Heidegger claimed that in the last days of the war he was sent to the front when the area commanders in Freiburg declared that he was thoroughly "dispensable."[116] No document has surfaced to support this claim. A noteworthy clue regarding Heidegger's behavior during the disintegration of National Socialism has been offered by Georg Picht:

On December 1944 just as dusk fell our doorbell rang. Outside stood Heidegger with his daughter-in-law and his assistant. They were fleeing from Freiburg, which had been bombed by the Allies, who were now threatening to invade it toward Messkirch. There were no means of transportation. They requested accommodations for the night. We passed a quiet and relaxed evening. On Heidegger's request my wife played Schubert's posthumous Sonata in B Major. As the music ended, he looked at me and said: "We cannot do that with philosophy." In our guestbook there is the entry: "Then death is different from decline. Every decline remains hidden in the beginning." *[Anderes denn ein Verenden ist das Untergehen. Jeder Untergang bleibt geborgen in den Anfang].*[117]

In a letter to Rudolf Stadelmann of July 20, 1945, Heidegger justified this attitude: "Everything now points to ruin. However, we Germans cannot go under, because we still have not risen; hence, we must persist through the night."[118] In another letter to Stadelmann on September 1, 1945, he added: "Moreover, I am of the conviction that out of our Swabian roots the spirit of the West will be awakened."[119] His popularity in France had convinced him: "I have for the time being here (and in the city) been 'fired upon.' The French, especially in Paris, are indignant. As the matter now stands, I am valued in Paris and France, where my philosophy is in 'vogue,' but hold out against its reception by my fellow-countrymen." And on November 30, 1945, he admitted—in the same way as in his "Ways to Language" of 1937—vis-à-vis Stadelmann: "The French know that my philosophical work of the past 25 years has determined and aroused the thinking and especially the attitudes of the young in spiritual matters."[120] However, he did not, by any means, forget the old feuds: "I would like to expressly warn you against Ed. Baumgarten (Königsberg) who repeatedly traveled out of Göttingen [changed course]."[121]

With the outbreak of the Cold War Heidegger faced a personal cold war of the spirit. In a letter from Heidegger to him on April 8, 1950, Jaspers noted:

The subject of evil is not at an end, but has now only entered a new arena. Stalin doesn't need to declare war any more; he wins a battle every day. This can no longer be avoided. Every word and every document constitutes a counter-attack although not in the political sphere, which for a long time has been outwitted in other relations of existence and now only leads a false existence. For the splendid proposal of a dispute by letter, the old story still

counts: the more simple the subject becomes, the more difficult it
is to think about it and to describe it. In the present-day state of
homelessness, it is not that nothing happens. Within this there
is hidden an Advent whose most distant sign we are perhaps
experiencing.[122]

Heidegger constantly declined to offer an explicit self-critique, appropriate to the horrors of Nazi fascism. This obstinancy is indicated by the
following anecdote, which comes from the theologian Rudolf Bultmann.
After the War Heidegger tried to make contact with Bultmann. In his
first telephone call he said:

"I want to apologize to you" . . . since [Bultmann reminisces]
everything was forgotten. If any motive might have connected him
with National Socialism, it was dissolved by his disillusionment.
Nothing stands between us anymore. And then, when, after we
said good-bye, I came back again to what he said to me on the
telephone: "Now you must," I said to him, "like Augustine write
retractions *[Retractiones]* . . . in the final analysis for the truth
of your thought." Heidegger's face became a stony mask. He left
without saying anything further.[123]

This report is all the more astonishing since Heidegger and Bultmann
edited the *Theologische Rundschau* together at a time when it was always
under the watchfully critical eye of Rosenberg's office. This is confirmed
in a letter, obtained from the archives of the Institute of Contemporary
History in Munich, from Dr. Erxleben to Brachmann dated February 5,
1942. At that time Heidegger's involvement in the periodical was carefully observed by a representative from Rosenberg's office.[124] (In this
connection Antje Bultmann-Lemke told me that among Rudolf Bultmann's literary remains in the university library in Tübingen there are
numerous letters in which Heidegger expressed his enthusiasm for National Socialism and in which he refers to the function the office of rector
at Freiburg had for him in this connection. However, as in other cases,
one cannot get authorization to inspect these documents.)[125]

Jaspers also tried without success to move Heidegger to recant. Disillusioned, he recognized that Heidegger was not able to grasp the depths
of his mistakes, or really to change, but only to arrive at a game of distortions and erasures.[126]

However, it would be incorrect to say that Heidegger had nothing to say about the Nazi's extermination practices. In his correspondence with Herbert Marcuse he compared the "Final Solution" of the Jewish question with the Allied Forces' measure in banishing the "East Germans."[127] Heidegger's letter to Marcuse on January 20, 1948, was the response to a letter from August 28, 1947, in which Marcuse demanded an opinion from Heidegger on the Shoah. In his first letter Marcuse wrote:

> You told me that you completely dissociated yourself from the Nazi regime after 1934, that you made exceptionally critical remarks in your lectures, and that you were under surveillance by the Gestapo. I will not doubt your word. But the fact remains that you very strongly identified with the regime from 1933 to 1934 and that today in the eyes of many you are seen as one of the most absolute spiritual supporters of the regime. Your own speeches, writings, and actions from this time are the proof. You have never publicly recanted—at least not since 1945. You have never publicly explained that you came to other views than those that you expressed and actualized [*verwirklicht*] in your activities in 1933 and 1934. You remained in Germany after 1934 though you would have found many prospects for work outside the country. You have not publicly denounced a single deed or idea [*Ideologie*] of the regime. Under these circumstances you are today still identified with the Nazi regime. Many of us have long awaited a word from you, a word to indicate that you are clearly and definitely free from this identification, a word that expresses your present attitude and what really happened. There has been no such word from you; at least it has never emerged from the private sphere.
>
> I myself—and very many others—have revered you as a philosopher and have learned an immeasurable amount from you. But we cannot make the separation between Heidegger the philosopher and Heidegger the man; this even conflicts with your own philosophy. A philosopher can go astray politically, but then he ought to expose his mistakes. But he cannot go astray regarding a regime that has killed millions of Jews merely because they were Jews, a regime where terror was made the norm and everything that was connected with the spirit, freedom, and truth was transformed into its bloody opposite, a regime that everywhere and in everything was the murderous caricature of that Western tradition that you yourself with so much insistence expounded

and justified. And if this regime was not a caricature but the actual fulfillment of this tradition, then there was no deception. You must now indict and renounce this tradition.

If one believes in a world spirit, one is inclined to see in it the glaring irony of a game, an irony that makes it one of the predecessors of Sartre. Must you thus enter into the history of the spirit? Every attempt to resist this strange misunderstanding founders on the general opposition to any serious involvement with the Nazi ideology. The common human understanding (as well as the spiritual) manifested by this opposition refuses to see you as a philosopher of the Nazi ideology, because it maintains that philosophy and Nazism are incompatible. In the end this conviction is right. Once again, you can only make a stand against (and we can only combat) the identification of you and your work with Nazism (and with it the annihilation of your philosophy) if you publicly acknowledge your change and transformation.

Heidegger's response came on January 20, 1948, and begins with the qualifying remark: "If I gather from your letter that you are seriously concerned with judging my work and my person, then your letter just shows how difficult a dialogue is with people who have not been in Germany since 1933 and who evaluate the beginning of the National Socialist movement from the perspective of its end." On his association with the Nazi regime Heidegger wrote:

I would like to say the following about the main points of your letter.

1. In regard to 1933: I expected from National Socialism a spiritual rejuvenation of all life, a reconciliation of social antagonisms, and the rescue of Western existence from the danger of communism. This thought was expressed in my Rector's Address (have you read it in its *entirety?*), in an address on "Das Wesen der Wissenschaft," and in two talks to the assistants and students of the local universities.[128] To that end there took place an election manifesto of about 25 to 30 lines that was published in the local student papers. Some of the propositions in this manifesto I regard today as slips.

That is all.

2. In 1934 I acknowledged my political errors and in protest against the state and party I resigned from my position as rector.

This was exploited in propaganda inside and outside the country; however, I was not aware of the way it was suppressed, and so the burden doesn't lie with me.

3. You are totally right that I have failed to offer a public and clear confession; it would have handed me and my family over to destruction *[ans Messer geliefert]*. As Jaspers has commented about this: That we live is our guilt.

4. I have in my lectures and practice from 1933 to 1934 taken an unequivocal stand so that my students did not succumb to Nazi ideology. Once my work from this period appears, it will show this.

5. A confession after 1945 was impossible for me, because the Nazi partisans demonstrated their change of heart in a disgusting manner, and I have nothing in common with them.

6. To the severe and justified reproach that you express "over a regime that has exterminated millions of Jews, that has made terror a norm and that transformed everything connected to the concepts of spirit, freedom, and truth into its opposite," I can only add that instead of the "Jews" one should put the "East Germans," and that is even more the case for one of the Allied Powers, with the difference that everything that happened since 1945 is known to all the world, while the bloody terror of the Nazis in reality was kept secret from the German people.

In Marcuse's response dated May 13, 1948, there is, among other things, the following remark:

For a long while I didn't know whether I should answer your letter of January 20th. You are correct: a dialogue with people who have not been in Germany since 1933 is obviously very difficult. Now I believe that the reason for this is not our ignorance of the conditions in Germany under the Nazis. We have known about these conditions very precisely—perhaps even better than those in Germany. The immediate contact that I had with many of these Germans in 1947 convinced me of this even further. It is, hence, not that we judge the beginning of the National Socialist movement from the perspective of its end. We knew, and I myself have seen, that the beginning already harbored the end; it was the end. Nothing has been added that was not already there in the beginning. The difficulty in the

discussion seems to me to rest more on the fact that people in
Germany were exposed to a total perversion of all concepts and
feelings, which so many among them so readily accepted. It
cannot be explained otherwise that you, who were able to
understand Western philosophers like no one else, could see in
Nazism "a spiritual rejuvenation of life in its totality," a "rescuing
of Western existence from the dangers of communism" (which
itself is an essential part of this existence!). That is not a political
problem, but an intellectual one—I almost want to say: a problem
of knowledge, of truth. You, the philosopher, have you confused
the liquidation of Western existence with its rejuvenation? Was
this liquidation not already obvious in every word of the "Führer,"
in every gesture and act of the SA long before 1933?

Marcuse elaborated on Heidegger's thesis on Shoah:

But now I want to examine a section of your letter more closely,
because my silence could be construed as an admission. You write
that everything that I say concerning the eradication of the Jews is
exactly the same for the Allies, if instead of "Jews" we put "East
Germans." Do you not situate yourself with this proposition
outside the dimension in which a discussion is possible between
people—outside of reason *[Logos]*? For only completely outside
this "logical" dimension is it possible to explain such a crime, to
adjust to, to "grasp," the fact that others could also have done
something like this. Further: how is it possible to compare
the torture, mutilation, and annihilation of millions of people with
the compulsory transplantation of groups of people who did not
face any of these crimes (perhaps disregarding some exceptions)?
The world today is such that the difference between the Nazi
concentration camps and the deportation and internment that
followed the war constitutes the whole difference between
inhumanity and humanity. On the basis of your argument, if the
Allies had been responsible for Auschwitz and Buchenwald—for
everything that took place there but in relation to those "East
Germans"—then your summation would be correct. If, however,
the difference between humanity and inhumanity is reduced to
this omission, then this is indeed the world-historical guilt of the
Nazi system, for the world has previously proven after over 2,000
years of Western existence what we can do to man. It appears as if

the seed has fallen onto fertile ground: perhaps we are still experiencing the completion of what began in 1933. I don't know if you will again treat this completion as a "renewal."

Heidegger's unreasonableness is even more striking and flagrant in a speech he gave in Bremen in 1949 where he said: "Agriculture is now a motorized *(motorisierte)* food industry, in essence the same as the manufacturing of corpses in the gas chambers and extermination camps, the same as the blockade and starvation of the countryside, the same as the production of the hydrogen bombs." [129]

Heidegger's most active student in France, Jean Beaufret, perpetuated this ominous tradition. He declared his solidarity with the right "revisionists" in two letters to the ideologue Robert Faurisson in 1978–1979, favoring the latter's thesis that under Hitler there were no concentration camps and no annihilation of the Jews, that Shoah is nothing other than a "historical dogma with the total aggression that is characteristic of a dogmatism." [130] Beaufret's opinion was known to his students in 1967, and certainly at least because of the preparations for a commemorative volume for Beaufret. A former student of Beaufret's, Roger Laporte, "provided information in 1967 to the philosopher Jacques Derrida that deeply shocked him. Jean Beaufret made remarks to him [Laporte] that today would be regarded as revisionistic and attacked the Jewish thinker Emmanuel Levinas in a way that far exceeded a justifiable critique." Nevertheless, this commemorative volume was published with contributions by Jacques Derrida and Roger Laporte (with a dedication to Levinas).

18 Return to Abraham a Sancta Clara

Reflections that occupied Heidegger during the end of his life are displayed in two complementary ways. While still working at the maximal level of abstraction, he now tried to bring the formal object of these reflections, that is, "the being of what is" *(das Sein des Seienden),* into the concrete world. As the pre-reflective basis of all thought, being can be perceived only if it reveals itself to be that which truly escapes thought, thus remaining absolutely indeterminate. Therefore, the history of being for Heidegger will be the history of signs, of traces left by being as it escapes thought.[1] The place, the frame in which Heidegger sought these signs, was the fatherland, his Swabian fatherland. And this was not because it was by chance the accustomed ground beneath Heidegger's feet, but because he considered it the center of the center, because it held within itself "the metaphysical people."

His speech "Homecoming" made it clear that the Swabian fatherland of Hölderlin was the true spiritual center of Germany. The signs that let us catch a glimpse of being are found in the local fatherland *(Heimat),* especially in its language, the mother tongue. Heidegger did not derive from that a philosophy of language that examines meanings with regard to true or false propositions; on the contrary, he pursued a thought that took careful account of the expressive singularity wherein signs can speak themselves. The language of the fatherland in this way becomes a sacred space, work *become* spirit. Doubly marked by the seal of the fatherland and the mother tongue, Heidegger's return to his origins is not limited to his dialogue with Hölderlin nor to his turning to J. P. Hebel. He returned, by way of having made a great circle, back to the subject of his first publication, to Abraham a Sancta Clara.

On May 2, 1964, Heidegger attended a meeting of former students of the Latin School of Messkirch, where he gave a speech that soon after was published by the town of Messkirch: "On Abraham a Sancta Clara" (Messkirch, 1964). Analysis of this text provides certain links between the essential themes of his reflections toward the end of his life and the permanent themes that recall his point of departure.

Although naming Vienna without ever returning to the subject, W. D. Gudopp has emphasized the role of this epicenter of the Catholic Reich in young Heidegger's education. The author mentions and comments on the text written by the young Heidegger on the occasion of the unveiling of the monument to Abraham a Sancta Clara, but he neglects to show the ties between this text and the 1964 writing on the Augustinian monk.

The speech opens with the quote from Abraham: "All those born under straw thatch do not have just straw in their heads."

Heidegger continued by saying that understanding Abraham does not mean just to count off the circumstances and events of his life. Understanding him means grasping his destiny, which then leads to a reflection on the era when he achieved his destiny.[2]

Heidegger depicts the times as follows:

"The second half of the seventeenth century, after the Peace of Westphalia in 1648, was not a time of peace. To the desolation and misery that followed the war, there followed new wars and threats, additional hunger and poverty. Foreign armies crisscrossed the land. The plague devastated Vienna. The Turks were at the gates. War and peace, terror in the face of death and the will to live, were close together."[3]

When Heidegger defined the times in which Abraham realized his destiny, and then left the entire tale without commentary, he simply remained silent about two essential elements in the familiar picture of Abraham sharing the suffering of others at the time: the Jews who were the cause of the plague, and the Turks who were the incarnate foreigner, the aggressive alien. We may well ask to what extent Heidegger's forgetfulness was conscious or not. Heidegger continued with the following shocking sentence: "This is why Abraham wrote at that time: 'Among us, poverty, wealth, and death ("May God take pity on us") are met in a single day.' Our peace is as far from war as Sachsenhausen is from Frankfurt."[4]

These are words that, to say the least, are troubling. *In 1964*, no one in Germany was unaware that Sachsenhausen, a suburb of Frankfurt, had been one of the most feared concentration camps in the Third Reich.

Also at this time no one was unaware that Frankfurt was the seat of a trial to investigate those responsible for the crimes perpetrated at Auschwitz. For a long time this subject was without question a great magnet for German public opinion. What could Heidegger have had in mind when he chose to join those two places in the mouth of Abraham? Could it be a matter of pure chance, a lapsus, or an open and frank provocation? I exclude the hypothesis that it was simply chance because we know the accuracy and virtuosity with which Heidegger used citation.

Could it be a slip of the tongue? One might surmise that Heidegger is quite aware of what he is doing, lets the well-known anti-semitism of Abraham slip by in silence, only to expose it unconsciously: by naming Sachsenhausen he is speaking of the Auschwitz crimes. He therefore does not speak directly of the connection between Abraham the anti-semite and Sachsenhausen/Auschwitz, but that buried and now-perceived relationship finally surfaces. With this trilogy, Abraham/Sachsenhausen/Auschwitz, Heidegger seems to say what he wants to say but cannot without taking the risk of linking the sacred fatherland with the greatest monstrosity mankind has ever been guilty of. The slip reveals what appears to be an unresolved, repressed situation. The question is all the more important because Heidegger chose the most significant and sensitive place to clarify things unconsciously: his birthplace. The scene unfolds in front of "the forces of the future" (the young of the fatherland), in the very school where Abraham and Heidegger had been in touch with the times of essential origination.

Could we be faced here with an unconscious retraction in Heidegger's expression? Does this "frailty" of Heidegger mean that he is refusing categorically to be an autocritic? Possibly.

There may be another answer. A characteristic stance of the philosopher is to defy "public opinion" consciously and openly so as to be understood only by those "capable of understanding." Could Heidegger have been trying in a "manly" way to take responsibility for the meaning of this trilogy by adopting a stance that only Himmler of all the Nazi leaders dared to take upon himself—suicide?

The question remains open and will remain so until more telling documentation becomes available.

Continuing our analysis of Heidegger's speech, we find Heidegger leading his hearers to quite novel themes:

> But on the other hand, during the second half of the seventeenth
> century, a new spirit was born, one that stubbornly turned
> toward the world in order to act and to create within it; this was

the spirit of the Baroque. Abraham was a contemporary of Bach and Handel. These great musical architects took up their work during the same time. The Baroque churches at Ottobeuren, Weingarten, Weissenau, Steinhausen, and Birnau were their edifices.[5]

We see in this another side of Abraham a Sancta Clara. His work is his language: "He spoke and wrote with the aid of his mastery of German, a language possessing extraordinarily creative possibilities." Going beyond this link with the Baroque, it is important "to be attentive to the way Abraham spoke; only then will we have an idea of the special power and richness of his language."[6] Abraham "thought in images. Through them he could make people *see* directly what he meant."[7] For example, he described the death that struck Vienna as a force transcending classes and noble houses, as a reaper cutting hay, high and low, striking like a thunderbolt both the roofs of palaces and those of thatch.[8]

With another image he lays bare the nothingness of human existence: "Man, that five-foot-tall nothing."[9] Only a superficial reader could think that Abraham was playing with words, for in fact he "was listening to language."[10] The example Heidegger chose to illustrate Abraham's linguistic virtuosity is rather sinister: "Rhyme and the harmony of words and syllables are used to strike an image. Father Abraham once wrote: 'A military chief struck the Turk's head with a whip; heads and scalps rolled like saucepans.'"[11] But for Heidegger the splendor of Abraham's language expresses itself in the phrase "the whiteness of the swan," which is revived by the image of the ephemeral whiteness of snow.[12]

In this way Heidegger achieved a curious synthesis. The fanatic priest loved swans; the cruel anti-semite sang of the snow's whiteness; he evokes the magic of the words and syllables by speaking about heads falling and banging like saucepans. Heidegger took from Abraham's and his own writings two examples of what Mitscherlich called "people unable to feel compassion." According to Heidegger the usual criticisms meted out to Abraham were grossly unjust: "A man usually described as coarse, one who condemned the behavior of people by calling up the devil and death."[13] Heidegger's conclusion was: "The road taken by Ulrich Megerle is a sign of the fidelity and rigor of Abraham in the face of the destiny he was given. We need to listen with care: Then we may find in this reunion not only a former pupil of a Messkirch school but a master for our own lives and a master of the language."[14]

In the 1910 text, Heidegger had painted Abraham from the perspective of the fatherland, underlining his role as a leading master and phy-

sician for the "salvation of the soul of the people," anticipating thereby
his own pedagogical scheme of "education by example" offered by eminent individuals.

Politically, Heidegger places Abraham a Sancta Clara in the same line
of anti-semitic Christian Socialism as the reformist populism of Karl Lueger, mayor of Vienna. With time Heidegger has transformed the objective social meaning of the image of Abraham. The first image of Abraham was drawn from the *Blütenlese* of Karl Bertsche, a specialist on Sancta
Clara and editor of the 1910 text in which Abraham is the "spiritual
bread" of the German warriors of the First War, and, later, of the Second. In a letter Bertsche wrote to the president of the Writers Union:

> The descendants of those Jews who struck Jesus are still punished
> today throughout the world. The fact that we persecute these
> damned perverts on all sides—Father Abraham says forthrightly—
> is in no way unjust, for, apart from the devil, Christians have no
> greater enemy than the Jews. Because of their many profanations,
> these beasts do not deserve anyone to be concerned about them,
> much less have contact with them.[15]

In his book *Abraham a Sancta Clara and Judaism* (1941), Franz Loidl
was, if possible, even more explicit and violent. After stating that "the era
of Abraham was extremely decisive for the Jews of Vienna,"[16] he added,
"the troubles of the Viennese led them to find a radical solution," because
it had become clear in the meantime that "neither martyrdom nor the
stake would separate them [the Jews] from their faith."[17]

In his writings *Lauberhütt* and *Weinkeller*, Abraham noted the auto-da-
fé of twenty-four Jews at Salzburg.[18] His information on Jewish life came
directly from his own experience. He knew the Viennese ghetto quite
well and could observe the Jews with his own eyes, even if only for a
short time, since, it is true, the Jews were expelled from Vienna soon
afterwards. When he arrived in Vienna in 1672, the serious problem had
been resolved; the city was almost emptied of Jews. Loidl says that this
was why Father Abraham said almost nothing more about them.[19] Loidl
reported that, thanks to "detailed research by Karl Bertsche," he was able
to ascertain that some publishers of Abraham's works had eliminated in-
sults about Jews.[20] But he is ready to recall them for us:

> The descendants of Jesus' assassins had to see how the seeds they
> had sown bore no fruit; on their graves no grass grew. The sons
> of those who had struck Jesus were born with a foreshortened

right arm. Others were born with pigs' teeth. The sons of those who gave him vinegar on the cross found their nostrils filled with worms on Holy Thursday. The sons of those who spat on him cannot spit without soiling their own faces. Those who whipped him had to watch their children suffer from 6,666 boils on their flesh every March 25.[21]

Since that time, all Jews have a peculiar odor, especially keen during Holy Week, their punishment for having witnessed Jesus' miracles without believing in him. Their claim that they are awaiting the Messiah has caused them much pain. There is the story of a Jewish girl pregnant by a student who persuaded others to believe that the child was the Messiah. Jews of the region came to watch and adore. But when they saw at the birth that the child was a girl, they seized the baby in anger and dashed her against a wall.[22]

Their sacrileges are beyond number: Jews demand that women who want to pawn their clothing bring consecrated hosts. During a Mass, a Jew profaned the host by biting it and then began to leap and howl in church like a dog until a saint took it from the Jew's mouth. Jews from Deggendorf (Bavaria) put needles into hosts, some in Paris (1290) burnt them. In Bohemia they spat on them and speared them on knives. At Nurenberg they crushed them in a mortar.[23]

Abraham accepted as true the claims, "worthy of belief," of the historian Antonius Bousinius, according to whom "when Jews circumcise the boy on the eighth day, the hemorrhage can be stopped only with the blood of a Christian."[24]

Loidl's lists of citations could continue endlessly. Still, it is important to note Loidl's particular way of "adapting" Abraham to the new world of 1941. When the Jews were finally expelled in 1670, the problem seemed to be but was not actually resolved. "Some years later the Jews returned to work and the problem began again at Vienna and the court. Since then the number of Jews has grown, and their money has extended their influence. Worse yet: the illuminism and liberalism of that time provided fertile ground which later offered protection to the Jews."

Loidl concludes: "With the third expulsion, the present one, the agitation that has provoked this peculiar people has reached a definitive resolution."[25]

Loidl's work was praised by Dr. Karl Eder in the Catholic review *Theo-*

logisch-praktische Quartalsschrift, edited by professors of theology and philosophy at the diocesan seminary at Linz,[26] who called it a "very timely writing." In addition, his work was published with the imprimatur of the Viennese archbishopric. Soon afterwards, Loidl and Karl Bertsche tried to have Abraham a Sancta Clara canonized.[27]

Certainly these citations from Loidl and Abraham cannot be imputed to Heidegger. But when Heidegger presented Abraham to the youth at Messkirch as an example for their lives, a man of destiny and master of the language, Heidegger took on the image of the Augustinian monk who incarnated the anti-semitic traditions of southern Germany and Austria. This anti-semitism was the very cradle of National Socialism.

The least that one could say is that Heidegger's writings contributed to the cult of a key figure of that anti-semitic tradition, linking Abraham to what in Heidegger's eyes was the summit of history, the *Heimat* (homeland).

Heidegger worked a certain abstractive operation on Abraham, yet Abraham remained what he had always been: a significant figure in the tradition. If Heidegger's goal was to illuminate Abraham's *essence,* he ought to have established first that his anti-semitism and xenophobia did *not* come from that essence, or at least were its negative side, something to be criticized. By maintaining the ambiguity, in 1964, Heidegger became a prestigious collaborator in the attempt to restore a sinister tradition.

We may continue our analysis of Abraham, now relying on Karl Bertsche's history of the works of the monk. After editing the sermons and other writings, Bertsche called on the Austrian Academy of Science to help him complete the edition. Documents in the archives of the Academy help us reconstruct the maneuvers and results of Bertsche's course of action. The documents offer a coherent set of facts, but we must again admit that not all documents were available to us.

Bertsche first wrote the Academy on June 28, 1936, and with the help of Josef Nadler, a member of the Academy, his request was heard. Bertsche and Nadler wrote the Academy on two occasions, July 2 and 5, 1936. The Academy answered Nadler on October 15, suggesting that possibly the finances could be got from an official decision by the Reich. Financial reasons seem to have stalled the dealings until 1938. We are led to believe that Bertsche and Nadler had no success in this quarter. The explanation is rather complicated and shows some of the inner contradictions of National Socialist cultural politics. We have already observed that Nadler defended the idea of the ethnic and cultural superiority of the region of southern Germany and German Austria. He saw the zone between the Rhine and the Danube as "the space in which since its beginnings the

Reich had undergone its greatest history: Staufer and Hapsburg, Charlemagne and Adolf Hitler."[28] Writing after the annexation of Austria, Nadler depicts southern chauvinism sympathetically. He links a genuinely racist interpretation with a rather refined cultural fascism, incorporating themes essential to the ideology he had taken from Richard von Kralik, whose disciple the young Heidegger had also been. It is in this sense that Nadler speaks of Abraham as an illustrious and exemplary man, providentially present at a time when the *Lebensraum* between the Rhine and the Danube was threatened by an implicit treaty between the French and the Turks:[29]

> Freiburg and Vienna, the city of the Black Forest and the city
> near the Kahlenberge, are separated by a great distance, yet they
> live in harmony with their differences. In spite of this, there have
> been for a long time good exchanges between them, thanks to the
> Germans, their royal houses and their governments. What once
> was true and then disappeared has now again become a
> reality: the new Reich. The majestic tower of the cathedral of
> Freiburg and the spire of Vienna's cathedral have today become
> brothers, the sign of their common mission.[30]

In spite of his pro-Nazi claims, the authorities considered Karl Bertsche an agent of Catholicism. Documents at the Center in Berlin show this. For these reasons the Union of Writers decided in 1937 to exclude Bertsche, obliging him to look elsewhere for funds and authorization to publish.

Bertsche's links to influential Catholic groups were well known. His *Anthology of Abraham a Sancta Clara (Blütenlese)* was published and often reprinted by the most important Catholic publishers in Germany, Herder at Freiburg. He was also a writer for the Viennese Catholic review *Schönere Zukunft*, which later refused to support the regime, although it held anti-semitic positions. In the December 24, 1939, issue, Bertsche himself wrote an article about Abraham's anti-semitism without offering a single criticism ("Abraham a Sancta Clara über die Lektüre").[31]

Contradictions between the Nazi regime and the Catholic Church had been apparent early at the ideological level in the serious polemics between Alfred Rosenberg and an important group of Catholic professors who had criticized his major writing, *The Myth of the Twentieth Century* (Munich, 1935). Making ironic remarks about the "scientific" nature of criticisms by Catholic critics, Rosenberg wrote several chapters analyzing links between the Church and the world of magic and sorcery. According to Rosenberg, the Church and its Jesuit avant-grade had invented this world of magic as a device for persecuting and exterminating heretics, mostly in northern Europe.[32] Rosenberg was attacking here one of Abraham's best-loved themes.[33] He had been a witness at witch trials, relating several stories of burning at the stake ("offerings to Vulcan"), enjoying them, and demanding that the work "of eliminating this bad seed" be continued.[34] In his longer chapter on "Demonology," Abraham exposed his flank to Rosenberg. Now it was clear that neither cultural authorizations from the regime nor the Catholic Church could finance the costly undertaking Bertsche was requesting.

Yet the situation had a different outcome when Austria was annexed in 1938. Just after signing the accords of Munich, when the easterners sold out Czechoslovakia, on December 30, 1938 (the Nazis called it "pacification day"), Bertsche wrote the new president of the Austrian Academy of Science, Heinrich von Srbik, "I have just read, on this day of world pacification, the news of your nomination as president of the Academy." After adding that Nadler had suggested he not push the plan to edit the works of Abraham "as long as the situation was not clear," Bertsche thought the moment had come to make the suggestion, "now that the annexation of Austria had given birth to Greater Germany, for so long your own desire." Since the "High Academy finally has a president," perhaps one could think of dedicating a monument "to the great builder of the bridge between Germany and Austria in the seventeenth century by editing his works . . . at the very moment when brothers, so long separated, have once again been united. Heil Hitler! Karl Bertsche."[35]

Karl Bertsche's hopes of obtaining Srbik's support were realistic. During the Weimar years, von Srbik was already a fierce anti-democrat. From Vienna he worked with Georg von Below in an anti-republican struggle for the founding of Greater Germany.[36] Von Srbik held to his expansionist ideals long after World War II. In his text *Humanism in Our Time* (*Humanismus bis zur Gegenwart,* 1951) he wrote about the annexation of Austria: "The people of the second Reich are hardly contained within the frontiers established by the state civil law, but they are aligned in the space of the blood and spirit of German manhood."[37]

Bertsche's efforts were successful. Although the Austrian Academy of Sciences was not in a position to fund the project, and had to reject it in a provisional decision, Baldur von Schirach, Reichsstatthalter at Vienna, intervened to propose complete funding for the edition. The question was resolved during the session of the Academy on February 7, 1942.

A document held in the Karl Bertsche dossier at the Document Center in Berlin reveals that Bertsche received authorization from the Union of

Writers of the Reich to edit Abraham a Sancta Clara's works, as von
Schirach had suggested.

The *Spiegel* interview

At the end of his life, Heidegger understood his philosophical
reflections to be a hermeneutics of being, irrevocably tied to the theme
of the sacred local fatherland and its spiritual directors. For our present
purpose, these reflections are closely connected with the interview Heidegger accorded *Der Spiegel*, the most widely read weekly in Germany.

To have given an interview about his relationship with National Socialism, an interview to be published posthumously, strongly indicates the
importance of the issue for Heidegger. By situating his "clarification of
facts of his past life" in juxtaposition with his own death Heidegger was
able to give a special solemnity to the interview. Potential detractors were
thus almost forced into the sad situation of profaning a tomb. The interview was organized and programmed with great care, certainly under
Heidegger's direction.

Even an attentive first reading of the published text gives the impression that the journalists involved hardly touched and certainly did not
plumb the relevant themes, and left the most important and embarrass-
ing question in the dark. This was perhaps not the doing of the journalists of *Der Spiegel*. In fact, as the editorial staff introduced the text of the
interview, it became clear that the published text was the result of a complex process. The questionnaire Heidegger was answering was different
from the one they had first sent him, and the answers he gave during the
interview do not match the published answers. *Der Spiegel* published with
the interview a photocopy of the text that Heidegger had corrected, giving us an idea of the quantity of changes made.

I contacted the archives of the journal to ask if I could consult the
documentation of the interview, but the director of the archives refused,
supporting his decision with ethical arguments.

I indicate these facts because it is so important to be able to compare
the published report with the original texts.

The published text itself, however, is not without interest. This posthumous publication assures the lasting influence of his philosphy on German society and on an international public already biased against National Socialism.

If this was in fact part of Heidegger's intention, a careful reading of
the text does not fail to reveal that in attaining this goal the philosopher

sacrificed none of his concerns of principle tied to the common values of National Socialism. Heidegger demanded in fact that his adherence to National Socialism be placed in the context of his reflections on the essence of technology fitted to a planetary scale. He thereby indicated that from the beginning National Socialism was engaged in a correct approach to the problems posed by the uncontrolled mastery of technology. After this heartening beginning, National Socialism was shackled by the philosophical ineptitude of its leaders.[38]

The published text leaves in the deepest shadows the meaning of this seemingly good beginning, the manner in which its objective could be managed politically, the persons who could be entrusted with such management. This too is essential: in his answers, Heidegger radically disqualifies other systems that try to take account of technology and its growth. When in 1962 Heidegger continued to affirm the grandeur of the beginnings of National Socialism ("its inner truth and grandeur"), as the single brief but successful attempt to face the central problem of "modern man," Heidegger renders a fundamental judgment whose explicit meaning cannot be ignored. Its meaning emanates from a thinker particularly sensitive to the significance of "beginnings," and who understands that such "beginnings" are examples that become the tasks of the future.

In this interview, Heidegger continued to state the fundamental distinction between "true National Socialism" and the deviationism that distorted it. This distinction is clear enough in the criticisms offered in the text, a final rendering of accounts with deviationism itself, and, as envisaged by Heidegger, as bearing on the solution by which to lift mankind from the mire. When the journalists asked him about Hölderlin's writing on "The Occult Law of the Historic Determination of the Germans," cited in his course on Nietzsche, Heidegger answered in a manner that was both soft in form and strict on content: The central problem of humanity can be solved only where humanity is born, in Europe, within Europe, at its center, where this time Heidegger does not give the name of a people, but names the language, the language of Hölderlin, the language of the Germans. For if the "beginning" *(Anfang)* was Greek, to reclaim it we must use an instrument adjusted to that end, which could only be the German language.[39] This is an open road to the coarsest sort of discrimination: "The French assure me of this truth again today: when they begin to think they speak German."[40] The French realize that "despite their rationalism they are unable to face the present world when it is a question of understanding it in the origin of its essence."[41]

Assuming that the whole text is carefully shaped, it is clear that at the determining point of his thought, Heidegger found expressions more virulent than the ones he formulated during his militant period. So, along with Mayor Kerber and the future French collaborators, he proposed to the French a dialogic model: the Germans would be the professors and the French the pupils chained to their desks.

To claim that German is absolutely untranslatable ("just as a poem cannot be translated, it cannot be otherwise with thought") can be "annoying" for those who do not speak it, but for Heidegger this reality ought not be hidden "but brought out clearly, on a grand scale. We need to think of the terrible consequences brought on us and still felt in our own days that derive from translating Greek thought into Roman Latin."[42]

Rainer Marten has shown better than anyone else that in its very essence Heidegger's philosophy cannot do without its fundamental will to discrimination.[43] The reasons are to be sought in the fact that Heidegger never broke his spiritual links with the ultimate possibility of the condition of National Socialism in all its forms: his sacralization of the Alemannic world and its use as an exclusive example. This appears in the problem that Heidegger considered fundamental in the interview. While disqualifying democracy as a political system because it is unable to face the technologizing of the world,[44] Heidegger claimed that National Socialism was able to do this from its beginning.

On page 206 of *Der Spiegel,* Heidegger claimed that technology had become independent of human control and that democracy was unable to regain control of it. On page 214, when he is asked *precisely* whether by using concepts "already outmoded" like the idea of the "local fatherland" *(Heimat),* he was not already distancing himself from any attempt to effect a solution to the problem of planetary technology, Heidegger answered: "It seems to me that you are using the word 'technology' in too absolute a sense. For me, I do not understand the problem of man in the world of planetary technology as an unexplainable curse from which we are to escape; I believe that within its proper limits thought ought to help man establish a satisfying relationship with technology. National Socialism certainly took that road."[45]

According to Heidegger, the link between *Heimat* and National Socialism, the generative impulse of the truth of the movement, has certainly retained its validity to the end. It is in this sense that one ought to understand the tight bond between Heidegger and the land and the fatherland, and not in the sense of mere metaphysical folklore: "All that is grand and essential has appeared only because man has had a fatherland and has been rooted in tradition."[46]

At the waning of his life, Heidegger's career has defined a great circle that comes back to its beginnings. His first text praised Abraham a Sancta

Clara as the physician "of the soul of the people," its director, its guide, its example. In the posthumous interview, the task of thought is to prepare the land on which "the saviour god," the only remedy, can appear.[47] To the extent that this god is not transcendant but like "everything that is grand and essential" produces "the fatherland," we must fear that this god is hardly distinct, in fact, from that other god, the one of Abraham a Sancta Clara in whom Heidegger saw the one who fulfills destinies.

Notes and index

Notes

Introduction

1. Guido Schneeberger, *Nachlese zu Heidegger* (Bern, 1962).

2. Karl Löwith, "Les implications politiques de la philosophie de l'existence chez Martin Heidegger," *Les Temps Modernes* (Paris) 2 (1946): 343–360; Löwith, "La polémique de Löwith avec De Waelhens," *Les Temps Modernes* 4 (1948): 370–373; Löwith, *Heidegger, Denker in dürftiger Zeit* (Frankfurt, 1953; 2nd ed., Göttingen, 1960); Georg Lukács, "Heidegger redivivus," *Sinn und Form* (Potsdam) 1 (1949): 37–62; Lukács, *Existentialismus oder Marxismus* (Berlin, 1951); Lukács, *Die Zerstörung der Vernunft* (Berlin, 1954).

3. Paul Hühnerfeld, *In Sachen Heidegger: Versuch über ein deutsches Genie* (Hamburg, 1959); Christian von Krockow, *Die Entscheidung: Eine Untersuchung über Ernst Jünger, Carl Schmitt und Martin Heidegger* (Stuttgart, 1958); Robert Minder, *Hölderlin unter den Deutschen und andere Aufsätze zur deutschen Literatur* (Frankfurt am Main, 1968); Theodor W. Adorno, *Jargon der Eigentlichkeit: Zur deutschen Ideologie* (Frankfurt am Main, 1964); Karl Jaspers, *Notizen zu Heidegger* (Munich/Zürich, 1978); J. P. Faye, "La lecture et l'énoncé," *Critique* (Paris) 237 (1967); Jürgen Habermas, *Philosophisch-politische Profile* (Frankfurt am Main, 1971).

4. François Fédier, "Trois attaques contre Heidegger," *Critique* 234 (1966); Fédier, "Une lecture dénoncée," *Critique* 242 (1967); J. M. Palmier, *Les Ecrits politiques de Heidegger* (Paris, 1968); Otto Pöggeler, *Philosophie und Politik bei Heidegger* (Freiburg/Munich, 1972); Alexander Schwan, *Die politische Philosophie im Denken Heideggers* (Cologne/Opladen, 1965).

5. Heidegger's manuscripts are in the Deutsche Literaturarchiv (Marbach). Their use is not authorized for academic purposes; no date is indicated when they might be available.

6. Berlin Document Center.

7. I would never have been able to achieve this work without the patient and effective help of those persons—whether as workers at research centers or simply as individuals—whose kindness helped me in my research. I cite: M. Pix at the

Document Center, Berlin/Dahlnen; Dr. Dieter Fitterling in Berlin; Mrs. Maria Keipert at the Koblenz Bundesarchiv and the Auswärtiges Amt Archiv at Bonn; Prof. Roman Bleistein in the Jesuit Archives of the German Federal Republic and in the Archbishop's Archives at Freiburg; Dr. F. Spiegeler (Bramsche) in the Archives of the Austrian Academy of Sciences in Vienna; Prof. Heinrich Heidegger (Saint Blasien); Prof. Dr. Hugo Ott (Freiburg); Prof. Dr. Rainer Marten (Freiburg); Prof. Dr. Hans-Martin Gauger (Freiburg); the Potsdam and Merseburg Zentrales Staatsarchiv; the Archives of Humboldt University; Prof. Dr. Norbert Kampe at the Göttingen University archives; Dr. Klingerhofer at the Hessisches Staatsarchiv (Marburg); Prof. Dr. Aaron Kleinberger at Jerusalem University; Dr. Wilfried Werner at the Heidelberg University Library; Prof. Andreas Oberländer OSB (Beuron) at the Generallandesarchiv at Karlsruhe; Georg Hauser of the Erzbichöfliches Studienheim of Saint Conrad in Konstanz; Mrs. Elke Naschold at the Liceum Heinrich-Suso in Konstanz; Prof. Dr. H. Maurer of the Bavarian State Library in Munich and the Konstanz State Archives; Prof. Dr. Wilhelm Schoeppe (Frankfurt am Main); Mrs. Josephine Grimme of the Karlsruhe State Library; Dr. O. F. Wiegand of the University Library (Kiel); Dr. Wolfgang Kreutzberger of the Munich Institut für Zeitgeschichte; Dr. Gundermann of the Prussian State Archives of Berlin; Dr. Guido Schneeberger, the Hoover Institute at Stanford; the Berlin State Library, and the State Archives of Messkirch; the Paris Center for Contemporary Jewish Documentation; Prof. Laetitia Boehm at the Archives of Munich University; the Marburg University Library; Prof. Golschmidt of the Max-Planck-Institut, Berlin; Dr. Rauch of the Archives at Tübingen University.

I would also like to express my special thanks to Prof. Dr. Ernst Tugendhat, who as administrator of Helene Weiss's archives granted me permission to consult in the archives the text of notes taken by Helene Weiss during Heidegger's 1933/34 course, and my thanks to Uwe Henning of the Max-Planck-Institut für Bildungsforschung, Berlin, for her frequent good counsel.

Chapter 1

1. G. Tümbült, *Geschichte der Stadt Messkirch* (Writings of the Society for History and Natural History in Baar and the Surrounding Areas in Donaueschingen, no. 19; Tübingen, 1933).

2. K. A. Barack (ed.), *Zimmerische Chronik* (Stuttgart, 1882).

3. Paul Motz, "Messkirch: Geschichte und Stadtbild," in *Badische Heimat,* vol. for 1934: *Zwischen Bodensee und Donau,* pp. 253–267.

4. See *Meyers Lexikon* (Leipzig, 1903), p. 390f.

5. Conrad Gröber, "Der Altkatholizismus in Messkirch: Die Geschichte seiner Entwicklung und Bekämpfung," *Freiburger Diözesan-Archiv* (Freiburg im Breisgau), N.S., 13 (1912): 135–198.

6. *Ibid.,* p. 186.

7. See G. Franz-Willing, "Der grosse Konflikt: Kulturkampf in Preussen," in O. Büsch and W. Neugebauer (eds.), *Moderne Preussische Geschichte: Eine Anthologie,* vol. 3 (Berlin/New York, 1981), pp. 1395–1457.

8. Gröber, "Altkatholizismus in Messkirch," p. 188.

9. *Ibid.,* p. 198.

10. *Ibid.*, p. 158.

11. *Ibid.*, pp. 149, 172.

12. See Hugo Ott, "Der junge Martin Heidegger: Gymnasial-Konviktszeit und Studium," *Freiburger Diözesan-Archiv*, 3rd ser., 104 (1984): 316f.

13. *Ibid.*

14. See Camille Brandhuber, "Das preussiche Kommunalabgabegesetz," *Kommunalpolitische Blätter* (Cologne), 1914–1915, pp. 242–249.

15. E. Föhr, "Zur Geschichte des St. Konradihauses in Konstanz," *Erzbischöfliches Studienheim St. Konrad* (Konstanz), 1962, p. 23.

16. *Ibid.*, p. 28f.

17. See Conrad Gröber, *Geschichte des Jesuitenkollegs und Gymnasiums* (Konstanz, 1904).

18. Günther Dehn, *Die alte Zeit, die vorigen Jahre: Lebenserinnerungen* (Munich, 1962).

19. *Ibid.*, p. 38.

20. *Ibid.*, p. 38f.

21. The ambivalence of this "movement" played itself out in the way it was received historically; see *Der Hotzenwald*, vol. 2 (Karlsruhe, 1940–1941). Cf. for contrast Th. Lehner (ed.), *Der Salpeterer: Freie, keiner Obrigkeit untertane Leut aus dem Hotzenwald; Geschichte und Dokumente einer demokratischen Bauernbewegung aus dem Südschwarzwald* (Berlin, 1977).

22. G. Loewy, *Die Katholische Kirche und das Dritte Reich* (Munich, 1965), and Klaus Breuning, *Die Vision des Reiches* (Munich, 1961).

23. See Martin Heidegger, *Unterwegs zur Sprache* (5th ed.; Pfullingen, 1975), p. 92.

24. See Richard Jonas, *Grundzüge der philosophischen Propädeutik* (Berlin, 1891), pp. 5, 6, 27.

25. Ott, "Junge Heidegger," p. 319f.

Chapter 2

1. Episcopal Archive (Freiburg), *Generalia*, Rubrik: Klerus: regarding the alumni of the theological seminary, vol. 7, 1908/9, 1910/11, B 2–32/174.

2. Fr. H. Koch, SJ, "Gedanken zur Kolonialpolitik," *Stimmen aus Maria Laach: Katholische Blätter* 16 (1909): 1–2.

3. *Ibid.*, p. 15.

4. *Ibid.*, p. 17.

5. *Ibid.*, p. 18.

6. *Ibid.*, p. 19.

7. *Ibid.*

8. *Ibid.*, p. 20.

9. Fr. V. Cathrein, SJ, "Materialismus und Sozialdemokratie," p. 32f, as well as "Die sozialdemokratische Moral," *Stimmen aus Maria Laach: Katholische Blätter* 16 (1909): 365–382.

10. Cathrein, "Die sozialdemokratische Moral," p. 381f.

11. B. Casper, "Martin Heidegger und die Theologische Fakultät, Freiburg, 1909–1923," *Freiburger Diözesan-Archiv* 100 (1980): 534–554.

12. Martin Heidegger, *Unterwegs zur Sprache* (5th ed.; Pfullingen, 1975), p. 96.

13. See C. Bauer, "Die Freiburger Lehrstühle der Geschichtswissenschaft," *Beiträge zur Geschichte der Freiburger Philosophischen Fakultät* (Freiburg), 1957, p. 183.

14. *Ibid.*, p. 190f.

15. *Ibid.*, p. 183.

16. See K. Töpner, *Gelehrte Politiker und politisierende Gelehrte: Die Revolution von 1918 im Urteil deutscher Hochschullehrer* (Frankfurt, 1970), p. 178ff.

17. H. Schleier, *Geschichtsschreibung der Weimarer Republik* (Berlin, 1975), p. 65.

18. See *ibid.*, p. 21.

19. "Jüdische Offiziere?," *Konservative Monatsschrift* 8 (May 1913), and "Judenfrage und Antisemitismus," *Konservative Monatsschrift* 8 (Dec. 1912).

Chapter 3

1. Martin Heidegger, "Abraham a Sancta Clara: Zur Enthüllung seines Denkmals in Kreenheinstetten am 15. August 1910," *Allgemeine Rundschau: Wochenschrift für Politik und Kultur* 35 (Aug. 27, 1910): 605.

2. See R. A. Kann, *Kanzel und Katheder: Studien zur österreichischen Geistesgeschichte vom Spätbarock zur Frühromantik* (Vienna/Freiburg/Basel, 1962), pp. 59–61.

3. See F. Loidl, "Abraham a Sancta Clara als Vorkämpfer für deutsche Art wider Türken und Fremdländerei," *Unsere Heimat* (Vienna) 14, no. 1/2 (Jan./Feb. 1941): 1. See also pt. 2 in *Unsere Heimat* 14, nos. 3/4 (1941): 44–55.

4. See Kann, *Kanzel und Katheder*, pp. 59–61.

5. *Ibid.*, p. 69.

6. *Ibid.*, p. 81.

7. *Ibid.* Cf. Manfred Arndorfer et al. (eds.), *Abraham a Sancta Clara: Eine Ausstellung der Badischen Landesbibliothek und der Wiener Stadt- und Landesbibliothek: Ausstellungskatalog* (in-house publication of the Badischen Landesbibliothek; Karlsruhe, 1982), pp. 150–152.

8. Karl Bertsche (ed.), *Abraham a Sancta Clara "Merck's Wien"* (1721; Leipzig, 1926), p. 25.

9. Abraham a Sancta Clara, *Judas III* (Salzburg, 1692), p. 339.

10. Abraham a Sancta Clara, *Abrahamische Lauberhütt I*, presented by P. Fr. Alexandro a Latere Christi, Prior of Taxa, Bishop's Archives, Vienna and Brünn, 1719–1723, p. 383.

11. O. Frankl, *Der Jude in den deutschen Dichtungen des 15., 16. und 17. Jahrhunderts* (Leipzig, 1905), pp. 69–71, 120, 131–132.

12. Abraham a Sancta Clara, *Lauberhütt II*, quoted in Loidl, "Abraham a Sancta Clara," pt. 2, pp. 47–48.

13. Abraham a Sancta Clara, *Reimb dich*, quoted in Loidl, "Abraham a Sancta Clara," pt. 2, p. 47.

14. Abraham a Sancta Clara, *Etwas für alle*, quoted in Loidl, "Abraham a Sancta Clara," pt. 2, p. 47f.

15. Abraham a Sancta Clara, *Lauberhütt II, Reimb dich, Etwas für alle,* and *Judas, Buch I*, quoted in "Abraham a Sancta Clara," pt. 2, p. 47ff.

16. See P. G. J. Pulzer, *Die Entstehung des politischen Antisemitismus in Deutschland und Österreich, 1867–1914* (Gütersloh, 1966).

17. *Ibid.*, p. 162.

18. See Sebastian Brunner, *Woher, Wohin?* (Vienna, 1855), vol. 1, p. 7.

19. See E. Weinzierl, "Der österreichisch-ungarische Raum: A. Katholizismus in Österreich," in H. Rengstorf and S. von Kortzfleisch (eds.), *Kirche und Synagoge: Handbuch zur Geschichte von Christen und Juden* (Stuttgart, 1970), vol. 2, pp. 484f, 499.

20. See Rudolf Till, "Die Anfänge der christlichen Volksbewegung in Österreich," in *Jahrbuch der Leo-Gesellschaft* (Vienna, 1937), pp. 57f, 65.

21. See Pulzer, *Entstehung*, p. 273.

22. *Ibid.*, p. 144.

23. See Weinzierl, "Der österreichisch-ungarische Raum," vol. 2, pp. 504f, 510.

24. See Pulzer, *Entstehung*, p. 166.

25. Adolf Hitler, *Mein Kampf*, Volksausgabe (10th ed.; Munich, 1942), p. 132f.

26. *Ibid.*; on Lueger see the well-known Nazi historian Walter Frank's *Hofprediger Adolf Stoecker und die christlich-soziale Bewegung* (Berlin, 1935), p. 149.

27. Protocol for the city council sessions of Vienna, no. 23, from July 12, 1901, p. 250ff, in the Vienna Stadt- und Landesarchiv.

28. See *Amtsblatt der k.u.k. Reichshaupt- und Residenzstadt Wien,* May 11 and Nov. 11, 1902.

29. See A. Pöllmann, OSB (Beuron), "Vom Abraham a Sancta Claras Denkmal," *Über den Wassern* 1 (1910): 18–20.

30. See *Historisch-politische Blätter* (Munich) 145 (1910): 538–540.

31. Heidegger, "Abraham a Sancta Clara," p. 605.

32. Karl Bertsche, *Abraham a Sancta Clara: Blütenlese aus seinen Werken* (Freiburg, 1910), p. 2.

33. *Ibid.*, pp. 11–12.

34. *Ibid.*, p. 17.

35. *Ibid.*, p. 69.

36. *Ibid.*

37. *Ibid.*, p. 87ff.

38. *Ibid.*, pp. 121–122.

39. *Ibid.*, p. 131.

40. Martin Heidegger, *Gesamtausgabe*, pt. I, in Heidegger, *Published Writings, 1910–1976*, vol. 13; *Aus der Erfahrung des Denkens (1910–1976)* (Frankfurt am Main, 1983), pp. 1–3.

41. See *Allgemeine Rundschau* 21 (May 24, 1913): 396, as well as 30 (July 26, 1913): 397, 733.

42. See *Allgemeine Rundschau* 9 (Feb. 27, 1932).

43. *Heuberger Volksblatt*, Dec. 3, 1909.

44. See N. Mikoletzky, "Richard von Kralik," in *Neue deutsche Biographie*, vol. 12 (Berlin, 1980), pp. 663–666.

45. See Carl Muth, "Vom Gral und dem Gralbund," *Hochland* 5 (Feb. 1905): 35–39, as well as Franz Eichert's "Gralfahrt-Höhenfahrt," *Der Gral* 1, no. 1 (Oct. 1906): 1–7.

46. See *Der Gral* 5, no. 2 (May 1911): 468f.

47. See G. Seewann, *Österreichische Jugendbewegung, 1908–1933*, vol. 1 (2nd ed.; Frankfurt am Main, 1974), pp. 26f, 32, 35, 140ff.

48. *Ibid.*, p. 322.

49. Richard von Kralik, "Der grossdeutsche Gedanke: Eine historische Übersicht," *Frankfurter zeitgemässe Broschuren* 30, no. 10 (July 1921): 213.

50. *Ibid.*, p. 241.

51. Richard von Kralik, "Das Recht der Kritik," *Der Gral* 2, no. 4 (Jan. 1908): 145–149.

52. See Richard von Kralik, "Das Rätsel der Romantik," *Der Gral* 6, no. 1 (Oct. 1911): 46–48.

53. Von Kralik, "Der grossdeutsche Gedanke," p. 242.

54. *Ibid.*

55. *Ibid.*, p. 241ff.

56. Richard von Kralik, *Abraham a Sancta Clara* (Vienna, 1922).

57. See Richard von Kralik, *Karl Lueger und der christliche Sozialismus* (Vienna, 1923), as well as "Vom deutsch-jüdischen Parnass," *Der Gral* 6, no. 7 (April 1912): 420–423.

58. See Richard von Kralik, "Ein literarisches Programm," *Der Gral* 1, no. 2 (Nov. 1906): 49–52.

59. See Richard von Kralik, "Volkspoesie und nationale Poesie," *Deutsche Arbeit: Monatsschrift für das geistige Leben der Deutschen in Böhmen* (Munich/Prague) 4 (Jan. 1904).

60. J. Weiss, *Lehrbuch der Weltgeschichte* (Graz, 1859–1898).

61. Karl Bertsche, "Ein Meister des Zungenhandwerkes: Abraham a Sancta Clara in rationalistischem Licht und Gewande," *Der Gral* 6, no. 5 (Feb. 1912): 282–289.

62. See Josef Nadler in *Der Gral* 4, no. 5 (Feb. 1910): 273–283.

Chapter 4

1. Martin Heidegger, "Per mortem ad vitam (Gedanken über Jörgensens 'Lebenslüge und Lebenswahrheit')," *Der Akademiker* (Munich) 5 (March 1910): 72f.

2. Martin Heidegger, "Zur philosophischen Orientierung für Akademiker," *Der Akademiker* 5 (March 1911): 66f.

3. Martin Heidegger, "Religionspsychologie und Unterbewusstsein," *Der Akademiker* 5 (March 1912): 66f.

4. Martin Heidegger, review of F. W. Foerster's *Autorität und Freiheit: Betrachtungen zum Kulturproblem der Kirche*, in *Der Akademiker* 7 (May 1910): 109f.

5. Martin Heidegger, review of A. J. Cüpper's *Versiegelte Lippen: Erzählung aus dem irischen Volksleben des 19. Jahrhunderts*, in *Der Akademiker* 1 (Nov. 1910): 29.

6. Martin Heidegger, review of J. Jörgensen's *Das Reisebuch: Licht und dunkle Natur und Geist*, in *Der Akademiker* 3 (Jan. 1911): 45.

7. Martin Heidegger, review of J. Gredt, OSB, *Elementa Philosophiae Aristotelico-Tomisticae*, vol. I: *Logica Philos. nat. Edit. II*, in *Der Akademiker* 5 (March 1912): 76f.

8. Martin Heidegger, review of Hellinghaus (ed.), *Bibliothek wertvoller Novellen und Erzählungen*, in *Der Akademiker* 3 (Jan. 1913): 45.

9. Anim Kausen, quoted from Lindl in *Der Akademiker* 1 (Nov. 1908): 1, as well as W. Prechtl's "'Der Akademiker': Unser Programm," *Der Akademiker* 1 (Nov. 1908): 2.

10. See J. Vormwald, "Die christologischen Irrtümer des Modernismus," *Der Akademiker* 9 (April 1910): 85–87, and Carl Braig, "Der Modernisteneid und die Freiheit der Wissenschaften," *Der Akademiker* 9 (July 1911): 141.

11. See Ph. Wagner, "Die Entstehung des Altkatholizismus in Deutschland,"

Der Akademiker 3 (Jan. 1910): 36f; *Der Akademiker* 4 (Feb. 1910): 55–57; and *Der Akademiker* 5 (March 1910): 68–70.

12. See K. Jakubczky, "Richard von Kralik: Ein Jahr katholischer Literaturbewegung," *Der Akademiker* 5 (March 1911): 77; an unsigned article, "Die deutschen Katholiken im Literaturleben der Gegenwart," *Der Akademiker* 1 (Nov. 1908): 12f; E. Baur, "Katholisches Literaturleben," *Der Akademiker* 1 (Nov. 1909): 11f; and A. Illinger, "Katholisches Literaturleben," *Der Akademiker* 2 (Dec. 1909): 25f.

13. See J. St., "Die Unmöglichkeit des Sozialismus," *Der Akademiker* 3 (Jan. 1911): 39–41, *Der Akademikes* 4 (Feb. 1911): 53f, and *Der Akademiker* 5 (March 1911): 70–72.

14. See J. Heiler, "Religiös-wissenschaftliche Vorträge für Akademiker," *Der Akademiker* 4 (Feb. 1911): 51.

15. See H. Auer, "Die sozial-caritativen Vereinigungen katholischer Studenten Deutschlands," *Der Akademiker* 2 (Dec. 1908): 31, *Der Akademiker* 3 (Jan. 1909): 48–49, and *Der Akademiker* 4 (Feb. 1909): 61–62.

16. See the essays of Prince Alois von Löwenstein, "Student und Mission," *Der Akademiker* 3 (Jan. 1911): 33–35 and *Der Akademiker* 4 (Feb. 1911): 49–50. In the last essay he summoned "the entire Catholic population to mobilize against Satan." See also W. Beier, "Die akademische Missionsbewegung auf dem Katholikentag zu Mainz," *Der Akademiker* 1 (Nov. 1911): 1–5.

17. See "Die Prophezeiungen zum Weltkrieg, 1914/15," *Der Akademiker* 4 (July 1915): 37–38.

18. See "Kriegsliteratur III," *Der Akademiker* 3 (May 1915): 26.

19. Engelbert Krebs, "Heinrich Mohrs Feldbriefe," *Der Akademiker* 1 (Dec. 1914): 7.

20. See N. Kampe, *Studenten und "Judenfrage" im Deutschen Kaiserreich: Die Entstehung einer akademischen Trägerschicht des Antisemitismus* (Göttingen, 1988).

21. See Joseph Eberle, "Dr. Lueger—und Studententum," *Der Akademiker* 1 (Nov. 1910): 2f.

22. See *Der Stürmer* 6 (March 1937).

23. Joseph Eberle, *Grossmacht Presse* (Munich, 1912).

24. *Das Neue Reich*, Jan. 16, 1919, quoted in E. Weinzierl, "Der österreichischungarische Raum: Katholizismus in Österreich," in H. Rengstorf and S. von Kortzfleisch (eds.), *Kirche und Synagoge: Handbuch zur Geschichte von Christen und Juden* (Stuttgart, 1970), vol. 2, p. 520.

25. Joseph Eberle in *Schönere Zukunft*, Nov. 27, 1938, quoted in Weinzierl, "Österreichisch-ungarische Raum," p. 524.

26. M. G. Lap, "Neuere Klassikerausgaben," *Der Akademiker* 8 (June 1914): 121.

27. See, further, pages 41–42, below.

28. See anonymous review of F. J. Völler's *Natur und Kultur* with an assessment of the essays contained in the book by Karl Bertsche, "Abraham a Sancta Claras Verhältnis zur Natur und Naturwissenschaft," *Der Akademiker* 6 (April 1911): 93.

29. See A. Himmelbach, "Die Akademischen Piusvereine einst und jetzt (Entwicklung und Zweckmässigkeit ihres Programms)," *Der Akademiker* 6 (April 1909): 85–86; Ph. Boos, "Existenzberechtigung der Akademischen Piusvereine," *Der Akademiker* 2 (Dec. 1909): 21–23.

30. See H. J. Patt, in K. Rahner and J. Höfer (eds.), *Lexikon für Theologie und Kirche*, vol. 8 (Freiburg, 1963), p. 544. On the pre-history of the Piusvereine, see E. Heinen, "Der Kölner Piusverein, 1848–1849: Ein Beitrag zu den Anfängen des

politischen Katholizismus," in *Jahrbuch des Kölnischen Geschichtsvereins*, vol. 57 (1968), pp. 147–242, and Morsey and Becker, *Christliche Demokratie in Europa* (Vienna, in press).

31. See Weinzierl, "Der österreichisch-ungarische Raum," p. 515.

32. *Reichspost*, Nov. 18, 1907, quoted in *ibid.*

33. See P. Hofrichter, "Die österreichischen Katholikentage des 20. Jahrhunderts (bis 1933)," unpub. diss., Vienna, 1966, p. 45, quoted in Rengstorf and von Kortzfleisch (eds.), *Kirche und Synagoge*, p. 515.

34. See Message of Pius X to the Akademische Piusvereine in Germany (Unio Piana), in *Der Akademiker* 3 (Jan. 1909): 1.

35. See *Der Akademiker* 4 (Feb. 1912): 58.

36. See *Der Akademiker* 8 (June 1912): 120.

37. See *Der Akademiker* 8 (June 1912): 121.

38. See *Der Akademiker* 3 (Jan. 1914): 45.

39. See *Der Akademiker* 3 (Jan. 1910): 38.

40. Martin Heidegger, "Per mortem ad vitam," p. 72.

41. A. von Roth, "Poetenstolz: Eine Plauderei," *Der Akademiker* 1 (Nov. 1910): 9. For the literary and historical context of Brandes and Jörgensen see H. M. and W. Svendsen's *Geschichte der dänischen Literatur* (Neumünster, 1964), pp. 354–362.

42. Heidegger, "Per mortem ad vitam," pp. 72–73. See also his review of Jörgensen's *Reisebuch*, p. 45.

43. Heidegger, review of Jörgensen's *Reisebuch*, p. 45.

44. See in *Sozialstudentische Chronik* the announcement of C. Sonnerschein's upcoming review of Foerster's book *Christentum und Klassenkampf* in *Der Akademiker* 1 (Nov. 1908): 8–10, which was to be published in *Der Akademiker* 3 (Jan. 1909): 44–46. A proof of the foreword to Foerster's *Autorität und Freiheit* appeared in *Der Akademiker* 5 (March 1910): 65f, and "Der Krieg und die sexuelle Frage," *Der Akademiker* 3 (May 1915): 32.

45. H. Donat, "Friedrich Wilhelm Foerster (1869–1966): Friedenssicherung als religiös-sittliches und ethisch-politisches Programm," in Rajewsky and Riesenberger (eds.), *Wider den Krieg: Grosse Pazifisten von Kant bis Böll* (Munich, 1987), pp. 167–183.

46. See B. Hipler (ed.), *Friedrich Wilhelm Foerster, Manifest für den Frieden: Eine Auswahl aus seinen Schriften (1893–1933)* (Paderborn, 1988).

47. Heidegger, review of Foerster's *Autorität und Freiheit*, pp. 109–110. See also his "Zur Orientierung für Akademiker," pp. 66–67.

48. Heidegger, "Zur philosophischen Orientierung für Akademiker," pp. 66–67. See also his review of Cüpper's *Versiegelte Lippen*, p. 29.

49. Heidegger, review of Cüpper's *Versiegelte Lippen*, p. 29.

50. Heidegger, review of Gredt, *Elementa Philosophiae Aristotelico-Tomisticae*, p. 76.

Chapter 5

1. B. Casper, "Martin Heidegger und die Theologische Fakultät, Freiburg, 1909–1923," *Freiburger Diözesan-Archiv* 100 (1980): 537.

2. *Ibid.*, p. 538.

3. *Ibid.*

4. Schneider's work on Albertus Magnus was published in Freiburg in 1903–1906.

5. Martin Heidegger, "Mein Weg in die Phänomenologie," in Heidegger, *Zur Sache des Denkens* (Tübingen, 1969), pp. 81–90.

6. Casper, "Martin Heidegger," p. 538.

7. See K. Böhme (ed.), *Aufrufe und Reden deutscher Professoren im Ersten Weltkrieg* (Stuttgart, 1975).

8. Abraham a Sancta Clara, in Karl Bertsche (ed.), *Kriegsbrot für die Seele aus den Werken des Abraham a Sancta Clara* (Freiburg im Breisgau, 1917), foreword, pp. 20, 22.

9. See K. Töpner, *Gelehrte Politiker und politisierende Gelehrte: Die Revolution von 1918 im Urteil deutscher Hochschullehrer* (Frankfurt am Main, 1970), pp. 142–143.

10. Engelbert Krebs, *Das Geheimnis unserer Stärke: Gedanken über den Grossen Krieg* (Freiburg, 1916).

11. Engelbert Krebs, *Le régime des prisonniers de guerre en Allemagne: Réponse basée sur des renseignements officiels et addressée à M. le Baron d'Anthuard, ministre plénipotentiaire* (Freiburg, 1917).

12. See Georg von Below, "Das gute Recht der Vaterlandspartei," *Preussische Jahrbücher* 172 (April 1918): 1–16.

13. See Heinrich Rickert, letter to Emil Lask, May 28, 1915, in Archives of the University of Heidelberg, Heid. Hs. 3820, literary estate of Emil Lask.

14. *Ibid.*

15. Casper, "Martin Heidegger," p. 538.

16. *Ibid.*

17. See E. Poulat, *Histoire, dogme et critique dans la crise moderniste* (Tournai/Paris, 1962); E. Weinzierl (ed.), *Der Modernismus* (Graz, 1974).

18. Carl Braig, *Der Modernismus und die Freiheit der Wissenschaft* (Freiburg, 1911).

19. Carl Braig, *Was soll der Gebildete vom Modernismus wissen?* (Freiburg, 1908).

20. Casper, "Martin Heidegger," p. 541.

21. *Ibid.*, p. 540.

22. See Martin Heidegger, records, Berlin Document Center, REM 1936.

23. Max Scheler, *Der Genius des Krieges und der deutsche Krieg* (Leipzig 1915).

24. *Ibid.*, p. 135. See also Max Scheler, *Krieg und Aufbau* (Leipzig, 1915), and H. Lübbe, *Politische Philosophie in Deutschland* (Stuttgart, 1963), p. 221ff.

Chapter 6

1. Georg Misch, "Alternative suggestions for professors," Oct. 28, 1920–Sept. 30, 1933, Archives of the University of Göttingen, XVI.IV B.7, vol. 2. What follows is also taken from the same source.

2. Edmund Husserl, letter to Paul Natorp, in Staatsarchiv Marburg, Sign. 307d/Acc. 1966/10, nos. 4, 28.

3. Concluding report of the appointment commission, Staatsarchiv Marburg.

4. *Ibid.*

5. See Martin Heidegger, "Zur Geschichte des philosophischen Lehrstuhles seit 1866," in H. Hermelink (ed.), *Die Philipps-Universität zu Marburg, 1527–1927* (Marburg, 1927), pp. 681–687.

6. Hans-Georg Gadamer, "Nur wer mitgeht, weiss, dass es ein Weg ist: Begegnungen mit Martin Heidegger," *Frankfurter Allgemeine Zeitung*, Sept. 28, 1974.

7. List of nominees, Aug. 5, 1925, in Zentrales Staatsarchiv Merseburg, Records of the Ministry of Education, vol. 19, Marburg University Subjects, sec. 4, no. 2, XIX, pp. 405ff.

8. See Martin Heidegger, "Mein Weg in die Phänomenologie," in Heidegger, *Zur Sache des Denkens* (Tübingen, 1969), p. 88.

9. Martin Heidegger, *Sein und Zeit* (10th ed.; Tübingen, 1963), p. 7.

10. Karl Löwith, *Heidegger, Denker in dürftiger Zeit* (2nd ed.; Göttingen, 1960).

11. Ernst Tugendhat, *Selbstbewusstsein und Selbstbestimmung* (Frankfurt am Main, 1979), p. 243.

12. Theodor W. Adorno, *Jargon der Eigentlichkeit: Zur deutschen Ideologie* (Frankfurt am Main, 1964), and Jürgen Habermas, *Philosophisch-politische Profile* (Frankfurt am Main, 1971).

13. Hans Ebeling, *Freiheit, Gleichheit, Sterblichkeit* (Stuttgart, 1982), pp. 26–41.

14. Heidegger, *Sein und Zeit*, p. 385. This excerpt is taken from Martin Heidegger, *Being and Time*, trans. John MacQuarrie and Edward Robinson (New York: Harper and Row, 1962), p. 437, which uses the 7th ed. of *Sein und Zeit*.

15. Heidegger, *Sein und Zeit*, p. 294.

16. *Ibid.*, p. 383.

17. *Ibid.*, p. 384.

18. *Ibid.*

19. *Ibid.*, p. 385.

20. See Erich Rothacker (ed.), *Briefwechsel zwischen Wilhelm Dilthey und dem Grafen Paul Yorck von Wartenburg, 1877–1897* (Philosophie und Geisteswissenschaften, vol. 1; Halle, [Saale], 1923).

21. Martin Heidegger, letter to Erich Rothacker, Jan. 4, 1924, in University of Bonn Archive, manuscript section, Rothacker I.

22. Count Paul Yorck von Wartenburg, quoted in Heidegger, *Sein und Zeit*, p. 403.

23. Adolf Hitler, *Mein Kampf*, Volksausgabe (10th ed.; Munich, 1942), pp. 92, 94, 96.

Chapter 7

1. Martin Heidegger, letter, Feb. 26, 1928, in Zentrales Staatsarchiv Merseburg, vol. 20, Marburg University Subjects, sec. 4, no. 2, XX, p. 268.

2. Toni Cassirer, *Aus meinem Leben mit Ernst Cassirer* (New York, 1950), p. 165, quoted in Guido Schneeberger, *Nachlese zu Heidegger* (Bern, 1962), p. 7.

3. Schneeberger, *Nachlese zu Heidegger*, p. 4.

4. See *ibid.*, pp. 9–11.

5. Otto zur Nedden, records, Berlin Document Center.

6. August Rumm, records, Berlin Document Center.

7. *Das Gesicht der Zeit: 10 Lithographien* (Karlsruhe, 1932).

8. Josef Mussler, records, Berlin Document Center.

9. Anton Fendrich, records, Berlin Document Center

10. Hans Blum, records, Berlin Document Center.

11. See Klaus Breuning, *Die Vision des Reiches* (Munich, 1969), p. 132f.

12. F. Muckle, *Der Geist der jüdischen Kultur und das Abendland* (Munich, 1923).

13. See E. Loewy, *Literatur unterm Hakenkreuz: Das Dritte Reich und seine Dichtung, Dokumentation* (Frankfurt am Main, 1966), p. 68.

14. See Schneeberger, *Nachlese zu Heidegger.*

15. *Ibid.*

16. Heinrich Berl, *Gespräche mit berühmten Zeitgenossen* (Baden-Baden, 1946), p. 67.

17. See Martin Heidegger, *Wegmarken* (Frankfurt am Main, 1967), p. 397.

18. *Ibid.*

19. *Karlsruher Tagblatt,* July 16, 1930.

20. H. W. Petzet, in *Bremer Nachrichten,* Oct. 11, 1930.

21. See H. W. Petzet, in *Bremer Nachrichten,* Oct. 5, 1930.

22. *Ibid.*

23. See H. Schleier, *Geschichtsschreibung der Weimarer Republik* (Berlin, 1975), p. 162.

24. Archives of Humboldt University, Records on Friedrich-Wilhelm-Universität, Berlin, regarding the professors of the philosophy faculty, letter P, no. 3, vol. 21, p. 368ff.

25. *Ibid.*

26. See Adolf Grimme, *Briefe* (Heidelberg, 1967), p. 32.

27. Zentrales Staatsarchiv Potsdam, vol. 2, rep. 76, Va. Sekt. 2, Tit. IV, University of Berlin Subjects, sec. 4, no. 68 A II.

28. *Ibid.*

29. *Ibid.*

30. See Grimme, *Briefe,* p. 36f.

31. Confidential State Archives, Preussischer Kulturbesitz, Berlin, handwritten documents section.

32. See A. Schölzel, "Zur Tätigkeit Nicolai Hartmanns an der Berliner Universität," *Wissenschaftliche Zeitschrift der Humboldt-Universität zu Berlin: Gesellschaftswissenschaftliche Reihe* 1 (1984): 62.

33. *Monistische Monatshefte* 15 (June 1930): 109ff.

34. See Hermann Herrigel, "Die politische Universität," in *Deutsche Zeitschrift: Unabhängige Monatshefte für die politische und geistige Gestaltung der Gegenwart* (Munich) 46 (1932–1933): 802–806.

35. Hannah Arendt, in W. Biemel, *Martin Heidegger in Selbstzeugnissen und Bilddokumenten* (Hamburg, 1973), p. 13.

36. Hannah Arendt, in *ibid.,* p. 11.

37. Hannah Arendt, in *ibid.,* pp. 11–12.

Chapter 8

1. Carl Friedrich von Weizsäcker, "Begegnungen in vier Jahrzehnten," in Günther Neske (ed.), *Erinnerung an Martin Heidegger* (Pfullingen, 1977), p. 245f.

2. Prof. Dr. Gerhard Ritter, remarks on the occasion of a visit with Dr.

H. Heiber, Freiburg, May 22, 1962, Archiv des Instituts für Zeitgeschichte, Munich, AZ 3078/62, pp. 8–9.

3. Adolf Hitler, quoted in H. Kuhn, "Die deutsche Universität am Vorabend der Machtergreifung," in Kuhn (ed.), *Die deutsche Universität im Dritten Reich* (Munich, 1966), p. 15.

4. Kuhn, "Die deutsche Universität," pp. 34, 38.

5. *Ibid.*, pp. 24, 26.

6. *Ibid.*, pp. 30, 35.

7. See O. Roegele, "Der Student im Dritten Reich," in Kuhn (ed.), *Die deutsche Universität*, p. 139; H. P. Bleuel and E. Klinnert, *Deutsche Studenten auf dem Weg ins Dritte Reich: Ideologien, Programme, Aktionen, 1918–1933* (Gütersloh, 1967); M. H. Kater, *Studentenschaft und Rechtsradikalismus in Deutschland, 1918–1933* (Hamburg, 1975).

8. Roegele, "Der Student im Dritten Reich," p. 139.

9. *Ibid.*, and K. D. Bracher, *Die nationalsozialistische Machtergreifung* (Cologne/Opladen, 1960), p. 420ff.

10. See Kuhn, "Die deutsche Universität," p. 40f.

11. See J. Pascher, "Das Dritte Reich erlebt an drei deutschen Universitäten," in Kuhn (ed.), *Die deutsche Universität*, p. 51.

12. Roegele, "Der Student im Dritten Reich," p. 140f.

13. See H. J. Düning, "Der SA-Student im Kampf für die Universität," in Roegele, "Der Student im Dritten Reich," p. 140.

14. *Ibid.*

15. *Ibid.*, p. 141.

16. *Ibid.*

17. G. Ruhle, *Das Dritte Reich: Dokumentarische Darstellung des Aufbaues der Nation*, vol. 1 (Berlin, 1933), p. 156, quoted in H. Maier, "Nationalsozialistische Hochschulpolitik," in Kuhn (ed.), *Die deutsche Universität*, p. 75.

18. Maier, "Nationalsozialistische Hochschulpolitik," p. 82.

19. See Bracher, *Die nationalsozialistische Machtergreifung*, pp. 383, 430f.

20. *Ibid.*, p. 434ff.

21. Wolfgang Kreutzberger, *Studenten und Politik: Der Fall Freiburg i. Br.* (Göttingen, 1972); A. G. von Olenhusen, "Die nationalsozialistische Rassenpolitik und die jüdischen Studenten an der Universität Freiburg, 1933–1945," *Freiburger Universitätsblätter* 6 (1964): 72ff.

22. E. O. Bräunche, W. Köhler, H. P. Lux, and Th. Schnabel, *1933: Die Machtergreifung in Freiburg und Südbaden* (exhibition catalogue Jan. 30–March 20, 1983; Freiburg, 1983).

23. *Ibid.*, p. 34.

24. *Ibid.*

25. *Ibid.*, p. 36.

26. *Ibid.*, p. 36f.

27. *Ibid.*

28. *Ibid.*, p. 37.

29. G. Tellenbach, *Aus erinnerter Zeitgeschichte* (Freiburg, 1981), p. 46.

30. *Völkischer Beobachter*, June 1, 1933; *Frankfurter Zeitung*, May 31, 1933.

31. See Internationaler Suchdienst Arolsen (1969) on the detention centers under the RF-SS, 1933–1945.

32. Bräunche et al., *1933*, p. 38.

33. *Ibid.*, p. 39.

34. P. Sauer, *Die Schicksale der jüdischen Bürger Baden-Württembergs während der NS-Verfolgungszeit, 1933–1945* (Stuttgart, 1969), p. 275.

35. See *Breisgauer Zeitung*, May 4, 1933.

36. Hugo Ott, "Martin Heidegger als Rektor der Universität Freiburg i. Br., 1933–1934: I. Die Übernahme des Rektorats der Universität Freiburg i. Br. durch Martin Heidegger im April 1933," *Zeitschrift des Breisgauer Geschichtsvereins Schau-ins-Land* 102 (1983): 121–136.

37. *Ibid.*, p. 123.

38. *Ibid.*, p. 125.

39. *Ibid.*

40. *Ibid.*, 127f.

41. See Wolfgang Schadewaldt, records, Berlin Document Center. On the course, see Schneeberger, *Nachlese zu Heidegger* (Bern, 1962), pp. 81, 96.

42. Ritter, remarks, p. 8.

43. Ott, "Heidegger als Rektor . . . 1933–1934," p. 130f.

44. Ritter, remarks, p. 8.

45. See Ott, "Heidegger als Rektor . . . 1933–1934," pp. 130–131.

46. *Ibid.*, pp. 123–124.

47. See Guido Schneeberger, *Nachlese zu Heidegger* (Bern, 1962), p. 144.

48. See *ibid.*, pp. 258–262.

49. See Kerber, records.

50. See Heinrich Himmler, telegram, in Franz Kerber, records, Berlin Document Center.

51. See the edited curriculum vitae by Kerber for the control of the SS, in Kerber, records.

52. On the application of the Führer principle in the university see Maier, "Nationalsozialistische Hochschulpolitik," p. 79ff.; H. Heigert, "Der Selbstmord der deutschen Studentenschaft," *Frankfurter Allgemeine Zeitung*, April 5, 1958; E. Y. Hartshorne, *The German Universities and National Socialism* (London, 1937); G. Kasper (ed.), *Die deutsche Hochschulverwaltung: Sammlung der das Hochschulwesen betreffenden Gesetze, Verordnungen und Erlasse* (Berlin, 1942–1943).

53. On Eucken see the opinion of Ritter, in remarks, pp. 16–18.

54. See Julius Wilser, records, Berlin Document Center.

55. Julius Wilser, "Angewandte Geologie im Feldzuge: Kriegsgeologie," *Natur-wissenschaft*, 1920, pp. 645–656.

56. See Julius Wilser, "Das Erdöl in der Weltwirtschaft II," *Geopolitik*, June 1927, p. 544f., which places in relief the warlike character of every economic rivalry.

57. Nicolas Hilling, records, Berlin Document Center.

58. Erik Wolf, records, Berlin Document Center.

59. Eduard Rehn, records, Berlin Document Center.

60. Georg Stieler, records, Berlin Document Center.

61. Wilhelm Felgenträger, records, Berlin Document Center.

62. Hans Mortensen, records, Berlin Document Center.

63. Hans Mortensen, "Die Litauerfrage in Ostpreussen," *Mitteilung der Geographischen Fachschaft der Universität Freiburg* 13–14 (1932–1933): 84.

64. Kurt Bauch, records, Berlin Document Center.

65. Otto Risse, records, Berlin Document Center.

66. H. W. Petzet, "Martin Heidegger," *Bremer Nachrichten*, Oct. 5, 1930.

67. Hans Spemann, "Die Wissenschaft im Dienste der Nation" (text of a speech on the first meeting of the Nazi German student group at the University of Freiburg, June 10–12, 1938), in Franz Kerber (ed.), *Alemannenland: Volkstum und Reich, ein Buch vom Oberrhein* (Stuttgart, 1939), pp. 79–83.

68. A. L. Schlageter, *Deutschland muss leben: Gesammelte Briefe von Albert Leo Schlageter* (Berlin, 1934), pp. 8, 9; quoted in Bräunche et al., *1933*, pp. 8, 9, 15.

69. A. L. Schlageter, *Gesammelte Aufsätze aus der Monatsschrift des CV* (Munich, 1932).

70. See *Frankfurter Zeitung*, May 29, 1933.

71. See Bräunche et al., *1933*, p. 8.

72. *Frankfurter Zeitung*, May 27, 1933.

73. Heidegger's speech on the tenth anniversary of Schlageter's death, quoted in Schneeberger, *Nachlese zu Heidegger*, p. 48.

74. Martin Heidegger, *Sein und Zeit* (10th ed.; Tübingen, 1963), p. 250.

75. *Ibid.*, para. 60.

76. *Ibid.*, paras. 51, 52.

77. Martin Heidegger, quoted in Schneeberger, *Nachlese zu Heidegger*, p. 48.

78. *Ibid.*

79. *Ibid.*

80. Heidegger, *Sein und Zeit*, para. 54, pp. 267ff.

81. *Ibid.*, p. 273.

82. Martin Heidegger, "Rede zu Ehren des Gedenkens an Schlageter," quoted in Schneeberger, *Nachlese zu Heidegger*, p. 49.

83. See Schneeberger, *Nachlese zu Heidegger*, p. 141.

84. Martin Heidegger, "Rede bei der Feierlichen Immatrikulation," reported by the *Freiburger Zeitung*, Nov. 27, 1933, and quoted in Schneeberger, *Nachlese zu Heidegger*, p. 157.

85. Adolf Hitler, *Mein Kampf*, Volksausgabe (10th ed.; Munich, 1942), p. 2.

86. *Ibid.*, p. 180ff.

87. H. Mörchen and O. F. Bollnow, "Philosophische Kriegsbriefe," *Blätter für Deutsche Philosophie* (Berlin) 15, no. 4 (1942): 444–455.

Chapter 9

1. See *Der Alemanne: Kampfblatt der Nationalsozialisten Oberbadens*, May 28, 1933, *Freiburger Zeitung*, May 29, 1933, and *Freiburger Studentenzeitung*, June 1, 1933, quoted in Schneeberger, *Nachlese zu Heidegger* (Bern, 1962), pp. 50–56.

2. See *Heuberger Volksblatt*, May 26, 1933.

3. Aaron Kleinberger, "Gab es eine nationalsozialistische Hochschulpolitik?," in M. Heinemann (ed.), *Erziehung und Schulung im Dritten Reich*, vol. 2 (Stuttgart, 1980), p. 8ff.

4. Alfred Bäumler, *Männerbund und Wissenschaft* (Berlin, 1934).

5. Ernst Krieck, *Bildung und Gemeinschaft* (Berlin, 1934), p. 31.

6. Ernst Krieck, *Nationalpolitische Erziehung* (Leipzig, 1932), pp. 165–167.

7. *Ibid.*, pp. 167–171. See also G. Müller, *Ernst Krieck und die NS-Wissenschaftsreform* (Frankfurt am Main, 1978).

8. H. Heiber, *Walter Frank und sein Reichsinstitut für Geschichte des neuen Deutschlands* (Stuttgart, 1966); H. Maier, "Nationalsozialistische Hochschulpolitik," in H. Kuhn (ed.), *Die deutsche Universität im Dritten Reich* (Munich, 1966), p. 168.

9. W. D. Gudopp, " 'Zum Fallen geneigt': Anmerkungen zu Heideggers Politik," in M. Buhr and H. J. Sandkühler (eds.), *Philosophie in weltbürgerlicher Absicht und wissenschaftlicher Sozialismus* (Cologne, 1985), p. 120.

10. Martin Heidegger, *Die Selbstbehauptung der deutschen Universität* (2nd ed.; Breslau, 1934), p. 5.

11. *Ibid.*, p. 5f.

12. *Ibid.*, p. 6f.

13. *Ibid.*, p. 8.

14. Adolf Hitler, *Mein Kampf*, Volksausgabe (10th ed.; Munich, 1942), p. 470.

15. Heidegger, *Selbstbehauptung*, p. 10.

16. *Ibid.*, p. 9.

17. *Ibid.*, p. 10ff.

18. *Ibid.*, p. 13f.

19. Rainer Marten, "Gross denken, gross irren? Rasse, Volk und Geist: Bemerkungen zur politischen Philosophie M. Heideggers," *Badische Zeitung*, Jan. 27, 1988, p. 12.

20. Heidegger, *Selbstbehauptung*, p. 14f.

21. *Ibid.*, p. 15ff.

22. *Ibid.*, p. 20.

23. See Sven Papcke, *Progressive Gewalt: Studien zum sozialen Widerstandsrecht* (Frankfurt am Main, 1973), p. 422f. On the agreement between Clausewitz and the "poetic head" of "the German movement" cf. the chapter "Brutalität und Transzendenz" in Wolf Kittler's *Die Geburt des Partisanen aus dem Geist der Poesie: Heinrich von Kleist und die Strategie der Befreiungskriege* (Freiburg, 1988), pp. 218–234.

24. Carl von Clausewitz, *Schriften, Aufsätze, Studien, Briefe*, vol. 1, ed. W. Hahlweg (Göttingen, 1966), p. 688.

25. Heinrich von Treitschke, *Deutsche Geschichte im Neunzehnten Jahrhundert*, pt. 1 (Leipzig, 1895), p. 392.

26. P. Schmitthenner, "Clausewitz, 1780–1831," in Willy Andreas (ed.), *Die grossen Deutschen: Neue deutsche Biographien* (Berlin, 1935), p. 634ff.

27. See Friedrich Meinecke, *Das Zeitalter der deutschen Erhebung, 1795–1815* (rev. 4th ed.; Bielefeld/Leipzig, 1906), p. 118.

28. Heinz Kammitzer, "Stein und das 'Deutsche Comittee' in Russland, 1812–1813," *Zeitschrift für Geschichtswissenschaft* 1 (1953): 56; Gabriele Venzky, *Die russich-deutsche Legion in den Jahren 1811–1815* (Wiesbaden, 1966).

29. See Walter Grab, *Ein Volk muss seine Freiheit selbst erobern: Zur Geschichte der deutschen Jakobiner* (Frankfurt am Main, 1984), p. 482ff.

30. Carl von Clausewitz, quoted in Karl Cerff (ed.), *Kulturpolitisches Mitteilungsblatt der Reichspropagandaleitung der NSDAP* (Berlin), Oct. 20, 1941, p. 7.

31. For an analagous interpretation of Röhm see Chapter 14, below.

32. *Deutschlands Erneuerung: Monatsschrift für das deutsche Volk* 3, no. 1 (1919): 1.

33. Hitler, *Mein Kampf*, p. 759f.

34. *Ibid.*, p. 760; Clausewitz, *Schriften, Aufsätze*, p. 688f.

35. Heidegger, *Selbstbehauptung*, p. 21.

36. *Völkischer Beobachter* (south German ed.), July 20, 1933.

37. *Der deutsche Student: Zeitschrift der Deutschen Studentenschaft* (Breslau), May 1934, p. 308. Reference is made to Adolf Rein, *Die Idee der politischen Universität* (Hamburg, 1933), and to Hans Heyse, *Idee der Wissenschaft und die deutsche Universität* (Königsberg, 1933).

38. See *Der deutsche Student*, Aug./Sept. 1933, p. 21. Cf. H. Freyer, *Das politische Semester: Ein Vorschlag zur Universitätsreform* (Jena, 1933), and J. W. Mannhardt, *Hochschulrevolution* (Hamburg, 1933).

39. E. Unger, *Das Schrifttum zum Aufbau des neuen Reiches, 1919–1934* (Berlin, 1934).

40. Albert Holfelder, "Die 'politische Universität' und die Wissenschaft," *Der deutsche Student*, Dec. 1933.

41. *Ibid.*, p. 9.

42. Richard Harder in *Gnomon*, 1933, pp. 440–441.

43. H. W. Petzet, *Auf einen Stern zugehen: Begegnungen und Gespräche mit Martin Heidegger (1929–1976)* (Frankfurt am Main, 1983), pp. 79, 81.

44. Heinrich Bornkamm, "Die Sendung der deutschen Universitäten in der Gegenwart," *Volk im Werden* 2 (1934): 32.

45. Erich Rothacker, "Politische Universität und deutsche Universität," *Kölnische Zeitung*, July 30, 1933.

46. Hermann Herrigel in *Deutsche Zeitschrift: Unabhängige Monatshefte für die politische und geistige Gestaltung der Gegenwart* 46 (1932–1933): 802–806.

47. *Rheinisch-Westfälische Zeitung* (Essen), Nov. 13, 1933.

48. Leading article from *Berliner Börsenzeitung*, Aug. 13, 1933.

49. *Zeitspiegel* (Leipzig) 2 (1933): 306.

50. R. König, "Zur Problemlage der Universitäts-Reform," *Das deutsche Wort: Der literarischen Welt* (Berlin), N.S., June 20, 1936, p. 571.

51. *Stuttgarter Neues Tageblatt*, July 15, 1933.

52. H. E. Karlinger, "Die neue Hochschule im Spiegel des Schrifttums," *Unitas* 3 (1935): 63.

53. *Die Hilfe: Zeitschrift für Politik, Wirtschaft und geistige Bewegung* (Berlin), Oct. 1, 1933, p. 504.

54. Hans Barth, "Geistige Führung," *Neue Zürcher Zeitung*, Aug. 6, 1933.

55. Eduard Baumgarten, "Der Bundestag in Bischofsstein," *Mitteilungen der Deutschen Altgilde Freischar* (Dortmund) 2 (1934): 5.

56. Benedetto Croce in *La Critica: Rivista di letteratura, storia e filosofia* (Naples) 31 (1933): 69–70.

57. Benedetto Croce, letter to Karl Vossler, Sept. 9, 1933, quoted in Guido Schneeberger, *Nachlese zu Heidegger* (Bern, 1962), p. 111f.

58. A. Lewkowitz, "Vom Sinn des Seins: Zur Existenzphilosophie Heideggers," *Monatsschrift für Geschichte und Wissenschaft des Judentums* (Breslau) 80 (1936): 187.

59. F. Weinhandl, "Universität und Wissenschaft," *Kieler Blätter*, edited by the community of Kiel professors (Publication of the Academy of Science of the NS Lectures at the Christian-Albrechts-Universität; Kiel, 1938), vols. 2–3, p. 127.

Chapter 10

1. Martin Heidegger, telegram to Robert Wagner, quoted in Guido Schneeberger, *Nachlese zu Heidegger* (Bern, 1962), p. 30.

2. See *Der Alemanne: Kampfblatt der Nationalsozialisten Oberbadens*, May 7, 1933, p. 11, quoted in Schneeberger, *Nachlese zu Heidegger*, pp. 28–29.

3. One may follow in some detail the debate about the interdiction of duels in the student review of the period *Burschenschaftliche Blätter*.

4. *Das deutsche Führer-Lexikon* (Berlin, 1934–1935).

5. Wolfgang Kreutzberger, *Studenten und Politik: Der Fall Freiburg i. Br.* (Göttingen, 1972), pp. 88–94.

6. See *ibid.*, p. 173.

7. Erich Stern, "Macht oder Recht? Die grundsätzliche Bedeutung jüngster Vorgänge in Freiburg."

8. *KC Blätter: Monatsschrift der im Kartell-Convent der Verbindung deutscher Studenten jüdischen Glaubens vereinigten Korporationen* (Berlin/Aix-la-Chapelle, 1925–   ).

9. See Neo-Friburgia, records of the University of Freiburg, XIV/1–146, summer semester 1933, quoted in Kreutzberger, *Studenten und Politik*, p. 173.

10. *Der Alemanne: Kampfblatt der Nationalsozialisten Oberbadens* (Sun. ed.), June 19, 1932.

11. See the documents in the Generallandesarchiv Karlsruhe (hereafter GLA) 235/8048.

12. *Ibid.*

13. *Ibid.*

14. See *Der Alemanne: Kampfblatt der Nationalsozialisten Oberbadens*, May 8, 1933.

15. See E. O. Bräunche, W. Köhler, H. P. Lux, and Th. Schnabel, *1933: Machtergreifung in Freiburg und Südbaden* (exhibition catalogue, Jan. 30–March 1, 1983; Freiburg, 1983), p. 49.

16. In the archival records of the city of Freiburg, from *ibid.*

17. *Breisgauer Zeitung*, May 12, 1933, p. 2, quoted in Schneeberger, *Nachlese zu Heidegger*, p. 33ff.

18. See *Deutsche Studentenschaft: Akademische Korrespondenz, Sonderdienst* (Berlin), April 25, 1933.

19. Martin Heidegger, speech at a rally at the University of Freiburg on the occasion of a speech by Hitler on Germany's withdrawal from the League of Nations, quoted in *Breisgauer Zeitung*, May 18, 1933, p. 3, and in Schneeberger, *Nachlese zu Heidegger*, p. 42f.

20. Kreutzberger, *Studenten und Politik*, pp. 40–45.

21. Martin Heidegger, speech at a mid-summer festival of the Freiburg students, quoted in *Freiburger Zeitung*, (evening ed.), June 26, 1933, p. 7, and in Schneeberger, *Nachlese zu Heidegger*, p. 71.

22. Karl Jaspers, *Philosophische Autobiographie* (Munich, 1977), p. 101, and *Notizen zu Heidegger* (Munich/Zürich, 1978), pp. 13, 50, 168, 274.

23. Martin Heidegger, "Deutsche Studenten," *Freiburger Studentenzeitung* 15 (8th semester), no. 1 (Nov. 3, 1933): 1, quoted in Schneeberger, *Nachlese zu Heidegger*, p. 135f.

24. See Schneeberger, *Nachlese zu Heidegger*, p. 118.

25. *Ibid.*, p. 18.

26. *Ibid.*, p. 60.

27. *Ibid.*, pp. 90–91.

28. *Ibid.*, p. 66.

29. *Ibid.*, p. 63.

30. *Ibid.*, p. 137.

31. *Ibid.*, pp. 166–167.

32. See Hugo Ott, in *Badische Zeitung*, Dec. 6, 1984, p. 10.

33. See Heidegger, letter to Dr. Fehrle, July 12, 1933, GLA 235/8819. Subsequent citations to this letter are also found there.

34. *Badische Zeitung*. An early reference to this letter occurs in Ott, *Badische Zeitung*, Dec. 6, 1984, p. 10.

35. Kreutzberger, *Studenten und Politik*, p. 166f.

36. See *Der Alemanne: Kampfblatt der Nationalsozialisten Oberbadens* (morning ed.), Nov. 25, 1933, p. 7, quoted in Schneeberger, *Nachlese zu Heidegger*, p. 154.

37. Schneeberger, *Nachlese zu Heidegger*, p. 156.

38. Martin Heidegger, speech on matriculation day, Nov. 25, 1933, quoted in the *Freiburger Zeitung* (morning ed.), Nov. 27, 1933, quoted in Schneeberger, *Nachlese zu Heidegger*, pp. 156–158.

39. Martin Heidegger, "Der Ruf zum Arbeitsdienst," *Freiburger Studentenzeitung* (8th semester), no. 5 (Jan. 23, 1934): 1, quoted in Schneeberger, *Nachlese zu Heidegger*, pp. 180–181.

40. *Ibid.*, p. 2.

41. *Ibid.*, p. 180.

42. *Ibid.*

43. *Ibid.*

44. For detailed and exact indications of the social and economic situation in Baden and Freiburg see Bräunche et al., *1933*, pp. 15–18.

45. See *ibid.*, p. 22f.

46. *Ibid.*, p. 23.

47. *Freiburger Zeitung* (morning ed.), Jan. 24, 1934, [p. 7], quoted in Schneeberger, *Nachlese zu Heidegger*, pp. 184–186.

48. *Freiburger Zeitung* (evening ed.), Jan. 17, 1934, [p. 4], quoted in Schneeberger, *Nachlese zu Heidegger*, p. 178.

49. See Schneeberger, *Nachlese zu Heidegger*, p. 204.

50. See *ibid.*, pp. 22–23.

51. See *ibid.*, p. 40.

52. See *ibid.*, p. 167.

53. See Helmut Haubold, memo, Nov. 11, 1942, in records, Berlin Document Center.

54. Martin Heidegger, "Nationalsozialistische Wissensschulung," *Der Alemanne: Kampfblatt der Nationalsozialisten Oberbadens* (evening ed.), Feb. 1, 1934, p. 9, quoted in Schneeberger, *Nachlese zu Heidegger*, p. 199. The following citation is also taken from this article.

55. Martin Heidegger, "Das Rektorat, 1933/34: Tatsachen und Gedanken," in Heidegger, *Die Selbstbehauptung der deutschen Universität* (Frankfurt am Main, 1983), p. 36.

56. *Ibid.*

Chapter 11

1. Martin Heidegger, letter to Fehrle, quoted in Hugo Ott, "Martin Heidegger als Rektor der Universität Freiburg i. Br., 1933/34," *Zeitschrift für Geschichte des Oberrheins* 132 (1984): 350.

2. Martin Heidegger, letter to Georg Plötner, April 24, 1933, quoted in Ott, "Heidegger als Rektor . . . 1933/34," p. 11.

3. Georg Plötner, letter to Martin Heidegger, May 23, 1933, in Archiv des Instituts für Zeitgeschichte, Munich, MA-228, p. 25071.

4. Georg Plötner, letter to Martin Heidegger, in Archiv des Instituts für Zeitgeschichte, Munich, MA-228, p. 25068.

5. See W. G. Oschilewski, *Zeitungen in Berlin: Im Spiegel der Jahrhunderte* (Berlin, 1975), p. 106ff.

6. See "Geht so Deutsche Studentenschaft?," *Deutsche Zeitung* (evening ed.), April 27, 1933.

7. Plötner, letter to Heidegger, June 1, 1933, in Archiv des Instituts für Zeitgeschichte, Munich, MA-228, p. 25066.

8. Martin Heidegger, telegram to Georg Plötner, June 3, 1933, in Archiv des Instituts für Zeitgeschichte, Munich, MA-228, p. 25064.

9. Martin Heidegger, letter to Georg Plötner, July 9, 1933, in Archiv des Instituts für Zeitgeschichte, Munich, MA-228, p. 25062.

10. See Guido Schneeberger, *Nachlese zu Heidegger* (Bern, 1962), pp. 76–77, for information on these addresses.

11. See Martin Heidegger, "Das Rektorat, 1933/34: Tatsachen und Gedanken," in Heidegger, *Die Selbstbehauptung der deutschen Universität* (Frankfurt am Main, 1983), p. 33.

12. See *Der Heidelberger Student* 6 (July 13, 1933).

13. See Joesph W. Bendersky, *Carl Schmitt: Theorist for the Reich* (Princeton, N.J., 1983), p. 203.

14. See "Die Universität im Neuen Reich: Ein Vortrag von Prof. Martin Heidegger," *Heidelberger Neueste Nachrichten* 150 (July 1, 1933): 4, quoted in Schneeberger, *Nachlese zu Heidegger*, pp. 73–75.

15. *Ibid.*, p. 74.

16. *Ibid.*

17. *Ibid.*, p. 75.

18. *Ibid.*

19. *Ibid.*

20. *Ibid.*

21. G. Tellenbach, *Aus erinnerter Zeitgeschichte* (Freiburg, 1981), pp. 41–42.

22. Schneeberger, *Nachlese zu Heidegger*, p. 75.

23. See Karl D. Erdmann, *Wissenschaft im Dritten Reich* (Publication of the Schleswig-Holstein Association of Universities, N.S., vol. 45; Kiel, 1967), p. 9.

24. See Lothar Wolf, *Die Stellung der Natur- und Geisteswissenschaften im Neuen Reich und die Aufgabe ihrer Fachschaften* (Kiel Addresses on the Questions of Nationality and the Border Country in the North Baltic Area; Neumünster, 1933).

25. Erdmann, *Wissenschaft im Dritten Reich*, p. 4.

26. *Ibid.*, p. 9.

27. See Hermann Heimpel, "Der gute Zuhörer," in Günther Neske (ed.), *Erinnerung an Martin Heidegger* (Pfullingen, 1977), p. 116.

28. *Norddeutsche Rundschau*, July 15, 1933; see also *Kieler Neueste Nachrichten*, July 16, 1933.

29. *Neues Tübinger Tagblatt und Steinlochwacht* 282 (Nov. 30, 1933).

30. Martin Heidegger, "Die Universität im nationalsozialistischen Staat," *Tübinger Chronik*, Dec. 1, 1933. The following quotations are also found in this article.

31. Association of German Universities, statement, April 22, 1933, in Bundesarchiv Koblenz, R 43 II.

32. See B. Reimann, "Die Niederlage der deutschen Universitäten," *Neue Zürcher Zeitung*, Dec. 3/4, 1983, p. 69.

33. *Ibid.*

34. See the letter of Prof. Tillmann and the response from the State Chancery, Bundesarchiv Koblenz, R 43 II. The following citations are also taken from this source.

35. See *Das deutsche Führer-Lexikon* (Berlin, 1934–1935), pp. 75–76, and R. Bollmus, *Das Amt Rosenberg und seine Gegner* (Stuttgart, 1970), p. 28.

36. See *Frankfurter Zeitung*, April 28, 1933.

37. See Ernst Krieck and Lothar Wolf, letters to Ministry Counsellor Prof. Achelis and Ministry Director Gerullis, June 18 and June 6, 1933, respectively, in Zentrales Staatsarchiv Potsdam, Association of German Universities, Rep. 76 Va., sec. 1, tit. IV, General University Subjects, sec. 4, no. 49.

38. See Zentrales Staatsarchiv Potsdam, 70 Re 8, Association of German Universities, Cultural and Political Work Community of German University Teachers. The following evidence is also taken from these files.

39. *Ibid.*

40. The complete list of members is to be found in the Zentrales Staatsarchiv Potsdam, 70 Re 8, Association of German Universities, Cultural and Political Work Community of German University Teachers.

41. On the rivalry between Ernst Krieck and Alfred Bäumler see H. Heiber, *Walter Frank und sein Reichsinstitut für Geschichte des neuen Deutschlands* (Stuttgart, 1966), pp. 580–590.

42. Zentrales Staatsarchiv Potsdam, date missing.

43. *Ibid.*

Chapter 12

1. See Guido Schneeberger, *Nachlese zu Heidegger* (Bern, 1962), pp. 138–139, 144–146, with a photograph, and 148–150. The following quote is taken from pp. 148–150.

2. K. D. Bracher, *Die nationalsozialistische Machtergreifung* (Cologne/Opladen, 1960).

3. See records referring to university affairs and studies in Germany, vols. 24 and 25, Science/University Affairs in Germany, Politisches Archiv des auswärtigen Amtes. For this information I am grateful to Uwe Henning of the Max-Planck-Institut für Bildungsforschung, Berlin.

4. Gerhard Ritter, "Freiburg als vorderösterreichische Stadt," in Franz Kerber

(ed.), *Reichsstrasse 31, von der Ostmark zum Oberrhein: Natur-Volk-Kunst* (Stuttgart, 1938), pp. 199–207.

5. Archiv der Friedrich-Wilhelm-Universität, Berlin, Records of the Professors of the Philosophy Faculty, Littr. P., vol. 25, Berlin/GDR.

6. See W. Petersen, records, Berlin Document Center, SS Membership, no. 279015.

7. Archiv der Friedrich-Wilhelm-Universität, Records of the Professors of the Philosophy Faculty.

8. Alfred Bäumler, evaluation of Martin Heidegger, Sept. 22, 1933, in Bäumler's private archive. The complete text of the evaluation will soon be published by Guido Schneeberger.

9. Bayerischen Hauptstaatsarchiv, Munich, Records of the Hiring Committee for a Successor for Richard Hönigswald, Sign. MK 39700. The following quotes are also taken from these records. I am grateful to Prof. Aaron Kleinberger of the University of Jerusalem for this information.

10. Bayerischen Hauptstaatsarchiv, Records of the Hiring Committee.

11. *Ibid.*

12. See H. Heiber, *Walter Frank und sein Reichsinstitut für Geschichte des neuen Deutschlands* (Stuttgart, 1966), p. 483ff.

13. Archiv der Friedrich-Wilhelm-Universität, Records of the Philosophy Faculty.

14. *Ibid.*

15. *Ibid.*

16. See J. Harms, "Vom Deutsch deutscher Philosophen," *Muttersprache: Zeitschrift des deutschen Sprachvereins* 49, no. 1 (Jan. 1934): 1–4, quoted in Schneeberger, *Nachlese zu Heidegger*, pp. 171–174.

17. See R. Deinhardt, "Deutsch denken und welsch reden, nein!: Man spricht Deutsch im Dritten Reich!," *Deutsche Bergwerks-Zeitung* (Düsseldorf) 20 (Jan. 25, 1934), quoted in Schneeberger, *Nachlese zu Heidegger*, pp. 191–193.

18. Ernst Krieck, "Vom Deutsch des Deutschen Sprachvereins," *Volk im Werden* 2 (1934): 128–129, quoted in Schneeberger, *Nachlese zu Heidegger*, pp. 182–184.

19. Hans Naumann, *Germanischer Schicksalsglaube* (Jena, 1934), pp. 82, 88.

20. Ernst Krieck, "Germanischer Mythos und Heideggersche Philosophie," *Volk im Werden* 2 (1934): 247–249, quoted in Schneeberger, *Nachlese zu Heidegger*, p. 226.

21. Hans Naumann, speech on the occasion of a book-burning in Bonn, in B. Zeller (ed.), *Klassiker in finsteren Zeiten* (2 vols.; Marbach, 1983), vol. 1, p. 116f.

22. See Karl Losemann, *Nationalsozialismus und Antike* (Hamburg, 1977).

23. On Krieck see in its entirety G. Müller's *Ernst Krieck und die nationalsozialistische Wissenschaftsreform* (Weinheim/Basel, 1978).

24. These two letters are in the Senkenbergische Bibliothek in Frankfurt.

Chapter 13

1. See Guido Schneeberger, *Nachlese zu Heidegger*, (Bern, 1962), p. 171.

2. Martin Heidegger, "Geleitwort der Universität [zum Jubiläum der 'Freibur-

ger Zeitung']," *150 Jahre Freiburger Zeitung*, Jan. 6, 1934, p. 10, quoted in Schnee-berger, *Nachlese zu Heidegger*, p. 151.

3. See "Professor Dr. Heidegger in Rundfunk," *Der Alemanne: Kampfblatt der Nationalsozialisten Oberbadens* (morning ed.), March 1, 1934, p. 6, quoted in Schnee-berger, *Nachlese zu Heidegger*, p. 215.

4. Martin Heidegger, "Schöpferische Landschaft: Warum bleiben wir in der Provinz?," *Der Alemanne: Kampfblatt der Nationalsozialisten Oberbadens* ("To New Shores: The Weekly Culture Supplement of the *Alemanne*"), March 7, 1934, [p. 1], quoted in Schneeberger, *Nachlese zu Heidegger*, p. 216. The subsequent quotes are also taken from this article. On August 11, Heidegger told Erich Rothacker that he "privately" planned a distribution of his "Rundfunkrede" and that he had "already reserved a copy" for Rothacker (Heidegger, letter to Rothacker, University of Bonn Archive, handwritten document section, Rothacker I).

5. See Robert Minder, *Hölderlin unter den Deutschen und andere Aufsätze zur deutschen Literatur* (Frankfurt am Main, 1968), pp. 119, 138f.

6. Adolf Hitler, *Mein Kampf*, Volksausgabe (10th ed.; Munich, 1942), pp. 151–152; cf. further Walther Darré, *Bauerntum als Lebensquelle der nordischen Rasse* (Munich, 1928).

7. The entire text appears in Schneeberger, *Nachlese zu Heidegger*, pp. 216–218.

8. *Völkischer Beobachter* (south German ed.), Oct. 31, 1933.

9. Schneeberger, *Nachlese zu Heidegger*, p. 135.

Chapter 14

1. See "Aufhebung des konfessionellen Prinzips bei den katholischen Studenten-verbänden," *Deutsche Studenten-Zeitung: Kampfblatt der deutschen Studenten* (Munich) 2, no. 5 (Feb. 10, 1934): 8, quoted in Guido Schneeberger, *Nachlese zu Heidegger*, (Bern, 1962), pp. 197–198.

2. In addition see Schneeberger's documentation, *Nachlese zu Heidegger*, p. 205.

3. *Ibid.*

4. *Ibid.*, p. 144.

5. A. Künzel, records, Berlin Document Center.

6. See Schneeberger, *Nachlese zu Heidegger*, p. 140, and Künzel, records.

7. Martin Heidegger, letter to the Reichsführer of the German student com-munity, Feb. 6, 1934, in Schneeberger, *Nachlese zu Heidegger*, p. 205f.

8. "Freiburger CV.-Abend," *Freiburger Zeitung* (evening ed.), Jan. 29, 1934, [p. 4], quoted in Schneeberger, *Nachlese zu Heidegger*, p. 195. There is another report on this evening on pp. 196–197.

9. Schneeberger, *Nachlese zu Heidegger*, p. 195.

10. See Wolfgang Kreutzberger, *Studenten und Politik: Der Fall Freiburg i. Br.* (Göttingen, 1972), p. 56ff.

11. *Ibid.*

12. *Ibid.*, p. 117.

13. See Klaus Breuning, *Die Vision des Reiches* (Munich, 1969).

14. The article on Schlageter is in *Academia* 1–3 (May–July 1933); cf. Dr. Grei-neder (lawyer to the Reichsführer SS), "SA und SS, Wesen und Aufgaben," *Aca-*

demia 5 (Sept. 1933); "Die Verfassung des CV," *Academia* 6–7 (Oct. 1933); and Prof. Dr. B. Dürken (director of the Institute for Mechanical Development and Genetics at the University of Breslau), "Vererbung beim Menschen und Rassenhygiene," *Academia* 11–12 (March–April 1934).

15. *Academia* 1–3 (May–June 1933), and 5 (Sept. 1933).

16. *Academia* 11–12 (March–April 1934).

17. Engelbert Krebs, "Die Aufgabe der Universität im Neuen Reich," *Academia* 4 (Aug. 1933): 93.

18. Engelbert Krebs, *Urkirche und Judentum* (Berlin, 1926; Die Morgen-Reihe/ 2. Schrift).

19. See "Ehrendolch für Dr.-Ing. Oskar Stäbel," *Der Alemanne: Kampfblatt der Nationalsozialisten Oberbadens* (morning ed.), Jan. 13, 1934, p. 6, quoted in Schneeberger, *Nachlese zu Heidegger*, p. 175.

20. See Wolfgang Sauer, "Die Mobilmachung der Gewalt," in Karl-Dietrich Bracher, Gerhard Schulz, and Wolfgang Sauer (eds.), *Die Nationalsozialistische Machtergreifung: Studien zur Errichtung des Totalitären Herrschaftssystems im Deutschland, 1933–1934* (Frankfurt/Berlin/Vienna, 1962), vol. 3, p. 264.

21. See "Studium und SA-Dienst: Dr. Staebel über wichtige Fragen der Studentenschaft," *Frankfurter Zeitung*, May 6, 1934, p. 1, quoted in Schneeberger, *Nachlese zu Heidegger*, pp. 230–233. Cf. Oskar Stäbel, "Kameraden!" *Deutsche Studenten-Zeitung: Kampfblatt der deutschen Studenten* 2, no. 15 (July 12, 1934): 2, quoted in Schneeberger, *Nachlese zu Heidegger*, p. 234.

22. Otto Strasser, *Die deutsche Bartholomäusnacht* (Zürich, 1935), p. 160f.

23. See Sauer, "Die Mobilmachung," p. 195f.

24. *Ibid.*

25. *Ibid.*, pp. 197–198.

26. See *ibid.*, p. 200.

27. *Ibid.*, p. 204.

28. *Ibid.*, pp. 205–207.

29. See *ibid.*, pp. 209–211.

30. See *ibid.*, pp. 213–214.

31. *Ibid.*, pp. 223–225.

32. Ch. Bloch, *Die SA und die Krise des NS-Regimes* (Frankfurt am Main, 1970).

33. Ernst Röhm, quoted in Bloch, *SA und die Krise*, pp. 48–50.

34. See U. D. Adam, *Hochschule und Nationalsozialismus: Die Universität Tübingen im Dritten Reich* (Tübingen, 1977), p. 89.

35. See *ibid.*, p. 90.

36. *Ibid.*, p. 91.

37. *Ibid.*, pp. 91–92.

38. *Ibid.*, p. 93.

39. See Bloch, *SA und die Krise*, pp. 53, 65.

40. "Rudolf Hess an die Studenten: Rede des Stellvertreters des Führers Pg. Rudolf Hess bei der Sondertagung des NS.D.St.B. auf dem Reichsparteitag in Nürnberg, 1934," *Deutsche Studenten-Zeitung: Kampfblatt der deutschen Studenten: Amtliches Nachrichten- und Schulungsblatt des Nationalsozialistischen Deutschen Studentenbundes* 2, no. 17 (Nov. 15, 1934): 5, quoted in Schneeberger, *Nachlese zu Heidegger*, pp. 244–246.

41. Georg Picht, "Die Macht des Denkens," in Günther Neske (ed.), *Erinnerung an Martin Heidegger* (Pfullingen, 1977), p. 198.

42. Martin Heidegger, "Das Rektorat, 1933/34: Tatsachen und Gedanken," in Heidegger, *Die Selbstbehauptung der deutschen Universität* (2nd ed.; Breslau, 1934), p. 40.

43. *Ibid.,* p. 18.

44. See Hugo Ott, "M. Heidegger als Rektor der Universität Freiburg i. Br., 1933/34," *Zeitschrift für Geschichte des Oberrheins* 132 (1984): 345; Martin Heidegger, interview, *Der Spiegel* (Hamburg), May 31, 1976, p. 204.

45. See Ott, "Heidegger als Rektor . . . 1933/34," p. 357.

46. "Rektoratswechsel an der Universität Freiburg," *Der Alemanne: Kampfblatt der Nationalsozialisten Oberbadens,* April 30, 1934, p. 3.

47. Heidegger, "Das Rektorat, 1933/34," p. 23.

48. Constantin von Dietze, "Die Universität Freiburg im Dritten Reich," *Mitteilungen der List-Gesellschaft* 3 (1960–1961): 96.

Chapter 15

1. "Deutsche Wissenschaftler hinter Adolf Hitler," *Völkischer Beobachter: Kampfblatt der nationalsozialistischen Bewegung Grossdeutschlands* (Berlin ed.) 47, nos. 231–232 (Aug. 19–20, 1934): 2. I am indebted to Uwe Henning of the Max-Planck-Institut für Bildungsforschung, Berlin, for this information.

2. Martin Heidegger, "Das Rektorat, 1933/34: Tatsachen und Gedanken," in Heidegger, *Die Selbstbehauptung der deutschen Universität* (2nd ed.; Breslau, 1934), p. 40.

3. Dr. Gross, letter to Thilo von Trotha, quoted in Leon Poliakov and Josef Wulf, *Das Dritte Reich und seine Denker* (Berlin, 1959), p. 548.

4. Alfred Rosenberg, letter to Minister Bernhard Rust, March 6, 1934, Archiv des Instituts für Zeitgeschichte, Munich, Rosenberg Office, MA 596, p. 318.

5. W. Rudolf, "Sinn und Aufgabe der Preussischen Dozentenschaft," *Der deutsche Student: Zeitschrift der Deutschen Studentenschaft,* Feb. 1934, pp. 86–90.

6. See A. Busch, *Die Geschichte des Privatdozenten: Eine soziologische Studie zur grossbetrieblichen Entwicklung der deutschen Universitäten* (Stuttgart, 1959), p. 137.

7. See Wilhelm Stuckart, records, Berlin Document Center.

8. Wilhelm Stuckart, "Zentralgewalt, Dezentralisation und Verwaltungseinheit," in *Festgabe für Heinrich Himmler* (on the occasion of his 40th birthday on the 5th anniversary of taking over the German police, June 17, 1941; Darmstadt, 1941), pp. 1–32.

9. Wilhelm Stuckart, *Nationalsozialistische Rechtserziehung* (Frankfurt am Main, 1935).

10. See Wilhelm Stuckart, "Der totale Krieg und die Verwaltung," *Deutsche Verwaltung* 1 (1943): 1–4.

11. In 1935 Stuckart became the state secretary in the Reichsinnenministerium. Cf. Walther Hofer, *Der Nationalsozialismus: Dokumente, 1933–1945* (Frankfurt am Main, 1978), p. 396.

12. See Zentrales Staatsarchiv Merseburg, Sign. Rep. 76 Va., sec. I, tit. IV, no. 71, pp. 506–511. The following quote is also taken from these files. Heidegger's answer is on pp. 499–505.

13. See G. A. Walz, records, Berlin Document Center; Werner Studenkowski, records, Berlin Document Center; Otto Reche, records, Berlin Document Center; W. Klausing, records, Berlin Document Center.

14. See Klausing, records.

15. See Volker Losemann, "Zur Konzeption der NS-Dozentenlager," in M. Heinemann (ed.), *Erziehung und Schulung im Dritten Reich*, vol. 2 (Stuttgart, 1980), pp. 87–109.

16. See Zentrales Staatsarchiv Merseburg, Sign. Rep. 76 Va., sec. 1, tit. 4, no. 71, pp. 506–511.

17. Generallandesarchiv Karlsruhe, literary estate of Ernst Krieck.

18. *Frankfurter Zeitung*, May 5, 1934; "Rechtsphilosophie als Waffe," *Berliner Tageblatt*, May 4, 1934. Cf. "Deutsche Rechtsmoral aus Blut und Boden," *Weimarische Zeitung* 103 (May 4, 1934), and "Ausschuss für Rechtsphilosophie der Akademie für Deutsches Recht gegründet," *Allgemeine Thüringische Landeszeitung Deutschland* 121 (May 4, 1934).

19. Charter for the Academy of German Law, in Hans Frank (ed.), *Akademie für Deutsches Recht, Jahrbuch 1* (Berlin/Munich/Vienna, 1933/34), pp. 188–189.

20. For a short presentation of the political development of the German universities (above all, in the democratic eras 1920–1932 and 1949–1952), see Ernst Jäckh and Otto Suhr, *Geschichte der Deutschen Hochschule für Politik* (Berlin, 1952).

21. Wilhelm Schoeppe, public letter, *Frankfurter Allgemeine Zeitung*, May 28, 1983.

22. *Ibid.*

23. Document in the literary estate of Eduard Baumgarten, administered by Prof. Wilhelm Schoeppe, Frankfurt am Main. Heidegger's evaluation is in the Archives of the University of Göttingen, records of "Dr. Baumgarten . . . Habilitation für Philosophie" (no record number); cf. H. Becker, H.-J. Dahms, and C. Wegeler (eds.), *Die Universität Göttingen unter dem Nationalsozialismus: Das verdrängte Kapitel ihrer 250 jährigen Geschichte* (Munich/London/New York/Oxford/Paris, 1987), p. 194, nn. 78 and 86, and pp. 37, 170, 179–185.

24. See Karl Jaspers, *Notizen zu Heidegger* (Munich/Zürich, 1978), p. 14ff.

25. Schoeppe, public letter.

26. *Ibid.*

27. See Rudolf Stadelmann, *Das geschichtliche Selbstbewusstsein der Nation* (Tübingen, 1934).

28. *Ibid.*

29. See Rudolf Stadelmann, "Hippolyte Taine und die Gedankenwelt der französischen Rechten," *Zeitschrift für die gesamte Staatswissenschaft* 92 (1932); 1–50.

30. See Rudolf Stadelmann, "Vom geschichtlichen Wesen der deutschen Revolutionen," *Zeitwende* 10 (1934).

31. See Rudolf Stadelmann, "Der Kampf um die Saar," *Deutsche Zeitschrift: Unabhängige Monatshefte für die politische und geistige Gestaltung der Gegenwart* 47 (1934): 657–668.

32. Guido Schneeberger, *Nachlese zu Heidegger* (Bern, 1962), p. 70.

33. Martin Heidegger, evaluation of Rudolf Stadelmann, July 1, 1935, Archives of the University of Göttingen, Records of the Trustees, XVI, IV.B.7, vol. 3, p. 33.

34. On Arnold Ruge, see Generallandesarchiv Karlsruhe, 450, no. 792.

Chapter 16

1. See the documents on the proceedings to hire a successor to Georg Misch, Archives of the University of Göttingen, records on "Nachfolge Misch" (personal records).

2. Hans Heyse, "Die neue Idee der Wissenschaft und die deutsche Universität," *Völkischer Beobachter* (North German ed.), May 6–7, 1934, supp.

3. See Archives of the University of Göttingen.

4. Martin Heidegger, lecture on Hölderlin, winter 1934/35, quoted in Otto Pöggeler, *Philosophie und Politik bei Heidegger* (Freiburg/Munich, 1972), p. 28f.

5. *Ibid.*, p. 108.

6. Martin Heidegger, *Einführung in die Metaphysik* (Tübingen, 1953), p. 8.

7. *Ibid.*, p. 8f.

8. *Ibid.*, p. 18.

9. *Ibid.*, p. 28f.

10. *Ibid.*, p. 29.

11. *Ibid.*, p. 32.

12. See Robert Minder, *Hölderlin unter den Deutschen und andere Aufsätze zur deutschen Literatur* (Frankfurt am Main, 1968), p. 132f.

13. Heidegger, *Einführung in die Metaphysik*, p. 34f.

14. *Ibid.*, p. 35.

15. *Ibid.*

16. Adolf Hitler, *Mein Kampf*, Volksausgabe (10th ed.; Munich, 1942), p. 68; on Russia as the "devil," see p. 752.

17. Heidegger, *Einführung in die Metaphysik*, p. 35f.

18. *Ibid.*, p. 152.

19. *Ibid.*, p. 36.

20. Hitler, *Mein Kampf*, p. 188f.

21. Heidegger, *Einführung in die Metaphysik*, p. 36f.

22. *Ibid.*, p. 10f.

23. Martin Heidegger, "Über das Wesen des Grundes," in Heidegger, *Wegmarken* (Frankfurt am Main, 1967), pp. 40–42.

24. Alfred Bäumler, "Die Dialektik Europas: Antwort an Jules Romains," in Bäumler, *Politik und Erziehung: Reden und Aufsätze* (4th ed.; Berlin, 1943), p. 53.

25. Heidegger, *Einführung in die Metaphysik*, p. 96.

26. *Ibid.*, p. 11.

27. *Ibid.*, p. 43.

28. *Ibid.*, p. 47f.

29. *Ibid.*, p. 47.

30. *Ibid.*, p. 101.

31. *Ibid.*, p. 102.

32. *Ibid.*, p. 117.

33. See Alexander Schwan, *Die politische Philosophie im Denken Heideggers* (Cologne/Opladen, 1965), pp. 94, 101.

34. See *ibid.*, p. 87f.

35. See *ibid.*, p. 92f.

36. Heidegger, *Einführung in die Metaphysik*, p. 152.

37. Martin Heidegger, interview, *Der Spiegel*, May 31, 1976, p. 204.

38. Rainer Marten, "Ein rassistisches Konzept von Humanität," *Badische Zeitung*, Dec. 19–20, 1987, p. 14.

39. See Elfride Heidegger-Petri, "Gedanken einer Mutter über höhere Mädchenbildung," *Deutsche Mädchenbildung: Zeitschrift für das gesamte höhere Mädchenschulwesen* 11, no. 1 (1935): 1–7. The following quotations are also taken from this article.

40. See the article by Karl Stracke in *Jahrbuch des Philologenverbandes: Kunze-Kalendar* (Breslau, 1942), p. 2.

41. See Karl Stracke, records, Berlin Document Center.

42. See Dr. E. Meyn von Westenholz, "Höhere Mädchenbildung als Forderung nationaler Einheit," *Deutsche Mädchenbildung* 11, no. 2 (1935): 49ff.

43. See H. Wendt, "Noch einiges Schrifttum über Nationalsozialismus und Frauenfrage," *Deutsche Mädchenbildung* 11, no. 6 (1935): 285ff.

44. See Dr. H. Voigts, "Schülercharakteristik und erbbiologischer Beobachtungsbogen," *Deutsche Mädchenbildung* 11, no. 7 (1935): 327ff.

45. See Alma Langenbach, "Der neue deutsche Frauentypus," *Deutsche Mädchenbildung* 11, no. 8 (1935): 338ff.

46. See Edith Ullbrich, "Biologisches Denken im evangelischen Religionsunterricht der höheren Schule," *Deutsche Mädchenbildung* 11, no. 8 (1935): 346ff.

47. Adolf Hitler, "Rede vor dem Frauenkongress in Nürnberg am 8. September 1934," *NS-Frauenwarte* (journal of the NS-Frauenschaft [German organization of Women]) 7 (Sept. 1934): 210–212.

48. Gertrud Scholtz-Klink, "Verpflichtung und Aufgabe der Frau im nationalsozialistischen Staat," *Schriften der Deutschen Hochschule für Politik* 23 (1936): 1–24.

49. Heidegger-Petri, "Gedanken einer Mutter über höhere Mädchenbildung," p. 1.

50. *Ibid.*

51. *Ibid.*, p. 2.

52. *Ibid.*

53. *Ibid.*, pp. 2–3.

54. *Ibid.*, p. 3.

55. *Ibid.*, p. 4.

56. *Ibid.*

57. *Ibid.*, p. 5.

58. *Ibid.*

59. *Ibid.*

60. *Ibid.*, p. 6.

61. *Ibid.*, p. 7.

62. See J. Stephenson, "Verantwortungsbewusstsein: Politische Schulung durch die Frauenorganisationen im Dritten Reich," in M. Heinemann (ed.), *Erziehung und Schulung im Dritten Reich*, vol. 2 (Stuttgart, 1980), pp. 194–205.

63. *NS-Frauenwarte* 2 (July 1932): 145 and (Oct. 1932): 168.

64. Dr. Schwab, "Gedanken zum Sterilisationsgesetz," *NS-Frauenwarte* 1 (Jan. 1934): 380ff.

65. Anonymous, "Ein Beitrag zum Rassenproblem," *NS-Frauenwarte* 2 (Feb. 1934): 406ff.

66. *N-S Frauenwarte* 1 (March 1934).

67. "Grundsätze der N.S. Frauenschaft [German organization of women]," *NS-Frauenwarte* 7 (July 1932): 26.

68. See F. Hundssnurcher and G. Taddey, *Die jüdische Gemeinde in Baden* (Stuttgart, 1968), pp. 92–93.

69. *Ibid.*, p. 93.

70. See F. Laubenberg and B. Schwineköper, "Geschichte und Schicksal der Freiburger Juden," *Freiburger Stadthefte*, no. 6 (Freiburg, 1963).

71. See W. Scheffer, *Judenverfolgung im Dritten Reich* (Berlin, 1964), p. 68f.

72. Karl Jaspers, *Notizen zu Heidegger* (Munich/Zürich, 1978), p. 87.

73. See *ibid.*, pp. 257, 274.

74. Martin Heidegger, *Spiegel* interview, p. 199.

75. Scheffer, *Judenverfolgung im Dritten Reich*, pp. 237–238.

76. H. W. Petzet, *Auf einen Stern zugehen: Begegnungen und Gespräche mit Martin Heidegger (1929–1976)* (Frankfurt am Main, 1983), p. 40.

77. See Aaron Kleinberger, "Gab es eine nationalsozialistische Hochschulpolitik?," in Heinemann (ed.), *Erziehung und Schulung*, pp. 14, 16.

78. Both documents are in the Zentrales Staatsarchiv Merseburg, University of Freiburg i. Br., 40-01 REM, vol. 1 (Sept. 1934–Dec. 1937), 1976, no. 10.

79. See Martin Heidegger, "Das Rektorat, 1933/34: Tatsachen und Gedanken," in Heidegger, *Die Selbstbehauptung der deutschen Universität* (Frankfurt am Main, 1983), p. 41.

80. See *Deutsches Bücherverzeichnis: Eine Zusammenstellung der im deutschen Buchhandel erschienenen Bücher, Zeitschriften und Landkarten*, vol. 20: *1936–1940* (Leipzig, 1942), p. 1091.

81. Martin Heidegger, letter to Maria Lietzmann, April 27, 1934, in the possession of Dr. F. Spiegeler, Bramsche.

82. R. Oberschelp (ed.), *Gesamtverzeichnis des deutschsprachigen Schrifttums, 1911–1965*, vol. 53 (Munich, 1978).

83. See Heidegger, *Spiegel* interview, p. 204.

84. See E. Loewy, *Literatur unterm Hakenkreuz: Das Dritte Reich und seine Dichtung, Dokumentation* (Frankfurt am Main, 1966), p. 310.

85. See *NS-Frauenwarte* 17 (1935/36): 17.

86. See Hildegard Brenner, *Ende einer bürgerlichen Kunstinstitution: Die politische Formierung der Preussischen Akademie der Künste* (Stuttgart, 1972), pp. 12–13, 170f.

87. See H. Schleier, *Die bürgerliche deutsche Geschichtsschreibung der Weimarer Republik* (Berlin, 1975), p. 104.

88. See *Tribuna* (Rome), Jan. 16, 1935.

89. See B. Zeller (ed.), *Klassiker in finsteren Zeiten* (exhibition catalogue of the German Literature Archives in the Schiller National Museum, Marbach, May 14–Oct. 31, 1983; Marbach, 1983), vol. 1, p. 348.

90. Deutsche Botschaft Rom, Bonn, Kw 7a, vol. 2 (Paket 1325a).

91. *Das innere Reich*, April 1934, quoted in Zeller (ed.), *Klassiker in finsteren Zeiten*, vol. 2, p. 176.

92. Zeller (ed.), *Klassiker in finsteren Zeiten*, vol. 1, p. 348.

93. See *Die Neue Literatur*, Feb. 1937, p. 468f.

94. B. Bauch, review of Heidegger's "Hölderlin und das Wesen der Dichtung," *Blätter für Deutsche Philosophie* 13, no. 1/2 (1939): 217f.

95. Dr. W. Könitzer, review of Heidegger's "Hölderlin und das Wesen der

Dichtung," *Wille und Macht: Führerorgan der NS-Jugend* 6 (March 15, 1937): 28–30.

96. Martin Heidegger, letter to B. Mascher, in Zeller (ed.), *Klassiker in finsteren Zeiten,* vol. 1, p. 352.

97. Martin Heidegger, records, Berlin Document Center. Cf. *Das Volk: Kampfblatt für völkische Kultur und Politik,* Verlag Nibelungen, Berlin/Leipzig.

98. See E. Unger, *Das Schrifttum zum Aufbau des neuen Reiches, 1919–1934* (Berlin, 1934), p. 148.

99. See Zentrales Staatsarchiv Merseburg, records on "Kant-Forschungen (1904–1934)," Preussiches Kulturministerium. More records on the "Kant-Gesellschaft" from the NS era can be found in the archives of the Martin Luther University, Halle-Wittenberg.

100. See Archiv des Instituts für Zeitgeschichte, Munich, Sign. MA 609.

101. See *ibid.,* pp. 56655–56657.

102. *Ibid.,* pp. 56654–56658.

103. *Ibid.,* p. 56653.

104. *Ibid.,* p. 56651.

105. *Ibid.,* pp. 56646–56648.

106. *Ibid.,* p. 56648.

107. Martin Heidegger, *Holzwege* (Frankfurt, 1963), p. 344.

108. *Ibid.*

109. *Ibid.*

110. *Ibid.*

111. Alexander Schwan, *Die politische Philosophie im Denken Heideggers* (Cologne/Opladen, 1965), p. 52.

112. See Pöggeler, *Philosophie und Politik,* p. 124.

113. Franz Kerber (ed.), *Alemannenland: Ein Buch von Volkstum und Sendung, für die Stadt Freiburg herausgegeben von Oberbürgermeister Dr. Kerber* (Stuttgart, 1937).

114. See Guido Schneeberger, *Nachlese zu Heidegger* (Bern, 1962), pp. 258–262.

115. See Franz Kerber, records, Berlin Document Center.

116. Franz Kerber, "Volk, Kultur und Gemeinde," in Kerber (ed.), *Alemannenland,* pp. 7–8.

117. *Ibid.*

118. *Ibid.,* p. 8.

119. *Ibid.,* pp. 7–8, 10, 11, 12.

120. See R. A. C. Parker, *Das Zwanzigste Jahrhundert, 1918–1945* (Fischer World History, vol. 34; Frankfurt am Main, 1967), p. 274ff.

121. Henri Lichtenberger, "Goethe und Frankreich," in Kerber (ed.), *Alemannenland,* p. 124ff.

122. Jean-Edouard Spenlé, "Nietzsche als geistiger Mittler zwischen Frankreich und Deutschland," in Kerber (ed.), *Alemannenland,* p. 140ff.

123. Alphonse de Chateaubriant, "Wie ich den Führer Adolf Hitler sehe," in Kerber (ed.), *Alemannenland,* p. 164ff.

124. Joseph M. Maitre, "Die französischen Frontkämpfer in Freiburg im Breisgau," in Kerber (ed.), *Alemannenland,* p. 171ff.

125. Chateaubriant, "Wie ich den Führer sehe," p. 164f.

126. Spenlé, "Nietzsche als geistiger Mittler," p. 156.

127. Franz Kerber, "Nachwort des Herausgebers" in Kerber (ed.), *Alemannenland,* p. 163.

128. Martin Heidegger, "Wege zur Aussprache," in Kerber (ed.), *Alemannen-land*, pp. 135–139, quoted in Schneeberger, *Nachlese zu Heidegger*, pp. 258–262. The following citations are also taken from this source.

129. See Pöggeler, *Philosophie und Politik*, p. 24.

130. Kerber (ed.), *Alemannenland*, p. 261.

131. *Ibid.*

132. *Ibid.*

133. Ph. Leibrecht, "Alemannenland," *Die Neue Literatur*, April 4, 1938.

134. "Alemannenland," *Die Buchbesprechung*, Feb. 1938, pp. 57–58.

135. "Alemannenland," *Schweizer Nationale Hefte* 5 (Jan./Feb. 1939).

136. Heidegger, "Rektorat, 1933/34," p. 42f; Heidegger, interview, *Der Spiegel*, May 31, 1976, p. 204.

137. See documents of the Reichsministerium for Science, Education, and Popular Education in Zentrales Staatsarchiv Potsdam, REM 49.01 (2940); Hoover Foundation, Stanford University, Sign. "Kongress-Zentrale."

138. See *Actes du huitième congrès international de philosophie à Prague* (Prague, 1936), Sept. 2–7, 1934.

139. Heidegger, *Spiegel* interview, p. 204.

140. Zentrales Staatsarchiv Potsdam.

141. *Ibid.*

142. Hoover Foundation, Sign. "Kongress-Zentrale."

143. Letter, Nov. 6, 1936, in Zentrales Staatsarchiv Potsdam.

144. Zentrales Staatsarchiv Potsdam.

145. *Ibid.*

146. *Ibid.*

147. *Ibid.*

148. Heidegger, *Spiegel* interview, p. 204.

149. Jaspers, *Notizen zu Heidegger*, p. 87.

150. See Heidegger, "Rektorat, 1933/34," p. 41, and *Spiegel* interview, p. 204.

151. Martin Heidegger, *Nietzsche* (2 vols.; Pfullingen, 1961).

152. Hitler, *Mein Kampf*, p. 293.

153. *Ibid.*, p. 293f.

154. *Ibid.*, pp. 379f, 629–633.

155. Heidegger, *Nietzsche*, vol. 1, p. 436.

156. *Ibid.*, p. 33.

157. *Ibid.*, p. 36.

158. Heidegger, *Einführung in die Metaphysik*, p. 152.

159. Heidegger, *Nietzsche*, vol. 1, p. 362f; Rudolf Hess, speech, in Schneeberger, *Nachlese zu Heidegger*, pp. 243-246.

160. Martin Heidegger, letter to Rudolf Stadelmann, April 20, 1939, in Bundesarchiv Koblenz, literary estate of Rudolf Stadelmann.

161. Heidegger, *Nietzsche*, vol. 1, p. 75.

162. *Ibid.*, p. 361.

163. *Ibid.*, p. 553.

164. *Ibid.*, p. 469f.

165. *Ibid.*, p. 124.

Chapter 17

1. R. Bollmus, *Das Amt Rosenberg und seine Gegner* (Stuttgart, 1970), *passim*.

2. Kurt Schilling, records, Berlin Document Center.

3. Martin Heidegger, "Das Rektorat, 1933/34: Tatsachen und Gedanken," in Heidegger, *Die Selbstbehauptung der deutschen Universität* (Frankfurt am Main, 1983), p. 42.

4. "Heidegger, Martin: 'Vom Wesen des Grundes,' " *Blätter für Deutsche Philosophie* 13, no. 1/2 (1939): 217.

5. Bruno Bauch, review of Heidegger's "Hölderlin und das Wesen der Dichtung," *Blätter für Deutsche Philosophie* 13, no. 1/2 (1939): 217f.

6. "F. Dornseiff: 'Wie wenn am Feiertage,' " *Geistige Arbeit* 19 (Oct. 5, 1942): 5.

7. *Die Literatur* (Stuttgart) 94, no. 6 (1982).

8. *Frankfurter Zeitung*, June 15, 1942.

9. *Scholastik* 18, no. 1 (1943).

10. Records of the committee to hire a successor to M. Büchner, 1941, Archives of the University of Munich, Sign. ON-10a.

11. On the appointment of Walther Wüst as SS-Standartenführer thanks to Himmler, see the corresponding communication in Wüst's records in the Berlin Document Center.

12. See Rudolf Till, records, Berlin Document Center.

13. SS-Obersturmbannführer Sievers, letter to the economic planning board of German bookdealers, May 21, 1942, in Till, records.

14. See Volker Losemann, "Zur Konzeption der NS-Dozentenlager," in M. Heinemann (ed.), *Erziehung und Schulung im Dritten Reich*, vol. 2 (Stuttgart, 1980), pp. 121, 133.

15. See Hugo Dingler, records, Berlin Document Center.

16. Hugo Dingler, "Max Planck und die Begründung der sogenannten modernen theoretischen Physik" (1939), typed text in Dingler, records.

17. *Ibid.*

18. Letter to the Reichsminister for Science, Education, and Popular Education, July 16, 1941, in the Archives of the University of Munich.

19. See Martin Heidegger, records, Berlin Document Center.

20. See Martin Heidegger, *Der Spiegel* interview, May 31, 1976, p. 204.

21. See records in the Archiv des Instituts für Zeitgeschichte, Munich, Sign. MA 40.

22. W. F. Otto, introduction, *Geistige Überlieferung*, vol. 1 (Berlin, 1940), pp. 17, 28f.

23. *Ibid.*

24. See Losemann, "Zur Konzeption," pp. 123ff, 216, 235f.

25. W. Erxleben, "Geistige Überlieferung: Ein Gemeinschaftswerk deutscher und italienischer Wissenschaftler," *Bücherkunde: Monatshefte für das deutsche Schrifttum*, 1942, p. 17f.

26. F. Dirlmeier, review of the yearbook *Geistige Überlieferung* in *Deutsche Kultur im Leben der Völker*, Dec. 1941, p. 458f. Cf. Giuseppe Bottai, "Ursachen und Gepräge des faschistischen Antisozialismus im Ideengut Mussolinis," and Ernesto Grassi, "Die Auseinandersetzung mit der deutschen Philosophie in Italien," both in *Na-*

tionalsozialistische Monatshefte: Zentrale politische und kulturelle Zeitschrift der NSDAP 140 (Nov. 1941): 883–887 and 898–911.

27. W. Erxleben, letter to Dr. Lutz, June 17, 1942, and Erxleben, remarks, July 3, 1942, both in Archiv des Instituts für Zeitgeschichte, Munich, Sign. MA 40.

28. *Ibid.*

29. Josef Goebbels, *Tagebücher, 1942–1943*, ed. L. P. Lochner (Zürich, 1948): 65f.

30. See Giuseppe Bottai, "Über das Lesen," in *Geistige Überlieferung* 2 (1942): 203–213.

31. See the article "Giuseppe Bottai" in G. Gentile and G. Trecanni (eds.), *Enciclopedia Italiana Trecanni*, vol. 7 (Rome, 1930), app. 1938, p. 575.

32. Bottai, *Pagine di critica fascista* (Rome, 1941), p. 214ff.

33. Bernhard Rust, "Preface" to Giuseppe Bottai's *Afrikanisches Tagebuch* (Berlin, 1940).

34. Bottai, *Afrikanisches Tagebuch*, p. 209.

35. *Ibid.*, p. 206.

36. Ernesto Grassi, "Die Bedeutung der Antike für unsere Überlieferung," foreword to Giuseppe Bottai's *Verteidigung des Humanismus: Die geistigen Grundlagen der neuen Studien in Italien* (Berlin, 1941), pp. 5–14.

37. *Ibid.*, p. 13.

38. See *Minerva: Jahrbuch der gelehrten Welt* (Berlin, 1930), p. 885; *Minerva: Jahrbuch der gelehrten Welt* (Berlin/Leipzig, 1934), p. 475.

39. Ernesto Grassi, *Il problema della metafisica platonica* (Bari, 1932).

40. Ernesto Grassi, *Dell'apparire e dell'essere* (Florence, 1933), p. 92.

41. *Ibid.*

42. *Kürschners Deutscher Gelehrten-Kalender* (Berlin, 1961), p. 587.

43. See Ernesto Grassi, *Vom Vorrang des Logos: Das Problem der Antike in der Auseinandersetzung zwischen italienischer und deutscher Philosophie* (Berlin, 1939).

44. See Ernesto Grassi, records, Berlin Document Center; Hans-Georg Gadamer, review of Grassi's book *Vom Vorrang des Logos*, in *Deutsche Literaturzeitung* 61 (1940): 893.

45. Walther Hofer, *Der Nationalsozialismus: Dokumente, 1933–1945* (Frankfurt am Main, 1978), p. 386.

46. *Kant-Studien*, N.S., 44 (1944).

47. Wilhelm Brachmann, "Der gegenwärtige Humanismus: Ein Beitrag zur Geistes- und Glaubensgeschichte der Gegenwart," *Kant-Studien*, N.S., 44 (1944): 15ff.

48. *Ibid.*, p. 15.

49. See *ibid.*, p. 33.

50. *Ibid.*, p. 34.

51. See Wilhelm Brachmann, records, Berlin Document Center.

52. Martin Heidegger, letter to Prof. Schuchardt, dean of the philosophy faculty, July 17, 1943, in Heidegger, records.

53. Prof. Schuchardt, letter to Martin Heidegger, July 19, 1943, in Heidegger, records.

54. Reichsminister for Science, Education, and Popular Education, letter to Baden Minister of Public Worship and Instruction, Oct. 21, 1943, in Heidegger, records.

55. See B. Zeller (ed.), *Klassiker in finsteren Zeiten* (2 vols.; Marbach, 1938), vol. 2, pp. 76–134.

56. See *ibid.*, pp. 120–122.

57. See *ibid.*, pp. 104–120.

58. See *ibid.*, p. 96f.

59. Paul Kluckhohn, "Zur Einführung," in Kluckhohn (ed.), *Hölderlin: Gedenkschrift zu seinem 100. Todestag* (2nd ed.; Tübingen, 1944), p. 3f.

60. Josef Weinheber, "An Hölderlin," in Kluckhohn (ed.), *Hölderlin*, p. 1f.

61. See Zeller (ed.), *Klassiker in finsteren Zeiten*, vol. 2, p. 176.

62. See Wilhelm Böhm, " 'So dacht' ich. Nächstens mehr': Die Ganzheit des Hyperionromans," in Kluckhohn (ed.), *Hölderlin*, pp. 224–239.

63. See Kurt Hildebrandt, "Hölderlins und Goethes Weltanschauung dargestellt am 'Hyperion' und 'Empedokles,' " in Kluckhohn (ed.), *Hölderlin*, pp. 134–173; Paul Kluckhohn, *Hölderlin: Philosophie und Dichtung* (Stuttgart, 1939), p. 240.

64. See Paul Böckmann, "Hölderlins mythische Welt," in Kluckhohn (ed.), *Hölderlin*, pp. 11–49; on Böckmann's *Hölderlin und seine Götter* (Munich, 1935), see the description in Zeller (ed.), *Klassiker in finsteren Zeiten*, vol. 1, pp. 333–334.

65. Martin Heidegger, "Andenken," in Heidegger, *Erläuterungen zu Hölderlins Dichtung* (2nd ed.; Frankfurt am Main, 1951); Kluckhohn (ed.), *Hölderlin*, pp. 267–324.

66. Heidegger, "Andenken," p. 92.

67. *Ibid.*, p. 137f.

68. *Ibid.*, p. 131f.

69. Quoted in *ibid.*, p. 83.

70. *Ibid.*

71. *Ibid.* The following citations are also taken from this source.

72. Martin Heidegger, second lecture on Hölderlin in 1942, quoted in Otto Pöggeler, *Philosophie und Politik bei Heidegger* (Freiburg/Munich, 1974), p. 110.

73. Robert Minder, *Hölderlin unter den Deutschen und andere Aufsätze zur deutschen Literatur* (Frankfurt am Main, 1968), p. 95f.

74. Martin Heidegger, "Heimkunft / An die Verwandten," in Heidegger, *Erläuterungen zu Hölderlins Dichtung*, p. 13.

75. *Ibid.*, p. 14.

76. *Ibid.*

77. *Ibid.*, p. 16f.

78. *Ibid.*, p. 22f.

79. *Ibid.*, p. 24.

80. *Ibid.*, p. 24f.

81. *Ibid.*, p. 26.

82. *Ibid.*, p. 28.

83. *Ibid.*, p. 29.

84. *Ibid.*, p. 29f.

85. Martin Heidegger, *Parmenides*, vol. 54 of Heidegger, *Gesamtausgabe* (Frankfurt am Main, 1982), p. 114.

86. M. Frings, commentary to Heidegger, *Parmenides*, p. 252.

87. Heidegger, *Parmenides*, p. 57.

88. *Ibid.*, p. 61.

89. *Ibid.*, p. 70.

90. *Ibid.*, p. 62.

91. *Ibid.*, p. 78.

92. *Ibid.*, p. 79.

93. See Alfred Rosenberg, *Der Mythus des 20. Jahrhunderts: Eine Wertung der seelisch-geistigen Gestaltenkämpfe unserer Zeit* (Munich, 1930).

94. Heidegger, *Parmenides*, p. 108.

95. Martin Heidegger, "Hölderlins Hymne 'Der Ister,' " in Heidegger, *Gesamtausgabe*, vol. 53 (Frankfurt am Main, 1984), p. 68.

96. Martin Heidegger, *Heraklit*, vol. 55 of Heidegger, *Gesamtausgabe* (Frankfurt am Main, 1979), p. 180f.

97. W. D. Gudopp, "Stalingrad–Heidegger–Marx," *Deutsche Zeitschrift für Philosophie* 31, no. 6 (1983): 678.

98. Heidegger, *Heraklit*, p. 123.

99. Heidegger, "Rektorat, 1933/34," p. 42.

100. Dr. Heinz Bollinger, letter to the author, Feb. 6, 1985.

101. Dr. Heinz Bollinger, letter to the author, Feb. 20, 1985.

102. *Badische Zeitung*, March 14, 1947.

103. See Hugo Ott, "Martin Heidegger und die Universität Freiburg nach 1945," *Historisches Jahrbuch der Görres-Gesellschaft* 105 (1985): 98.

104. *Ibid.*, p. 99.

105. *Ibid.*, p. 100.

106. See *ibid.*, p. 102.

107. See *ibid.*, p. 106.

108. See report in K. A. Moehling, "Martin Heidegger and the Nazi Party: An Examination," Ph.D. diss., Northern Illinois University, 1972, app.

109. See Ott, "Heidegger und die Universität Freiburg," pp. 107–108.

110. *Ibid.*, p. 113.

111. *Ibid.*

112. *Ibid.*

113. See *ibid.*, pp. 116–117.

114. See the records in the Archives of the University of Tübingen, Proceedings of the Senate, Sign. VAT 47/41, and records of the Academic Chairs, VAT 205/6.

115. See Martin Heidegger, letters to Rudolf Stadelmann, July 20, Sept. 1, and Nov. 30, 1945, in Bundesarchiv Koblenz, literary estate of Rudolf Stadelmann.

116. Heidegger, *Spiegel* interview, p. 204.

117. Georg Picht, "Die Macht des Denkens," in Günther Neske (ed.), *Erinnerung an Martin Heidegger* (Pfullingen, 1977), p. 204ff.

118. Heidegger, letter to Stadelmann, July 20, 1945.

119. Martin Heidegger, letter to Stadelmann, Sept. 1, 1945.

120. *Ibid.*, Nov. 30, 1945.

121. Heidegger, letter to Stadelmann, July 20, 1945.

122. Karl Jaspers, *Notizen zu Heidegger* (Munich/Zürich, 1978), p. 289.

123. Rudolf Bultmann, quoted from A. Fischer-Barnicol, "Spiegelungen—Vermittlungen," in Neske (ed.), *Erinnerung an Martin Heidegger*, pp. 95–96.

124. Archiv des Instituts für Zeitgeschichte, Munich, Sign. MA 141, no. 0348756.

125. See Otto Pöggeler, "Den Führer führen?: Heidegger and kein Ende," *Philosophische Rundschau* 32 (1985): 39.

126. H. Saner, report, in Jaspers, *Notizen zu Heidegger*, p. 18.

127. Heidegger-Marcuse correspondence in Stadt- und Universitätbibliothek Frankfurt am Main, literary estate of Herbert Marcuse.

128. On this speech, see Heidegger's letter of July 25, 1933, to Prof. Löhlein, the dean of the medical faculty at Freiburg, and the text of a speech by Löhlein of July 1933, which is connected to Heidegger's speech. Both documents are located in the Heeres-Sanitätsinspektion, Bundesarchiv/Militärarchiv, stock H. 20/1074. In his speech Löhlein referred to "the fundamental statement that the Rector had briefly made in lecture hall 5 of the university in which he indicated that the German universities must not shift in the middle of the stormy developments all around us, or change in their outward behavior, thereby exhibiting a kind of external correction. That would not correspond with their dignity and their highest task vis-à-vis the whole [nation], merely to endure passively a fundamental change in their internal and external life. Rather, it is in the interest of preserving the universities and their esteemed position, in regard to larger tasks, always to take upon themselves the spiritual development of our people. It is an obvious duty that the universities take an active and leading role in the spiritual transformation of young Germany and with these regenerative acts they should never forget their own objectives and their own ways."

129. Martin Heidegger, quoted in W. Schirmacher, *Technik und Gelassenheit* (Freiburg, 1985), p. 25.

130. Jean Beaufret to Robert Faurisson, in *Annales d'histoire révisionniste*, autumn-winter 1987, pp. 204–205.

Chapter 18

1. Martin Heidegger, *Zur Sache des Denkens* (Tübingen, 1969), pp. 72–80.

2. Martin Heidegger, *Über Abraham a Sancta Clara* (Messkirch, n.d.).

3. *Ibid.*, p. 5.

4. *Ibid.*

5. *Ibid.*

6. *Ibid.*, p. 7.

7. *Ibid.*, p. 8.

8. *Ibid.*, p. 9.

9. *Ibid.*

10. *Ibid.*

11. *Ibid.*, p. 11.

12. *Ibid.*, p. 14.

13. *Ibid.*

14. *Ibid.*, p. 15.

15. See Karl Bertsche, records, Berlin Document Center. See also Franz Loidl, *Menschen im Barock: Abraham a Sancta Clara über das religiössittliche Leben in Österreich in der Zeit von 1670 bis 1710* (Vienna, 1938); Loidl, *Abraham a Sancta Clara und das Judentum: Studie über das Judentum in Wien und Österreich im Barock* (Vienna, 1941); and Loidl, *Abraham a Sancta Clara als Vorkämpfer für deutsche Art wider Türken und Fremdländerei* (Vienna, 1941).

16. Loidl, *Abraham a Sancta Clara und das Judentum*, p. 10.

17. *Ibid.*

18. Loidl, *Menschen im Barock*, p. 257.

19. Loidl, *Abraham a Sancta Clara und das Judentum*, pp. 13–14.

20. *Ibid.*, p. 15.

21. *Ibid.*, pp. 15–16.

22. *Ibid.*, p. 17.

23. *Ibid.*, pp. 18–19.

24. *Ibid.*, p. 19.

25. *Ibid.*, p. 26.

26. Dr. Karl Eder, in *Theologisch-praktische Quartalsschrift* 4 (1941): 341.

27. See Franz Loidl, *Aspekte und Kontakte eines Kirchenhistorikers: Kirche und Welt in ihrer Begegnung* (Vienna, 1976), p. 20.

28. Josef Nadler, "Westmark und Ostmark: Grenzen, Fugen, Klammern," in Franz Kerber (ed.), *Reichsstrasse 31, von der Ostmark zum Oberrhein: Natur, Volk, Kunst* (Stuttgart, 1939), p. 136.

29. *Ibid.*, p. 144.

30. *Ibid.*, p. 146.

31. Karl Bertsche, "Abraham a Sancta Clara über die Lektüre," *Schönere Zukunft*, Dec. 1939, p. 151.

32. Alfred Rosenberg, *An die Dunkelmänner unserer Zeit: Eine Antwort auf die Angriffe gegen den 'Mythus des 20. Jahrhunderts'* (Munich, 1935).

33. *Ibid.*, pp. 3–5, 50, 80, 88ff.

34. Abraham a Sancta Clara, *Judas I*, p. 304, quoted in Loidl, *Menschen im Barock*, p. 257.

35. Archives of the Austrian Academy of Science, Sign. 360/1938, C. 2536, 2537.

36. See H. Schleier, *Die bürgerliche deutsche Geschichtsschreibung der Weimar Republik* (Berlin, 1975), p. 114.

37. Heinrich von Srbik, *Humanismus bis zur Gegenwart* (Munich/Salzburg, 1951), p. 338f.

38. Martin Heidegger, interview, *Der Spiegel*, May 31, 1976, p. 214.

39. *Ibid.*, p. 217.

40. *Ibid.*

41. *Ibid.*

42. *Ibid.*

43. Rainer Marten, "Heideggers Heimat—eine philosophische Herausforderung," in Ute Guzzoni (ed.), *Nachdenken über Heidegger: Eine Bestandsaufnahme* (Hildesheim, 1980), p. 154.

44. Heidegger, *Spiegel* interview, p. 206.

45. *Ibid.*, p. 214.

46. *Ibid.*, p. 209.

47. *Ibid.*

Index